ON GREEK MARGINS

HERMES, EURYDICE, AND ORPHEUS
Greco-Roman copy of late-fifth-century relief, in Museo Nazionale, Naples

ON
GREEK MARGINS

C. M. BOWRA

OXFORD
AT THE CLARENDON PRESS
1970

Oxford University Press, Ely House, London W.1

GLASGOW NEW YORK TORONTO MELBOURNE WELLINGTON
CAPE TOWN SALISBURY IBADAN NAIROBI DAR ES SALAAM LUSAKA ADDIS ABABA
BOMBAY CALCUTTA MADRAS KARACHI LAHORE DACCA
KUALA LUMPUR SINGAPORE HONG KONG TOKYO

© OXFORD UNIVERSITY PRESS 1970

PRINTED IN GREAT BRITAIN

TO
ANTONY AND
ALISON ANDREWES

PREFACE

An elderly writer may perhaps be excused for wishing to gather into a single volume such *obiter scripta* as he still has some affection for. The student who wishes to consult them can of course look them up in the periodicals and other publications where they first appeared, but even he may find it convenient to have them brought together under one cover. In the vast mass of specialist periodicals, which has been aptly described as being 'both Limbo and Lethe', these unassuming contributions may suffer from a neglect which, at least in their author's eyes, is not always deserved. They may sometimes be by-products of more substantial work done in books; they often deal with subjects which are restricted or peripheral, though not necessarily the worse for being so. In this volume I have collected a number of articles, written in the last thirty years, though most are comparatively recent. Most of them treat self-contained subjects, such as single poems, or passages, or themes. They deal for the most part with matters that have long engaged my attention, notably Homer and lyric and elegiac poetry. This gives some kind of unity and, I hope, justifies their collection into a book. I have rejected some other articles, partly because they have found a place in larger contexts, partly because they have faults beyond remedy. Those that I have kept I have on the whole left as they were at their first publication, but I have made a number of small alterations, such as giving the latest references for editions of fragments and the like, omitting repetitious matter between one article and another, adding a few notes on recent work when they seemed to be indispensable, and removing obvious slips and errors. In the few places where I have changed my views, I have drawn attention to it. I have kept certain inconsistencies of spelling, especially of Greek names, between one chapter and another. Most of these articles are controversial, and some have in fact provoked controversy, and may do so again. This seems to me a good reason for summoning them from their shadowy hiding-places and setting them in the critical light of day.

The original provenance of each article is given at its start, and I am grateful for permission to reprint to the editors and proprietors of *Journal of Hellenic Studies*, *Mnemosyne*, *Glotta*, *Classical Quarterly*, *Anales de filología clásica*, *Classical Review*, *Philologus*, *Hermes*, *Historia*, *American Journal of Philology*, *Museum Helveticum*, *Journal of Roman Studies*, *Byzantinische Zeitschrift*, to F. W. Cheshire, Melbourne, and to the British Academy.

In a book of this kind the author owes obligations past number to those who have over the years helped him with information, advice, and criticism. Some of these are acknowledged in individual contexts, but some other obligations are more extensive, and I would like to mention specially my indebtedness to Professor A. Andrewes, Professor Hugh Lloyd Jones, Mr. W. G. Forrest, and Mr. T. C. W. Stinton. I could only wish that the results were more worthy of their generous help. Finally, I am delighted to thank the staff of the Clarendon Press for their skill and patience in producing the book, and Mr. Edward Greene for his unfailing care and good temper in compiling the Indexes.

C. M. B.

Oxford

CONTENTS

Hermes, Eurydice, and Orpheus. Greco-Roman copy of late-fifth-century relief, in Museo Nazionale, Naples. Photograph by Alinari. *Frontispiece*

I.	Homeric Epithets for Troy	1
II.	Ἐϋκνήμιδες Ἀχαιοί	14
III.	Γλῶσσαι κατὰ πόλεις	27
IV.	Two lines of Eumelus	46
V.	The Fox and the Hedgehog	59
VI.	A Couplet of Archilochus	67
VII.	A Fragment of the *Arimaspea*	72
VIII.	The Two Palinodes of Stesichorus	87
IX.	Two Poems of Theognis	99
X.	Xenophanes on the Luxury of Colophon	109
XI.	Asius and the Old-fashioned Samians	122
XII.	Euripides' Epinician for Alcibiades	134
XIII.	A Love-duet	149
XIV.	Arion and the Dolphin	164
XV.	A Cretan Hymn	182
XVI.	Melinno's Hymn to Rome	199
XVII.	Orpheus and Eurydice	213
XVIII.	Εἴπατε τῷ βασιλῆι	233
XIX.	Palladas and the Converted Olympians	245
XX.	Palladas and Christianity	253
	Index Auctorum	261
	Index Verborum	267
	General Index	273

I

HOMERIC EPITHETS FOR TROY[1]

THE publication of the fourth volume on the excavations at Troy by the University of Cincinnati in the years 1932–8[2] enables us to review with more confidence the historical events which lie, no matter at how great a distance, behind the *Iliad* and to reconsider the Homeric epithets for Troy in the light of new knowledge. We may at the start agree with the writers that no site in the Troad except Hisarlik has any reasonable claim to be that of Troy,[3] and it is now clear that Troy VI, which was gravely damaged by an earthquake c. 1275 B.C.,[4] was succeeded by Troy VIIa, which had a real continuity with VI and was largely a rebuilt version of it, until it perished itself from fire c. 1240 B.C.[5] VIIa has thus a substantial claim to be the Homeric city, and the date of the destruction agrees with that given by Herodotus for the Trojan war as κατὰ ὀκτακόσια (ἔτεα) μάλιστα ἐς ἐμέ (2. 145. 4). We may ask how relevant the Homeric epithets are to Troy as we now know it to have been, and when they may have been introduced into the oral tradition which Homer inherited and used in the eighth century. At the start we may say that, while all of them are at least adequate for a walled city on the site of Hisarlik, and some are much to the point, not all are equally individual, and we may classify them according to their use for cities in general and for Troy in particular. In doing this we must remember that in the Homeric poems cities have epithets as gods and heroes do, and that there is bound to be a certain overlap between one city and another in the epithets attached to them. Though we may postulate a pool of adjectives suitable for cities from which the poet draws those that meet his

---

[1] First published in *Journal of Hellenic Studies*, lxxx (1960), 16–25.
[2] C. W. Blegen, C. D. Boulter, J. L. Caskey, M. Rawson, *Troy*, iv (Princeton, 1958).
[3] Ibid. iv 11.
[4] Ibid. iii. 11.
[5] Ibid. iv. 11, 50, 90, 176. See also C. W. Blegen, *Troy and the Trojans*, 163, where he suggests 'about 1260 B.C., if not indeed somewhat earlier'.

needs most adequately, there are some which are confined to Troy and others which are especially appropriate to it.

1. Conventional epithets for places

(a) The application of ἐϋκτίμενος to Troy occurs in the formulaic ἐϋκτίμενον πτολίεθρον at Δ 33, Θ 288, Φ 433 and has recently come into prominence because of its possible connection with the Mycenaean *ki-ti-me-na*, which is used with reference to the ownership of land.[1] But the Homeric use of ἐϋκτίμενος for Troy does not conform to any of the meanings suggested for the Mycenaean word. It cannot be applied to 'private' as opposed to 'communal' land, or to 'cultivated' as opposed to 'uncultivated'. If it is historically connected with *ki-ti-me-na*, it has changed its meaning. When it is applied to cities, such as Phere (E 543), Arisbe (Z 13), Iolkos (B 712), Lyktos (P 611), Pylos (γ 4), and Nerikos (ω 377), it can conceivably mean 'well founded' or 'well built', but it can hardly have this meaning for Lemnos (Φ 40, θ 283), Lesbos (δ 342, ρ 133), or Ithaca (χ 52). It seems, therefore, to have some rather vague meaning, 'well established', and this is supported by the words νῆσον ἐϋκτιμένην ἐκάμοντο (ι 130) for Scherie. It clearly has no special significance for Troy, and looks as if it were drawn from a pool of epithets suitable for cities. Even if it has an ancient origin, its meaning has been distorted and dimmed by time.

(b) ἐρίβωλος (I 329, Σ 67, Ψ 215) is certainly applicable at least to the Trojan plain, but it is not very distinguishing, and it is not surprising that it is applied also to districts like Phthia (I 363), Paeonia (Φ 154), and Scherie (ε 34).

(c) ἐριβῶλαξ is a variant on ἐρίβωλος, used for its different scansion in oblique cases, accusative at Γ 74, 257, and dative at Z 315, Π 461, Ω 86. It is evidently common currency since it is used for Larisa (B 841, P 301), Phthia (I 363), Tarne (E 44), Askanie (N 793), Paeonia (P 350), and Thrace (Y 485).

(d) ἐρατεινή at E 210 has an emotional connotation, but is in no sense descriptive, and is applied to places so various as Augeia (B 532, 583), Araithureë (B 571), Arene (B 591), Mantinea

[1] M. Ventris and J. Chadwick, *Documents in Mycenaean Greek*, 233; L. R. Palmer, *Mycenaean Greek Texts*, 83, 85, 93, 186 ff., 217.

(B 707), Emathia (Ξ 226), Maeonia (Γ 401, Σ 291), Lakedaimon (Γ 239, 443), and Scherie (η 79).

(e) εὔρεια, used of Troy at N 433, Ω 256, 494, 774, α 62, δ 99, ε 307, λ 49, is limited to regions with a certain amount of open land and is therefore suited to countries like Lycia (Z 173, 210, Π 455, 673, 683), and Crete (N 453), but also to cities with open land around them, appropriately for Knossos (Σ 591) and Sparta (λ 460), but less so for Helike (B 575). It certainly suits the Troad.

(f) ἱρή is used twenty-one times in the *Iliad* and twice in the *Odyssey* for Troy and may be connected with it as the seat of a temple of Athene. It also lies behind the phrase Τροίης ἱερὰ κρήδεμνα (Π 100). It too is common currency and used for Onchestos (B 506), Thebe (A 366), Sounion (γ 278), Pylos (φ 108), Athens (λ 323), and the Echinades (B 625). Its frequent appearance in the *Iliad* for Troy is probably due to its happy and useful union with Ἴλιος at the end of the line.

In these cases epithets applied to Troy are evidently drawn from a common stock which was available for most places. They are all appropriate enough but never very individual or illuminating. (a) refers to the good work which has gone to the making of Troy; (b) and (c) to the fertile land around it; (d) to its general amenities; (e) to the extent of its open lands and (f) to its cults. All of them are consistent with what we know of Troy VI and VIIa, and partly of VIIb and VIII. But they do not differentiate it very firmly from other cities which are well established, have lands around them, and are known for their cults. If the demands of oral composition meant that Troy had to have epithets, these are adequate enough but do not suggest any special knowledge.

2. *Epithets confined to Troy*

(a) ἐΰδμητος, which appears in ἐϋδμήτοιο πόληος at Φ 516, is normally used of towers (Π 700, X 195), walls (M 36, υ 302, χ 24, 126), and altars (A 448), but in this single case is applied to a whole city, as in Hesiod fr. 235. 4 W.–M. It suggests the solid work which can be seen in its buildings, and is abundantly justified by the remains of Troy VI and VIIa. It is not used of any other city as such, and looks as if it were given special duties for a clear impression of Troy in its strength and solidity.

(b) ἐϋτείχεος at A 129, B 113, 288, E 716, Θ 241, I 20 is more specific than ἐΰδμητος. The walls of Troy VI, which survived with some patching in Troy VIIa,[1] show how well deserved the epithet is, and help to explain why the Achaeans took ten years to capture the city. Its absence from other cities does not indicate that they lacked walls but suggests that those of Troy were particularly noteworthy.

(c) εὔπυργος at H 71 may be taken to refer to towers in the fortifications, such as existed in VI in at least four places, known as VIg, VIh, VIi, VIk, and survived into VIIa. We do not know how high they were, but they were an integral and important feature in the defences of Troy and must have presented an impressive spectacle. Towers also existed at Mycenae and Tiryns, but, since they were built in connection with gates, which were fewer than at Troy, the towers also were probably fewer. The number of them at Troy certainly contributed to the impression of it as a 'well-towered city'.

(d) ὀφρυόεσσα occurs only once in a highly dramatic passage, when the Trojans burst into lamentations as they see the dead body of Hector dragged behind the chariot of Achilles:

τῷ δὲ μάλιστ' ἄρ' ἔην ἐναλίγκιον, ὡς εἰ ἅπασα
Ἴλιος ὀφρυόεσσα πυρὶ σμύχοιτο κατ' ἄκρης.

(X 410–11)

The adjective seems to be derived from such phrases as ἐπ' ὀφρύσι Καλλικολώνης (Υ 151), and is explained by the Townleian scholiast as ἐπὶ ὀφρυώδους τόπου κειμένη. It was used in the seventh or sixth century by a Delphic oracle for Acrocorinth (Hdt. 5. 92 β 3), and by "Hesiod" for Corinth (fr. 204. 48 W.–M, and not only conveys a vivid impression of Troy on its ridge overlooking the plain but helps to strengthen by contrast the menace of its coming doom. It is a general comment on the forbidding aspect which the city presented, especially to any possible attackers.

(e) ἄστυ μεγά (B 803, H 296, I 136, 278, O 681, P 160, Φ 309, X 351) is not very appropriate to the site of Troy if it refers simply to extent. The remains of VI and VIIa measure some 200 yards at their widest diameter and cover not more than five acres, nor does it take more than a quarter of an hour to walk round them without hurrying. It is true that in the *Iliad* Homer suggests that a very large force is housed in this small area, and

[1] *Troy*, iv. 6, 48, 73, 88.

we may agree with Thucydides when he says: εἶκος ἐπὶ τὸ μεῖζον μὲν ποιητὴν ὄντα κοσμῆσαι (1. 10. 3). But μεγά need not refer to extent, and may well refer to height and mass, as it is used for a tower (Z 386) or a mountain (Π 297). Such a meaning would suit Troy very well, with its formidable fortifications and the appearance which these presented to anyone on the plain below.

(f) εὔπωλος (E 551, Π 576, β 18, λ 169, ξ 71) belongs to rather a different category from the preceding cases, since it is concerned not with the appearance of Troy but with its breeding of horses. As such it is connected with the adjective ἱππόδαμοι, which is used of the Trojans twenty-one times in the *Iliad*. εὔπωλος is fully justified by history. Though no bones of horses have been found in the first five settlements, they are abundant in Troy VI[1] and VIIa[2] but become rare in VIIb.[3] It has been surmised with good reason that the people who built Troy VI owed their success to their use of the domesticated horse,[4] and they seem to have left this legacy to their descendants who held the city till the destruction of VIIa.

The epithets in this class are more precise and more distinctive than in the preceding. Taken together they suggest actual observation and local knowledge. They are more than merely appropriate to Troy, and were surely chosen with an eye to its appearance and character. Since none of them is applied to other cities which might seem to deserve them, it looks as if they were intended to give from different angles an impression of Troy in its striking individuality, with its well-made walls and towers, its threatening look, and its breeding of horses.

3. *Epithets suitable to Troy but not confined to it*

A third class of epithets differs from the first in not being obviously drawn from stock, and from the second in not being confined to Troy. None the less they suit it very well and are in this respect close to the second class. The aspects which they stress are shared with other places, but are none the less characteristic of Troy.

(a) αἰπή (N 625, γ 130, λ 533, ν 316), αἰπύ (O 71), and αἰπεινή (I 419, N 773, O 558, P 328) have the same meaning, and their usage is determined entirely by requirements of scansion. They

---

[1] *Troy*, iii. 123, 136, 182, 188, etc.
[2] Ibid. iv. 199.
[3] Ibid. iv. 10.
[4] Ibid. iv. 51, 66, 70, 73, 117, 123.

are apt for Hisarlik, which rises steeply from the plain on the north and west sides, and certainly must have risen noticeably on the east and south sides also before the builders of Troy IX did their great levelling. αἰπύ is confined to Troy, but αἰπεινή is applied also to Calydon (*N* 217), Gonoessa (*B* 573), and Pedasos (*Z* 35), and is relevant enough to what we know of these places. αἰπή has a similar range, and is justifiably applied to Dion in northern Euboea (*B* 538), where the modern village of Lithada is set on the edge of a precipice; to Pylos (γ 485, ο 193), which deserves the reference if it is to the Mycenaean site of Epano Englianos; and to the mythical home of the Laestrygonian Lamos in a mountainous fjord (κ 81). Its application to Troy may have been suggested by the view which it presents to anyone who approaches it from the north or the west, as travellers who come by sea usually do.

(*b*) ὑψίπυλος (*Π* 698, *Φ* 544) is explained by Hesychius as meaning ὑψηλὰς πύλας ἔχον, and his assumption that it refers to the number, as well as to the height, of gates is important for Troy. In Troy VI excavation has revealed the remains of gates VIr in the north-east, VIs in the east, VIt in the south, VIu in the south-west, VIv in the west, VIy in the south, and VIz in the south-west. Not all of these existed at the same time, but there must have been at least four at most periods in the life of Troy VI, and such seem to have lasted through Troy VIIa. Nor can we rule out the possibility that there were other gates in the north wall which do not survive. The only other city to which Homer applies ὑψίπυλος is the Mysian Thebe (*Z* 416), and on this we are in no position to say whether it is justified or not, though Thebe had close relations with Troy and may have resembled it in its manner of fortifications for its strategic position at the head of the Adramyttian Gulf. The adjective might, we would think, have been applied to other citadels such as Mycenae, Tiryns, and Athens, but in fact it is not. The fortifications of Mycenae, which present so striking a spectacle to-day, are not hinted at, nor are those of Athens, while Tiryns is called, very appropriately, τειχιόεσσα (*B* 559) without any hint of its gates. The reason for this must be that Troy was exceptional in the number of its gates, while these other cities had only one main gate and a postern entry. A series of lofty gates at Troy would earn the epithet ὑψίπυλος. The nearest approaches to it are the Boeotian Thebes, which is called ἑπταπύλοιο (*Δ* 406) in accordance with legend and the importance attached to each gate in the war of the Seven, and the Egyptian Thebes, which is ἑκατόμπυλοι (*I* 383), as befits so remarkable a city outside the familiar confines of the Greek world.

(*c*) ἠνεμόεσσα, which is found in the formula Ἴλιον ἠνεμόεσσαν (*Γ* 305, *Θ* 499, *M* 115, *N* 724, *Σ* 174, *Ψ* 64, 297), is, as anyone who has visited Troy knows, remarkably apt, and engaged the special attention of Schliemann, who made meteorological inquiries about it. The north wind, which the modern Greeks call Θρᾳκιάς in the winter and μελτέμι, in the summer, blows powerfully at most seasons of the year and provides ample justification for the epithet. But it is not attached uniquely to Troy. It is applied also to the mountain of Mimas (*γ* 172), which is on the Ionian coast near Erythrae and was the scene of a violent storm recorded by Thucydides (8. 34. 5), and to Enispe in Arcadia (*B* 606), whose exact position is not known to us, as it was not known to Strabo (388), but of course in Arcadia the adjective may easily be deserved.

(*d*) εὐρυάγυια, which is applied to Troy eight times in the *Iliad* and twice in the *Odyssey*, presents a special problem. It used to be thought that it referred to Troy VI, in which there is an unoccupied space between the walls and the buildings enclosed by them.[1] This might call for notice and deserve a special epithet. But this interpretation is hardly tenable, since the adjective is applied also to Mycenae (*Δ* 52) and Athens (*η* 80), where there is no such space. Moreover, in VIIa this open space was covered with houses when the city was rebuilt after the earthquake of *c*. 1275 B.C.,[2] and this suggests that εὐρυάγυια must have another meaning, which can only be 'with broad streets'. One of the most noteworthy features of the rebuilding in VIIa is the construction of well-paved and well-drained streets, notably Street 710, which leads from the South Gate to the citadel, and may indeed have been one of the ways by which the Achaeans entered Troy, since a bronze arrow-head has been found in it.[3] This street, together with the remains of others, suggests that Troy VIIa was well planned for internal communications, and this alone would justify the epithet. It is significant that εὐρυάγυια is applied also to Mycenae, where a royal road led through the Lion Gate to the summit, and to

---
[1] W. Leaf, *Troy*, 150–1.   [2] *Troy*, iv. 6–7.   [3] Ibid. iv. 48–51.

Athens, which had a well-made approach. Homeric notions of width in streets were not the same as ours, and it is likely that any city which had a system of streets would be thought remarkable. In Troy, as in Mycenae and Athens, the epithet is amply justified and seems to fit Troy VIIa better than Troy VI.

(*e*) εὖ ναιόμενον, which is applied to Troy in the formula εὖ ναιόμενον πτολίεθρον (*A* 164, *B* 133, *I* 402, *N* 380), seems to mean 'well populated'. It is used also for the island of Cos, where Heracles arrives after the first Trojan War (*Ξ* 255, *O* 28), and for Sidonie (*ν* 285). The first may have been chosen to suggest a flourishing city worthy of capture by Heracles (Apollodor. *Bibl.* 2. 7. 1; Strab. 531; Eustath. 985, 35), and the second, even if it is not the same as the historical Sidon, must surely be a city on the Phoenician coast and as such assumed to be prosperous and worthy of this epithet. Troy VI cannot have been very populous, as even its small area left room for houses to stand in their own space without overcrowding, but VIIa was different. Houses were smaller and more crowded; empty spaces were covered by them; their stores were kept indoors in jars below the surface of the floor. When the city was refashioned after the earthquake of *c.* 1275 B.C., special steps were taken to make it accommodate more inhabitants without extending the circuit of its walls.[1] It is possible that this is what is meant by εὖ ναιόμενον.

Even if some epithets for Troy are so conventional as to be not very informative, others are much to the point and chosen with an eye for what Troy really was. Just as Pylos is called ἠμαθόεσσα because of the sandy beaches below the hill on which the 'Palace of Nestor' stands, and Mycenae has been abundantly justified in its epithet πολυχρύσοιο by Schliemann's discoveries, so Troy has epithets which are always consistent with its site and appearance and often illuminating and picturesque. They indicate that at some stage or stages a poet or poets knew the site and found the right adjectives for it. This need not have happened within a short space of time, but we ought to be able to decide roughly when some of these epithets were brought into poetical use. We can do something towards this by asking how appropriate they are to the successive cities on the site of Hisarlik. Of these VI and VIIa, which may be treated as a continuous settlement, provided

[1] *Troy*, iii. 38; iv. 9.

obvious opportunities. The walls and towers and gates, the well-paved streets, the crowded houses, even the breeding of horses, are all reflected in the epithets. Troy VI–VIIa was in contact with the Mycenaean world, as the finds of pottery show,[1] and if information from travellers was not enough, it could be supplemented by warriors who fought at Troy in the middle of the thirteenth century. This, and especially the parts of it which we call Troy VIIa, is the obvious Troy for the epithets, but we must first enquire whether some of them might not come from a later date. Troy VIIb continued in a diminished and presumably poverty-stricken form the life of VIIa and maintained some relations with mainland Greece.[2] It is therefore not impossible that wandering bards, whose repertory already contained episodes from the tale of Troy, supplemented the existing epithets with others formed from a knowledge of the site, which might indeed be partly ruined but still suggest something of its former glory. This period would be from c. 1240 B.C. to c. 1100 B.C.[3] In it fell the beginning of the Dark Age, the vast destruction of c. 1200 B.C., and the subsequent movements of Greek peoples, but the poetical tradition, which was already at work in Mycenaean days, survived the catastrophes, and there is no *a priori* reason why poets should not have known about Troy and made use of their knowledge in songs of the heroic past. From c. 1100 B.C. to a little after 750 B.C., when it was refounded by Greek colonists,[4] Troy seems to have been deserted, and even if poets visited it, which must have been rare at the best, its remains would not have conveyed much to them. Nor is it easy to believe that the poet of our *Iliad* could have seen much of the ancient town. If, as is likely, he lived in the second half of the eighth century, he would in all probability have found nothing but a desolate, overgrown heap of rubble, and certainly not sufficient ruins to provide him with the exact knowledge which the more special epithets imply. He could see the actual position where Troy had stood and grasp its relation to the surrounding landscape, but he would not see complete towers or gates or streets. We are forced to conclude that in so far as the epithets reveal a real knowledge of Troy, this must have been gained during the existence of VI or VIIa, with perhaps some small reinforcements from VIIb.

[1] *Troy*, iii. 38; iv. 9. [2] Ibid, iv. 145.
[3] Ibid. iv. 249. [4] J. Boardman, *The Greeks Overseas*, 133.

We need not shrink from the notion that some Homeric epithets go back to the Mycenaean age. An oral, formulaic style, like that of the *Iliad* and the *Odyssey*, may last for many centuries and preserve in fixed phrases much information which dates from a remote past. Just as the poems carry unexpected details about Mycenaean civilization[1] into a time when some of them must have been almost unintelligible, so they preserve information on Troy and the Trojan War, which must go back to men who knew about them from their own experience on the spot. We cannot say exactly for what kind of poem these epithets were chosen and fashioned into formulas, but they look as if they were made for hexameters, and this suggests that the hexameter existed in Mycenaean times, and the poems would have been κλέα ἀνδρῶν, which, whether they were sung in praise of the living or as tales of the heroic dead, told of great doings at Troy. That the one kind of poem passes easily into the other is proved by poetical practice in many parts of the world[2] and is indeed a natural process as the high exploits of the present recede into the past. It is clear that the tale of Troy became a subject for song at an early date, and it is no less clear that certain details and episodes, which are fully intelligible only in the light of what we know about Troy VI–VIIa, were preserved for centuries as an integral part of the tradition, despite their minor relevance to the main story. It is no accident that the faulty structure of the western fortifications of Troy, which has been revealed by excavation,[3] was known to Homer's Andromache:

λαὸν δὲ στῆσον παρ' ἐρινέον, ἔνθα μάλιστα
ἀμβατός ἐστι πόλις καὶ ἐπίδρομον ἔπλετο τεῖχος (Z 433–4)

or that the batter of the walls, which is not nearly so steep as at Mycenae and Tiryns and provides an easy climb up to the angle, or ἀγκών, where the perpendicular battlements on top of them begin,[4] was enshrined in Patroclus' attempts to scale them:

τρὶς μὲν ἐπ' ἀγκῶνος βῆ τείχεος ὑψηλοῖο
Πάτροκλος, τρὶς δ' αὐτὸν ἀπεστυφέλιξεν Ἀπόλλων. (Π 702–3)

[1] T. B. L. Webster, *From Mycenae to Homer*, 64–90.
[2] C. M. Bowra, *Heroic Poetry*, 9–23.
[3] *Troy*, iii. 102–4, 109–113. See W. Leaf, *Troy*, 156.
[4] *Troy*, iii. 87; D. Gray, in J. L. Myres, *Homer and his Critics*, 258.

If the tradition preserved details such as these from Mycenaean times, and it can hardly have done so from any other, it is even more likely to have preserved formulas for the city itself, since these were indispensable for any oral song about Troy.

In trying to decide which of these epithets are early we may start with those which give a visual impression of Troy as a fortified citadel. They are ὀφρυόεσσα, εὐτείχεος, ὑψίπυλος, εὔπυργος, ἐΰδμητος. Some of these may be Mycenaean. The prefix εὐ- occurs a number of times in Linear B tablets from Knossos and Pylos.[1] -τείχεος looks as if it were related to *to-ko-do-mo* (*toikhodomoi*, 'builders'),[2] and -δμητος to *de-me-o-te* (*demeontes*, 'who are to build').[3] All five of these epithets suit Troy VI–VIIa, and if we add εὐρυάγυια and εὖ ναιόμενον, both of which are peculiarly suitable to VIIa, we get a fairly comprehensive picture of Troy as it would look from without and within in the middle of the thirteenth century. εὔπωλος also must be early, since it comes from the time when the Trojans were renowned for their horses, and this does not seem to have been the case after the destruction of VIIa. It too may be an ancient word, since the dual *po-ro* appears on a tablet from Knossos.[4] All these epithets look as if they went back to Mycenaean times and were adapted to poetry when the events of Troy were still fresh in men's minds, and the memory of the city which the Achaeans had besieged and burned was fixed in these apt and convincing words.

Against these we may set other epithets which cannot be ascribed with equal confidence to Mycenaean times and may indeed come from any period when men knew that there had once been a city of Troy on a hill in the Troad. They none the less record impressions of the actual scene and setting. Of these the most striking is ἠνεμόεσσα, which at least looks like an ancient word, since it is related to the Mycenaean *a-ne-mo*[5] and may embody the memories of men who knew the hardships of a campaign in the Troad, but we cannot rule out the possibility that it might also convey an impression formed at a later date by travellers who knew Troy and its wind. Its highly restricted use in the text suggests that it is perhaps less fully acclimatized

---

[1] Ventris–Chadwick, 418.
[2] Id. 182 (PY An 70).
[3] Id. 174 (PY An 35. 1).
[4] Id. 210 (KN 82 Ca 895).
[5] Id. 306 (KN Fp 1).

than, for instance, εὐρυάγυια, which is used in more than one formula, and that its entry into the poetical tradition did not come very early. αἰπεινή and its cognate words suggests knowledge of the hill but not necessarily of the city, while ἐριβώλαξ and ἐρίβωλος refer only to the countryside, and for this reason we cannot assign them with certainty to Mycenaean times and must concede that they could have been added to the repertory at any date up to Troy VIII.

Once suitable epithets for Troy had been found, it was helpful, for reasons of oral composition, to supplement them with others, and some of these look as if they were introduced by men who did not know the look of Troy and therefore used noncommittal words like ἐϋκτίμενος, ἐρατεινή, εὔρεια, and ἱρή, which come from a general stock of epithets for cities and their territories and imply no specific knowledge of Troy. Some of them may indeed be ancient words, but others have a modern air, as ἐϋκτίμενος seems to have lost any close connection with the Mycenaean *ki-ti-me-na*, and ἱρή in its contracted form is later than the Mycenaean *i-je-ro*.[1] But, whether ancient or recent, these unspecific epithets were evidently adopted by poetry when bards had no actual acquaintance with Troy and, feeling a need to widen the range of phrases for it, made use of more or less standardized words which would be appropriate enough but not very distinctive or revealing. None of them makes an unusual point. They belong to traditional ways of handling cities, and their application to Troy may have come when the city and the landscape were no longer familiar and had to be treated with a cautious vagueness.

If we think that the *Iliad* was composed in the eighth century by a man called Homer, it is clear that he had very little part in bringing these epithets for Troy into the epic language. They belong to a tradition which he inherited and no doubt expanded and enriched. In this matter, as in others, he seems to have been content to operate with formulas which were for the most part fixed and regularized before he began to compose, and his task was rather to use them with the utmost effect for his own version of the wrath of Achilles and its dire consequences. It is out of the question that Homer saw Troy in its heyday or even ruins substantial enough to give him a clear notion of what it had been

[1] KN Fp 363.

five hundred years before his own lifetime. But this does not mean that he did not know the country round the hill where Troy had once stood. Indeed it is difficult to imagine how he could have composed the *Iliad* in its present form unless he had in his mind a much clearer picture of the Troad than that of Ithaca in the *Odyssey*, and the clarity of the picture, which helped him to some of his most dramatic effects, may have been enhanced by personal knowledge. It is conceivable that he saw Troy VIII in its early years, and perhaps he knew the Troad when it was becoming a home for new Greek colonists. But all that is another question. For the moment we may be content to recognize that the Homeric epithets for Troy go back in part to the Mycenaean age and reflect the sight which the city presented to at least one generation of Achaeans.

II

ΕΥΚΝΗΜΙΔΕΣ ΑΧΑΙΟΙ[1]

IN demonstrating his important thesis that in Homer 'l'emploi de l'épithète fixe, c'est-à-dire de l'épithète ornamentale (et non l'épithète particularisée) dépend uniquement de sa commodité pour la versification',[2] Milman Parry did not pay much attention to those classes of nouns combined with adjectives in which Homer presents real alternatives in the sense that the needs of meaning, case, and position are met by more than one formula, which is metrically interchangeable with other formulas performing the same duties. A special example of this may be seen when the Achaeans appear in the nominative after a word ending with a consonant, and with their accompanying epithet occupy the second half of the line after the bucolic caesura. For this there are three formulas: ἐϋκνήμιδες Ἀχαιοί occurs 17 times in the *Iliad* and 4 in the *Odyssey*; ἀρήϊοι υἷες Ἀχαιῶν 7 times in the *Iliad* and once in the *Odyssey*; ἀριστῆες Παναχαιῶν 6 times in the *Iliad* and not at all in the *Odyssey*. The first and third of these are also used in the accusative, which has the same metrical value as the nominative—the first 14 times in the *Iliad* and 4 in the *Odyssey*, the third twice in the *Iliad*. It is obvious that of these three possible formulas for the Achaeans at this place in the hexameter ἐϋκνήμιδες Ἀχαιοί is the most common and might therefore be thought to be the most firmly established. We must ask when it entered the repertory of epic language: is it Mycenaean, or does it date from the introduction of hoplite armour after 700 B.C.? The question is relevant to the dating of the Homeric poems, at least in their final form. If the formula is Mycenaean, it is but another example of a survival through the centuries, which has proved its usefulness, but if it comes from after 700 B.C., it means that the text of the poems was at this date changed to take note of a contemporary feature

---

[1] First published in *Mnemosyne*, S. iv, vol. xiv (1961), 97–110, slightly altered.
[2] *L'Épithète traditionelle dans Homère*, 27.

of defensive armour. The evidence for greaves soon after 700 B.C. is clear if not abundant. They are depicted on a proto-Attic amphora in Berlin, dated to c. 680 B.C.,[1] and on a *deinos* of much the same date.[2] From Kavousi and Praisos in Crete come remains of actual bronze greaves, which have been dated to c. 650 B.C.[3] Our task is to enquire which is the more likely time— Mycenaean or seventh century—for such an epithet as ἐϋκνήμιδες to have found so regular a function in the Homeric poems.

For those who are sceptical of Mycenaean elements in Homer the answer is easy. Carl Robert,[4] who is followed up to a point by H. L. Lorimer,[5] regarded ἐϋκνήμιδες as a later substitute for one of the other conventional epithets and pointed out that at *H* 385, ψ 272 and 658 the MSS. have a variant of ἀριστῆες Παναχαιῶν. But of course this proves nothing about the date of ἐϋκνήμιδες and does no more than show that rhapsodes or copyists knew both formulas and slipped naturally enough from one to the other. None the less we may ask whether on general grounds we should conclude that ἐϋκνήμιδες is late and intrusive in the epic language. First, it could be argued that it is well suited to the age of hoplite armour when iron weapons were combined with a defensive armour of bronze and the appearance of warriors so accoutred made a powerful impression on those who were not accustomed to it. An echo of this can be seen in the oracle which Herodotus reports as having been given c. 655 B.C. to Psammetichus I, ὡς τίσις ἥξει ἀπὸ θαλάσσης χαλκέων ἀνδρῶν ἐπιφανέντων (2. 152. 3). Bronze greaves would contribute to this effect, and the adjective ἐϋκνήμιδες may have been coined and circulated at this time to suit this new phenomenon. Yet the epithet is not necessarily bound to this date, for it could with equal relevance be ascribed to any period when greaves were a marked feature of Greek accoutrement. Secondly, it could be argued that since ἐϋκνήμιδες is much more distinctive than Ἀρήϊοι υἷες and differentiates the appearance of the Achaeans in war from that of other peoples, it would be well suited to a time when they wore greaves and others did not. This is true and important, and it might point to the seventh century, but equally

---

[1] H. L. Lorimer, *Homer and the Monuments*, 250.
[2] Id. *P.B.S.A.* xlii (1947), 90, fig. 6.
[3] A. M. Snodgrass, *Early Greek Armour and Weapons*, 87.
[4] *Studien zur Ilias*, 46.
[5] *Homer and the Monuments*, 252.

it could point to the thirteenth. Certain factors indicate that a Mycenaean date calls for serious consideration.

First, since the Homeric style is traditional and contains elements which go back for some five centuries before the poet's own time, it is possible that ἐϋκνήμιδες, which is deeply embedded in the text, is ancient and displaced by alternatives simply because at certain periods greaves were not worn and some other formula was fashioned with a more contemporary appeal. This could have happened at almost any date between the end of the Mycenaean age and the beginning of the seventh century, and there is no fundamental difficulty about it. Secondly, Homer tends to be conservative in his formulas for arms and armour. His bronze weapons, tower-like shields, silver-studded sword-hilts, and plumed and horned helmets, are Mycenaean and remain in his text because they belong to the poetical tradition and are canonized by usage, and this may in principle be true of ἐϋκνήμιδες. Thirdly, it seems to be characteristic of an oral style, like that of the Homeric poems, that once a formula has proved its usefulness it comes to stay and may endure long after the conditions from which it was born have passed away. Since ἐϋκνήμιδες occurs so commonly in the poems, we should expect it to be ancient and its alternatives, which are less favoured, to be later introductions. This point must not be pressed too far, and we cannot argue with certainty that a more distinctive epithet is likely to be more ancient than a less distinctive one. But at least it looks as if the case for an ancient origin should be treated seriously. Though Parry is right in saying that conventional epithets have no special force in their particular contexts, their introduction into the epic repertory cannot have been unmotivated in the first place, and their remarkable character shows that much skill and discrimination have gone to their choice. When the Achaeans are called 'well-greaved', the reason must be that at some time this was not merely true of them but distinguished them from other peoples who were not. There is a good case for reconsidering the matter and seeing if we can reach any firm conclusion.

There are no signs of greaves in representations of Minoan warriors, and we may conclude that they were not worn, because the big body-shield protected the shins as well as the body. Nor are they found on representations of fighting in earlier

ΕΥΚΝΗΜΙΔΕΣ ΑΧΑΙΟΙ

Mycenaean art, where the big shield is still the main means of defence. But in the thirteenth century they make an impressive appearance, and the evidence indicates that there was more than one kind of them. The commonest class is that displayed on some monuments from Mycenae:

A 1. On both sides of the Warrior Vase,[1] in combination with some kind of corslet, trews, and two different kinds of shield, one on each side, but both apparently circular. The greaves cover the calf from just below the knee to above the ankle and are painted a dark colour. They are evidently made to fit closely.

A 2. On the Warrior Stele,[2] which closely resembles the reverse of the Warrior Vase and may follow the same design.[3] The greaves resemble those on the Vase and are painted the same colour.

A 3. On the fragment of the Groom Vase,[4] where the alleged groom, who holds an accoutred horse, wears greaves which are similarly painted dark. The bottoms are missing, but the rest fits the calves closely. The term 'groom' must not be pressed. The man is a warrior, whatever his standing.

A 4. On the fragment of another vase from Mycenae,[5] which shows parts of a warrior. He wears greaves of the same colour, and though the bottoms are lost, they are evidently of the same kind as those enumerated above.

We may supplement these with three other cases which do not come from Mycenae but conform to the general pattern above:

A 5. Fragment of a mixing-bowl from Lefkandi,[6] *c.* 1200 B.C., with warrior wearing trews and greaves like those on the Warrior Vase.

A 6. Remains of a fresco of warriors from the late Mycenaean palace at Epano Englianos near Pylos, *c.* 1200 B.C.[7] The design resembles that of the examples from Mycenae, but the colour is lighter.

[1] H. L. Lorimer, *Homer and the Monuments*, pl. iii. 1 *a, b*.
[2] Ibid., pl. iii. 2.
[3] T. B. L. Webster, *From Mycenae to Homer*, 40.
Lorimer, pl. xii. 1.   [5] Ibid., pl. xiii. 2.
[6] *Archaeological Reports 1966–67*, 13, fig. 18; *Excavations at Lefkandi, Euboea, 1964–66*, fig. 39. There are traces of a like figure on fig. 41, but the man on fig. 40 does not look like a warrior.
[7] *Illustrated London News*, 16 Jan. 1954, 89, fig. 13. See D. L. Page, *History and the Homeric Iliad*, 245, 283; C. W. Blegen and M. Rawson, *The Palace of Nestor*, i. 2, fig. 197.

A 7. An ivory relief from Delos.[1] Its origin is not known, but the style of the greaves is of the normal Mycenaean kind, and the work itself is probably Mycenaean.

Different from these is a representation which raises special questions.

B 1. The fresco of a falling warrior from the megaron at Mycenae.[2] The greaves are painted white and have a projection upwards to cover the knees in front. The figure also wears what look like close-fitting boots and are different from the foot-gear on the Warrior Vase and the Warrior Stele.

These representations show that the Mycenaeans wore some sort of protection on their legs, but they leave undecided whether this consisted of metal greaves or was no more than some kind of gaiter. If the figure on the Groom Vase is no more than a groom, then the chances are that he wears not greaves but gaiters. But fortunately these cases may be supplemented by examples of actual bronze greaves:

C 1. Remains of a pair of bronze greaves found in 1960 at a tomb at Dendra, which may be dated *c.* 1400 B.C., together with bronze body-armour and a boar's-tusk helmet.[3]

C 2. From Nicosia in Cyprus,[4] lower part of one greave shaped to fit the ankle, with holes pierced for lacing and remains of lacing wires. The date seems to be the end of the thirteenth century B.C.

C 3. From Enkomi in Cyprus,[5] slightly different in style from above but of about the same date. There seem to have been originally two pairs of greaves.

C 4. From Khalandritsa in Achaea,[6] from a tomb in a Mycenaean cemetery, dated *c.* 1200 B.C. They resemble the Enkomi greaves in design but have a more elaborate ornament. The lacing is of the same kind.

These archaeological finds show that bronze greaves were in use in 1400 B.C. and again in 1200 B.C. in districts so far apart as the Peloponnese and Cyprus, and since bronze was all too likely

[1] R. Hampe, *Gymnasium*, lxiii (1956), 14, Taf. x.
[2] H. L. Lorimer, *Homer and the Monuments*, pl. xii. 3.
[3] First published in *Tò Βῆμα*, 22 May 1960. See H. W. Catling, *Cypriot Bronzework in the Mycenaean World*, 141; E. Vermeule, *Greece in the Bronze Age*, 135, pl. xxi A.
[4] Catling, 140.   [5] Ibid. 140.
[6] *B.C.H.* lxxviii (1954), fig. 25; Catling, 141.

ΕΥΚΝΗΜΙΔΕΣ ΑΧΑΙΟΙ

to be melted down, the survival of even a few greaves means that once they were in quite common use. There is no doubt that greaves, often of bronze, were worn by Mycenaeans in the thirteenth century and may well have been worn by Achaeans in the Trojan War, which may be dated to the middle part of that century. These greaves are not all made to precisely the same pattern, but we need not trouble about the varieties of decoration on the actual specimens, since such variety would be natural to any warrior-class whose members prided themselves on their equipment. But two other points call for notice.

First, in Class A 1–4 the dark colour in which the greaves are painted has prompted the suggestion that they are more likely to have been made of leather or of felt than of bronze.[1] This might be due to the difficulty of getting bronze from abroad, and the pattern of the greave from Khalandritsa suggests that leather greaves provided the model for it. Yet on the Warrior Vase the greaves are painted the same shade as the spear-points, which can only have been of bronze, and this suggests that they are of the same material. If bronze greaves existed, as we know that they did, an artist, whose subject was the advance of warriors to battle, would presumably depict their equipment at its highest, rather than its lowest, level. If the Mycenaeans could get enough bronze for helmets, shields, swords, and corslets, they could presumably get enough also for greaves, and the abundant references to bronze in the Pylos tablets show that there was no shortage of it, even if its distribution was carefully accounted for and recorded.[2] Bronze greaves need not have been worn by the rank and file, if indeed such existed in Mycenaean armies, but there is a good case for believing that they were worn by eminent warriors such as those on the monuments from Mycenae seem to have been. Nor is there now any need to regard the bronze greaves from Cyprus as exceptional and beyond the scope of Mycenaean usage.[3] They are almost certainly of Mycenaean workmanship[4] and resemble in all essential respects their counterparts on the mainland.

Secondly, in B 1 the greaves of the falling warrior on the

[1] H. L. Lorimer, *Homer and the Monuments*, 251.
[2] M. Ventris and J. Chadwick, *Documents in Mycenaean Greek*, 352 ff.; L. R. Palmer, *Mycenaean Greek Texts*, 279 ff.
[3] H. L. Lorimer, *Homer and the Monuments*, 251; D. L. Page, *Sappho and Alcaeus*, 213. [4] H. W. Catling, *Cypriot Bronze-work in the Mycenaean World*, 140.

fresco are painted white, and this means that they were made of a material different from that of the dark greaves in A 1–5. Miss D. Gray suggests that possibly the white colour represents padded linen,[1] but the fresco, with the warrior's well-shaped calf and slender ankle, suggests that if the greaves were padded, the padding was very thin, and anyhow linen is a much feebler protection than bronze against weapons with a considerable piercing or thrusting or slashing power. We may therefore take up a hint from Homer and ask whether these greaves were made of tin, like those fashioned for Achilles by Hephaestus: τεῦξε δέ οἱ κνημῖδας ἑανοῦ κασσιτέροιο (Σ 613), which save him from being wounded in the leg by the spear of Agenor, ἀμφὶ δέ οἱ κνημὶς νεοτεύκτου κασσιτέροιο | σμερδαλέον κονάβησε (Φ 592–3). If these are what the fresco represents, they might well be painted white, but the notion of tin greaves presents difficulties.

First, Miss Gray argues, 'I do not think that the long leggings with kneeguards on the Mycenaean frescoes, coming right up to the crook of the knee behind and tied there, could have been worn if they had been made of metal.' This is not quite a fair account of the fresco. The greaves do not come right up to the crook of the knee behind, but stop just short of it and leave room to bend the knee. In later classical times metal greaves were often shaped to cover the kneecap in front,[2] and the Mycenaean specimen is an early experiment in this direction. But even if we reject this objection, a more substantial one remains. Tin provides a very feeble protection, and Homer may have been vaguely conscious of this when he called it ἑανοῦ. If he really represents ancient tradition on this point, we must choose between two possible alternatives. The first is that κασσίτερος is not really tin but bronze with a high alloy of tin. This would be explicable in Mycenae where both bronze and tin must for the most part have been imported from abroad.[3] An alloy of this kind might have sufficiently bright a surface to justify painting it as white, or at least have had so polished a surface that the painter's limited palette could not depict it otherwise. The second possibility is that tin was used as a surface decoration on a stronger basis such as bronze. Miss Gray suggests this for the θώρηξ which

---

[1] *J.H.S.* lxxiv (1953), 5.
[2] A. Hagemann, *Griechische Panzerung*, i. 134 ff.
[3] E. Vermeule, *Greece in the Bronze Age*, 227 ff.

Achilles takes from Asteropaeus (Ψ 561) and the tin οἶμοι on the θώρηξ of Agamemnon (Λ 24), and we can apply her idea to the greaves of Achilles. In that case they could be made of bronze but plated with tin for decorative purposes or even to make it easier to keep them clean, since any equipment made of bronze is likely to suffer seriously from the weather on active service. Of these alternatives the second looks stronger, since the Greek word κασσίτερος, which is derived from the Babylonian *kassi-tira* (Sanskrit *kastiram*), must surely mean 'tin' and not refer to some alloy, and anyhow a high admixture of tin would weaken bronze greaves beyond the legitimate safety-point. It seems that Homer may not have been entirely wrong to speak of tin greaves. What he did not say, and may not really have known, is that the tin was only a surface, for decorative purposes, on a sound foundation of bronze.[1]

We may, then, conclude that in Mycenaean times bronze greaves were worn at least by superior warriors and fell into two classes. The first is that of A 1–7 and C 1–4, the second that of B 1. We may assume that in both kinds the fastening was done by a wire lace up the back and that the greaves were of a reasonably close, though not tight, fit round the calf. The rarity of type B 1 may be due to the clumsiness of its kneeguard, which may have protected the knee but would impede the wearer's speed and freedom of movement. Though the two kinds are different, and the second looks like an elaborated version of the first, they show that metal greaves were part of the equipment of a Mycenaean warrior in the thirteenth century. It is true that no word or ideogram for 'greave' has been found in Linear B texts, but, since the same is true of 'shield', nothing can be deduced from it. On the other hand no late Mycenaean representation of warriors shows them without greaves. An apparent exception is a late sherd from Tiryns,[2] which depicts two men with shields and spears but no greaves, but this proves nothing, since the presence of a dog shows that they are equipped not for war but for hunting. There is thus no inherent difficulty in the epithet ἐϋκνήμιδες going back to Mycenaean times.

The epithet indicates that Achaean greaves were not only distinctive but good, and this would suit a time when they were

---

[1] It is possible, but not very likely, that the same workmanship is represented on the Pylos fresco.   [2] H. Schliemann, *Tiryns*, Taf. 14.

commonly, if not always, made of bronze. Equally it would not suit the period between c. 1200 and c. 700 B.C., when bronze was not easily available, and if greaves existed, they were probably made of leather. Leather greaves may be better than none, but they are neither very distinguished nor very distinguishing on the battlefield. We do not know that in this period greaves were worn, since no examples survive and even when in the eighth century painting begins again to portray warriors, the linear methods of the artists convey nothing clear or decisive. It is true that a terra-cotta shield from Tiryns[1] shows a warrior with coverings on his calves, but the cross-hatching suggests that they are not of metal and may even not be leather gaiters but some kind of wrapping. Nor are they likely to be earlier than 700 B.C. There is no need to think that greaves of some sort did not exist in this period, but equally there is no reason to think that they were universally worn or worthy of special attention.

We are in the end forced to choose between the late Mycenaean age and the seventh century as the time when the epithet ἐϋκνήμιδες was introduced. It looks as if Homer was not very well acquainted with greaves and their use but relied upon oral tradition for his references to them. When his narrative calls for an account of a warrior arming himself, he allows some liberty in developing the theme, but he begins with lines which are traditional and formulaic:

> κνημῖδας μὲν πρῶτα περὶ κνήμῃσιν ἔθηκε
> καλάς, ἀργυρέοισιν ἐπισφυρίοις ἀραρυίας.

This is applied without variation to Paris (Γ 330–1), Agamemnon (Λ 17–18), Patroclus (Π 131–2), and Achilles (Τ 369–370). On the other hand, when it comes to actual fighting, greaves, except in the special case of Achilles at Φ 592, are not mentioned and may even be forgotten. We need not complain that nothing is said about a greave when Diores is struck on the shin by a large stone (Δ 519), since such a missile would make short work of any protective armour, but when Pandarus hits Menelaus with an arrow and the blood spurts out, Homer does not speak of him as wearing greaves but says:

> τοῖοί τοι, Μενέλαε, μιάνθην αἵματι μηροὶ
> εὐφυέες κνῆμαί τε ἰδὲ σφυρὰ κάλ' ὑπένερθε. (Δ 146–7)

[1] H. L. Lorimer, *Homer and the Monuments*, pl. x. 1.

We are forced to the conclusion that Homer knew something about greaves from the poetical tradition and mentioned them at certain places, but he seems to have lived at a time when they were not worn, and in his realistic accounts of fighting he says next to nothing of them, even when we might expect him to do so. In that case the use of ἐϋκνήμιδες as the normal adjective of Ἀχαιοί must be part of the traditional repertory and have been well and firmly established long before the appearance of hoplite armour in the seventh century.

Though Homer knew something about greaves, he did not know much, and this partial ignorance may account for a familiar problem, the presence of χαλκοκνήμιδες with Ἀχαιοί at *H* 41. This of course is not an alternative to ἐϋκνήμιδες since it has a different scansion, but neither is it, so far as we can see, the normal way to speak of Achaeans at this place in the hexameter. The regular formula must be μένεα πνείοντες Ἀχαιοί, which occurs at *Γ* 8, *Λ* 508, *Ω* 364 and looks as if it were the more deeply entrenched form. It is easy to assume that χαλκοκνήμιδες is a single, late importation from the age of hoplites, and this may well be the case. It makes no special point in the context and is certainly not what Parry called 'une épithète particularisée'. It could have been introduced after the *Iliad* had taken its main shape and its origin may lie in the desire of some bard in the seventh century to present his heroes as up-to-date in the best modern way. Yet it is no less possible that it is a survival from Mycenaean times when Achaeans wore bronze greaves, and that it lost its place when these fell out of use and references to them meant little to bards and their audiences. Its appearance at this place may be Homer's almost unconscious tribute to an element in the tradition which meant next to nothing to him and which for that reason he did not exploit. We may fairly assume that he did not really think of the Achaeans as wearing bronze greaves, since he never mentions them, and the only metal greaves which he names are those of Achilles and made of tin. In using ἐϋκνήμιδες he followed tradition and may in his own mind have had no very precise notion of its meaning, but the epithet seems to have come to him from a distant past when greaves were made of bronze, and that is why the creators of the epic formulas drew attention to them.

An epithet of this kind may be presumed to have come into use because it stressed something which differentiated the Achaeans from other peoples, and evidently it was thought that the wearing of greaves did this. This would hardly be apposite after the adoption of the hoplite greave in the seventh century since it was not confined to Greece or the Greeks. A votive-shield from the Idaean cave in Crete, which seems to come from the middle of the eighth century, may conceivably be Greek work, but the warriors whom it portrays are almost certainly foreigners from northern Syria, and there is no doubt that they wear greaves.[1] Similarly, enamelled bricks from the Phrygian site of Pazarli, dating from the end of the seventh century, show warriors with greaves[2] and, though for this reason they have been thought to be Greeks, there is no good argument that they are. Equally, in the West bronze greaves have been discovered at Torre Galli and Veio in central Italy and dated to the second half of the eighth century.[3]

Similar greaves have been found in Yugoslavia, at Ilijak from between 800 and 650 B.C.[4] and at Čitluci from the seventh century.[5] In the first part of the seventh century bronze greaves were not a Greek peculiarity, and in that case there would be little point in creating for Achaeans a new formula which drew attention to their leg-protection as something distinctive and unusual. On the other hand, in the thirteenth century greaves seem to have been characteristic of the Achaeans and of no other Aegean people. Outside the Mycenaean armies they are hardly to be found. They are not worn by the Hittites or the Egyptians or their Shardana mercenaries or the Sea Raiders or the corsleted warrior who fights a griffin on the ivory mirror-handle from Enkomi.[6] It is true that in the north-west greaves make a relatively early appearance and that finds of them in Hungary at Rinyaszentkirály and Kuřim have been dated c. 1150–1050 B.C.,[7] but even if we accept the dating, these examples are later than any of our Mycenaean ones and much later than the pair from Dendra. There is no real case for believing that greaves came to

---

[1] J. Boardman, *The Cretan Collection in Oxford*, 138–9.
[2] Hamit Kosay, *Les Fouilles de Pazarli* (Ankara, 1941).
[3] G. von Merhart, *Ber. d. röm. germ. Komm.* xxxvii–xxxviii (1956–7), 126. I owe my acquaintance with this article to Mr. H. W. Catling.
[4] Ibid. 93.   [5] Ibid. 136.
[6] H. L. Lorimer, *Homer and the Monuments*, pl. ii. 4.
[7] von Merhart, 134.

the Aegean from the north-west, nor need we accept Pliny's belief that they were a Carian invention (*N.H.* 7. 56. 200). In the eastern Mediterranean world the Mycenaeans alone exploited them. There is indeed one famous exception, which comes from nearly two hundred years later, *c.* 1020 B.C., when the Philistine champion, Goliath of Gath, in addition to his helmet of brass, his coat of mail, and his spear 'like a weaver's beam', wears 'greaves of brass upon his legs' (1 Samuel 17: 6). If he inherited the traditions of the Sea Raiders, it is clear that they learned the virtues of greaves too late and would have done better if they had worn them against the archers of Ramesses III. But Goliath is an extraordinary exception, and we may suspect that even in his time and country he was an oddity who maintained the style of a past age. In the thirteenth century it was entirely appropriate that poets, wishing to find some distinctive epithet for the Achaeans, should call them ἐϋκνήμιδες. Such indeed they were, as no other people of the Mediterranean seems to have been. The epithet was specially suitable for them as ἱππόδαμοι was for the Trojans, who from the beginning of Troy VI to the destruction of Troy VIIa must have owed much of their wealth and renown to the breeding of horses on the plain which was still used some sixty years ago by the Sultan Abdul Hamid II for the same purpose.

When we set the case for the thirteenth century against that for the seventh, the thirteenth has the advantage, and it looks as if the appearance of ἐϋκνήμιδες in the epic repertory dated from Mycenaean times. The appearance of greaves with the panoply of Dendra may have been meant for some special ceremonial purpose, since it is difficult to imagine any warrior fighting with all that equipment on him.[1] The real change came later, probably in the thirteenth century B.C., when the large body-shield was replaced by the small round shield and the corslet. Once a warrior was freed from the burden of the large shield, he could distribute weight about himself in other ways and combine greater mobility with more adequate protection. Most peoples of the eastern Mediterranean adopted the round shield and some kind of corslet, but the advantages of greaves were appreciated

---

[1] It might equally have been devised for defensive war but proved to be too cumbrous even for that. This may have delayed the introduction of the new armour for a century or so.

only by the Achaeans. In Homer's time this form of armour was known from tradition, and his references to greaves can best be explained by his acquaintance with formulaic phrases which embodied a memory of them. With the exception of the greaves of Achilles, which have a special interest because they are made by a god, Homer pays little attention to their use in war. If he is inconsistent in his treatment of them, the same may be said of his treatment of the large shield. He knew of such things through formulaic phrases which recalled them, but he need not necessarily have given much thought to them or worked them closely into his narrative. When he calls the Achaeans ἐϋκνήμιδες, he preserves a genuine feature from a time when the revolution in defensive armour was more thoroughly exploited by the Achaeans than by any other people of the Near East. Because even the comparatively humble greaves were connected with the heroic exploits of the thirteenth century, they too passed into the repertory of heroic song.

III

ΓΛΩΣΣΑΙ ΚΑΤΑ ΠΟΛΕΙΣ[1]

IN his *Anecdota Graeca*, iii. 1095–6 Immanuel Bekker published from a Codex Urbinas in the Vatican Library a list of one hundred glosses divided unequally between twenty-two districts. This list has been used by writers on Greek dialects, such as Hoffmann, Meister, and Bechtel, to supplement other sources of information on regional vocabularies, and also for their own special purposes by a few writers on Homer.[2] It has also received serious, if limited, attention in special contexts from Ahrens,[3] Sittl,[4] and W. Schulze,[5] but the only basic and comprehensive discussion is that of K. Latte,[6] who has laid his foundations so firmly that it remains only to supplement or amplify him on certain points and to attempt some advance from his position in directions which were not in his purview. First, we may examine what the list is and what it attempts to do. Secondly, we may try to dig deeper into the problem of its origins and sources and to ask more precisely what these may have been. Thirdly, since Latte has already demonstrated the reliability of the List on a few points, we may strengthen his case with other evidence and examples, and assess its value as an instrument for the examination of poetical and especially Homeric vocabulary. Fourthly, since the List plainly contains some archaic words, we may try to relate some of these to what has in recent years been discovered from the decipherment of the Linear B tablets and to ask whether any of these words can be credited with an ancient lineage and proved to be current in Mycenaean times. Since the text is needed for reference in any

---

[1] First published in *Glotta*, xxxviii (1959), 43–60, altered.
[2] M. Kleemann, *Vocabula Homerica in Graecorum dialectis servata* (Colmar, 1876); T. W. Allen, *Homer: the Origins and the Transmission* (Oxford, 1924) 100; M. Leumann, *Homerische Wörter*, Basel, 1950) 262–74.
[3] *Kleine Schriften*, i. 268. [4] *Philologus*, xliii (1884), 2.
[5] *Gött. Gel. Anz.* 1897, 876.
[6] *Philologus*, lxxx (1924–5), 136–75.

detailed discussion and may not always be readily available, we may first reproduce it in full:

Ποῖαι γλῶσσαι κατὰ πόλεις

αὗται καλοῦνται γλωσσηματικαί.

Ἀθηναίων. ἄγαν· λιάν. ἅλις· ἀρκεῖ. λωπός·[1] ἱμάτιον. ὀθνεῖος· ἀλλότριος. πέδον· γῆ.
Ἀργειῶν. αἶσα· μοῖρα. κτύπος· ψόφος. μῆλα· πρόβατα.
Ἀρκάδων. ἄορ· ξίφος. θήγει· ἀκονᾷ. ἴς· ἰσχύς. λέκτρον· κλίνη. λυκάβας· ἐνιαυτός. ξυνόν· κοινόν. οἷος· μόνος.
Ἀχαιῶν. αὔει· φωνεῖ. ἄτερ· χωρίς. λάζω· λαμβάνω.
Αἰτωλῶν. δέμας· σῶμα. οὖλας· ἔλαφος.[2] πάλος· κλῆρος.
Ἀκαρνάνων. ἐνέπει· λέγει. στεῖχε· πορεύου. κῆρ· ψυχή.
Ἀμβρακιωτῶν. αἴθεται· καίεται. βίος· τόξον. χαίτη· τρίχες.
Αἰολέων. αἰχμή· λόγχη. γόος· κλαυθμός. δῶμα· οἶκος. κεκρυφαλέος· ἀριστερόν.
Ἑρμιονέων. ἴθι· πορεύου. κνίσα· ἐπίπλους.
Θεσσαλῶν. αἶψα· ταχέως. ἄνευθε· χωρίς. βροτός· ἄνθρωπος. ἑκάς· πόρρω. καλπίς· ὑδρία. κίρκος· ἱέραξ. κρᾶτα· κεφαλήν. λάτρις· δοῦλος.
Κυπρίων. ἀλαός· τυφλός. ἄλγος· ὀδύνη. ἄλοχος· γυνή. δέπας· ποτήριον. ἔμαρψεν· ἔλαβεν. ἠβαῖον· ὀλίγον. ἕζε· κάθισον. ἰός· βέλος. θής· λάτρις. ταρβεῖ· φοβεῖται. πέδιλα· ὑποδήματα. φάσγανον· ξίφος. χθών· γῆ. τόργος· γύψ. δούπησεν· ἀπέθανεν.
Βοιωτῶν. ἀγορεύει· λέγει. ἄνεω· ἥσυχοι. ἦρι· πρωί. κοίρανος· βασιλεύς. μέθου· οἶνος. πελειά· περιστερά.
Δωριέων. ἔπετε· εἴπατε. φύς· ὀσφύς (ὀσφὺς δὲ λέγονται αἱ ψύαι παρὰ τὸ φύειν τὰ παιδία ἀπὸ τῆς κατιούσης ἐκεῖθεν γονῆς, ὅπερ φησὶ καὶ Πλάτων)[3]
Ἰώνων. κοῦρος· παῖς. νέκυς· νεκρός.
Κλειτορίων. ἆται· ἄνεμοι. αὐδή· φωνή. δέδορκεν· ὁρᾷ. ἕστιοι· νεκροί.[4] ἐσθλόν· ἀγαθόν. λεύσει· ὁρᾷ. πάροιθεν· ἔμπροσθεν. χῆλος· κιβωτός. ὦκα· ταχέως. ὠλέναι· βραχίονες.
Κρητῶν. γονυτος·[5] θήκη, φαρέτρα. ἕλπομαι· δοκῶ. ἔντεα· ὅπλα. θέραπες· δοῦλοι. λᾶς· λίθος. μείων· ἐλάσσων. μόχθος· πόνος. σάκος· ἀσπίς. φῶς· ἀνήρ. σκῆπτρον· βακτηρία.

[1] Latte proposes to change this to the Homeric form λώπη, but the list is not confined to Homeric words, and since λωπός is a genuine form, it is wiser to leave it.
[2] Latte suggests the emendation οὖδας· ἔδαφος.
[3] It is impossible to say how this exegetical note found its way into the text, but it is plainly not at home in it.
[4] Latte proposes ἔνεροι for ἕστιοι, but O. Hoffmann, Gr. Dial. i. 103 may be right in comparing Soph. O.C. 1726, τὰν χθόνιον ἑστίαν, and connecting it with the spirits of the dead who haunt the hearth.
[5] γονυτος is a vox nihili, and the early emendation γωρυτός looks right in the context.

Κορινθίων. ἔτυμον· ἀληθές. φᾶρος· ἱμάτιον.
Κερκυραίων. κώπη· λαβὴ ξίφους. φάλανθος· φάλακρος. φηγός· δρῦς.
Λακώνων. ἀγλαός· καλός.
Μαγνητῶν. αἶα· γῆ. νηδύς· γαστήρ.
Σικελῶν. κόρσας· κεφαλάς. μέλαθρον· οἰκία. ναίει· οἰκεῖ. φόρμιγξ· κιθάρα.
Φλιασίων. ἄμφω· ἀμφότεροι. ἀντικρύ· ἐναντίον.

I

If we examine the structure and the contents of this List, its purpose emerges at once. It consists of words which are familiar from poetry, but are also, according to the Compiler, current in various local vernaculars. His aim is to show that words which are thought to be poetical are in fact still used, or were once used, in certain parts of Greece. Of his 100 words 86 are to be found in Homer, though most of them are not confined to him but appear in other poetry. The rest are the Attic ἄγαν (Theogn. 335; Aesch. *P.V.* 180 etc.), λωπός (Hippon. fr. 2 D.; Anacr. fr. 441 96 b P.) and ὀθνεῖος (Eur. *Alc.* 532–3, 646); the Aetolian πάλος (Aesch. *Sept.* 458); the Thessalian λάτρις (Theogn. 302; Soph. *Trach.* 70; Eur. *Supp.* 639); the Cypriot τόργος (Call. fr. 647 Pf.; Lyc. Alex. 88, 357, 1080); the Corcyrean φάλανθος (Anon. *A.P.* 9. 317. 1); the Cretan μόχθος ('Hes.' *Scut.* 306; Alc. frs. 38. 9; 121. 11 L.–P.) and θέραπες (*Gr. Vers- Inschr.* 1089. 3 Peek; Eur. *Ion*, 94, *Supp.* 762); and the Doric ἔπετε (Nicand. *Al.* 429, 490; *Ther.* 508 in the form ἔπουσι, 'they call'). If we dismiss as almost certainly corrupt the Aeolic κεκρυφάλεος, the Doric φύς, and the Aetolian οὔλας, we are left only with the Clitorian ἔστιοι, which does not occur in any known poetry but may have had a place in some lost work. The List looks as if it were designed for those who are interested in the vocabulary of poetry, and though this poetry is primarily Homeric, it is not always or necessarily so. The Compiler aims at showing that a number of words, evidently not in common parlance, survive in this or that dialect. This is a genuine task of lexicography and is here conducted with neatness and dispatch.

It is clear that the Compiler has formed the List from other than literary sources. Of the 22 dialects from which he draws, only those of Athens, Boeotia, Aeolis, Laconia, and Ionia produced a poetry which had a special local stamp. The remaining

17 belong to relatively unimportant places, which are unlikely to have developed a vernacular poetry of their own and must surely have used a standard, inter-regional language such as we find in the epic and in most choral verse. This does not exclude the possibility that the Compiler sometimes used obviously vernacular verse if it contained obviously vernacular words. But we cannot be sure that he did, and in general his selection of places suggests that he was interested in their actual speech. It is from the living vernaculars that he draws the material by which he hopes to show that his 100 words, which are commonly thought of as exclusively or predominantly poetical, are in fact used in this or that district.

II

We do not know who the Compiler was, but we can learn something of his methods by comparing his entries with the corresponding entries in Hesychius. From this the following points emerge:

1. All the words in the List are to be found in Hesychius except the suspected οὖλας, κεκρυφάλεος, φύς, and ἔπετε and ἔστιοι. Since ἔπετε is known to us only from Nicander and ἔστιοι from no extant author, these words are plainly very rare, and perhaps Hesychius thought them not worthy of attention.

2. The meanings given by the Compiler to individual words are nearly always identical with one of the meanings given by Hesychius to the same words, but Hesychius often gives more than one meaning. For instance, against the Compiler's ὦκα· ταχέως we can set Hesychius' ὦκα· ταχέως, ὠκέως, ὀξέως, and against ἴς· ἰσχύς we can set ἴς· ἰσχύς, δύναμις, νευρά, βία.

3. Hesychius gives examples of the same noun in different cases or of the same verb in different persons or tenses as, μέλαθρα and μέλαθρον, or στεῖχε, στείχειν, and στείχωμεν, but the Compiler consistently gives one example only of each word.

4. Although Hesychius often ascribes words to dialects, it is remarkable that in no single case does he agree with the ascriptions in the List. For the most part, where the List gives ascriptions, Hesychius does not, and when exceptionally he does,

as for τοργός, he differs from the List in making it not Cypriot but Sicilian.

5. The List draws its words from 22 regions, all of which except Clitor and Phlius, are drawn upon by Hesychius for other words.

The List has plainly some connection with Hesychius, but no less plainly is not derived directly from him, since in that case there would not be the different ascriptions of τοργός nor would ἔστιοι and ἔπετε appear as they do, nor would we hear of Clitor and Phlius. On the other hand the similarity between the explanations given to the words in the List and Hesychius and the general likeness between the mass of words selected suggests some relatively close relation. The obvious answer is that Hesychius and the List drew from a common source, from which Hesychius drew much more freely in the different examples of single words and in the number of synonyms for each. This common source would be a copious work which contained some words not even in Hesychius, ascriptions to dialects which he does not mention, and a full supply of synonyms, from which the List makes only its careful selection. Even the recalcitrant τοργός can be brought into this scheme, since it is possible that the source ascribed it both to Sicilian and to Cypriot. It is tempting to think that this source is Diogenianus, to whom Hesychius expresses his indebtedness in his Preface. Diogenianus seems to have compiled on a greater scale than Hesychius and completed what the *Suda* s.v. Διογενιανός calls λέξις παντοδαπὴ κατὰ στοιχεῖον ἐν βιβλίοις ε'. Such a book would naturally contain words from dialects, and its wide scope might allow full lists of synonyms and of ascriptions to dialects. Hesychius says of him that he gave τὰς ἐζητημένας τῶν λέξεων οὐκ ἐχούσας τά τε τῶν κεχρημένων ὀνόματα καὶ τὰς τῶν βιβλίων ἐπιγραφὰς ἔνθα φέρονται. This does not actually say that Diogenianus did not ascribe words to dialects, but, if he did not ascribe them to authors or works, it is at least likely that he treated dialects in the same way. Indeed if Diogenianus had ascribed words to dialects, it is likely that Hesychius would have said so in his preface; for he is careful to explain that Diogenianus drew from a wide stock of material, and specifically mentions his use of Homeric, comic, tragic, and lyric poetry, the orators, the medical writers, and the historians. He gives the impression that Diogenianus covered the whole field of literature, but he does not hint that he was interested in the non-literary, spoken word of different Greek regions. This argument is not final, but on such knowledge as we have we must beware of concluding that Diogenianus was concerned with dialects or ascribed words to them in his work, and in that case our List, no less than Hesychius, got its information from elsewhere.

The *Suda* says that the work of Diogenianus was an ἐπιτομή... τῶν Παμφίλου λέξεων βιβλίων ε΄ καὶ ϟ΄. Pamphilus was a scholar of vast industry and prodigious output, who flourished *c*. 50 A.D. and according to the *Suda* (s.v. Πάμφιλος) ἔγραψε περὶ γλωσσῶν ἤτοι λέξεων βιβλία ἐνενήκοντα πέντε. Athenaeus knew this work and refers to it variously as περὶ γλωσσῶν καὶ ὀνομάτων (14. 650 e), περὶ ὀνομάτων καὶ γλωσσῶν (9. 387 d), περὶ ὀνομάτων (3. 89 d, 121 b; 8. 360 b), and γλῶσσαι (2. 53 b, 62 d, 69 d; 11. 470 d). The distinction between γλῶσσαι and ὀνόματα leaves little doubt that Pamphilus was concerned, among other matters, with dialect words, and it may have been from his collection that Hesychius got some of his own ascriptions to dialects. The task would have been easier if Hesychius used not the original work but the epitome made in the reign of Hadrian by C. Iulius Vestinus in his four books of Ἑλληνικὰ ὀνόματα (*Suda*, s.v. Οὐηστῖνος). The same may be true of our Compiler. Either Pamphilus or Justinus would provide material for γλῶσσαι that appealed to a collector of them. So learned and comprehensive a work would explain both the similarities between our List and Hesychius and the differences between them. It is a tenable hypothesis that both, either directly or indirectly, relied on Pamphilus, but not in quite the same way. That is why, though both are interested in certain words and there is a considerable overlap between them, they do not handle them absolutely alike. Pamphilus would provide enough materials for them to choose what appealed to their individual tastes and suited their conception of the work before them.

Pamphilus was not the first Greek lexicographer to collect γλῶσσαι from dialects, and no doubt he based much of his work on earlier scholars. He belonged to a long and distinguished tradition, which goes back at least to Zenodotus, whose interest in γλῶσσαι is clear from Schol. Ap. Rhod. 2. 1005 στυφελήν· τραχεῖαν καὶ σκληράν· οὕτως Κλειτόριοι λέγουσιν, ὥς φησι

Ζηνόδοτος ἐν Γλώσσαις. Κυρηναῖοι δὲ τὴν χέρσον.[1] This illustrates how the collectors of γλῶσσαι worked. First, since στυφελός is not found in Homer but makes its first appearance for us in Theognis 1194, it has a special appeal, and Zenodotus, like the Compiler of the List, tracks down words which are commonly regarded as poetical to a local source. Secondly, his ascription of it to the Clitorians indicates that he was more interested in small local distinctions than in larger linguistic units like Arcadian, and his precedent may account for the way in which our List classes some words as Ἀρκάδων and others as Κλειτορίων. It looks as if the Compiler found the one set in what was ultimately a different source from the other. Thirdly, it is possible, though not certain, that Zenodotus ascribed the word also to Cyrene. Our Compiler's desire for neatness seems to have prevented him from ascribing any word to more than one dialect, and in this he differed from the earlier, more copious compilers of γλῶσσαι. In general we may conclude that our Compiler worked in a tradition which went back to Zenodotus and that his immediate source of supply may have been Pamphilus. If this is so, he deserves some attention. This was still a high world of Alexandrian scholarship, which had at its disposal vast masses of material not available to us. Our List, preserved by some strange whim of chance, is derived from this age and worthy of respect for its ancestry.

III

It is not enough to claim that the List comes from a good stock; we must also try to establish its reliability at those points where we can check it. These are not many. The sparse number of inscriptions in most of the dialects with which it deals means that in many cases we have no evidence with which to test it. Nor indeed are most of its words of a kind to get into inscriptions. What inscriptions offer for evidence is certainly of first importance but it is necessarily scanty, and must be supplemented from other sources which may be less reliable. We may begin with the better authenticated words and move on to those which inspire less confidence. In this process we shall incidentally see how poetical these words are in their classical career.

[1] Zenodotus collected γλῶσσαι and arranged them alphabetically. See now R. Pfeiffer, *History of Classical Scholarship*, 115.

1. Ἀργείων. αἶσα· μοῖρα. (L)[1]

In Homer αἶσα has, among other meanings, that of 'portion', and this makes rare appearances in poetry (Pind. *P.* 9. 56) and in prose inscriptions from Cyprus (Hoffmann, no. 148, Masson, no. 285) and Arcadia (*I.G.* v. ii. 40. 43; 41. 17; 263. 33; 269. 26, 28). In the Argolid it is found in a treaty at Tylissos between the men of Tylissos and of Knossos about 450 B.C., Schwyzer, *D.G.E.* 84. 10 συν]βάλλεσθαι δὲ τὰν τρίτ[αν αἶσ]αν τὸς Ἀργείος τᾶν ψάφōν and 15 συνβάλλεσθαι δὲ τὸνς ἐκ Τυλισō τᾶν ψάφōν τὰν τρίταν αἶσαν. The word was also used in a slightly more specialized sense, as we know from Hegesandrus: τὴν συμβολὴν τὴν εἰς τὰ συμπόσια ὑπὸ τῶν πινόντων εἰσφερομένην Ἀργεῖοι χῶν καλέουσι, τὴν δὲ μερίδα αἶσαν (Athen. 8. 365 d). It is clearly Argive in the sense of 'portion', and its appearance also in Arcadian and Cypriot indicates that it has a high antiquity.

2. Κρητῶν. λᾶς· λίθος. (L)

λᾶς may be a corruption of either λᾶας or λᾶος. Both words are Homeric, λᾶας being found 12 times and λᾶος twice, while the genitive plural λάων, which may belong to either, is found 4 times. Otherwise both words are rare, but λάου is found at Soph. *O.C.* 196 and λάϋς at Corinna, fr. 654 (a) i 34 P. For the presence of λᾶος in Crete there is good evidence in the Law of Gortyn, Schwyzer, *D.G.E.* 179 x 36 ἀπὸ τō λάō δ ἀπ' ἀγορεύοντι, 'from the stone from which they make the proclamations'.

3. Κρητῶν. μείων· ἐλάσσων. (L)

μείων appears in Homer at *B* 528, 529, *Γ* 193 and in Hesiod, *Op.* 690, *Theog.* 447, and is common in other poetry. Its Cretan character is fully attested by the Law of Gortyn, Schwyzer, *D.G.E.* 179. ix. 49–50 τō μείονος (twice) and x. 16 μεῖον.

4. Κλειτορίων. λεύσει· ὁρᾷ.

Homer uses λεύσσειν in various parts, and it is common in poetry at most periods, but does not appear in literary prose. The spelling with one σ is not a mistake of our Compiler or of his copyists, since it is frequently found in MSS. and appears on an inscription from Smyrna (*C.I.G.* 3284), as well as in Hesychius'

---

[1] The sign (L) indicates that the word is discussed by Latte, though not necessarily in the same way or at the same length as here.

ΓΛΩΣΣΑΙ ΚΑΤΑ ΠΟΛΕΙΣ 35

entries λεύσοντες· βλέποντες, λεύσουσα· βλέπουσα, λεύσει· βλέψει. The presence of the word in Arcadia is guaranteed by the Tegean decree of 218 B.C. *I.G.* v. ii. 16. 10 ὅπως οἱ λοιποὶ λεύσοντες τὰν τῆς πόλεως εὐχαριστίαν ἄνδρες ἀγαθοὶ γίνωνται, and it is worth noting that, so far as we know, there is no other word for 'see' in Arcadian.

5. Ἀθηναίων. ὀθνεῖος· ἀλλότριος.

ὀθνεῖος is not in Homer, and in other extant poetry is confined to a single play of Euripides (*Alc.* 532–3, 646, 810). This suggests that it belongs essentially to prose, and in Attic prose it appears in Plato (*Prot.* 316 c; *Rep.* 5. 470 b; *Legg.* 1. 629 e), Isaeus (4. 18), Lycurgus (25), and more officially in *I.G.* i^2 6. 54 χρήμασιν τῶν ὀθνείων καὶ Ἀθηναίοισιν ἅπασιν. It looks not so much conversational as public and even legal, and it is certainly Attic. Its absence from Herodotus suggests that it is not indigenous to Ionic, and its occasional presence in Democritus (frs. 60, 80, 90 D.–K.) may be due to Attic influence.

6. Βοιωτῶν. μέθου· οἶνος.

μέθυ in Homer means 'wine'. As such it is not found in prose and only scantily in poetry (Xenophan. fr. 5. 2 D.–K.; Aesch. *Supp.* 953; Eur. *Alc.* 757, *Cyc.* 149, *Ion* 1198). The form μέθου, as the List gives it, is indisputably Boeotian, since the Berlin papyrus of Corinna writes ου for υ in such words as κρουφίαν, ἀούσας, δουῖν, ἀδούτων. In presenting the word in this way the List gives assurance of its Boeotian character. Though it could easily have had a place in poetry, there is no reason to think that it was not also current in Boeotian speech.

7. Ἀρκάδων. οἶος· μόνος. (L).

οἶος is common in Homer and classical poetry (Pind. *O.* 1. 71; *P.* 1. 93; Aesch. *Ag.* 131; Soph. *Ai.* 750; fr. 22 P.), but does not occur in literary prose. Nor is it actually found in Arcadian in the sense of 'alone'. But its existence is implied in the Arcadian place-name Οἰὸν τῆς Σκιριτιδός, whose inhabitants were Οἰᾶται (Xen. *Hell.* 6. 5. 24; Paus. 8. 45. 1). No less significantly it is found in the related dialect of Cyprus, Schwyzer, *D.G.E.* 679. 14 *kase onasiloi oivoi aneu tokasikenetone*, i.e. κὰς Ὀνασίλοι οἴϝοι ἄνευ τô(ν) κασιγνέτōν. If the word existed in Cyprus and was a place name in Arcadia, there is a good chance that it belonged to Arcadian speech.

8. *Ἀργείων. μῆλα· πρόβατα.* (L)

μῆλα is very common in Homer and frequent in the lyric poets and tragedians. Its presence in Argos gets some support from Hesychius: μηλοσόη· ὁδός, δι' ἧς ⟨τὰ⟩ πρόβατα ἐλαύνεται. Ῥόδιοι, for, since Rhodes was colonized from the Argolis, its presence there looks like an ancient survival from an original usage on the mainland.

9. *Ἀρκάδων. ἄορ· ξίφος.* (L)

ἄορ with φάσγανον and ξίφος is one of Homer's favourite words for 'sword', but outside Homer it is rare even in poetry (Hes. *Theog.* 283, *Scut.* 221, 257; Eur. *El.* 476) and not found in prose. Its appearance in Arcadian is confirmed by schol. T. ad Ξ 385, καὶ Ἀρκάδες καὶ Αἰτωλοὶ πᾶν ὅπλον ἄορ καλοῦσιν. This elastic use of the word seems to have been known to Alexandrian and later poets, since Callimachus applies it to a trident (*H.* 4. 31) and Oppian to the horn of the rhinoceros (*Cyn.* 2. 553).

10. *Ἀθηναίων. ἅλις· ἀρκεῖ.*

ἅλις is common in all kinds of poetry but in the special sense of ἀρκεῖ it is conversational Attic, as at the end of an argument in Plat. *Polit.* 287 a καὶ τούτων μὲν ἅλις, and we may detect the influence of the vernacular in such tragic passages as Soph. *O.T.* 1061 ἅλις νοσοῦσ' ἐγώ and Trag. Adesp. 76 N. ἅλις ἐγὼ δυστυχῶν.

11. *Αἰολέων. δῶμα· οἶκος.*

Alcaeus fr. 48. 15 L.–P. has Ἀίδαο δῶμα, but δῶμα is not the only word for 'house', since δόμος occurs at Sapph. frs. 1. 7 and 55. 3 L.–P. and Alc. 42. 9 and 357. 2 L.–P. and looks as if it were the normal word. In Ἀίδαο δῶμα Alcaeus clearly echoes the Homeric δῶμ' Ἀίδαο (Ο 251, μ 21), while Sappho keeps closer to the vernacular when at fr. 55. 3 she writes κἀν Ἀίδα δόμῳ. But though Ἀίδαο is a loan from the epic, it does not necessarily follow that δῶμα is the same, or that in Lesbian there were not two words for 'house'.

ΓΛΩΣΣΑΙ ΚΑΤΑ ΠΟΛΕΙΣ 37

12. Αἰολέων. γόος· κλαυθμός.

γόος is very common both in Homer and the tragedians, but does not appear in prose before the Septuagint, and then but rarely. Neither it nor related words have been found in Lesbian, but it is at least possible that when Erinna, *Lament for Baucis*, 18, writes στονα]χεῖσα γόημι he follows a Lesbian example; for, as the *Suda* says s.v. ῎Ηριννα, she writes in a mixture of Doric and Aeolic, and γόημι, which has an unquestionably Aeolic form, looks like an Aeolic word.

13. Θεσσαλῶν. αἶψα· ταχέως.

αἶψα, which is common in Homer and makes spasmodic appearances in other poetry (Theogn. 663, 1001; Aesch. *Supp.* 481; Emped. fr. 35. 11 D.-K.), does not appear in prose before a late text from Gortyn (*Mon. Ant.* 18. 322). There is no evidence for it in Thessaly but it is used in the cognate dialect of Lesbos by Sappho frs. 1. 13 and 60.5 L.-P., and possibly by Alcaeus fr. 346. 2. It may also have appeared in the Boeotian of Corinna in the form ἦψα (*B.K.T.* v. ii. 36), and this combination of evidence suggests that it is an original Aeolic word.

14. Σικελῶν. ναίει· οἰκεῖ.

ναίειν is very rare in prose, but so frequent in poetry that it looks as if it came from a common stock of poetical words. Yet it may be Sicilian. At least it appears in two Sicilian poets, Empedocles fr. 112. 1–2 D.-K. ὦ φίλοι, οἳ μέγα ἄστυ κατὰ ξανθοῦ Ἀκράγαντος ναίετ' ἀν' ἄκρα πόλεος, and Epicharmus fr. 130 K. Ζεὺς ἄναξ, ἀν' ἄκρα ναίων Γαργάρων ἀγάννιφα. Moreover, if we believe, as for various reasons we may, that *Olympian* 5 is the work not of Pindar but of a Sicilian imitator, the word makes another appearance there at 19, σωτὴρ ὑψινεφὲς Ζεῦ Κρόνιόν τε ναίων λόφον. Its authenticity is not certain, but there is something of a case for it.

15. Θεσσαλῶν. λάτρις· δοῦλος. (L)

λάτρις, which is not found in Homer, is not uncommon in other poetry (Theogn. 302, 486; Soph. *Trach.* 70) and occurs 18 times in Euripides, which might be enough to establish it as a familiar poetical word. It is indeed he who gives some evidence for its

Thessalian origin; for he seems to have used it to amplify the Thessalian word πενέστης in the line

λάτρις πενέστης ἁμὸς ἀρχαίων δόμων.   (fr. 830 N.)

16. *Ἰώνων. νέκυς· νεκρός.*

Homer uses both νέκυς and νεκρός, and so does Herodotus. Yet there is some slight indication that νέκυς is the more strictly Ionic form. It is used by Simonides fr. 80. 5 D. κρυερὸς νέκυς and by Heraclitus fr. 86 D.–K. νέκυες γὰρ κοπρίων ἐκβλητότεροι. Neither of these is really conclusive, since Simonides may have got the word from a common poetical vocabulary and at fr. 63 Heraclitus uses νεκρός. But since νεκρός has a wide circulation outside Ionic and νέκυς is comparatively rare outside poetry, it may be the more authentically Ionic word of the two.

17. *Λακώνων. ἀγλαός· καλός.*

ἀγλαός is common in epic, elegiac, and lyric poetry, but rare in tragedy, and then only in choral passages (Soph. *O.T.* 152; Eur. *Andr.* 135), and the same restriction applies to comedy (Aristoph. *Lys.* 640). Its absence from iambic verse suggests that it was regarded as reserved for special duties, and that is why it is not found in prose. If it existed in Laconian, its meaning of 'beautiful' rather than 'bright' gets some support from Tyrtaeus, who at fr. 7. 28 D. applies it to youth: ὄφρ' ἐρατῆς ἥβης ἀγλαὸν ἄνθος ἔχῃ and at fr. 9. 36 to victory: νικήσας δ' αἰχμῆς ἀγλαὸν εὖχος ἔχῃ. Both these cases look as if they were derived from the common stock of epic and elegiac poetry, and it is hard to think that such a word was current in Laconian vernacular. Yet Tyrtaeus wrote his songs for Spartans, and we must not rule out the possibility that his use of ἀγλαός echoed something in their own native practice.

Not all these cases are equally cogent. The best are those which are guaranteed by inscriptions and the weakest those for which the evidence comes from poetical texts which may be suspected of drawing on more than their native vernacular. The examples which come from literary texts raise the question whether the Compiler did not himself use these as well as spoken vernaculars. He may well have done, but even then a poetry so markedly local as Lesbian is a good authority, which he was

ΓΛΩΣΣΑΙ ΚΑΤΑ ΠΟΛΕΙΣ 39

fully justified in quoting. In the mass these cases present a strong argument for the well-informed character of the List and leave the impression that it is a serious and scholarly work, composed by someone who had ample materials at his disposal, knew what he was doing, and may be treated as an authority on the usage of certain words in Greek dialects. His method was to collect words which appear in Homer and other poets and to ascribe them to their local sources. No doubt they struck him by their unusual air and excited his interest for this reason. Greek scholars were much interested in the vernacular use of words and observed the varieties with some care. Our Compiler evidently used good sources and reported them, so far as we can judge, correctly.

IV

The List prompts questions about the historical background of the words in it. They are quoted for their unusual air, and since most of them are found in Homer, they have already a respectable age. We may perhaps venture behind him and ask whether we cannot trace some of them to a considerably earlier time. It was only natural that local Greek vernaculars should preserve words which once belonged to a common stock but fell out of use except in poetry, where they survived through its conservative character and especially the oral tradition which kept the epic alive. That some of the words are as old as the Mycenaean age is clear from their appearance in tablets of Linear B. Such as they are, they illustrate the capacity of Greek words to survive the centuries.[1]

1. *Αἰολέων. αἰχμή· λόγχη.*
The tablet PY Jn 829. 3, which tells how various groups of people are to make contributions of bronze, states that one of the objects for which it will be used is *ai-ka-sa-ma*, i.e. *aixmans*, spear- or arrow-points. This is the meaning of *αἰχμή* in Homer, and its extension to cover the whole spear is natural enough. It can be seen in Herodotus (3. 78. 2; 4. 71. 4) and Xenophon (*Cyr.* 4. 6. 4), but both these may be suspected of being influenced by poetry. As a local colloquial word *αἰχμή* in the sense of 'spear' is

[1] In this section I am grateful for help from Professor L. R. Palmer.

a survival from Mycenaean usage, even if it has slightly changed its meaning.

2. Κυπρίων. δέπας· ποτήριον.

The word *di-pa*, i.e. *dipas*, occurs both at Knossos (KN K 875) and at Pylos (PY Ta 641) and is associated 'with a pictogram of a deep vessel, usually fitted with ring handles'.[1] The word is rare in poetry outside Homer (Stes. fr. 181/4. 1 P.; Antimach. fr. 66. 1 W.; Aesch. frs. 69. 3; 74. 3 N.), and has slightly changed its meaning into some sort of vessel like a φιάλη. Its colloquial use in Cyprus is not surprising, since Cypriot kept many ancient words from the time of its Achaean colonization, and it is significant that the cognate form δέπαστρον, which Silenus and Clitarchus report παρὰ Κλειτορίοις τὰ ποτήρια καλεῖσθαι (Athen. 11. 468 a), existed in Arcadian.

3. Κυπρίων. πέδιλα· ὑποδήματα.

The Mycenaean origin of πέδιλα is now assured by the appearance of *pe-di-ra* in the nominative plural (PY Ub 1318), *pe-di-ro*, possibly dual (ibid.), and *pe-di-ro-i* in the dative plural (ibid.).

4. Κρητῶν. ἔντεα· ὅπλα.

The word ἔντεα is common in epic and lyric poetry but appears only once in tragedy, where it is applied to harness (Aesch. *Pers.* 194). In Mycenaean it forms the base of two compound words, *e-to-wo-ko*, i.e. *entoworgoi* (KN Fh 462, PY An 39. 5, Fn 50. 6) and *e-te-do-mo*, i.e. *entesdomos* (KN Uf 432, Ea 808).

5. Κρητῶν. μείων· ἐλάσσων.

The word *me-u-jo* i.e. *mewjon* (KN Ak 612 etc.) is used with reference to children and goblets in the sense of 'smaller'. μείων, as we have seen, survived in Crete, and also in Arcadia (*I.G.* v ii 3. 15 and 18).

6. Κρητῶν. λᾶς· λίθος.

Though the relevant noun has not yet appeared on Linear B tablets, the adjective *ra-e-ja* (PY Ta 642) appears in lists of building materials and has been equated with λαεία, 'of stone'.

---

[1] J. Chadwick, *Minoica*, 119.

ΓΛΩΣΣΑΙ ΚΑΤΑ ΠΟΛΕΙΣ 41

7. Ἰώνων. κοῦρος· παῖς.

ko-wo, i.e. *korwos*, *korwoi*, is frequent in Mycenaean (KN Ag 87, PY Aa 60) and seems to be applied to young slaves or servants. The form is closely paralleled by the feminine Κόρϝα in Arcadian (*I.G.* v. ii. 554). The masculine had some circulation in various parts of Greece, Eustath. 1535. 49 κῶρος Αἰολικῶς καὶ Δωρικῶς ὁ νέος; Scholl. ad N 95 οἱ δὲ Λάκωνες τὸ κοῦροι ἀντὶ τοῦ εὐγενεῖς; Eustath. 23. 37 οἱ Ἀχαιοὶ τοὺς ἐφήβους κούρους καλοῦσιν. It seems to have a more specialized meaning in Achaean and Doric than in Mycenaean or perhaps in Ionic.

8. Κορινθίων. φᾶρος· ἱμάτιον.

Tablets from Cnossus (Lc 532, Le 786) and Mycenae (Oe 127) combine the ideogram for 'cloth' with the word *pa-we-a*, i.e. *pharwea*, φάρϝε(h)α. In later times φᾶρος is common in poetry, but despite its appearance in Aristophanes (*Thesm.* 890) and Herodotus (2. 122. 3; 9. 109. 1) is not colloquial. Its survival in Corinth may be an idiosyncrasy which dates from Mycenaean times.

9. Κυπρίων. φάσγανον· ξίφος.

Tablets from Knossos (KN Ra 1540) give the ideogram for sword combined with the word *pa-ka-na*, i.e. *phasgana*. In classical Greek φάσγανον is confined to poetry, and its appearance in Cypriot is yet another indication of the archaic character of this dialect.

V

The interrelations between Greek dialects are so complex and in some respects so problematical that we must beware of trying to prove too much from our List. But if we restrict ourselves to well-defined lines of enquiry, we may achieve some small results.

Though Arcadian and Cypriot are branches of a single language which was spoken in the Peloponnese before the Dorian invasion, both must have changed in many respects between Mycenaean times and the fifth century B.C., when our first evidence appears, and the presence of a word in one or the other does not guarantee its Mycenaean ancestry. If, however, a word from one or the other of them is found also in the speech of a region which had little to do with Arcadia or Cyprus, it deserves consideration. This is particularly true of Aeolic, especially Lesbian, which is known to have had some original relation to Arcado-Cypriot but is quite distinct from it. Words common to Arcado-Cypriot and Lesbian, especially if they are rare elsewhere, may go back to before the Aeolian colonization of the Asia Minor coastlands. We may consider the following:

1. Κλειτορίων ἆηται· ἄνεμοι.

The feminine form ἆηται is found in both Sappho (frs. 2. 10; 20. 9 L.–P.) and Alcaeus (fr. 249. 5). It is not easy to distinguish its meaning from ἄνεμος (Sapph. fr. 47. 2; 37. 2; Alc. frs. 38. 13, 249. 11; 326. 1; 319), and Lobel can hardly be right when he says that it means 'blasts' or 'hurricanes',[1] since this does not fit Sapph. fr. 2. 10–11 αἰ δ' ἆηται μέλλιχα πνέοισιν. There is, however, no need to dispute that ἆηται is a genuinely Lesbian word. It differs in form and gender from the Homeric ἀήτης, and there is no real reason why Lesbian should not have had more than one word for 'wind'.

2. Κλειτορίων. αὐδή· φωνή.

Both in Homeric and in later Greek αὐδή is used often of the human voice as opposed to ὀμφή, which is a divine voice. When the Compiler gives φωνή as a synonym for αὐδή, he may mean that it covered both meanings as φωνή does. In any case it is a good Lesbian word, used by Sappho with reference to herself, fr. 1. 16 L.–P, τὰς ἔμας αὔδας.

3. Κλειτορίων. πάροιθεν· ἔμπροσθεν.

Alcaeus once uses πάροιθα (fr. 6. 11 L.–P.), but he also uses πάροιθεν (frs. 112. 20; 325. 3). The existence of these alternatives helped poetry, since the last syllable of πάροιθα could be short before a consonant or elided before a vowel, but there is no reason to think that both forms are not indigenous.

4. Κυπρίων. χθών· γῆ.

Alcaeus uses the accusative χθόνα at fr. 34. 5 L.-P. and the genitive χθόνος at frs. 38. 10 and 130. 29. As Lobel has shown,[2] in Lesbian χθών means 'land' in the strict sense of excluding the sea, while

---

[1] Ἀλκαίου μέλη, xxxiv. [2] Ibid. xxxv–xxxvi.

γᾶ and γαῖα mean 'earth' in the wider sense of both land and sea. The Compiler might seem to suggest that in Cypriot χθών has this wider sense, and though we cannot press the point, it is possible that it developed differently from its Lesbian counterpart.

5. *Κυπρίων. ἔμαρψεν· ἔλαβεν.*
ἔμαρψε appears at Sapph. fr. 58. 21 L.–P. and μάρψαι seems to appear at Alc. fr. 61. 14. The general Aeolic character of the word is illustrated by two glosses of Hesychius, καμμάρψαι· καταλαβεῖν and κάμμαρψις· μέτρον σιτικόν, τὸ ἡμιμέδιμνον Αἰολεῖς.

6. *Κυπρίων. ταρβεῖ· φοβεῖται.*
The same root is found in Lesbian, though the form is that of a -μι verb, at Alc. frs. 119. 115 and 302 ii 12 τάρβημμι, and at fr. 206. 7 the infinitive τάρβην.

These words which are common to Arcado-Cypriote and the Lesbian branch of Aeolic surely go back to a common origin, which is likely to be the language of the Greek mainland before the Aeolian colonization.

VI

A second possible source of information on Mycenaean vocabulary may be found in those Cretan glosses which occur also in other dialects, especially when these are outside the Dorian group. We have seen that the Mycenaean tablets contain words like ἔντεα and κῶρος, which were current in historical Crete, and it is likely that other words were equally ancient. Though their vogue is restricted, they appear in more than one dialect, and this suggests an ancestry which goes back to a time before the classical dialects had found their familiar shape or Crete had been subjected to Dorian influences and ceased to use the Mycenaean language. A few such words may be suggested.

1. *Κρητῶν. μόχθος· πόνος.*
μόχθος is used in Lesbian by Alcaeus, fr. 38. 9 L.–P. μόχθον ἔχην and 129. 11 ἐκ δὲ τῶνδε μόχθων. It has a certain vogue in prose (Democr. fr. 223 D.–K.; Xen. *Symp.* 2. 4, *Cyr.* 1. 6. 25), but this

looks 'literary' and is generally regarded as 'poetical'. That it existed in the Lesbian vernacular we can hardly doubt.

2. *Κρητῶν. σάκος· ἀσπίς.*

No word for 'shield' has yet appeared in the Mycenaean documents, but σάκος seems to be of some antiquity. Not only was it used in Crete but it appears at Epidaurus in an Argive inscription, Schwyzer, *D.G.E.* 108 g. 1. 11 στορὰν τô σακô. Argos is sufficiently distant and different from Crete for the coincidence to be striking, and here too we may suspect an ancient survival.

3. *Κρητῶν. ἔλπομαι· δοκῶ·*

This use of ἔλπομαι is to be found also in Lesbian, where Alcaeus fr. 69. 8 L.–P. has ἤλπετο, and the letters ἠλπ[at Sappho fr. 23. 1 suggest the same word.

4. *Κρητῶν. φῶς· ἀνήρ.*

φῶς is a highly poetical word, which does not appear in prose before the second century A.D. Its appearance in Crete is matched by its appearance in the Asclepieum at Epidaurus, *I.G.* iv 1488. 46 ἐπὶ τῶν διόπων φώτων.

5. *Κυπρίων. ἰός· βέλος.*

The existence of ἰός in Cyprus is matched by its existence in Crete in a curse on anyone who steals arrows, *G.D.I.* 1038 ὅστι[ς] ἀποστερί[δδ]οι τῶν ἰὸν ἔμ(μ)ανιν ἤμε̄[ν] αὐτοῖ τ[ὰν] Ἀθ[α]ναίαν. This looks like an ancient use, but we must note that the only Mycenaean word for 'arrow' known hitherto from the tablets is *pa-ta-ja*, i.e. πάλταια (KN Ws 1704).

6. *Λακώνων. ἀγλαός· καλός.*

Though the List ascribes ἀγλαός to Laconian, it is worth noting that Hesychius has the entry ἀγλαόν· γλαφυρόν. Κρῆτες καὶ Κύπριοι. In Cretan and in Cypriot ἀγλαός has the rather special meaning of γλαφυρός, which is presumably 'smooth'. This slight variation in sense is evidence for the antiquity of the word and its independent development in more than one place.

It is not surprising that Mycenaean words should have survived in Crete, and in these cases their survival elsewhere indicates that behind their several appearances lies a common stock. It is a far cry from Cretan to Cypriot or Arcadian, and the presence of certain otherwise rare words on both sides of the divide indicates a Mycenaean ancestry. It is tempting to try to construct similar ancestries for other words in the List, but for the present the evidence seems inadequate for the venture to have much hope of success. Nor can we be certain that the Greek of Mycenaean times was a single homogeneous language. When in the present context we speak of Mycenaean, we mean the language of the Linear B tablets from Knossos, Pylos, and Mycenae, and we assume that this was a pre-Dorian language of the Peloponnese and Crete and the common ancestor of Arcadian and Cypriot. Relics of it are embodied in the language of the Homeric poems, whence they passed into later poetry, but other relics survived in isolated, local usage, and were duly noted and collected by Alexandrian scholars. Their air of antiquity confirms the impression that the Compiler and his authorities liked to track down archaic words and had a keen instinct for their detection.

IV

TWO LINES OF EUMELUS[1]

AMONG the scanty remains of poetry attributed to Eumelus of Corinth two lines (fr. 13 Kinkel; fr. 1 Bergk, Diehl, Edmonds; fr. 696/1 Page)[2] stand out as different from the rest, first because they are concerned not with the legendary past but with an actual, present occasion, and secondly because they are composed not for Corinthians but for Messenians. Our evidence comes from Pausanias and may be set out at the start:

4. 4. 1. ἐπὶ δὲ Φίντα τοῦ Συβότα πρῶτον Μεσσήνιοι τότε τῷ Ἀπόλλωνι ἐς Δῆλον θυσίαν καὶ ἀνδρῶν χόρον ἀποστέλλουσι· τὸ δέ σφισιν ᾆσμα προσόδιον ἐς τὸν θεὸν ἐδίδαξεν Εὔμηλος, εἶναί τε ὡς ἀληθῶς Εὐμήλου νομίζεται μόνα τὰ ἔπη ταῦτα.

4. 33. 2. ἄγουσι δὲ (οἱ Μεσσήνιοι) καὶ ἑορτὴν ἐπέτειον Ἰθωμαῖα, τὸ δὲ ἀρχαῖον καὶ ἀγῶνα ἐτίθεσαν μουσικῆς· τεκμαίρεσθαι δ' ἔστιν ἄλλοις τε καὶ Εὐμήλου τοῖς ἔπεσιν· ἐποίησε γοῦν καὶ τόδε ἐν τῷ προσοδίῳ τῷ ἐς Δῆλον·

τῷ γὰρ Ἰθωμάτᾳ καταθύμιος ἔπλετο μοῖσα
ἁ καθαρὰ καὶ ἐλεύθερα σάμβαλ' ἔχουσα.

οὐκοῦν ποιῆσαί μοι δοκεῖ τὰ ἔπη καὶ μουσικῆς ἀγῶνα ἐπιστάμενος τίθεντας.

The text, as quoted by Pausanias, raises one or two problems, whose solution affects our view of the lines. Since the manuscripts give both σάμβαλα and μοῖσα which are not epic forms but suggest an Aeolic affinity, the first being found at Sappho fr. 110 (a) 2 L.-P., and the second at frs. 103. 8; 127, and 128, we are clearly right to follow Dindorf in changing ἔχουσα to ἔχοισα. This does not, however, mean that we should go further with

---

[1] First published in *Classical Quarterly*, n.s. xii (1963), 145–53.
[2] In recent years the fragment has not received much attention. The best treatment of it is still that of H. W. Smyth, *Greek Melic Poets*, 163–4. See also Schmid–Stählin, *Gesch. d. gr. Lit.* I. i. 291; H. Flach, *Gesch. d. gr. Lyr.* 93–4; U. von Wilamowitz-Moellendorff, *Textg. d. gr. Lyr.* 38–9; M. Wellman, *R.-E.* vi. 1081; T. J. Dunbabin, *J.H.S.* lxviii (1948), 67; G. L. Huxley, *Early Sparta*, 114, n. 199.

TWO LINES OF EUMELUS

Bergk and assume that the second line must have been a hexameter and may be emended to

ἁ καθαρὰ⟨ν κίθαριν⟩ καὶ ἐλεύθερα σάμβαλ' ἔχοισα.

When Pausanias speaks of τοῖς ἔπεσιν and ἔπη he need not necessarily mean dactylic hexameters. Though the word is commonly used in this sense, it can also be used for other kinds of line, as we see from Ps.-Plut. *Mus.* 3, which may not be very far from Pausanias in time and illustrates his technical vocabulary: καθάπερ Στησιχόρου τε καὶ τῶν ἀρχαίων μελοποιῶν οἱ ποιοῦντες ἔπη τούτοις μέλη περιετίθεσαν. This shows that ἔπη could be used for lines in lyric poetry, and this seems to be the case with Pausanias' account of our piece. If we take the text as it stands, it makes perfectly good sense without any alteration,[1] and gives a dactylic hexameter and a dactylic pentameter. This is exactly what we find, for instance, at the beginning of the first strophe and antistrophe in the parodos of Aeschylus' *Agamemnon*:

κύριός εἰμι θροεῖν ὅδιον κράτος αἴσιον ἀνδρῶν
ἐντελέων, ἔτι γὰρ θεόθεν καταπνείει . . .   (*Ag.* 104–5)

and that it was thought to be characteristic of Aeschylus may be seen from Aristophanes' use of it, with very small variations, in all four strophes of a choral song in the Aeschylean manner at *Frogs* 814–29.[2] That Eumelus' poem was composed on a scheme which included such dactylic metra is not only tenable but likely. The προσόδιον was a choral song (Procl. ap. Phot. *Bib.* 320ª18 ff. Bekker; *Et. Mag.* 690. 41; Schol. Lond. Dion. Thrac. 451. 17 Hilgard),[3] and it is likely to have been composed at an early date, not in heroic hexameters like epic monody, but in a choral metre, even if this was of a simple kind. Moreover, if we keep the traditional text, it has an admirable sense and balance. The Muse herself is called 'pure', and this is much more effective than if the adjective were applied to her lyre. Nor is it at all certain that she would have a lyre, since προσόδια were traditionally sung to the flute.

If, as Pausanias says, the lines were composed by Eumelus, it is important to examine his date. On this we have four statements:

1. Paus. 4. 4. 1. puts Eumelus in the time of Phintas, king of

---
[1] Smyth, 164.   [2] See also Phrynichus fr. 735/1(a) P.
[3] H. Färber, *Die Lyrik in der Kunsttheorie der Antike*, i. 48–9, ii. 29–30.

Messenia, and since at 4. 4. 4 he puts Phintas a generation before the outbreak of the First Messenian War, and at 4. 13. 7 puts the war from 743 to 724 B.C., his date for Phintas, and with him for Eumelus, is about 773 B.C.

2. Eusebius–Jerome 150. 21 Fotheringham: Ol. 5. 3 (757 B.C.) *Eumelus poeta qui Bugoniam et Europiam et Arctinus qui Aethiopidem composuit et Ilii Persis agnoscitur.*
3. Eusebius–Jerome 155. 4 Fotheringham: Ol. 9. 1 (743 B.C.) *Eumelus Corinthius versificator agnoscitur et Sibylla Erythraea.*
4. Clem. Alex. *Strom.* 1. 131. 8 S. Εὔμηλος δὲ ὁ Κορίνθιος πρεσβύτερος ὢν ἐπιβεβληκέναι Ἀρχίᾳ τῷ Συρακούσας κτίσαντι. Since Clement puts the foundation of Syracuse in 734 B.C. and ἐπιβεβληκέναι means 'overlapped', he indicates that Eumelus was alive at the time, but belonged to an older generation than Archias.

We cannot expect to find any exact chronology for the eighth century B.C., but of these four dates two look less convincing than the other two. First, when Pausanias puts Eumelus about 773 B.C. he makes him conform to his own chronology of the First Messenian War, but, though his actual dates for this, 743–723 B.C., may not be far off the mark, there is too much romance in his general account to allow trust in it[1] or in its handling of individual characters. Secondly, when Eusebius–Jerome gives two dates, the earlier is open to suspicion because of the connection which it makes between Eumelus and Arctinus. Since both were believed to have written epic poems, it was easy to bring them together, and the case might appear all the stronger because the *Titanomachia* was ascribed to both (Athen. 7. 277 d). On the other hand Clement's association of Eumelus with Archias looks as if it deserved respect, since the foundation of Syracuse was a verifiable event, and there is no call to dispute its date in 734 B.C. Archias was honoured as its founder, and, if Eumelus was connected with him, this would be a solid fact. For this there is some supporting evidence. Eumelus was, as Pausanias says, τῶν Βακχιδῶν καλουμένων (2. 1. 1), and this means that he belonged to the powerful clan of the Bacchiads who ruled Corinth for some two hundred years and controlled the politics of the city until they were dispossessed by Cypselus in 657 B.C.

---

[1] See especially F. Jacoby, *F. Gr. Hist.* iii a 136 ff.

(Hdt. 5. 92. 3; Nic. Dam. 90 F 57–60 Jacoby; Paus. 2. 4. 4; Diod. 7. 9. 4; Strab. 378).[1] Archias himself was a Heraclid (Thuc. 6. 3. 2), but there seems to be no difference between a Heraclid and a Bacchiad, since the Bacchiads were descended from Heracles (Diod. 7. 9. 4) and credited with the foundation of Syracuse (Timaeus, 566 F 80 Jacoby). Eumelus would thus belong to the same ruling class as Archias and may well have played some subsidiary role in the Syracusan venture or at least have been remembered for his connection with Archias. Such a date is not very far from the second date given by Eusebius–Jerome, 743 B.C. Indeed the connection between Eumelus and the Erythraean Sibyl may not be so accidental as it looks, since she must have come from Erythrae and may have been connected with the early days of colonization in the West.[2] It is also perhaps worth noting that the preceding entry in Eusebius–Jerome in Ol. 8. 3 (745 B.C.) says *Lacedaemonii contra Messenios uicennale bellum habebant*, and it looks as if Eusebius–Jerome had in mind some association between Eumelus and the First Messenian War. Such as the external evidence is, it suggests that Eumelus flourished in the third quarter of the eighth century, but, being older than Archias, was by this time of mature years.

Though Eumelus seems to have lived at this time, it does not necessarily follow that he wrote the lines which Pausanias so confidently ascribes to him. We might indeed be disposed to doubt Pausanias' word on the matter, since, in another context, speaking of the verses on the Chest of Cypselus, he says: τὰ ἐπιγράμματα δὲ τὰ ἐπ' αὐτῆς τάχα μέν που καὶ ἄλλος τις ἂν εἴη πεποιηκώς, τῆς δὲ ὑπονοίας τὸ πολὺ ἐς Εὔμηλον τὸν Κορίνθιον εἶχεν ἡμῖν, ἄλλων τε ἕνεκα καὶ τοῦ προσοδίου μάλιστα ὃ ἐποίησεν ἐς Δῆλον (5. 19. 10). Here Pausanias shifts a little from his earlier position that the poem for Delos is probably the only authentic work of Eumelus (4. 4. 1) and suggests that the lines on the Chest may also be his. But this is out of the question. The Chest, which must have been a remarkably fine piece of work, cannot conceivably have been made in the eighth century and is much more likely to come from the early years of the sixth,[3] and in that

---

[1] H. Toepfer, *R.-E.* ii. 2783 ff.; P. N. Ure, *The Origin of Tyranny*, 192 ff.: T. Lenschau, *R.-E.* Supp. iv. 1013 ff.; A. Andrewes, *The Greek Tyrants*, 43–9.

[2] J. Pollard, *A.B.S.A.* lv (1960), 198 ff.

[3] H. Payne, *Necrocorinthia*, 351, ascribes the Chest to the first quarter of the sixth century.

case the verses cannot have been written by Eumelus. They are in the epic tradition, like the other hexameter fragments attributed to him, and if there was any similarity of style between them and the προσόδιον, it would be due simply to the use of epic words or phrases in both. Pausanias in fact does no more than offer a tentative personal suggestion, and there is nothing in it. This is not the case with his attribution of the προσόδιον to Eumelus. At 4. 4. 1 he says that it is the common view, νομίζεται, that this is his only genuine work. That this was in accordance with the views of ancient scholars has some supporting evidence. First, at 2. 1. 1. Pausanias has doubts about Eumelus' alleged authorship of ἡ Κορινθίων συγγραφή, and well he may, since this was a prose paraphrase of a poetical work or works, and such is inconceivable in the eighth century. Secondly, though Schol. Ven. A on Z 131 regards Eumelus as the author of the *Europia*, both Pausanias, who speaks of ὁ τὰ ἔπη ἐς Εὐρώπην ποιήσας, and Clement, who speaks of ὁ τὴν Εὐρωπίαν ποιήσας (*Strom.* 1. 151), evidently feel misgivings and express themselves with caution. Thirdly, as we have seen, Athenaeus (7. 277 d) says that the *Titanomachia* was ascribed variously to Eumelus and Arctinus and ὅστις δήποτε χαίρει ὀνομαζόμενος. Since these doubts are all concerned with epics about the heroic past, they mark the difference between such poems, which were liable to be ascribed to almost any famous poet, and our fragment which deals with quite a different class of theme and might well be ascribed to a historical author. It is understandable that, just as the *Thebais, Epigoni*, and *Cypria* were ascribed to Homer, so in Corinth poems about the past were ascribed to Eumelus just because of his eminence. This means not that he did not compose any such poems but that those which were ascribed to him were probably not his. Behind them lay an oral tradition in which bard after bard sang of much the same themes, and when at last texts were written down, they would easily be attributed to some great poet of the past, who may indeed have had a hand in shaping the story but whose actual work these poems were not. The authorship of such poems was rightly more disputed than that of the προσόδιον, which dealt with a historical occasion and may have mentioned real personalities.

Nor is it convincing to argue that a Bacchiad aristocrat like Eumelus would not have composed such a poem as the προσόδιον, since it would have been below his social dignity to do so.[1] The early lyric poets were often men of some standing. Arion was held in high honour by Periander (Hdt. 1. 24. 1); Stesichorus was sufficiently established to come into conflict with Phalaris (Aristot. *Rhet.* 1393^b); Ibycus came from a noble family at Rhegium (Strab. 257; Ps.–Plut. *de Nob.* 2). However exclusive the Bacchiads may have been, there is no reason to think that they would shrink from producing songs and choirs on important occasions. When Pausanias thinks that the προσόδιον is the only authenticated work of Eumelus, we are wise to take his word. How the poem survived is a question to which there is no sure answer, but there is no difficulty in its having done so. The new alphabet came to Greece in the middle of the eighth century and was very soon applied to inscribing verses on pots and stone and bronze. There is no reason to think that poems were not also inscribed on more perishable materials such as skins and papyrus and wood, and it may well be the case that Eumelus' poem was inscribed after performance and preserved, possibly at Delos.[2] In his knowledge of it Pausanias clearly goes outside his dubious sources for parts of the First Messenian War, and we have no reason to assume that he did not know the actual text or that its preservation from the distant past was in any way impossible.

Short though the fragment is, it yields some points of interest on the style of choral poetry at this early date. On the one hand there are in it words which have clearly Aeolic affinities, notably σάμβαλα and ἔχοισα, to which we may add Μοῖσα.[3] ἔπλετο is actually found at Sappho, fr. 94. 26 L.–P. and other forms of the word at frs. 50. 1; 81 (b) 3, and 79. 5, and at Alcaeus, frs. 360. 1, 373, and 113. 6 L.–P., but since it is common in Homer, it may have a past in the epic. καθαρά does not actually occur in Sappho and Alcaeus, but it need not be fundamentally alien to Aeolic. So too Ἰθωμάτας, which may be a genuine Messenian form, since it is found in Messenia in the third century B.C. (Schwyzer, *D.G.E.*, no. 71. 23), is not difficult to absorb into an Aeolic setting, since Alcaeus uses the similarly formed ὠμήστας for Dionysus (fr. 129. 9 L.–P.). On the other hand καταθύμιος

---

[1] E. Bethe, *R.-E.* vi. 1080
[2] Wilamowitz, *Textg. d. gr. Lyr.* 38.
[3] Alcman commonly uses the termination -οισα and this perhaps illustrates the description of him by Apollonius Dyscolus 1. 1. 107. 13 Schneider–Uhlig as συνεχῶς αἰολίζων.

belongs to a different category. The prefix κατα- is not normal in Sappho or Alcaeus, and for καταθύμιος we should expect κατθύμιος on the analogy of κατθναίσκει (Sappho, fr. 140. 1 L.–P.).[1] καταθύμιος is, however, to be found in Homer at K 383, P 201, and X 292. These bits of evidence, slight though they are, indicate that there was in Eumelus' language an element of Aeolic, which calls for explanation. First, we might claim that, though Corinth was predominantly a Dorian city, it had once been Aeolian (Thuc. 4. 42. 2) and in later times almost prided itself on having produced Sisyphus Αἰολίδαις (Alcaeus, fr. 38. 5 L.–P.) and Bellerophon Αἰολίδας (Pind. O. 13. 67), while Aeolic elements have been found in the Corinthian dialect.[2] In that case Eumelus' Aeolic forms may be traditional to Corinth, either in poetry or in the spoken vernacular. Secondly, there are, as is well known, Aeolic elements so deeply sunk in the epic language that they may go back to a remote past, and though the epic, as we know it, is predominantly Ionic, it may outside Ionia have kept a strong portion of Aeolic forms. Eumelus would take these over because the epic was probably the dominating art of his time. Thirdly, it is possible that even in the eighth century Lesbos had already begun to practise lyric song and to win a name for it. Early in the next century it was to produce Terpander and Arion and with them to gain a great reputation (*Suda*, s.v. μετὰ Λέσβιον ᾠδόν; Sappho, fr. 106 L.–P. πέρροχος ὡς ὅτ' ἄοιδος ὁ Λέσβιος ἀλλοδάποισιν), and was known to Archilochus in the Λέσβιον παιήονα (fr. 76 D.). Yet, even if we rule out this possibility, there are good enough reasons for Eumelus' use of occasional Aeolic forms, and when he does so he anticipates the mixed language which was to be the medium of such choral poets as Stesichorus, Simonides, and Pindar. He certainly did not write either in his own vernacular or in that of the Messenians, and no doubt the epic, in whatever form he knew it, would have some influence on him.

Pausanias says that Eumelus' words come from a προσόδιον sung by a choir sent by the Messenians to Delos. That it was a real song, not something recited or spoken, is clear from his calling it an ᾆσμα, but we do not know to what instrument, if

---

[1] It is true that at fr. 44. 12 L.–P. Sappho writes κατὰ πτόλιν, but the poem is full of anomalies, and this is one of them; so too is καταστείβοισι at fr. 105 (c) 2; see E. Lobel, *Ἀλκαίου μέλη*, xiv–xv.   [2] C. D. Buck, *Greek Dialects*[2], 4.

any, it was performed. In later times a προσόδιον was normally sung to the flute (*Et. Mag.* 690. 33; Ioh. Sard. in Aphth. *Progymn.* 8 Rabe), but this need not always have been the practice. If there was a musical accompaniment, it would be more primitive than the music of the lyre after the reforms of Terpander (Timoth. *Pers.* 234 ff.; Ps.-Plut. *Mus.* 3; *Suda*, s.v. νόμος) or of the flute after the reforms of Clonas (Ps.-Plut. *Mus.* 4). Though Homer mentions choral songs of more than one kind, he suggests that they need not always be accompanied by instruments. At least he says nothing about them in connection with the Paean (*A* 473) or the Dirge (*Σ* 50–1, 314–16, *Ω* 723, ω 60). On the other hand, on the Shield of Achilles, when a ὑμέναιος is sung and young dancers turn cart-wheels,

ἐν δ' ἄρα τοῖσιν
αὐλοὶ φόρμιγγές τε βοὴν ἔχον.   (*Σ* 494–5)

But a προσόδιον was a more solemn affair than a ὑμέναιος, and, since in later times its music was restricted to the flute, this may always have been the practice, which Greek conservatism, strong in such matters, saw no reason to alter.

Pausanias says that the song was composed in the time of Phintas, son of Sybotas, and that it was the first occasion when the Messenians sent a sacrifice and a choir of men to Apollo at Delos. The second item of information may conceivably have come from the song, which may, like other choral songs composed for special occasions, have mentioned its performers at some point, and such a departure from Messenian custom might call for attention. But the mention of Phintas is more open to suspicion. Though Pausanias says little about him, he must have died before the outbreak of the war, which was carried on by his sons. It is of course possible that the song was connected with him in Corinthian tradition, but we may doubt whether he would be sufficiently important to be remembered in this way at Corinth, and it is more likely that on this point Pausanias has taken him from a later, less reliable source and given him a place in the story. The reference to him has determined the conventional date for the song, since Pausanias says, ἐγένετο δὲ καὶ πρὸς Λακεδαιμονίους ἐπὶ τῆς Φίντα βασιλείας διαφορὰ πρῶτον (4. 4. 1). That such a date was known is clear from the way in which Eusebius–Jerome places Eumelus just before the war, and it is natural that this date has been accepted for it.[1] Yet we shall see that there are great difficulties in accepting this. Phintas may or may not have been a historical figure, but we may doubt whether he had anything to do with Eumelus.

Before we look more closely at the possible date of the lines, we may establish one small point. When Pausanias says that this was the first time that the Messenians sent a choir to Delos, this seems right. We have good evidence for an early festival there in the Homeric Hymn to Apollo, which surely comes from the seventh century and at 147 indicates that this is essentially an Ionian festival:

$$\text{ἔνθα τοι ἑλκεχίτωνες Ἰάονες ἠγερέθονται.}$$

At 152, when it speaks of Ἰάονες ἀθρόοι, it suggests that this is not merely Ionian but Panionian. This would in the ordinary course of events exclude a Messenian choir whose song was composed by a Corinthian, and it can only have been in special circumstances that this was allowed. The choir sent from Messenia is intimately related to the rites of Zeus Ithomatas, who had his sanctuary on Mount Ithome and his festival of the Ἰθωμαῖα at which the Messenians held their μουσικῆς ἀγών, and his importance may be gauged by the sacrifice to him of three hundred prisoners by Aristomenes in the Second Messenian War (Clem. Alex. *Protrept.* 42. 2 S.). The choir has the highest credentials and offers to the god of Delos the goodwill of the god of Ithome. The need of the Messenians was great, and steps were taken to make the offering as impressive as possible.

Three points now emerge from the text. First, what is the precise meaning of ἔπλετο? Smyth[2] and others take it as an aorist which means 'became' and therefore 'is'. This is well known from Homer, but we may doubt if it is right here. For though it occurs some eighteen times in Homer, it is invariably combined with a present indicative or an optative or an imperative, and there is no doubt of its meaning. When it is not so combined, it has its natural meaning of 'was'. This is what it must have here. It is combined with καταθύμιος, and this must mean that the Muse 'was in the mind' of the god of Ithome, in the sense

---

[1] T. J. Dunbabin, *J.H.S.* lxviii (1948), 67, with a reservation in n. 71, suggests that the lines may have been written before the war. G. L. Huxley, *Early Sparta*, 114, n. 199, puts them in the generation before the outbreak.
[2] *Greek Melic Poets*, 164.

that he cared greatly for her; for this is the meaning of the word in χ 392, Theognis 617, 1086, 1238, 1283, Hdt. 5. 39. 1., Democr. fr. 277 D.–K. But if we press, as we must, the past meaning in ἔπλετο, it suggests that song can no longer be practised at Ithome as it used to be and that therefore the god is deprived of something which he used to love. For this there must be good reasons. Though we need not necessarily refer the words to the blockade of Ithome by the Spartans when the Messenians shut themselves up in it (Paus. 4. 9. 1), we must surely assume that something has happened to hamper and diminish the traditional musical performance in honour of Zeus, and this can hardly be anything else than the presence of a Spartan army in Messenia. The Ἰθωμαῖα may have been discontinued in a time of urgent need, and the regular cult of music and song reduced to meagre proportions, if not altogether abandoned. This rules out any suggestion that the song comes from before the outbreak of war and indicates that Pausanias is wrong in connecting the song with Phintas and the events that preceded the fighting. The lines come from the dark period when the Messenians are feeling the pressure of the Spartan invaders and look back to a better time when Zeus of Ithome still received the songs in which he delighted.

Secondly, the Muse is called καθαρά, and since this is not an adjective given to her elsewhere, it is not merely decorative but must serve some special purpose. In accordance with established usage it implies cleanliness from guilt or pollution and may be illustrated by the way in which Apollo is washed after birth ἁγνῶς καὶ καθαρῶς (Hom. Hymn, 3. 121), or a sacrifice is conducted in the same words (Hes. *Op.* 337), or Xenophanes insists that men should sing to the gods καθαροῖσι λόγοις (fr. 1. 14 D.–K.), or an Attic σκόλιον hopes that the singer may become a golden lyre carried by a woman καθαρὸν θεμένη λόγον (fr. 901/17 P.) with reference to some such rite as the Panathenaic procession. Yet since Eumelus prefixes a definite article and suggests that such purity is not so much an adjunct of the occasion as an element in the Muse's character, we may read something precise and purposeful into what he says. He would not have used the word in this striking way without deliberate intention, and we may surmise that through it he implicitly denies any stories which told that the war began because of impious acts committed by the Messenians. Two such acts were recorded of them, the first the murder of the Spartan king Teleclus when he came to sacrifice at Messene, and the second the violation of some maidens who had come to sacrifice at the sanctuary of Artemis. Both acts are reported not only by Pausanias (4. 4. 2) but by Strabo (279 and 362), who gets his information on the second from Antiochus of Syracuse (555 F 9 Jacoby), and this double authority inspires confidence. The war may well have been inflamed by stories of such behaviour, and Eumelus' use of καθαρά looks as if he were defending the Messenians against accusations of this kind. He claims that their Muse comes clean of pollution, as if some of those present might complain that she did not. This too suggests that the poem was written after the outbreak of war, and this gains a little additional support from Antiochus, who differs from Pausanias in not associating the affair of the maidens closely with the death of Teleclus but adding that the former took place shortly before the destruction of Messenia by the Spartans and the foundation of Rhegium, which may be placed about 730 B.C. (Strabo 257; Diod. 8. 23. 2).[1] Though the dates of the war are much disputed, it lasted for nineteen years (Tyrt. fr. 4. 4 D.) and may possibly be dated from 740 B.C. to about 720. In that case there is a second slight piece of evidence that our song was composed during it, and indeed before 730 B.C., when the position of the Messenians was already bad.

Thirdly, something of importance must lie behind the words ἐλεύθερα σάμβαλ' ἔχοισα. That the Muse, who is embodied in a choir marching in procession, should wear sandals is appropriate enough, but the epithet ἐλεύθερα is not so easily disposed of. It might, of course, have a purely technical meaning and refer to the kind of movement which accompanies the song and is for some reason regarded as 'free', perhaps because it is not restricted to a single place but moves from one to another in procession. But this explanation is not only feeble in itself but an anticlimax after καθαρά. It is more likely that ἐλεύθερα suggests quite simply the freedom recently enjoyed by the Messenians and now gravely threatened by the Spartans. That ἐλεύθερα can mean 'of free men' or 'of freedom' can be seen from Pind. *P.* 2. 57

---

[1] T. J. Dunbabin, *The Western Greeks*, 13. 2; L. Kroymann, *Sparta und Messenien*, 11.

ἐλευθέρᾳ φρενί, 8. 98 ἐλευθέρῳ στόλῳ, Aesch. *Pers.* 592–3 λέλυται γὰρ λαὸς ἐλεύθερα βάζειν, *Ag.* 328–9 οὐκέτ' ἐξ ἐλευθέρου δέρης, and Eur. fr. 495. 38 N. φασγάνοις ἐλευθέροις. Such parallels justify us in taking Eumelus' words to mean 'wearing the sandals of freedom', and the movement of the choir is itself an outward sign of the independence which the Messenians still cherish and claim to have been dear to their god. This point also suggests that the song was written during the war, at a stage when the Messenians realized how serious the Spartan threat to their liberty was. The evidence, then, leads to the conclusion that the song cannot have been written, as Pausanias suggests and some modern scholars agree, before the war. It was written during it at a time when the danger to Ithome was sufficiently deadly for a special mission to be sent to Apollo at Delos.

We may well ask how the Messenians were able to do this when they were beleaguered at home and must have found it difficult to equip a choir and send it to Delos. We cannot deny that this could have happened or that in so grim an emergency the Messenians may have thought the god's help sufficiently important to call for a great effort on their part and to succeed in making it. Yet a tempting alternative has been suggested to me by Professor A. Andrewes, who thinks that the choir may have been sent not from Messenia itself but by Messenian exiles temporarily resident in Euboea and soon to set off to the West with Chalcidian colonists. This is clearly stated by Antiochus of Syracuse (555 F 9 Jacoby), who adds that it was carried out at the bidding of the Delphian Apollo, and that these Messenians constituted the ruling class of Rhegium until the time of Anaxilas, who himself claimed to be descended from them and invited other Messenians to come to his city. If the song was sent by these Messenians, there is perhaps a special point in καθαρά, for they dissociated themselves from the rest of their countrymen in the affair of the violated maidens and consulted Apollo about ways to escape punishment for it. The time to send a choir to Delos would be not after the decision to sail to the West but before it and before the god of Delphi had issued his instructions. At such a moment the Messenian exiles in Chalcis may well have turned to Apollo, with whom they were especially concerned in the matter of the maidens, but approached him first in Delos in the hope that he might inspire the Ionians to help them. In this they were not entirely disappointed, since the Chalcidians found for them a lasting home and a dignified independence in Rhegium. The goodwill of the Chalcidians was displayed no less effectively in their provision of transport for Messenians still in the Peloponnese so that they could join their fellow countrymen in Rhegium (Heracl. Pont. 55 Rose). We cannot be certain that the choir was sent from Chalcis, but it was surely sent in a time of war when Chalcis was active in friendship for the troubled Messenians.

There remains a final question: how and why did the Messenians ask the Corinthian Eumelus to write the song for them? If we are to believe Pausanias, the Corinthians were the only people to fight on the Spartan side in the war (4. 11. 1), but we need not pay too much attention to this, since it may have been transferred to the First Messenian War from the Second. Yet the problem about Eumelus remains. In a later age he would no doubt, like Simonides and Pindar, have been invited to give his professional services for a fee, but this seems out of the question for a Bacchiad in the eighth century. More probably, because Corinth had already formed that friendship with Chalcis which enabled both powers to combine in establishing their power in the West,[1] and was soon to align herself on the side of Chalcis in the Lelantine war,[2] this appealed to Eumelus as the friend of Archias and persuaded him to do what the Chalcidians asked of him for their troubled friends. On the Messenian side there were obvious advantages in getting a distinguished figure like Eumelus to compose a song for them. In such a crisis they must give the god the best that they could, and this would include a song by a famous poet. The interrelations of Greek states at this date are beyond our grasp, but it seems to be clear that in their desperate need the Messenians appealed to the Delian god of the Ionian people and used as their intermediary a member of the ruling class at Corinth.

[1] A. Andrewes, *The Greek Tyrants*, 40.
[2] W. G. Forrest, *Historia*, vi (1957), 160–75.

V

THE FOX AND THE HEDGEHOG[1]

AMONG the remains of Archilochus is an iambic trimeter as mysterious as it is fascinating. Zenobius, who quotes it (5. 58), says that it was written by Homer and quoted by Archilochus in an epode, μέμνηται ταύτης Ἀρχίλοχος ἐν ἐπῳδῇ· γράφει δὲ καὶ Ὅμηρος τὸν στίχον ... λέγεται δὲ ἡ παροιμία ἐπὶ τῶν πανουργοτάτων. If Zenobius is telling the truth, and there is no reason to doubt it, the line must, as Bergk saw,[2] come from the *Margites*, and it is even possible that Archilochus said so, since he is known to have said that this poem was the work of Homer (Eustrat. in Aristot. *Nic. Eth.* 6. 6, p. 320 Heylbut). But the origin and original purpose of the line need not concern us, since we are not likely to know any more about them. The important point is that Archilochus quoted it, and we ought to be able to discover how he did. What was his precise intention when he quoted

πόλλ' οἶδ' ἀλώπηξ, ἀλλ' ἐχῖνος ἓν μέγα,   (fr. 103 D.)

what contrast did he draw between the Fox and the Hedgehog, and to what purpose did he put it? Zenobius gives two clues, but neither is easy to follow. First he says that the line was used as a proverb ἐπὶ τῶν πανουργοτάτων, and secondly he quotes as relevant some lines from the *Phoenix* of Ion of Chios about the Hedgehog:

ἀλλ' ἔν τε χέρσῳ τὰς λέοντος ᾔνεσα
ἢ τὰς ἐχίνου μᾶλλον οἰζυρὰς τέχνας,
ὃς εὖτ' ἂν ἄλλων κρεισσόνων ὁρμὴν μάθῃ,
στρόβιλος ἀμφ' ἄκανθαν εἰλίξας δέμας
κεῖται δακεῖν τε καὶ θιγεῖν ἀμήχανος.

(fr. 38 N.; 81 von B.)

Let us see what can be made of this.

The words ἐπὶ τῶν πανουργοτάτων imply that both the Fox

---

[1] First published in *Classical Quarterly*, xxxix (1940), 26–9, substantially altered.
[2] *P.L.G.* ii⁴. 418.

and the Hedgehog are types of οἱ πανουργότατοι. This is easy enough for the Fox, to whom the adjective πανοῦργος is applied by Aristotle (*H.A.* 488ᵇ20) and whose ancient reputation for mischief deserves the epithet in a bad sense, but to us the Hedgehog seems as harmless a creature as it did to Aristotle, who praised it for its skill as a weather-prophet (*H.A.* 612ᵇ4) and says nothing against its character, while others admired its prescience in storing food for the winter (Tzetz. ad Lyc. *Alex.* 1093; Plin. *N.H.* 8. 37. 133). But this was not the only view of it. Tzetzes says explicitly ὁ ἐχῖνος ζῷόν ἐστι πανοῦργον, and Aelian goes further when he couples it with the Fox, ἡ ἀλώπηξ πονηρὸν ζῷόν ἐστιν ... πονηρὸν δὲ καὶ ὁ χερσαῖος ἐχῖνος (*N.A.* 6. 64). We need not take the adjective πανοῦργος too seriously, nor in the worst sense for either creature. It could almost have a hint of admiration like the English 'rogue', as when in Menander's *Epitrepontes* (318) the slave Onesimus greets Habrotonon's plan for outwitting her master: πανούργως καὶ κακοηθῶς, Ἁβρότονον. It seems clear and indeed reasonable that πανοῦργος should be used almost as a term of praise by those who admired a subtle or even unscrupulous display of wits. That it was applied to the Fox is easy to understand; for its other name was Κερδώ (Pind. *P.* 2. 78; Aristoph. *Equ.* 1068; Ael. *N.A.* 7. 47), and it was a familiar example of craftiness, but the application of πανουργία to the Hedgehog calls for discussion.

There is not much ancient lore about the Hedgehog. The Greeks were impressed by its prickles and by its gift of rolling itself into a ball (Emped. fr. 83 D.-K.; Aristoph. *Pax*, 1086; Opp. *Cyn.* 2. 599–600; Aristot. *H.A.* 490ᵇ29). The latter trick was perhaps enough to qualify the Hedgehog for πανουργία, though we might feel that it is not comparable with the Fox's multifarious guile. But the Hedgehog's exploitation of this talent was admired, and it was noted how it could be turned to the purposes of an active defence. Oppian (*Hal.* 2. 359–86) describes at length how the Hedgehog, who is the enemy of the Snake, rolls up at the sight of it; the Snake encircles the Hedgehog but is pierced by its prickles and eventually dies. Sometimes the Hedgehog dies too, but more often it escapes:

> πολλάκι δ' ἐξήλυξε καὶ ἔκφυγε δεινὸς ἐχῖνος,
> ἐκδὺς ἑρπυστῆρος ἀλυκτοπέδης τε κελαινῆς,
> εἰσέτι τεθνηῶτος ἔχων περὶ σάρκας ἀκάνθαις.   (384–6)

The same trick is reported by Tzetzes (ad Lyc. *Alex*. 1093), who also draws attention to the hedgehog's chances of survival, ὁ δὲ νοῦς ἑλίσσεται δίκην σφαίρας καὶ ταῖς ἀκάνθαις ἐμπλακέντα τὸν ὄφιν ἀνελὼν σῴζεται, and uses this, like other of its habits, to show that the Hedgehog is πανοῦργος. Since this seems to have been the Hedgehog's only means of defence against enemies, it may well be called ἓν μέγα and be what Archilochus has in mind.

In their different ways both the Fox and the Hedgehog might be regarded as types of πανουργότατοι and be classed together for their cunning and their ability to outwit their foes. But are they allies or enemies? On this point Zenobius says nothing, and we must look elsewhere. On first thoughts we might expect them to be friends, since, according to Aristotle (*Rhet*. $1393^{b}28$), Aesop told a fable in which the Hedgehog in a friendly spirit offers to remove the ticks which are sucking the Fox's blood. But against this we must set weighty evidence on the other side. Plutarch (*de Soll. Anim*. 16) says that the Hedgehog rolls itself into a ball when the Fox approaches, and the word προσιούσης certainly suggests something like attack. There seems to have been a traditional hostility between the two creatures, and what forms it could take may be seen from two passages of Aelian, which tell of the unscrupulous methods by which the Fox seeks to penetrate the Hedgehog's defences:

δολερὸν χρῆμα ἡ ἀλώπηξ. ἐπιβουλεύει γοῦν τοῖς χερσαίοις ἐχίνοις τὸν τρόπον τοῦτον. ὀρθοὺς αὐτοὺς καταγωνίσασθαι ἀδύνατός ἐστι. τὸ δὲ αἴτιον, αἴ ἄκανθαι ἀνείργουσιν αὐτήν. ἡ δὲ ἡσύχως καὶ πεφεισμένως ἔχουσα τοῦ ἑαυτῆς στόματος ἀνατρέπει αὐτοὺς καὶ κλίνει ὑπτίους, ἀνασχίσασά τε ἐσθίει ῥᾳδίως τοὺς τέως φοβερούς. (*N.A*. 6. 24)

A little later he gives an account of an even more poignant struggle:

καὶ ὁ μὲν ἑαυτὸν συνειλήσας κεῖται, θεασάμενος ἤκουσαν τὴν ἀλώπεκα, ἡ δὲ χανεῖν τε καὶ ἐνδακεῖν οὐ δυναμένη, κᾆτα οὔρησεν αὐτοῦ ἐς τὸ στόμα· ὁ δὲ ἀποπνίγεται, τοῦ πνεύματος ἔνδον ἐκ τῆς συνειλήσεως κατεσχημένου καὶ ἐπιρρέοντος οἱ τοῦ προειρημένου, καὶ μέντοι τὸν τρόπον τοῦτον κακὸν κακὴ περιελθοῦσα τὸν ἐχῖνον ἡ ἀλώπηξ ᾕρηκεν αὐτόν. (*N.A*. 6. 64)

From these two passages we may conclude that the enmity between the Fox and the Hedgehog had a place in common lore and that Plutarch, who knew the line from Archilochus, either found such a reference in his text or interpreted the lines by knowledge of the topic from elsewhere.

Archilochus, as we are told, brought this line into an Epode. Since his Epodes concerned his personal affairs and were largely directed against his enemies such as Lycambes, Cheidos, Pericles, and an unknown seer, we can well imagine that such a line could have a place in the pursuit of some feud. It would be comforting if we could assign it to an Epode about which something is known, and this F. Lasserre has ingeniously tried to do.[1] He argues that it belongs to *Epode* 2 and bases his case on Horace's *Epode* 6 and the Virgilian *Catalepton* 13. In the first of these occur the words:

> caue, caue: namque in malos asperrimus
>   parata tolle cornua,
> qualis Lycambae spretus infido gener.   (11–13)

and in the second, addressed to the pervert Lucienus, we find the lines:

> nunc laede, nunc lacesse, si quidquam uales.
>   en nomen adscribo tuum.   (33–4)

Lasserre is surely right in thinking that both these poems owe something to Archilochus' *Epode* 2, but it is not so clear that our line comes from this poem. First, in Horace's poem the metaphor comes from neither a Fox nor a Hedgehog but from some horned animal, and this suggests a different source. Secondly, in the Virgilian poem there is no hint about the vengeance which the writer will take, and it is on this point that Lasserre bases his argument. Thirdly, both these poems suggest an open declaration of hostilities, but the line of Archilochus, whatever its context, has clearly a more subtle and more complex meaning. Even if Archilochus' *Epode* 2 had the character which Lasserre ascribes to it, there is no final reason to ascribe our line to it.

That Archilochus used the line with reference to himself is surely beyond dispute. His *Epodes* dealt with personal matters, and in them he used animal lore to point his situations and conclusions. In fr. 88 D., for instance, he addresses Lycambes by name, and in all probability the *Epode* in which this occurs told the fable of the Fox and the Eagle, while Lucian (*Pseudolog.* 1) says that in a poem about a man and a cicada, of which five

---

[1] *Les Épodes d'Archiloque*, 52 ff.; *Archiloque: fragments*, 51.

lines certainly survive, Archilochus compared himself with the cicada. On general principles it is possible that he compared himself with the Fox or the Hedgehog, and we must consider both on their merits.

There is nothing surprising if Archilochus compares himself with the Fox. After all, if we may trust Aelian, the Fox wins in his encounter with the Hedgehog, and we should expect Archilochus to proclaim his superiority to this adversary. More important, Archilochus is known to have compared himself with a Fox. Plato recognizes the aptness and justice of the comparison when he says τὴν τοῦ σοφωτάτου Ἀρχιλόχου ἀλώπεκα ἑλκτέον ἐξόπισθεν κερδαλέαν καὶ ποικίλην (*Rep.* 2. 365 c), and that the comparison was not regarded as degrading but almost as noble can be seen from the remark of Dio Chrysostom: τὴν Ἀρχιλόχου ἀλώπεκα τοῖς λέουσι καὶ ταῖς παρδαλέσι παραβαλλόμεν καὶ οὐδὲν ἢ μὴ πολὺ ἀποδεῖν φάμεν (*Or.* 55. 10). How Archilochus made the comparison may be seen from the fragments of two *Epodes*. In one, directed against Lycambes, he told the fable of the Fox and the Eagle to illustrate the theme of friendship destroyed by treachery. The story, which Aristophanes attributes to Aesop (*Av.* 651 ff.), survives in more than one version and is made clear by the summary in 'Aesop' (*Fab.* 5 Halm; 3 Chambry). From Archilochus' poem enough fragments survive (frs. 85–95 D.) to show how he treated the story. The Fox and the Eagle make a bond of friendship, but the Eagle violates it by eating the Fox's young, and in due course the Fox gets its revenge by doing the same to the Eagle. If we may judge by the prayer which the Fox makes to Zeus (fr. 94 D.), Archilochus sympathized with the Fox and made him a dignified figure with right on his side. Again, Archilochus (frs. 81–83 D) made use of the fable of the Fox and the Monkey. The version of 'Aesop' (*Fab.* 43–4 Halm; 39 Chambry), gives only the beginning of the tale, in which the two characters boast of their ancestry, and the Monkey says that its were slaves. The sequel can be found elsewhere, when the Monkey thinks that it is a king (*Fab.* 38 Chambry) and is mocked by the Fox, who leads it to a trap where it is caught. Here again the Fox triumphs, and the moral is one which Archilochus would be likely to draw in a quarrel with someone whom he likens to a monkey.

There are, then, quite persuasive reasons for thinking that, when Archilochus spoke of the Fox and the Hedgehog, he may have identified himself for the moment with the Fox. But there are arguments hardly less cogent on the other side, which suggest that he could no less reasonably identify himself with the Hedgehog. Though the Hedgehog is called πανοῦργος, this is no more damaging than 'méchant' in the familiar couplet:

> Cet animal est très méchant;
> Quand on l'attaque, il se défend.

The πανουργία of the Hedgehog is its *méchanceté* in defending itself when attacked. It is not a type of treachery, like the Eagle in Archilochus' *Epode*, nor a type of boastful vanity like the Monkey. It is by most standards a perfectly honourable and respectable creature. It gains in esteem from its hostility to the Snake, and there is nothing disreputable in its methods of warfare. There is no good reason why Archilochus should choose it to typify some enemy or indeed why it should not in some way stand for himself.

That it does so may perhaps be argued from the position and emphasis of the words ἓν μέγα, which suggest that the single, big thing known by the Hedgehog is worth as much as all the knowledge of the Fox. This cannot be proved beyond dispute, but it gets support from a line ascribed variously to Semonides and Simonides by the MSS. of Stobaeus, *Flor.* 4. 34:

> ἓν δὲ τὸ κάλλιστον Χῖος ἔειπεν ἀνήρ,

where ἕν certainly draws attention to the special eminence of the line from Homer (*Z* 146), which the poet then proceeds to quote. So also in two lines from Sophocles' *Danaë*,

> οὐκ οἶδα τὴν σὴν πεῖραν· ἓν δ' ἐπίσταμαι,
> τοῦ παιδὸς ὄντος τοῦδ' ἐγὼ διόλλυμαι,   (fr. 165 P.)

ἕν gives emphasis to what is most important in the speaker's mind. In Archilochus' line the special knowledge of the Hedgehog is certainly stressed and may well be singled out for praise. We may perhaps pursue the point a little further. Diehl aptly quotes as parallel another fragment of Archilochus:

> ἓν δ' ἐπίσταμαι μέγα,
> τὸν κακῶς μ' ἔρδοντα δεινοῖσ' ἀνταμείβεσθαι κακοῖς.[1]
>   (fr. 66 D.)

---

[1] I give the line not as Diehl prints it but with Pfeiffer's convincing correction of μ' ἔρδοντα for με δρῶντα.

What could be more natural than that the ἓν μέγα of the Hedgehog should be a remarkable gift for doing a bad turn to its enemies? Could it not, for instance, treat the Fox in the same crafty way as it treats the snake? Or at least could it not have so good a defence against its adversaries that they suffer from it? The objection to this is that fr. 66 suggests a more active and more offensive policy than rolling up into a ball, but since Archilochus applies ἓν μέγα to himself here, it makes it more likely that he does the same elsewhere. It indicates not that he always behaves in the same way but that he has up his sleeve a big trick for certain situations, and it is not unfair to relate this to his hatreds and feuds. So though there are good arguments for thinking that he dramatizes himself as the Fox, there are equally good arguments for thinking that he dramatizes himself as the Hedgehog. After looking at the matter fairly and squarely from both sides, we find ourselves neatly balanced between opposing views, and we must ask if the evidence is sufficient to allow them to be reconciled.

In the passage quoted by Zenobius from the *Phoenix* of Ion of Chios the speaker says simply that he would rather behave like a Lion than like a Hedgehog: in other words, he would rather conduct a bold offensive than a passive defence. He makes his point through two antithetical cases, the King of the Beasts and the humble Hedgehog, whose self-protecting devices prevent it from being bitten or even touched by its adversary. The contrast between the Fox and the Hedgehog is not on this scale, since the Fox lacks the heroic stature of the Lion and is the embodiment not of the offensive spirit but of cunning. It would be difficult to combine the qualities of the Lion and the Hedgehog, but a man might resemble the Fox in some respects and the Hedgehog in others. This surely is what Archilochus means. He quotes the traditional line of the *Margites* and applies it to himself in both its references. In his favourite role of the Fox he knows how to deal with his enemies, but in some circumstances the wiles of the Fox are worthless in comparison with the single great trick of the Hedgehog, and this is what Archilochus now proposes to copy. So long as he is in pursuit of his enemies, he will behave like the Fox, but when they attack him, he will turn to the defensive like the Hedgehog. In combining the qualities of the two animals he is not hampered by any legendary hostility between them, and indeed his present position gains from the paradox that he has something in common with both of the traditional adversaries. He gives a new point to the line from the *Margites* by showing that its two kinds of πανουργία are not incompatible in a single character. It is no criticism to say that one of the characters is disreputable and the other of little account; for such considerations do not count for much with Archilochus, who, as Dio Chrysostom says, πρῶτον αὑτὸν ψέγει (*Or.* 33. 12). The candour which he lavished on his enemies he applied also to himself, and in this case, by comparing himself with two not very dignified animals, he proclaims both his resource in attack and his stubborn resistance in defence.

VI

A COUPLET OF ARCHILOCHUS[1]

In his copious discourse on wine Athenaeus (1. 30 f.) says that Archilochus compares Naxian wine with nectar, and then proceeds to quote a couplet by him:

ἐν δορὶ μέν μοι μᾶζα μεμαγμένη, ἐν δορὶ δ' οἶνος
Ἰσμαρικός, πίνω δ' ἐν δορὶ κεκλιμένος. (fr. 2 D.)

The text presents no difficulty, and the words are simple enough, but the lines have suffered from an interpretation canonized by a succession of editors and passed from one to another without any hint of its inadequacy. It has been common form to illustrate the lines by the famous song of Hybrias, where he says of his shield:

τούτῳ γὰρ ἀρῶ, τούτῳ θερίζω,
τούτῳ πατέω τὸν ἁδὺν οἶνον ἀπ' ἀμπέλω,
τούτῳ δεσπότας μνοίας κέκλημαι. (fr. 909. 3–5 P.)

It is claimed that just as Hybrias lives by his shield, so Archilochus lives by his spear, which wins him bread and wine and on which he reclines as he drinks. Such an interpretation is in keeping with what we know of Archilochus' life and habits, but it suffers from grave defects.

First, there is a stylistic difficulty. When ἐν δορί appears three times in a couplet, we reasonably expect it to have the same meaning on each appearance, especially in so careful a writer as Archilochus. But that is not what the traditional interpretation gives. J. M. Edmonds gives a fair sample of the common view when he translates: 'In the spear is my kneaded bread, in the spear my Ismarian wine, I recline when I drink on the spear.'[2]

[1] First published in *Anales de filología clásica*, vi (1954), 37–43.
[2] *Elegy and Iambus*, ii. 99. For other more recent views, see J. A. Davison, *C.R.* lxxiv (1960), 1 ff., 'equipped with my spear' or 'in my ship'; V. Ehrenberg, *Cl. Phil.* lvii (1952), 179–80; T. B. L. Webster, *Greek Art and Literature*, 30; D. A. Campbell, *Greek Lyric Poetry*, 'In my spear is my kneaded barley-bread, in my spear is my Ismaric wine (i.e. my spear provides my bread and wine), on my spear I lean when I drink it.' He adds: 'Archilochus' couplet is neat enough even if his uses of

With the Greek in front of us we cannot but feel that such a version ruins the formal elegance of the triple ἐν δορί by suggesting that it is no more than a verbal device which has no function for the meaning. This alone should make us suspicious of the usual interpretation and suggest that we should look for another.

Secondly, there is a serious objection from linguistic usage. ἐν δορὶ κεκλιμένος is taken to mean 'reclining on my spear', but we may doubt whether this is possible. We should expect simply δορὶ κεκλιμένος on the analogy of such Homeric phrases as ἀσπίσι κεκλιμένοι (Γ 135), πόντῳ κεκλιμένοι (O 740), στήλῃ κεκλιμένος (Λ 371), φηγῷ κεκλιμένος (Φ 549). When T. Hudson-Williams comments: 'In our passage ἐν δορί is added to make the repetition more emphatic',[1] he recognizes the difficulty but does not explain it, since the repetition could hardly make anything more emphatic by using ungrammatical, if not unintelligible, Greek. ἐν δορὶ κεκλιμένος is not the same as δορὶ κεκλιμένος and is unlikely to have been put in its place just to secure a perfunctory reappearance of ἐν δορί for the third time.

Thirdly, the alleged parallel from Hybrias is delusive. His fourfold τούτῳ does indeed emphasize how he lives through his shield and gets his livelihood from it, but he uses τούτῳ by itself without ἐν and gives it precisely the same function on each appearance. Moreover, in this immediate connection he speaks not about his spear and sword but about his shield, and we can hardly doubt that the song was meant to be accompanied by some play with his shield, which the repeated τούτῳ helped to stress. Archilochus would hardly have done the same kind of thing with his repeated ἐν δορί, since its last appearance would create an anticlimax and destroy the elegance of his couplet. For these reasons the accepted explanation is unsatisfactory, and we ought to be able to find another which meets our needs.

Our second difficulty was felt by U. Bahntje, who saw that Hybrias provides no real parallel and that the common explanation is clumsy and inadequate. He himself suggests that Archilochus:'imaginem proposuit militis excubantis cui quibus opus est ab hasta pendent';[2] in other words, that he literally carries his food and drink on his spear as he lies down on it to enjoy them.

ἐν δορί are not all alike and even if they are somewhat forced.' I still find the alleged conclusion an anticlimax.
[1] *Early Greek Elegy*, 82.   [2] *Quaestiones Archilocheae* (Göttingen, 1900), 11.

Though the picture is not absolutely clear or convincing, it has perhaps some truth to campaigning conditions, when a soldier might use his spear to carry his rations. It has at least the merit that it gives a possible sense to ἐν δορί in all three cases, but it suffers from giving the third case a different meaning from the other two, and this is a serious obstacle to accepting it.

In introducing the couplet Athenaeus is more confusing than helpful. He seems to have in mind some other passage than this, since the couplet says nothing about nectar, and Ismarian wine does not come from Naxos. Fortunately the lines are quoted by Synesius (*Ep.* 130, p. 717 H.; cf. *Suda*, s.v. ὑπνομαχῶ), who says of himself: ἀλλ' ἱπποκρατεῖται μὲν ἅπαντα καὶ τὴν χώραν ἔχουσιν οἱ πολέμιοι, ἐγὼ δὲ ὑπὸ μεσοπυργίῳ τεταγμένος ὑπνομαχῶ. " ἐν . . . κεκλιμένος·" οὐκ οἶδ' εἰ μᾶλλον Ἀρχιλόχῳ προσήκοντα ἦν ταῦτα εἰπεῖν. Synesius applies Archilochus' lines to himself at a time of war, when he is at his post on some fortification. The precise point of comparison must be that, like Archilochus, Synesius spends his life under arms and takes his meals at 'action stations'. This is clearly at variance with the traditional interpretation, since it assumes that ἐν δορί refers neither to the means by which Archilochus gets his bread and wine nor to his manner of carrying them, but to the place and circumstances where he puts them to their proper use. If we follow this hint from Synesius, we may perhaps find a more satisfying explanation of the couplet.

We have seen that ἐν δορί should have the same meaning each time that it occurs. If it could mean something like 'under arms' or 'at my post', we could understand why Synesius quotes it as he does. Nor in fact is it very far from having such a meaning. A certain use of ἐν indicates that it means not 'in 'but 'at' or 'by', and then 'at my spear' gives us just what we want. This is a Homeric use, notably ἐν ποταμῷ (Σ 521, ε 466), 'at the river', or ἐνὶ καυλῷ (Ν 608), 'at the shaft'.[1] If we apply this meaning to the couplet of Archilochus, it makes excellent sense. At his spear are his food and drink and at his spear he drinks. This gives the same meaning to ἐν δορί at each appearance and agrees with Synesius' quotation of the passage to illustrate his own situation.

If the couplet speaks of Archilochus' life under arms at his post, some of its other implications still need to be unravelled. In what temper does he speak of his food and drink? and what

[1] Kühner–Gerth, *Ausf. gr. Gramm.* ii. 1. 464.

precise importance should be attached to the rations which he mentions? First let us take μᾶζα μεμαγμένη. This is barley-meal, kneaded but not baked, as we see from Herodotus' words on the Babylonians: καὶ ὃς μὲν ἂν βούληται αὐτῶν ἄτε μᾶζαν μαξάμενος ἔδει, ὁ δὲ ἄρτου τρόπον ὀπτήσας (1. 200). A μᾶζα was contrasted with a wheaten loaf, as by Hippocrates (*Vet. Med.* 8), and thought inferior to it, as the proverb ἀγαθὴ καὶ μᾶζα μετ' ἄρτον (Zenob. 1. 12) shows, though it had a certain dignity on old-fashioned occasions, as in Solon's insistence that it should be eaten instead of ἄρτος in the Prytaneum (Athen. 4. 137 e). But it was, in the normal view, a humble food, the fare of slaves and soldiers. This does not necessarily mean that Archilochus despises it; for in another place it is the allegedly superior ἄρτος which he says reeks of servitude, δούλιον ἄρτον ἔδων (fr. 79. 6 D.). If a μᾶζα smacked of humble life and simple circumstances, that was in certain lights to its credit. Xenophon knew that to the hungry it makes little difference whether bread is made of barley or of wheat: ἀναμνησθήτω πῶς μὲν ἡδὺ μᾶζα καὶ ἄρτος πεινῶντι φαγεῖν (*Cyr.* 1. 2. 11), and that a μᾶζα μεμαγμένη might be quite palatable can be seen from Aristophanes' description of the way in which Cleon has appropriated the glory due to Demosthenes for the victory at Pylos:

καὶ πρώην γ' ἐμοῦ
μᾶζαν μεμαχότος ἐν Πύλῳ Λακωνικήν,
πανουργότατά πως περιδραμὼν ὑφαρπάσας
αὐτὸς παρέθηκε τὴν ὑπ' ἐμοῦ μεμαγμένην.   (*Equ.* 54–7)

There would be no point in this if a μᾶζα was universally despised and regarded as a very poor food. The point is that it is simple and nourishing. When Archilochus adds to the noun the participle μεμαγμένη, he suggests that, such as it is, it is properly prepared and ready to be eaten. He does not complain of it but hints that in war it is good to have any rations at all and that this kind of food will suffice.

The μᾶζα μεμαγμένη may be nothing out of the way, but there can be no doubt about the Ismarian wine; for this was a wine with a history. It is what Odysseus gave to the Cyclops, ἡδύν, ἀκηράσιον, θεῖον ποτόν and which had an ὀδμὴ θεσπεσίη (ι 205, 210–1). Homer's authority was recognized by Virgil (*G.* 2. 37), Propertius (2. 33. 32), and Ovid (*Met.* 9. 642). Since it came from Thrace, and Archilochus knew the country from his own

A COUPLET OF ARCHILOCHUS

experience, this looks like one of the consolations which he found for the hardships of war. The food is nothing out of the ordinary, but the wine is first-class, and that is why Archilochus keeps it to the last, when he develops his theme with the word πίνω. It is the wine which makes the occasion worthy of notice.

This takes us to the last word κεκλιμένος. κλίνεσθαι is used regularly for reclining to eat or to drink. If the actual business of getting down is expressed in the aorist as in Eur. *Cyc.* 543 κλίθητί νύν μοι πλευρὰ θεὶς ἐπὶ χθονός and at Hdt. 1. 211. 2 κλιθέντες ἐδαίνυντο, the perfect is used when the eaters and drinkers have taken their places. So Theocritus describes a rustic repast:

> τὸν Πτελεατικὸν οἶνον ἀπὸ κρατῆρος ἀφύξω
> πὰρ πυρὶ κεκλιμένος. (7. 65–6)

The word κεκλιμένος suggests lying down as the Greeks lay down for a feast, and Archilochus' point is that in his own special conditions he does something of the kind. His only furniture is his spear, and this provides the setting. His food is humble enough, but the wine is splendid, and that is his main interest. Even in these circumstances he can enjoy himself as if he were at some convivial occasion. He was a man who knew how to make the best of unpromising conditions, and just as when he is on watch in a ship at sea, he looks forward to a good evening,

> οὐδὲ γὰρ ἡμεῖς
> νήφειν ἐν φυλακῇ τῇδε δυνησόμεθα,   (fr. 5 A 8–9 D.)

so on land, when war is close to him, and he has military duties to perform, he is not discouraged, but enjoys the situation because he has something good to drink.

VII

A FRAGMENT OF THE *ARIMASPEA*[1]

THE longest extant fragment of the *Arimaspea* consists of six lines quoted by 'Longinus' in *On the Sublime*, 10. 4. He does not mention its author by name but contents himself with a guarded reference to ὁ τὰ Ἀριμάσπεια ποιήσας, as if he himself had doubts about the authenticity of its ascription to Aristeas of Proconnesus. In this he is in good company, since Dionysius of Halicarnassus classes the poem with the works ascribed to Cadmus of Miletus as a case in which the alleged authorship does not meet with general acceptance (*de Thuc.* 23). Such doubts were natural in a scholarly age. The legend of Aristeas, as Herodotus tells it (4. 14), would tax the credulity of critical historians, and it would be only natural to have suspicions about a work said to be written by him. On the other hand Herodotus certainly believed in the authorship of Aristeas (4. 13. 1), and no doubt his belief was shared by his contemporaries. In our present enquiry the name of the author is of no great importance. The six lines which concern us (fr. 1 Kinkel) come from a work called *Arimaspea*, and we can hardly doubt that this is the work known to Herodotus. Not only does it deal with the same remote peoples, but, when Herodotus says that Aristeas got his information about the Arimaspians from the Issedones, it cannot be a mere coincidence that in four lines quoted by Tzetzes from the *Arimaspea* (frs. 1–3 Kinkel), the first puts the Ἰσσηδοί in the nominative, and the next three speak of the Arimaspians in *oratio obliqua*.

The *Arimaspea* was composed in three books (*Suda*, s.v. Ἀριστέας) and told of matters which claimed to be historical and geographical but must have been to a large degree fabulous. It was used on the one hand by such pioneers of historical inquiry as Hecataeus (1 F 193 Jacoby), Hellanicus (4. F 187), and Damastes (5 F 1) for its account of peoples and places from the

[1] First published in *Classical Quarterly*, N.S. vi (1956), 1–10, slightly altered. For a full and able discussion of Aristeas see now J. D. P. Bolton, *Aristeas of Proconnesus* (1962).

Scythians of the Euxine to the Hyperboreans and the Northern Sea. For this purpose Herodotus also used it (4. 13 ff.), though he did not believe everything that it said. On the other hand it contained legendary matter which appealed to poets. Both Pausanias (1. 24. 6) and Pliny (*N.H.* 7. 2. 10) say that Aristeas told of unceasing war between the Arimaspians and the gold-guarding griffins,[1] and he is probably responsible for Aeschylus' reference to them (*P.V.* 803–6). Since Aristeas told of the Hyperboreans, he may be the source of Pindar's remarkable account of them (*P.* 10. 30 ff.), and Pindar certainly knew of him (fr. 284 Bo.; 271 Sn.). Though the historians treat the Rhipaean mountains simply as a geographical feature, poets, such as Sophocles (*O.C.* 1248), see them more romantically as the home of night,[2] and a dependence on Aristeas may explain the mythical attributes which Aristotle noted in accounts of them (*Meteor.* 350^{b}7). The Φορκίδες, who with their single eye never see the light of either sun or moon, as Aeschylus describes them (*P.V.* 794–7), have a Central Asian counterpart in 'swan-maidens' who live in the dark and have eyes of lead,[3] and may come from some Scythian tale culled by Aristeas. Scanty though these references are they suffice to show that the *Arimaspea* fitted remote and largely fabulous peoples into a kind of geographical plan. For some of his information Aristeas quoted his own experience when he visited the Issedones (Hdt. 4. 13. 1), and for much else beyond their frontiers he claimed their authority (Hdt. 4. 16. 1). His reports on these unknown peoples were so striking that early historians could not entirely neglect them.

On the other hand, Aristeas seems not to have been content

---

[1] A. Alföldi, *Gnomon*, ix (1933), 517 ff., shows that the one-eyed Arimaspians and the gold-guarding griffins are genuine creatures of Asian folklore. If so, stories of them may have penetrated into Greek lands long before Aristeas, since the late Mycenaean ivory mirror-handle from Enkomi in Cyprus (H. L. Lorimer, *Homer and the Monuments*, pl. 11. 4) shows a warrior, who is not, however, one-eyed, fighting a griffin.

[2] Alcman also refers to them (fr. 90 P.), and since he is known to have been interested in fabulous peoples (Strab. 43; Aristid. 2. 508), it is tempting to think that he drew on Aristeas. But no certainty is possible, because we lack firm information on the date of both poets. If with H. T. Wade-Gery, *The Poet of the Iliad*, 75, we put Aristeas at the earliest in the second quarter of the seventh century, and with D. L. Page, *Alcman: the Partheneion*, 166, Alcman in the middle, it is possible that some influence took place. See Bolton, 40 ff.

[3] N. K. Chadwick, *J.R.A.L.* lxvi (1936), 313–16; E. R. Dodds, *The Greeks and the Irrational*, 162.

with this but to have claimed supernatural powers. Even Herodotus says that he went to the Issedones φοιβόλαμπτος (or φοιβόληπτος) γενομένος (4. 13. 1) and this implies some kind of divine possession. When the *Suda* says τούτου φασὶ τὴν ψυχὴν ὅτε ἐβούλετο ἐξιέναι καὶ ἐπανιέναι πάλιν (s.v. Ἀριστέας), when Pliny says that his soul could take the form of a bird (*N.H.* 7. 52. 174), and when Strabo calls him ἀνὴρ γόης εἴ τις ἄλλος (589), we are not surprised that he should claim to be more than an ordinary traveller and to have more than usual sources of information. Such are indeed described by Maximus of Tyre (38. 3 Hobein), who tells with relish how Aristeas' soul could leave his body, fly into the air, and traverse sea and land until he came to the Hyperboreans; by such means he was able to learn not only about natural phenomena but about the ways of men. Perhaps Maximus has given some rein to his fancy, but his high-flown account must have some foundation in either the poetry or the legend of Aristeas, and since he expressly mentions the Hyperboreans, the poetry may be his source. There might seem to be some contradiction between Herodotus' account of a traveller who gets information by hearsay and Maximus' account of a shaman who gets it by vision,[1] but the answer is not far to seek if we assume that Aristeas presented himself in both roles and that Herodotus stressed the one and Maximus the other. A poet who makes such claims is likely to have an unusual approach to experience, and the six lines quoted from the *Arimaspea* by 'Longinus', which look innocent enough at first sight, may well contain more than meets the unsuspecting eye.

'Longinus' quotes the lines to make a contrast with five lines from Homer which tell, in a simile, of men in a ship during a storm at sea (*O* 624–8), and his point is that, whereas Homer creates a real sense of terror, Aristeas does not. 'Longinus' admits that he tries to do so, but adds παντὶ οἶμαι δῆλον, ὡς πλέον ἄνθος ἔχει τὰ λεγόμενα ἢ δέος (*de Sub.* 10. 4). This is his only critical comment, and it says very little. It is therefore not surprising that scholars have disagreed about the interpretation of the lines. In themselves they present no difficulties of text or syntax and look simple enough:

[1] For Greek shamanism in general and for Aristeas' relation to the beliefs of his age see Dodds, 135–78.

A FRAGMENT OF THE *ARIMASPEA*

θαῦμ' ἡμῖν καὶ τοῦτο μέγα φρεσὶν ἡμετέρῃσιν.
ἄνδρες ὕδωρ ναίουσιν ἀπὸ χθονὸς ἐν πελάγεσσι·
δύστηνοί τινές εἰσιν, ἔχουσι γὰρ ἔργα πονηρά.
ὄμματ' ἐν ἄστροισι, ψυχὴν δ' ἐνὶ πόντῳ ἔχουσιν.
ἦ που πολλὰ θεοῖσι φίλας ἀνὰ χεῖρας ἔχοντες
εὔχονται σπλάγχνοισι κακῶς ἀναβαλλομένοισι.

(fr. 1 Kinkel)

In a poem like the *Arimaspea*, of whose contents and construction we are lamentably ignorant, it is almost impossible to say what the context is. Our only clue is that 'Longinus', by comparing and contrasting the lines with five from Homer, indicates that at some point they must deal with a similar theme. If we press the words ἐπὶ τῶν χειμώνων, which precede the quotation from Aristeas, it looks as if both poets were concerned with men in trouble during a storm at sea. Beyond this we can hardly go, since Aristeas does not even mention a ship and his account of stormy weather is more implied than stated. What really interests 'Longinus' is the difference of temper between the two passages. While Homer evokes a real sense of horror, Aristeas does no more than create effects which have an ἄνθος or elegance. This clue is by no means negligible, since it tells us something about Aristeas' spirit and manner of writing, but so far as the elucidation of the passage is concerned, 'Longinus' gives only a small and not very illuminating hint. Our only hope is to look carefully at the lines and ask what they mean.

As befits the study of such a poet, ingenious interpretations are not lacking. It has, for instance, been suggested that Aristeas tells of the inhabitants of pile-dwellings in lakes and dwells on the miseries of their existence.[1] In his travels he could have seen such methods of life as Herodotus describes on Lake Prasias (5. 161–2) and 'Hippocrates' on the Phasis (*Aer.* 15). For this view it may be argued that, since Herodotus uses πέλαγος for a large tract of flooded country (2. 97. 1; 3. 117. 3; 7. 129. 3), there is no reason why Aristeas should not use ἐν πελάγεσσι of a marsh or a lake. Equally ἀπὸ χθονός means no more than 'away from the land', and though χθών is normally used in contrast with θάλασσα, there is no reason why it should not be contrasted with some other tract of water. Of such pile-dwellers it might reasonably be said that they ὕδωρ ναίουσιν, and the misery described by

[1] Schmid–Stählin, *Gr. Lit. Gesch.* I. i. 303; H. Meuli, *Hermes*, lxx (1935), 121 ff.

Aristeas is perhaps not ultimately different from the exhaustion and weariness which 'Hippocrates' notices. On the other hand this view is open to serious objections. First, it is unlikely that a marsh or a lake would be called πόντος, which is always used of the open sea and not of inland waters. Secondly, the miseries of such an existence as Aristeas describes between water and sky seem to have little relation to pile-dwellers. They may indeed have peculiar sufferings but his words are not really applicable to them. Thirdly, if he refers to pile-dwellers, there is no point in 'Longinus'' words ἐπὶ τῶν χειμώνων or in his comparison with Homer. Even in the roughest weather a pile-dwelling is hardly comparable to a ship in a storm. On close consideration pile-dwellers do not seem to be likely candidates for Aristeas' mysterious people.

It has also been suggested that Aristeas refers to 'fabulous sea-dwellers'.[1] Though this is a little vague, a case can be made for it. The Greeks of the seventh century were much interested in monsters both on land and in the sea. The art of the time displays several varieties of Tritons,[2] and if Tritons were accepted, other strange marine beings may have followed in their train. We might even indulge a flight of fancy and suggest that the Στεγανόποδες, to whom Alcman is known to have referred (Strab. 43), were not 'Shelter-feet', rather like the Σκιάποδες or 'Shadow-feet', to whom he also referred (Aristid. 2. 508),[3] but simply some web-footed race. This is the only meaning of the word in classical times, and it may have been the meaning that Alcman gave to it. Creatures of this kind would qualify for dwelling in the sea as Aristeas' people do, and it would not be beyond him to dilate on the misery of their existence. A difficulty about such a view is that Aristeas calls his people ἄνδρες.

[1] E. Bethe, *R.-E.* ii. 877.
[2] A. Lesky, *Thalatta*, 110 ff.
[3] See also Plin. *N.H.* 7. 2. 23: 'idem hominum genus qui Monocoli uocentur singulis cruribus, mirae pernicitatis ad saltum; eosdem Sciapodas uocari, quod in maiore aestu humi iacentes resupini umbra se pedum protegant.' Hecataeus (17 F 327 Jacoby) puts them in Aethiopia. See also Aristoph. *Av.* 1553; Scylax ap. Philostrat. *Vit. Ap.* 3. 47. As we know nothing about the Στεγανόποδες there is no good reason for identifying them with the Σκιάποδες or even for assuming that they are similar. If Alcman used two different names, he probably implied two different kinds of creature. Lucian, *V.H.* 2, invents his own fanciful variation of 'Cork-feet', καθορῶμεν ἀνθρώπους πολλοὺς ἐπὶ τοῦ πελάγους διαθέοντας, ἄπαντα ἡμῖν προσεοικότας καὶ τὰ μεγέθη, πλὴν τῶν ποδῶν μόνων· ταῦτα γὰρ φέλλινα εἶχον· ἀφ' οὗ δὴ οἶμαι ἐκαλοῦντο Φελλόποδες.

Now the word could be extended beyond normal men to include one-eyed Arimaspians (Paus. 1. 24. 6), men with wings (Pind. *P.* 4. 182), the Cyclops (ι 494), and even, in Alexandrian times, dog-men (Simias, fr. 1. 9 Powell), but it seems unlikely that it could be stretched to beings who were hardly human in any real sense but led a unique life in the sea. The limitations of the word can be seen from Homer's contrast between Κενταύροισι and ἀνδράσι, which shows that though the Centaurs were half human, they were still not ἄνδρες. It may well be possible that Aristeas spoke of strange and monstrous beings, but we are not entitled to assume that he does so here.

It looks then as if Aristeas' people are in some sense human, even if their situation is highly unusual. Since no known people corresponds with them in ancient literature, we must ask whether perhaps they are after all ordinary human beings presented in a very unfamiliar light. Hermann Fränkel suggests that 'plainly a sea-people is meant, which never comes on land; Aristeas will have heard of ships with dwelling-cabins. This has greatly surprised him, and he is sorry for the poor people who have to exist in this way.'[1] Yet this is not quite satisfying. It is difficult to conjecture where Aristeas, in speaking of the lands north of the Euxine, could have placed a sea-bound people, and it is unlikely that any Greek poet would regard even so excessively nautical a life as this as 'a great wonder'. Yet this kind of approach may prove profitable if we apply it in a different way, and ask whether perhaps these people are after all ordinary human beings presented from an unfamiliar angle in a strange light. This is the suggestion of W. Rhys Roberts,[2] who says that 'the curious passage . . . is a description of a storm from the point of view of an inland people, probably the Arimaspi themselves, whose country the adventurous Aristeas had visited and described in hexameter verse. In the last line seasickness may possibly be intended; cf. ἐμοῦντος τοῦ ἑτέρου καὶ λέγοντος τὰ σπλάγχνα ἐκβάλλειν in Plutarch *De vitando aere alieno*, 8.' Before we consider the main substance of this, we may point out that Aristeas did not claim to have visited the Arimaspians, except perhaps in vision. Herodotus is quite clear on the point: οὐδὲ οὗτος προσωτέρω Ἰσσηδόνων αὐτὸς ἐν τοῖς ἔπεσι ποιέων ἔφησε

---

[1] H. Fränkel, *Dichtung und Philosophie des frühen Griechentums*[2], 278.
[2] *Longinus on the Sublime*, 218.

ἀφικέσθαι (4. 16. 1). So, if this is the view of an inland people, it is more likely to be that of the Issedones, whom Aristeas knew, than of the Arimaspians, whom he did not. Nor need we assume that the passage refers only to a storm. The present tenses, ναίουσιν, ἔχουσι, εὔχονται suggest that this is a more or less permanent condition, and it is wiser to suppose that it is not a storm which is in question but the whole business of life at sea, as it is misunderstood by those who know of it only by hearsay. But with these reservations Rhys Roberts' suggestion deserves serious attention. There is no inherent difficulty in an inland people's having very odd views about life at sea or in Aristeas' making much of it. The theory can be restated, modified, and amplified in such a way as to give a coherent view of the passage. As unfortunately Rhys Roberts did not do this, we may perhaps take up his task where he left it.

It might reasonably be argued that, though it is quite possible that the words are spoken by some inland people and that Aristeas in fact reports what the Issedones or their like have said to him, we cannot prove that these lines were so spoken. What are the precise implications of ἡμῖν and ἡμετέρῃσιν in the first line? We might assume that Aristeas is speaking either of himself or of the Greeks at large, and that he describes something that amazes either himself or them. Neither of these uses of ἡμεῖς is to be found in Homer, who maintains a characteristic objectivity in excluding them. But Aristeas' poem was not heroic in the Homeric manner and must have had more in common with the personal, instructional manner of Xenophanes, Parmenides, and Empedocles, who also wrote in hexameters. Xenophanes uses ἡμετέρη of his own wisdom (fr. 2. 12 D.–K.), and Parmenides ἡμέτερος when his goddess speaks of herself and her companions (fr. 1. 25 D.–K.); but in Empedocles the situation is more instructive, since he uses ἡμέτερος three times (frs. 4. 2; 131. 2; 133. 2 D.–K.), all in the sense of 'my' with reference to himself, as is natural in a man who had a message peculiarly his own and claimed prophetic authority for it. But this is hardly what Aristeas does here. He may well feel amazement at what he is going to describe, but there is no point in his emphasizing this wonder as peculiarly his own. In this context it would be certainly more appropriate if he used ἡμῖν and ἡμετέρῃσι not of himself but of Greeks in general, of the whole public which he addresses or the society to which he belongs. But for this there is no parallel in early Greek poetry, and indeed the Greeks seem to have avoided it except in speeches with a public or political content, when the speaker, with his audience before him, makes them share his own views. Nor do ἡμεῖς and ἡμέτερος seem to have been used by poets for an experience shared with their hearers. It is true that at *N*. 6. 6. and possibly at *O*. 9. 106 Pindar uses ἄμμε to refer vaguely to all men, but that is no parallel; for there is no point in Aristeas' so using the word here. Though in dealing with ἡμεῖς and its adjective a considerable range of meanings is to be expected, it is on the whole unlikely that a poet like Aristeas would use it either of himself and his countrymen or of himself and his audience, and since one or the other of these meanings is required by the view under discussion, we may reject it and assume that the speaker is not the poet but someone else, in all probability the spokesman of some people whose views he professes to expound.

If, then, the lines are spoken by some inland people, it is tempting to examine how Aristeas sets about his unusual task and what he makes of it. There is an ingenuity in his methods which betrays the conscious craftsman. He is out to interest and surprise, and he makes the most of his theme. For those who have never seen the sea the thought of existence on it is strange and disturbing. So he stresses certain points and emphasizes certain paradoxes by a deft selection of words and ideas. When, for instance, he says that his seafarers ὕδωρ ναίουσιν, he omits any mention of ships and almost gives the impression that these people actually live in the sea rather than on it. Just as Bacchylides calls dolphins ἁλιναιέται (17. 97), or Euripides speaks of Poseidon as ναίων ἅλα (*Hel.* 1584), or a Sophoclean chorus asks whether Heracles ναίει ποντίας αὐλῶνας (*Trach.* 99–100), so Aristeas suggests that his seafarers dwell in the sea as ordinary men dwell on the land and emphasizes the paradox by calling them ἄνδρες. Moreover, to make the situation absolutely clear, he adds ἀπὸ χθονὸς ἐν πελάγεσσι. If by ἀπὸ χθονός he means 'away from the land' and simply stresses the severance between this life and that of normal men, ἐν πελάγεσσι suggests that his people have something in common with those who really dwell in the sea, since it is closely related to the formula ἁλὸς ἐν πελάγεσσι, which Homer uses of Leucothea (ε 335), and the Homeric

Hymn to Apollo uses of Delos, when she is afraid that Apollo will sink her in the depths (Hom. Hymn, 3. 73). Aristeas builds up his picture of a strange unnatural existence by an adroit use of words, which is based on tradition but put to new purposes in a way which helps to create an impression of untutored simplicity.

The life of these seafarers is paradoxical and unpleasant, and the unpleasantness arises from the paradox that, instead of living on the earth as ἀνέρες ἀλφησταί should, they pass their days divided between sea and sky, to neither of which they belong. Aristeas makes his point neatly:

δύστηνοί τινές εἰσιν, ἔχουσι γὰρ ἔργα πονηρά,
ὄμματ' ἐν ἄστροισι, ψυχὴν δ' ἐνὶ πόντῳ ἔχουσιν.

The last words recall a famous line of Archilochus, which Aristeas need not necessarily have known,[1] but with which he presents an illuminating contrast:

ψυχὰς ἔχοντες κυμάτων ἐν ἀγκάλαις.   (fr. 21 D.)

When Archilochus says that sailors 'have their lives in the arms of the waves', he compares men at sea with children dandled in their mothers' arms and speaks with the assurance and the affection of a man who knows the sea. Aristeas matches ψυχὰς ἔχοντες by ψυχὴν ἔχουσι and produces exactly the opposite effect by suggesting that existence on the sea is spent in continual risk and affliction. His words are nicely adjusted to the feelings of those who do not know the sea and have an undefined horror of it. The difference between the two passages lies largely in the difference between ψυχάς and ψυχήν. The plural, as Archilochus uses it, means no more than the 'lives' of sailors' in the sense of what they do and suffer; the singular, as Aristeas uses it, means the state of their feelings in the presence of danger and death. In the singular ψυχή has an emotional connotation which it does not have in the plural. This is why it is applied to such conditions as love (Eur. *Hipp.* 505) or courage (Pind. *P.* 1. 48) or appetite (Aesch. *Pers.* 841) or poverty of spirit (Hdt. 5. 124. 1). So Aristeas uses it correctly to mark the misery of his seafarers. Instead of having their feelings engaged in ordinary

[1] For the date of Archilochus, with a *floruit c.* 650 B.C., see F. Jacoby, *C.Q.* xxxv (1941), 97–100.

A FRAGMENT OF THE ARIMASPEA

human activities, they are absorbed by the horrors of the unescapable sea.

This is one side of their existence. The other is that their eyes are fixed on the stars. What is for every sailor part of his normal routine becomes in the view of the ignorant landsman a whole existence. Odysseus may steer his craft by watching the constellations, but these people have their eyes fixed on the stars as an inevitable part of their double and divided life. The skill with which Aristeas depicts their quandary may be seen more clearly if we look at another passage much later in date but not utterly dissimilar in subject and perhaps ultimately derived from him. Talking of fishermen, Oppian says:

δούρασι δ' ἐν βαιοῖσιν ἀελλάων θεράποντες
πλαζόμενοι, καὶ θυμὸν ἐν οἴδμασιν αἰὲν ἔχοντες,
αἰεὶ μὲν νεφέλην ἰοειδέα παπταίνουσιν,
αἰεὶ δὲ τρομέουσι μελαινόμενον πόρον ἅλμης. (*Hal.* 1. 41–4)

Oppian starts at a disadvantage because he is trying to enlarge on the horrors of life at sea to those who know something about it. He therefore cannot indulge in such hyperboles and drastic simplifications as Aristeas. He tries instead to make events at sea as dramatic as he can without departing too far from the truth, with the result that we are presented not with a purely fanciful situation but with a rhetorical description of familiar facts. Like Aristeas, Oppian plays with the notion of a life divided between sea and sky and filled with continual anxiety. But his details are less striking and less unusual. The θυμός which fishermen have in the waves is less comprehensive than Aristeas' ψυχή. The endless watch on the violet-coloured cloud is less mysterious and less imaginative than the eyes fixed on the stars. The mention of ships is less bold than the hint of people actually living in the sea. Oppian does his best, but his words show how good a performer Aristeas is in extracting an entirely new mystery from something known to everyone.

The misery of Aristeas' seafarers expresses itself in prayer, but this prayer takes an unusual form. They lift their hands to the gods, but what else happens is less obvious. In suggesting that in the last line Aristeas refers to seasickness and in quoting Plutarch to enforce his case, Rhys Roberts is on the right track, but the problem is less simple than he implies. Plutarch uses ἐκβάλλειν transitively in the sense of 'vomit', and that this is normal may be seen from Timotheus' Persian, who, after falling overboard in the battle of Salamis, suffers sadly before he dies:

βλοσυρὰν δ' ἐξέβαλλεν ἄ-
χναν ἐπανερευγόμενος
στόματι βρύχιον ἅλμαν.   (Pers. 83–5 P.)

Aristeas uses not ἐκβάλλειν but ἀναβάλλειν, and uses it in the passive with σπλάγχνα. By some means, and in some connection, which is not fully clear, the bowels of his seafarers are 'thrown up'. This may be connected with seasickness, but it is not fully illustrated by the passage from Plutarch. Aristeas may well mean the preliminaries or symptoms of seasickness, but the fatal crisis is not mentioned. Perhaps he is restrained by poetical propriety, but we may suspect that he has something more subtle in mind.

More serious than this is a question of syntax. σπλάγχνοισι ἀναβαλλομένοισι is in the dative and must be treated as such. It is unfortunate that in his edition of *On the Sublime* Rhys Roberts gives not his own translation but that of A. S. Way:

Often I ween to the gods are their hands upraised on high,
And with hearts in misery heavenward-lifted in prayer do they cry.

This is open to more than one objection. First, whatever σπλάγχνοισι may mean, it cannot have the English meaning of 'hearts', especially when they are said to be lifted heavenwards, which evokes ecclesiastical echoes of *sursum corda* and is quite alien to the real meaning of σπλάγχνα as 'bowels'. Secondly, the Greek text gives no authority for the words 'do they cry'. εὔχονται may suggest it, but does not explicitly state it.

It is clear that much turns on how we take σπλάγχνοισι ἀναβαλλομένοισι. It has been suggested that this is 'a dative of accompanying circumstances' like the Homeric ἀπονόσφιν ἔβη τετιηότι θυμῷ (Λ 555).[1] This is an established usage,[2] and certainly gives simpler sense than if we take the dative as instrumental.[3] Behind Aristeas' words lie such epic formulas as

αἱ δ' ὀλολυγῇ πᾶσαι Ἀθήνῃ χεῖρας ἀνέσχον,   (Ζ 301)

where the uplifting of hands in prayer is accompanied by a cry. So Aristeas, more ingeniously, says that when the seafarers pray,

---

[1] Bolton, *Aristeas*, 15.
[2] Kühner–Gerth, *Ausf. gr. Gramm.* ii. 2. 435.
[3] This was my first view, but I have abandoned it.

their prayer is accompanied by physical reactions of a painful and undignified character. With this unexpected stroke our fragment ends, and we do not know what Aristeas went on to say. But it throws a small ray of light on his methods of composition. Just as elsewhere he must have amazed his Greek readers by tales of wonders beyond their ken, so here he reverses the process and provides men accustomed to the sea with a shock of surprise by showing what seafaring means to the imagination of peoples who do not know it in reality.[1]

We can well understand that in these lines 'Longinus' found nothing to inspire fear, but his judgement that they have ἄνθος is more interesting. The word indicates some kind of elegance or brilliance or charm. They have indeed an individual quality, a sophisticated agility in presenting an unprecedented situation, a neatness in making their point and making the most of it. They are not exactly amusing, and there is no reason to think that they are meant to be, but they certainly titillate and engage the curiosity. They owe much to Aristeas' dexterous style and suggest that, though he knew the formulaic language of epic poetry, he used it in his own way, not slavishly repeating its phrases but making innovations and adjustments in them. In this he resembles post-Homeric writers of epic, but he is more adroit and works towards a more calculated and more familiar end. His effects are more vivid and more violent. Take, for instance, a line on the Arimaspians:

χαίτῃσιν λάσιοι, πάντων στιβαρώτατοι ἀνδρῶν.
(fr. 4. 2 Kinkel)

This looks Homeric because all its words are used by Homer, but in fact Aristeas treats them in a new and different way. Homer applies λάσιος only to animals and to parts of the human body, such as the chest (*A* 189). In applying it to a whole class of men, Aristeas suggests that they are like shaggy animals such as sheep (*Ω* 125) and rams (*ι* 433). This is perfectly fair for the outlandish Arimaspians, and gets unexpected support from the representation of them on a silver mirror from Kelermes in the Kuban,

[1] Professor A. Andrewes points out to me that καὶ τοῦτο may suggest that the speakers have other things to mention which they find peculiar to ways of life not their own and that perhaps, while Aristeas expresses his amazement at what they say about their neighbours, they retort that a lot of reported Greek activities seem improbable to them.

now in the Hermitage at Leningrad. Here a griffin has on either side a sturdy, unusually hairy figure, who seems to be fighting him.¹ The mirror comes from the middle of the sixth century and may well be based on the *Arimaspea*. It illuminates also the adjective στιβαρώτατοι. Homer uses στιβαρός for parts of the body but not for the complete man, and Aristeas anticipates what looks like a colloquial use in Aristophanes (*Thesm.* 639) in transferring the word to people who are uncommonly muscular. In this one line he advances from Homeric convention in two directions, and both moves secure something more surprising and more sensational than strict Homeric precedent allowed.

What Aristeas does with words, he also does with his themes. His conception of men praying with upcast bowels is adventurous enough for any taste, but a similar audacity, on a smaller scale, can be seen in his treatment of the one-eyed Arimaspians. Any Greek on hearing of them would connect them in his mind with the Cyclopes and feel that there must be something rude and bestial about them. Strabo indeed advances the paradoxical view that Homer derived his Cyclopes from the Arimaspians and transferred them from Scythia to their lonely island (21). The opposite seems more likely—that Aristeas learned of the Cyclopes from Homer, and, seeing that his Arimaspians might easily be confused or compared with them, went out of his way to make them different. For instance, while the Cyclopes have indeed many goats but otherwise get no benefit from the rich soil of their land (ι 116), Aristeas makes his Arimaspians

ἀφνειοὺς ἵπποισι, πολύρρηνας, πολυβούτας.

(fr. 3. 3 Kinkel)

If they are to be compared with Homeric characters at all, it is with the prosperous inhabitants of the Pylian cities which Agamemnon offers to Achilles—

ἐν δ' ἄνδρες ναίουσι πολύρρηνες, πολυβοῦται—

(*I* 154, 296)²

or, if we want a parallel from post-Homeric epic, with the rich man in the *Carmen Naupactium*:

ἀλλ' ὃ μὲν οὖν ἐπὶ θινὶ θαλάσσης εὐρυπόροιο
οἰκία ναιετάασκε πολύρρην, πουλυβοώτης. (fr. 2 Kinkel)

¹ Bolton, *Aristeas*, 6, pl. I.
² The same line occurs at Hesiod, fr. 243. 3 M.–W., of the Hellopians.

Despite their remote home and their ghoulish appearance, the Arimaspians are presented as enjoying a Greek way of life. Indeed even their appearance is made less fearsome than we might expect, when Aristeas says

ὀφθαλμὸν δ' ἕν' ἕκαστος ἔχει χαρίεντι μετώπῳ. (fr. 4. 1)

They may have only one eye each, but it is set in a charming face. The adjective χαρίεν attached to μέτωπον recalls Homer's words about Achilles:

ἀλλ' ἀνδρὸς θείοιο κάρη χαρίεν τε μέτωπον. (Π 798)

Though the surviving lines of the *Arimaspea* are indeed scanty, they show that Aristeas, who knew the epic language, used it in his own way to produce new effects and to introduce new subjects in such a manner as to acclimatize them, despite all their oddity, to a familiar world of poetry.

That Aristeas told remarkable stories we cannot doubt, and perhaps unacknowledged traces of them may be found in Herodotus' account of the Scythians no less than in poetry.[1] From such a magician we should expect no less. But the surviving fragments suggest that in relating his wonderful tales he adopted an easy, persuasive manner, which has no traces of mystification or desire to impress such as we find, for instance, in the fragments of Epimenides. Aristeas sets about his task with an air of being sensible and practical and makes his remote peoples more intelligible by describing them through their likeness to the Greeks, as when he speaks of the Issedones,

Ἰσσηδοὶ χαίτῃσιν ἀγαλλόμενοι ταναῇσι, (fr. 2)

which recalls Xenophanes' account of the Colophonians in their luxurious heyday,

αὐχαλέοι, χαίτῃσιν ἀγαλλόμεν' εὐπρεπέεσσιν.

(fr. 3. 5 D.-K.)

Of course the Issedones were a real people about whom something could be known from travellers, but Aristeas shows good sense in

---

[1] It is tempting to surmise that Herodotus' account of Kolaxais, the ancestor of the Scythian kings (4. 5. 2), comes from Aristeas, since, if Alcman indeed knew the *Arimaspea*, his otherwise obscure reference to a ἵππος Κολαξαῖος (fr. 1. 59 P.), which D. L. Page, *Alcman, the Partheneion*, 90, thinks must apply to an illustrious breed of horses 'familiar to Alcman's audience', would then be a simple literary reference from a work which had recently come into circulation. See Bolton, *Aristeas*, 43.

presenting them so simply. Again, when he reports what is said about the Arimaspians, he approaches the subject with a plain factual assurance:

> καί σφεας ἀνθρώπους εἶναι καθύπερθεν ὁμούρους
> πρὸς Βορέω, πολλούς τε καὶ ἐσθλοὺς κάρτα μαχητάς,
> ἀφνειοὺς ἵπποισι, πολύρρηνας, πολυβούτας. (fr. 3)

If such was his manner, it is the more likely that his strange account of seafarers is not his own report on people whom he himself has seen but something which he alleges to have been told him by others and claims to report as they told it, with all the oddities which, in their puzzled ignorance, they found in it. It may also help to explain why, despite his shamanistic claims, Aristeas was treated more or less seriously by serious authors. A man who spoke in this disarming, plausible manner might after all seem to have something to say that was worth hearing.

VIII

THE TWO PALINODES OF STESICHORUS[1]

THE publication of a papyrus from Oxyrhynchus containing the remains of a commentary on Stesichorus[2] is a salutary lesson on the dangers of speculation on the fragments of Greek lyric poetry; for although many scholars have discussed the famous Palinode, none has suggested that there was not one but two. The papyrus states this beyond question and quotes Chamaeleon as its authority. Chamaeleon was a slightly ambiguous figure. On the one hand he seems to have had a taste for gossip about men of letters and to have purveyed it even when he did not himself believe it, as in the alleged love of Anacreon for Sappho (Athen. 13. 599 c), but even in this case he says that it is the opinion of some people and does not give his own authority to it. On the other hand he has the great virtue that his interest in writers extends to their writings and that he quotes passages which we do not know from other sources, notably a substantial part of Pindar's ἐγκώμιον for Xenophon of Corinth (fr. 107 Bo.; 122 Sn.), two fragments of Anacreon (frs. 359/13; 371/27 P.), and three fragments of Aeschylus (frs. 309–11 N.). His reliability in assigning texts is to some extent guaranteed by his rightly sceptical attitude to some alleged lines of Sappho, which, as he sees, cannot possibly be her work (Athen. 13. 599 d). Though he liked gossip, he liked to back it with a text, and though his interpretations may be faulty, his texts usually are not. Stesichorus had an obvious appeal for such a man, since his *Helen* and his Palinode provided material for an unusual, dramatic story. We may therefore put some trust in his information about the two Palinodes, which comes presumably from his work περὶ Στησιχόρου, of which we know only that it existed and that in it he said that the work of early poets used to be sung (Athen. 14.

---
[1] First published in *Classical Review*, N.S. xiii (1963), 1–10, slightly altered.
[2] D. L. Page, *Poetae Melici Graeci*, 106, no. 193/16; *Ox. Pap.* xxix. 35–6. See now M. Doria, *P.P.* 1963, 81–93; F. Sisti, *Stud. Urb.* xxxix (1965), 301 ff.; J. A. Davison, *From Archilochus to Pindar*, 222–5.

620 c). In the papyrus he says that there existed διτταὶ παλιν-ωιδ⟨ίαι δια⟩λλάττουσαι, of which the first began

δεῦρ' αὖτε θεὰ φιλόμολπε,

and the second

χρυσόπτερε παρθένε,

and that the first attacked Homer because he sent Helen to Troy, while the second attacked Hesiod for some unspecified reason. It is not certain that one further item of information on the papyrus comes from him, but it must in any case be treated with respect. With this new knowledge we must look again at the traditional versions of what Stesichorus said in recantation and ask what light the papyrus throws on it.

In considering the first fragment we must decide to whom it is addressed, and we might be tempted to think that it is Helen. It is to her that Stesichorus speaks in the second person in the fragment of a Palinode already known to us (fr. 192/15 P.), and the new words are not inappropriate to her. That she can be called θεά is clear from Euripides' *Helen*, where the Dioscuri tell her that when she dies, θεὸς κεκλήσῃ (1667), and φιλόμολπε suits a divine being who is believed both by Euripides (*Hel.* 1465–7) and by Aristophanes (*Lys.* 1308–15) to dance by the waters of the Eurotas. αὖτε has then a special force; for it hints or forecasts that on this occasion she will hear a very different song from the last, when the *Helen* was sung. Nor is even δεῦρο out of place, since the song may have been performed at some season or festival at which Helen is believed to be present, as she is in Pindar's *Olympian* 3. Yet though the individual words are suitable enough for Helen, the tone is not right for a song in which Stesichorus is going to make a humble apology for having insulted her, and in that case an obvious alternative is the Muse. That she can be called θεά is clear from Homer (α 10), while Hesiod speaks of the Muses in the plural as θεαί (*Theog.* 24) and Pindar as θεᾶν (*I.* 8. 66). Though φιλόμολπος is applied by Pindar to Aegina because of her love of songs and dances (*N.* 7. 8), it is directly applicable to the Muse, whose special concern these are. In summoning her with the word δεῦρο Stesichorus does very much what Sappho does when she calls the Muses and the Graces, δεῦτέ νυν ἄβραι Χάριτες καλλίκομοί τε

Μοῖσαι (fr. 127 L.–P.) and βροδοπάχεες ἅγναι Χάριτες δεῦτε Διός κόραι (fr. 53 L.–P.), or Aristophanes when he makes his choruses sing ὦ Διὸς ἐννέα παρθένοι, ἁγναὶ Μοῦσαι . . . ἔλθετ' (Ran. 875–9) and Μῶα μόλε Λάκαινα (Lys. 1298). Stesichorus then appeals to the Muse very much as he does at the start of his Oresteia (fr. 210/33 P.) and of another poem, which may be the 'Ἰλίου πέρσις[1], and begins δεῦρ' ἄγε Καλλιόπεια λίγεια (fr. 240/63 P.). All is then straightforward and coherent and the sense is clinched by the word αὖτε. This does not inevitably mean that Stesichorus summons the Muse back to give a new version of the story of Helen, since it could conceivably mean that he needs her just for some new song. So indeed Sappho says δεῦρο δηὖτε Μοῖσαι χρύσιον λίποισαι . . . (fr. 127 L.–P.), but in this special context αὖτε may well suggest that the Muse must sing another song because Stesichorus wishes to repudiate or amend what he has said about Helen. The Muse is certainly a good candidate for the opening words of this Palinode, and whether they are addressed to her or to Helen, they are unquestionably the start of a new song, and we must dismiss any theory that the Palinode was no more than a part or an epilogue of the poem in which Stesichorus said the wrong things about Helen.[2] Any passages which seemed to support this view must now be reconsidered, and we see that, when Isocrates says that Stesichorus reviled Helen ἀρχόμενος τῆς ᾠδῆς (Hel. 64), this was in a different ᾠδή from the Palinode; that, when Dio Chrysostom says that the recantation was ἐν τῇ ὕστερον ᾠδῇ (Or. 11. 40), this means not 'in the later part of the song' but 'in the song which came later'; that when Philostratus says that the Palinode was ἐναντίον τῷ προτέρῳ λόγῳ (Vit. Apollon. 6. 11), he means 'contrary to the earlier piece'. It is clear that both this Palinode and the next are new and separate songs.

The second Palinode also began with an invocation, χρυσόπτερε παρθένε, which must be addressed to a divine being. The only being so called in early poetry is Iris, who is χρυσόπτερος in Homer (Θ 398; Λ 185), and in the Homeric Hymn to Demeter (314). But though Iris is not inappropriately called a virgin, it is hard to see why she should be summoned here, unless it is to

[1] Bergk, P.L.G.[4] 223.
[2] I made this mistake in my Greek Lyric Poetry[2], 112; see also J. Vürtheim, Stesichoros' Fragmente und Biographie, 59.

bring some message from Olympus to Stesichorus and his company; and even so it is unlikely that he would actually summon her in this way, which would be without precedent or parallel and perhaps even offensive to the gods in its assumption that their messenger is at the call of a human being. That the word could be used of other divine beings is clear from Aristophanes' attachment of χρυσόπτερος to Eros (*Av.* 1738), and if that can be done, it leaves the door open for other candidates. As Page suggests, there is a possible ray of light from Himerius, who was well instructed in Greek poetry and often picks up its phrases and images for his own use. When he says ὦ Διὸς παῖδες, ἴτε, ἴτε Μοῦσαι χρυσοπτέρυγοι (*Or.* 48. 37 Colonna), he may well have some passage of poetry in mind, and indeed suggests this by saying that his invocation is ποιητικόν. In that case the Muse or the Muses could be called 'golden-winged'. Stesichorus also calls her 'maiden', and this is suitable enough since Pindar speaks of Ἑλικώνιαι παρθένοι (*I.* 8. 63), Bacchylides of κλυτοφόρμιγγες ... παρθένοι ... Πιερίδες (1. 1–2), and Aristophanes of παρθένοι ἁγναὶ Μοῦσαι (*Ran.* 875–6). So the second Palinode summons the Muse at the start, as the first also does; and though this may be no more than Stesichorus' normal practice, it is tempting to think that he has a special reason for doing so—because it is she who must now put right what he has said before and help him to produce a more respectful version of the doings of Helen. Indeed, if we may judge by the first words of his *Oresteia*, he expects the Muse to join him in his work and take a share of it (fr. 210/33 P.), and that would be very much his attitude here.

The discovery of the first lines of the two Palinodes calls for the reconsideration of a passage which is certainly concerned with Stesichorus and has been connected with his *Helen* and its sequel. At the beginning of a speech Aristides says that it is a pleasant task to welcome a traveller from abroad, and then proceeds: μέτειμι δὲ ἐπὶ ἕτερον προοίμιον κατὰ Στησίχορον. σκιαμαχεῖν μὲν οὖν πως οἶδ' ὅτι δεῖ, πρὸς οὓς γὰρ εἰρήσεται τὰ λεγόμενα οὐχ ἤκουσιν· ὥστε συμβαίνει ἅμα μὲν σχεδὸν ὥσπερ ἂν εἰς μάτην γίγνεσθαι τοὺς λόγους, ἅμα δ' εἶναι σαφέστατον ὡς ὀρθῶς καὶ προσηκόντως εἰρήσονται (*Or.* 33. 3). It has long been recognized that the words μέτειμι ἐπὶ ἕτερον προοίμιον are either a direct quotation from Stesichorus or a fairly close paraphrase of something that he said, and with this goes a possibility that εἰς μάτην comes from the same source,[1] since it stands out oddly in the text of Aristides, and Stesichorus is said to have used the accusative plural μάτας after εἰπών or εἶπον in the sense of 'talking nonsense' (fr. 257/80 P.). Since Aristides proceeds to a defence of himself, it is a reasonable supposition that Stesichorus does the same and that the words, or their substance, come from a Palinode. It is now clear that if they come from either Palinode, they are not its actual opening, but of course they might come soon afterwards. Even so it is not clear from which Palinode they come. Even if εἰς μάτην is drawn from the same source, as it may be, they could come from either, since in both Stesichorus must have had something to recant and could well proclaim that he had talked nonsense, whether misled by Homer or by Hesiod. If the words come from the first Palinode, they would suit the use which Aristides makes of them, since his tone changes from confidence to self-defence, and this would suit a parallel change from the *Helen* to the first Palinode. But a similar change would be just as appropriate in the second Palinode, in which Stesichorus also apologizes for something he has said earlier. In favour of the second Palinode, we can argue that, when Stesichorus, as quoted by Aristides, says that he is going to make a second προοίμιον, his 'second prelude' should be comparable with something of its own kind, and this would be better suited to a ἕτερον Palinode, which performs a function not unlike that of the first, than to the first Palinode, which performs a function very different from that of the *Helen*, and is not easily compared with it as another example of a single kind. It is therefore possible that Aristides knew the two Palinodes and distinguished between them. If so, he is unique among the more than twenty writers of antiquity who mention a Palinode, but always as if there were no more than one.[2]

Of the first Palinode we know at least as much as the papyrus, and therefore Chamaeleon, says of its contents. In it Stesichorus μέμ]φεται τὸν Ὅμηρο[ν ὅτι Ἑλέ]νην ἐποίησεν ἐν Τ[ροίαι] καὶ οὐ τὸ εἴδωλον αὐτῆ[ς (2–5). Since Stesichorus blames Homer for not saying that it was a phantom of Helen present at Troy, it follows that he himself said that it was, and to this extent the papyrus confirms what we already knew from Plato, τὸ τῆς Ἑλένης

---

[1] Both points were first made by Bergk, *P.L.G.*⁴ 222–3.
[2] An ample list may be found in O. F. Kleine, *Stesichori Himerensis Fragmenta* (Berlin, 1828), 95–6, and this is completed by Bergk, *P.L.G.*⁴ 218–19.

εἴδωλον ὑπὸ τῶν ἐν Τροίᾳ Στησίχορός φησι γενέσθαι περιμάχητον ἀγνοίᾳ τοῦ ἀληθοῦς (*Rep.* 9. 586 c), and from Aristides, ὥσπερ οἱ Στησιχόρου Τρῶες οἱ τὸ τῆς Ἑλένης εἴδωλον ἔχοντες ὡς αὐτήν (*Or.* 45. 54). Stesichorus clearly tried to absolve himself by blaming Homer, and he must have done so by name, rather as in a later generation Pindar complains that the renown of Odysseus is greater than his sufferings because of the sweet words of Homer (*N.* 7. 20–3). If Pindar could do this, perhaps using Stesichorus as a precedent, there is no doubt that Stesichorus himself could speak out on what was for him a matter of great importance. In the second Palinode Stesichorus blamed Hesiod, ἔν τε τ[ῆ]ι ἑτέραι τὸν Ἡσίοδ[ον] μέμ[φετ]αι (5–7), but, since we are not told what his complaint was, we are very much in the dark. Stesichorus can hardly have blamed Hesiod, as he did Homer, for not introducing the Phantom, since it looks very much as if, at some point, he did; for the paraphrase of Lycophron, *Alex.* 822, says πρῶτος Ἡσίοδος περὶ τῆς Ἑλένης παρήγαγε τὸ εἴδωλον (p. 71 Scheer; Hes. fr. 358 M.–W.), and since παρήγαγε must mean 'introduced', it suggests that Hesiod said something about a Phantom and may have invented it.[1] It follows that Stesichorus must have censured Hesiod for something else, and that we shall have to consider later. The papyrus then goes on to give some other information, but does not say from which Palinode it comes, though, since it deals with what happened to Helen during the Trojan war, it looks as if it came from the first. At least it tells what Stesichorus did with an important element in the story: αὐτὸ[ς δ]έ φησ[ιν ὁ] Στησίχορο[ς] τὸ μὲν ε[ἴδωλο]ν ἐλθεῖ[ν ἐς] Τροίαν τὴν δὲ Ἑλένην π[αρὰ] τῶι Πρωτεῖ καταμεῖν[αι (12–16). This is not quoted as coming from Chamaeleon, though there is no reason to doubt that it does, and it certainly must be derived, directly or indirectly, from the text of Stesichorus, since otherwise the papyrus would not say αὐτὸς δέ φησιν. At least we may now rule out modern notions that Proteus was introduced into the story after Stesichorus,[2] and the construction certainly

---

[1] A. M. Dale, *Euripides: Helen*, xxiii, dismisses this passage as worthless and thinks that 'Hesiod' is a blunder for 'Stesichorus'. Stesichorus certainly has all the credit for the Phantom, and may well have invented it. The point does not affect our argument.

[2] Wilamowitz, *Sappho und Simonides*, 241, n. 1; Schmid–Stählin, *Gesch. d. gr. Lit.* II. i. 476. T. Hopfner, *Orient und griechische Philosophie* (Leipzig, 1925), 50, ascribes the story to the influence of Egyptian priests.

implies that the arrival of the Phantom at Troy and the sojourn of Helen with Proteus are related and more or less contemporaneous. Since Proteus is connected with Egypt, where Homer places him (δ 383 ff.), it follows that among his other innovations Stesichorus started the career of the Egyptian Helen. The papyrus is very far from telling even the main outline of what Stesichorus said in his Palinode, but it gives two or three solid pieces of information, against which we must set what we can gather of the story from other sources.

In saying that Helen stayed in Egypt with Proteus the papyrus is not alone. This was known to Euripides and stated explicitly by him (*Hel.* 44 ff.), and further details are given by Tzetzes (ad Lyc. *Alex.* 113) and by a scholiast on Aristides (ad *Or.* 13. 131), both of whom quote Stesichorus as their authority. According to them, when Paris carried off Helen, he brought her by ship to Egypt, where Proteus deprived him of her. This sounds plausible enough, but at this point the two sources diverge. While Tzetzes says that Proteus gave the Phantom to Paris, who sailed off with it to Troy, the scholiast says that Proteus gave Paris a picture to comfort him for his loss. This disagreement stirs suspicions about both accounts, and though we may feel that Tzetzes is more likely to be right than the scholiast, it is clear that even when Stesichorus is quoted by name, we cannot always accept what is attributed to him. But there is a more serious difficulty than this. Though we do not know exactly what Stesichorus said about Helen that caused so much trouble and inspired the recantation, at least he ἐβλασφήμησε her (Isocr. 10. 64). His first poem was regarded as *uituperatio* (schol. Cruq. ad Hor. *Epod.* 17. 42), and this must have been directed in part against her behaviour to Menelaus in running away with Paris, to which Stesichorus refers in a fragment which surely comes from the *Helen*[1] and speaks of her and her sister as διγάμους τε καὶ τριγάμους καὶ λιπεσάνορας (fr. 223/46, 4–5 P.), but if in his revised version he still sent her with Paris as far as Egypt, his recantation is partial and inadequate and would hardly be acceptable in circles where he was thought to have spoken very ill of her. We may therefore try to find an alternative version which is more in the authentic spirit of a Palinode, and

[1] So Bergk, *P.L.G.*⁴ 215.

it still[1] seems that the right clue lies in a statement of Dio Chrysostom: καὶ τὸν μὲν Στησίχορον ἐν τῇ ὕστερον ᾠδῇ λέγειν ὅτι τὸ παράπαν οὐδὲ πλεύσειεν ἡ Ἑλένη οὐδαμόσε, ἄλλοι δέ τινες ὡς ἁρπασθείη μὲν Ἑλένη ὑπὸ τοῦ Ἀλεξάνδρου, δεῦρο δὲ παρ' ἡμᾶς εἰς Αἴγυπτον ἀφίκοιτο (*Or.* 11. 40). If we read this without proper attention, we are liable to assume that it must be wrong because it seems to rule out the possibility that Helen went to Egypt, and we are then forced to assume that she must have spent the war in concealment,[2] perhaps in Therapna,[3] or that this was the end of her career on earth and she was transported either to the sky to join the Dioscuri[4] or to the Islands of the Blest.[5] Though she may well have ended her days in one or the other of these ways, there is now no need to assume that this took place so early, and her position during the war is settled by a closer look at what Dio says. In it the important word is πλεύσειεν. Dio says not that Helen did not *go* anywhere, but that she did not *sail* anywhere. It follows that she did not sail away with Paris and her reputation is saved. That Dio is right follows from the only quotation known to us from a Palinode before the recent discovery:

οὐκ ἔστ' ἔτυμος λόγος οὗτος,[6]
οὐδ' ἔβας ἐν νηυσὶν εὐσέλμοις,
οὐδ' ἵκεο πέργαμα Τροίας.   (fr. 192/15 P.)

This presumably comes from the first Palinode, since it denies Helen's presence at Troy, and it comes with the unquestionable authority of Plato (*Phaedr.* 243 a). With it, as with Dio, it is a question not of Helen's not *going* anywhere but of her not *sailing* anywhere, that is neither to Troy nor to Egypt. We can avoid this conclusion only if we assume that Dio has misunderstood his text, which is unlikely, or that the quotation made by Plato is a contorted way of saying that Helen did not sail to Troy. This is surely impossible in a statement which is intended to be a solemn recantation of an error and must be made with rigour and clarity. The conclusion is that Helen certainly went to Egypt and presumably spent the war there, but she did not go by sea.

[1] A. von Premerstein, *Philologus*, lv (1896), 641.
[2] V. Pisani, *Riv. fil.* n.s. vi (1928), 476 ff.
[3] E. Preuss, *De Euripidis Helena* (Diss. Leipzig, 1911), 48 ff.
[4] Bowra, *Greek Lyric Poetry*², 109–10.
[5] Vürtheim, *Stesichoros*, 67 ff.
[6] λόγος οὗτος refers forward to the following words.

Helen, then, must have come to Egypt by some other means than a ship, and what this was may be deduced from Euripides, who gives an entirely adequate alternative when he makes Helen say of herself:

> λαβὼν δέ μ' Ἑρμῆς ἐν πτυχαῖσιν αἰθέρος
> νεφέλῃ καλύψας—οὐ γὰρ ἠμέλησέ μου
> Ζεύς—τόνδ' ἐς οἶκον Πρωτέως ἱδρύσατο.   (*Hel.* 44–6)

This is perfectly consistent with the papyrus on the one hand and with Dio and the fragment on the other, and though we must not press the details too far, we can hardly doubt that Stesichorus transferred Helen to Egypt by divine agency. The device solved more than one problem. Menelaus, left alone without her, could still go to fight at Troy; Helen's reputation is saved because she has never yielded to Paris, and it must be of this that Aristides is thinking when he says ὥσπερ τῶν ποιητῶν φασί τινες τὸν Ἀλέξανδρον τῆς Ἑλένης τὸ εἴδωλον λαβεῖν, αὐτὴν δὲ οὐ δυνηθῆναι (*Or.* 13. 131). It follows that the Phantom began its career at Sparta when Paris absconded with it and that it continued its career at Troy, where Greeks and Trojans fought for it. In that case both Tzetzes and the scholiast on Aristides are wrong in saying that Stesichorus made Proteus create the Phantom and send either it or a picture of it with Paris when he sailed to Troy.

If such is the outline of the revised tale of Helen as Stesichorus told it, we have still to account for the other version or versions known to Tzetzes and the scholiast. The story in general must have been told by poets other than Stesichorus and Euripides, and indeed this follows from Dio's remark that the alternative story of Helen's going to Egypt with Paris was told by ἄλλοι τινές (*Or.* 11. 40). We may surmise how such a result was reached. The primary source is Herodotus, who reports the story as he heard it from the priests at Memphis. They must have got much of it from Greek travellers, and their story has a distinctly Greek look.[1] It says that Helen and Paris came to Egypt on their voyage to Troy (2. 113. 1) and were received at

---

[1] That not only Helen but Menelaus was honoured in Egypt follows from Plut., *de Mal. Her.* 13, where, speaking of a tale told against Menelaus, he continues ἀλλὰ πολλαὶ μὲν Ἑλένης πολλαὶ δὲ Μενελάου τιμαὶ διαφυλάττονται παρ' αὐτοῖς, but this looks as if it referred to his own time. For Helen in Egypt, see W. J. D. Vissert, *Götter und Kulte*, 19, 84.

Memphis by Proteus, who took Helen from Paris and sent him off without her to Troy (2. 112–15). In this we may detect an expansion of Homer's statement that Helen and Paris sailed to Troy (*Z* 291–2) into their sailing first to Egypt, and a full exploitation of Stesichorus' version that Helen stayed with Proteus. The second has been rationalized and moralized, and taken with the first provides a common basis for the stories recounted by Tzetzes and the scholiast. Then the Phantom, of whom Herodotus says nothing, was brought back, not as Stesichorus told but as a creation of Proteus. Such a refashioning must be the work of poets, and the added touch about the picture, given by the scholiast, suggests an Alexandrian poet interested in the varieties of love. The development of the story on these lines looks like the work of Greek poets in Egypt, who picked up a story which connected Helen with their country, combined two versions, and added fresh details to make it more interesting. That the authentic story told by Stesichorus should be confused with these later variations is not surprising. Neither Tzetzes nor the scholiast need have known the actual text of Stesichorus, as Plato certainly did, and they are quite likely to have drawn their information from handbooks of mythology, in which different versions could easily be confused and lead even serious scholars to ascribe to Stesichorus what was in fact the work of other and later poets.

So far the new information in the papyrus helps to tidy up what Stesichorus did in his Palinodes to refashion the story of Helen. But it also raises a new question. If Stesichorus blamed Homer for saying that Helen went to Troy, for what did he blame Hesiod? We might of course argue that it was for the same reason. Hesiod, after all, says that Zeus sent the race of heroes over the sea to Troy Ἑλένης ἕνεκ' ἠυκόμοιο (*Op.* 165) and is quite outspoken about her faithlessness to Menelaus, ὡς δ' Ἑλένη ᾔσχυνε λέχος ξανθοῦ Μενελάου (fr. 176. 7 M.–W.). Neither of these passages hints at the Phantom, which may be the invention not of Hesiod himself but of some member of his school. Yet since Stesichorus presumably knew of it from a poet whom he thought to be Hesiod, it seems unlikely that he would blame him for sending Helen to Troy, still more that he would make this the theme of a second Palinode when he had already dealt with it in a first. A more promising possibility is that what Stesichorus blames Hesiod for is the story, told in the original

Helen, that Helen was first married to Theseus and, having given birth to Iphigeneia, handed her over to Clytaemestra to look after (fr. 191/14 P.).[1] Such a story would confirm Stesichorus' earlier judgement that Helen was not merely δίγαμος but τρίγαμος and he might well feel that he must retract it and apologize for having told it. Moreover, there is some slight evidence that this story was told by Hesiod. Though it was certainly current in Argos, where it was supported by local rites and traditions (Paus. 2. 22. 6), a fragmentary text of Philodemus says: Στη[σίχορο]ς δ' ἐν 'Ορεστεί[αι κατ]ακολουθήσας ['Ησιό]δωι τὴν Ἀγαμέ[μνονος 'Ι]φιγένειαν εἶ[ναι τὴ]ν Ἑκάτην νῦν [ὀνομαζ]ο-μένην (fr. 215/38 P.). If Stesichorus said this in his *Oresteia*, it should supplement what he said in his *Helen*, and up to a point it is quite consistent. The joint story that emerges is that by Theseus Helen bore Iphigeneia, who was transformed into Hecate, and the last part is supported by Pausanias (1. 43. 1), who records that, according to Hesiod, Iphigeneia was saved by Artemis and became Hecate. If Stesichorus got the latter part of the story from Hesiod, it is quite likely that he also got the first, and indeed there would be no difficulty if Philodemus did not expressly call Iphigeneia the daughter of Agamemnon. It looks as if Philodemus, in recalling briefly the Stesichorean and Hesiodic transformation of Iphigeneia into Hecate, forgot that Stesichorus had made her the daughter of Theseus and referred to her, without thinking about it, in her much more usual role as the daughter of Agamemnon. If this is right, then it is probable that Stesichorus got from Hesiod both the transformation into Hecate and the love-affair of Helen and Theseus. This Hesiodic source cannot have been the same as fr. 23 (a) M.–W., since there Agamemnon is indicated as the father of Iphigeneia and she is called not Iphigeneia but Iphimede and transformed not precisely into Hecate but into Ἄρτεμις εἰνοδίη, which is not quite the same. There is in principle no objection to the existence of more than one version of this story of the birth of Iphigeneia, and Hesiodic poets may have treated the theme with their own variations. But it is clear that the early love-affair of Helen may have been a Hesiodic theme. This is very far from being a solid case, but, so far as it goes, it would explain why Stesichorus

---

[1] The story was told by Euphorion (fr. 90 Powell), Alexander Aetolus (fr. 90 Powell), and Apollodorus, *Bibl.* 3. 10. 7. See also Hellanicus, 4 F 134 Jacoby.

blames Hesiod in his second Palinode. The story was as discreditable to Helen as her flight with Paris to Troy and particularly unwelcome in any place where she was honoured as ἁγνὰ χοραγὸς εὐπρεπής (Aristoph. *Lys.* 1315). Stesichorus might feel that in this also he had gone too far and must retract what he had said and put the blame on Hesiod for misleading him. In that case there was a real need for two Palinodes. The first acquitted Helen of any responsibility for the Trojan War, the second of an early love-affair with Theseus.

IX

TWO POEMS OF THEOGNIS[1]
(805–10 and 543–6)

IN 805–10 Theognis speaks authoritatively to Cyrnus about consulting the Delphic Oracle. It is his only reference to it and comes from a time when the Oracle's prestige was high and contemporary references to it are few. The text, as Douglas Young prints it in his Teubner edition of 1961,[2] keeps close to the MSS. and is metrical and grammatical, but a nice small improvement is secured in 807 by adopting T. Hudson-Williams' alteration of κέν to κ' ἐν.[3] We then get

805 τόρνου καὶ στάθμης καὶ γνώμονος ἄνδρα θεωρὸν
    εὐθύτερον χρὴ ‹ἔ›μεν, Κύρνε, φυλασσόμενον,
    ᾧτινί κ' ἐν Πυθῶνι θεοῦ χρήσασ' ἱέρεια
    ὀμφὴν σημήνῃ πίονος ἐξ ἀδύτου·
    οὔτε τι γὰρ προσθεὶς οὐδέν κ' ἔτι φάρμακον εὕροις
810 οὔτ' ἀφελὼν πρὸς θεῶν ἀμπλακίην προφύγοις.

Before we attempt a translation we must examine the meaning of certain words.

First, in 805 θεωρόν is taken by Liddell–Scott–Jones to mean 'spectator', but since the lines are concerned with consulting the Delphic Oracle, this interpretation does not in itself mean very much, and we may reasonably expect the word to be more specific in its intention. It is surely used of a man who makes enquiries of the god as in Soph. *O.C.* 413, where Ismene speaks of ἀνδρῶν θεωρῶν Δελφικῆς ἀφ' ἑστίας or *O.T.* 114, where the word is applied to Laius apparently with reference to his enquiry at Delphi whether the son who is fated to kill him is in fact dead or not. Though θεωρός is related to religious activities, these can be of various kinds, and it ties it down too tightly and too irrelevantly if we translate it as 'spectator'. One of the duties of a θεωρός

---

[1] First published in *Philologus*, ciii (1959), 157–66.
[2] In 806 Young is surely right in preferring Ahrens' ἔμεν to Crusius's ἴμεν, because it suits better the imagery of 805, where the examples of straightness are all fixed and not moving.
[3] *The Elegies of Theognis*, 226.

might be to consult the Oracle, and this is clearly what is meant here.

Secondly, 807–8 raise a problem in the meaning and construction of ὀμφήν. Does it refer to the voice of the priestess or of the god, and is it governed by σημήνῃ or χρήσασα? Edmonds translates: 'to whom the priestess of the God declareth her answer'[1] and Carrière: 'à qui la prêtresse rend sa réponse et révèle l'oracle'.[2] Neither of these is quite satisfactory. First, since ὀμφή is always used of the voice of a god as opposed to that of a man, which is αὐδή, and this usage is enshrined in the Homeric formula θεοῦ ὀμφῇ (γ 215, π 96), in our poem ὀμφήν is more likely to be constructed with θεοῦ than to be connected in any way with the priestess. Secondly, σημαίνειν does not seem to be used with such an object as ὀμφήν, nor is there any need so to treat ὀμφήν, since it is easily and naturally taken as the object of χρήσασα in a construction like that of Hom. Hymn, 3. 132, χρήσω δ' ἀνθρώποισι Διὸς νημερτέα βουλήν. Thirdly, σημήνῃ does not mean 'declareth' or 'révèle', but refers to the allusive language of oracles and is well illustrated by Heraclitus, ὁ ἄναξ οὗ τὸ μαντεῖόν ἐστι τὸ ἐν Δελφοῖς οὔτε λέγει οὔτε κρύπτει ἀλλὰ σημαίνει (fr. 93 D.–K.). This absolute use of σημαίνειν in the sense of 'hint' or 'indicate' or 'give a sign' is too common to call for further illustration.

After this preliminary clearance, we may attempt a bald translation:

> Straighter than compass-line or carpenter's rule or square must that man be, Cyrnus, and keep on his guard, who consults the Oracle, even he to whomsoever at Pytho the priestess has given a sign when she declares the voice of the god from his rich shrine. For neither by adding anything would you find any further remedy, nor by taking away would you escape fault in the eyes of the gods.

The difficulty of the poem lies in its meaning. What does the declaration to Cyrnus really amount to? Against what precisely does Theognis utter a warning? At the start it is tempting to think that what he stresses is the correct interpretation of the oracular message, that those who receive it must do nothing either more or less than it enjoins. Greek history provides many examples of men who did one or the other and came in

---

[1] *Elegy and Iambus*, i. 326. [2] *Théognis: poèmes élégiaques*, 64.

consequence to disaster. For instance, the Spartan Dorieus erred on the side of excess. He was told by Delphi that he would take the place to which he went, and by this it meant the district of Eryx, but he attempted the more formidable task of attacking Sybaris and was killed. The moral drawn by Herodotus is that παρὰ τὰ μεμαντευμένα ποιέων διεφθάρη (5. 45. 1). Conversely, it was dangerous not to pay full attention to everything that an oracle said. When Arcesilas of Cyrene in exile consulted the Pythia about restoration to his kingdom, she answered that he would be restored but told him to be gentle to his opponents. He forgot or disobeyed her instructions and treated his adversaries abominably, with the result that they killed him, and Herodotus comments εἴτε ἑκὼν εἴτε ἀέκων ἁμαρτὼν τοῦ χρησμοῦ ἐξέπλησε μοῖραν τὴν ἑωυτοῦ (4. 164. 4). Such errors are not inconsistent with the warnings implied in Theognis' use of προσθείς and ἀφελών. But this is not what Theognis says, nor is he really concerned with the action taken to put an oracle into effect. First, though he is certainly interested in the correct treatment of an oracle once it has been given, he is concerned solely with that of the θεωρός and not with that of the city which sends him and will presumably take action about what the god says. Secondly, though Herodotus emphasizes the danger of misinterpreting or neglecting an oracle, he does not suggest that either should be called ἀμπλακίη. The Theognidean corpus presents ἀμπλακίη at 204, 386, 404, and 630, and in each case for something morally wrong. When in 810 Theognis adds the words πρὸς θεῶν, he means that such an action is wrong in the eyes of the gods, as we can see from such parallels as Thuc. 1. 71. 5 ἄδικον οὐδὲν οὔτε πρὸς θεῶν τῶν ὁρκίων οὔτε πρὸς ἀνθρώπων and Xen. *Anab.* 1. 6. 6 ὅ τι δικαιόν ἐστι καὶ πρὸς θεῶν καὶ πρὸς ἀνθρώπων. Theognis is concerned not merely with the danger of failure but with the moral wrongness of some action connected with the treatment of oracles.

This prompts a second explanation,—that what concerns Theognis is not the interpretation of an oracle but its transmission from Delphi to the place which sent the θεωρός. In this connection it is tempting to explain the poem by the entry τὰ τρία in the *Suda*, which says ὅτι ὁ μαντευόμενος ἐν Δελφοῖς ἐλάμβανε τοὺς χρησμούς, καὶ προείρητο αὐτῷ, εἰ λύσει, μία τῶν τριῶν· ἢ γὰρ τῶν ὀφθαλμῶν αὐτὸν ἔδει στερηθῆναι ἢ τῆς χειρὸς ἢ τῆς γλώττης. This startling piece of information gets almost no support from other sources, and we do not know to what date it refers or whether it really contains any truth. Yet even if it has authority, it suggests a different procedure for dealing with oracles from that which prevailed in the sixth and fifth centuries. It implies that the text is so sacred that the θεωρός who receives it must not open it or, presumably, even know its contents. Such secrecy is in conflict with actual methods in more than one respect. First, though the texts of oracles were not written down by the enquirers themselves, they were written down for them at Delphi, and this is why the middle form συγγραψάμενοι is used for the agents of Croesus (Hdt. 1. 48. 1), and the Athenian θεοπρόποι before Salamis (id. 7. 142. 1), and ἐξεγραψάμην for Heracles when he gets the oracle of the Selli (Soph. *Tr.* 1167), or for Pisthetaerus from Apollo (Aristoph. *Av.* 982). If the inquirers had their answers written down or them it is probable that they knew the contents. Secondly, though such texts were no doubt sealed, it was the agents who sealed them, as we know from an Athenian inscription about the Eleusinian rites (*I.G.* ii[2]. 1096). Thirdly, the Athenian θεοπρόποι must have broken the seals themselves, since they reported, ἀπήγγελλον, the contents to the people. Even if we modify the *Suda*'s words εἰ λύσει into εἰ λύσει πρὸ τῆς νενομισμένης ἡμέρας, as Zenobius, quoting Aristides, does (*Cent.* 6. 11), we do not get much further. The procedure suggested in the entry τὰ τρία does not agree with what seems to have been normal practice, nor does it illuminate what Theognis says beyond asserting that an oracular text must be treated with the utmost care and respect.

What Theognis means is that once an oracle has been given, the θεωρός who receives it must not tamper with it in any way either by addition or by subtraction.[1] That additions to oracles met with strong disapproval is clear from the way in which Hipparchus banished Onomacritus for inserting lines into an oracle of Musaeus (Hdt. 7. 6. 3), and since every word in an oracle might count, it was no less heinous to omit lines. Both actions are equally dishonest and would presumably be equally distasteful to the god of Delphi, τὸν οὐ θεμιτὸν ψεύδει θιγεῖν (Pind. *P.* 9. 42). It is therefore surprising that Theognis seems to distinguish between the gravity of addition, which is apparently no worse than useless, and of subtraction, which is an ἀμπλακίη in

---

[1] J. Kroll, *Theognis-Interpretationen*, 260: 'es bei der θεωρία nach Delphi mit dem Überbringen des Orakels möglichst genau zu halten'.

the eyes of the gods. If he really makes such a point, it is hard to see why he does, and it diminishes the grave authority of his opening lines. But we may doubt whether this is what he means. It is easier to assume that he expresses himself in a somewhat condensed and elliptical manner and that what he means is that both addition and subtraction are not only useless but positively wrong. The construction οὔτε . . . οὔτε binds the two clauses together and makes it easier to treat them as referring to a single futile and impious class of conduct.

If this is Theognis' conclusion, we should be in a better position to consider his opening lines, where much depends on εὐθύτερον, which Edmonds translates 'nearer to the line', adding a note that 'the idea is "more accurate"', and Carrière translates 'il doit s'efforcer à plus d'exactitude'. In their view εὐθύτερον means 'more exact' or 'more accurate', and implies no more than an absolute adherence to the words of the oracle, which must be brought home exactly as it was delivered at Delphi. This certainly suits the main theme of the poem, and the metaphors τόρνου καὶ στάθμης καὶ γνώμονος are consistent with it. But we may doubt whether this interpretation gives to εὐθύτερον some of its more important associations. When it is applied to behaviour, it seems to have some ethical connotation, to mean not so much 'accurate' or 'exact' as 'honest' or 'straight' as the antithesis of 'crooked'. This is clear enough from two Theognidean couplets. The first tells how poverty tests a good man:

τοῦ μὲν γὰρ τὰ δίκαια φρονεῖν νόος, οὔτέ περ αἰεὶ
ἰθεῖα γνώμη στήθεσιν ἐμπεφύῃ,   (395–6)

and the second expounds that a slavish outlook is never straight:

οὔποτε δουλείη κεφαλὴ ἰθεῖα πέφυκεν,
ἀλλ' αἰεὶ σκολιὴ καὐχένα λοξὸν ἔχει.   (535–6)

A similar point is made by the Attic σκόλιον on the Crab and the Snake where the Crab enforces with action its belief that the only straight snake is a dead snake:

ὁ καρκίνος ὧδ' ἔφα,
χαλᾷ τὸν ὄφιν λαβών·
εὐθὺν χρὴ τὸν ἑταῖρον ἔμ-
μεν καὶ μὴ σκολιὰ φρονεῖν.   (fr. 892/9 P.)

That this is a normal meaning of εὐθύς in contexts referring to behaviour is clear from such passages as Pind. O. 13. 12, P. 3. 28; Aesch. Eum. 433; Hdt. 1. 96. 2; 2. 161. 4; Thuc. 3. 43. 2. These indicate that in our poem εὐθύτερον should have more than a merely intellectual connotation.

This is consistent with two of Theognis' metaphors of comparison. Though στάθμη is often used metaphorically of accuracy (Aesch. Ag. 1045; Soph. fr. 474.5 P.; Tr. Fr. Adesp. 287 N.; Theocr. 25. 194),[1] it can also be used of honest and decent behaviour. So a Theognidean poem uses it with reference to impartiality in public affairs:

εἶμι παρὰ στάθμην ὀρθὴν ὁδόν, οὐδετέρωσε
κλινόμενος· χρὴ γάρ μ' ἄρτια πάντα νοεῖν.
πατρίδα κοσμήσω, λιπαρὴν πόλιν, οὔτ' ἐπὶ δήμῳ
τρέψας, οὔτ' ἀδίκοις ἀνδράσι πειθόμενος, (945–8)

and so Pindar applies it to the young Thrasybulus, who

πατρῴαν μάλιστα πρὸς στάθμαν ἔβα (P. 6. 5)

and attains the standard of behaviour which his father expects of him. Though στάθμη is commonly applied to intellectual accuracy, in other contexts it can have ethical associations. The same seems to be true of γνώμων, which Lucian uses with such an intention when he asks ὁποῖον χρὴ τὸν κανόνα εἶναι καὶ γνώμονα τοῦ κατὰ τὴν ἀρετὴν βίου (Hermot. 76). In our poem εὐθύτερον suggests that we have to do with more than mere accuracy or precision and that what Theognis has in mind is honesty or intellectual integrity which, in its refusal to tamper with the sacred words, is absolutely 'straight'. In such a notion intellectual precision is certainly implied, but it is also a moral virtue, appropriate to those who deal with the god of Delphi. Just as it was deceitful of Glaucus, son of Epicydes, to approach the Pythia with a question about carrying out a wicked plan (Hdt. 5. 92), and Xenophon was chidden by Socrates for asking how to pursue a given course instead of whether he should pursue it, as if this showed a lack of candour (Xen. Anab. 3. 1. 7), so also, once an oracle had been given, the enquirer had to maintain an absolute honesty and report exactly what had been said to him with no embellishments or omissions. This is the lesson of

---

[1] See E. Fraenkel, Aeschylus: Agamemnon, ii. 474.

Theognis, and it is in accord with the ethical standards upon which the Delphic oracle insisted.

We know nothing of the circumstances in which Theognis composed this poem, but it is tempting to think that he was himself a θεωρός and that he lays down his own conception of his duties. The poem shows marked similarities to another, 543–6, and since the two seem to imply that he held some sort of office, they may be related. The second poem resembles the first in being addressed to Cyrnus, in using the imagery of στάθμη and γνώμων, in referring to ἀμπλακίη, and in being concerned, somehow or other, with discovering the will of the gods:

χρή με παρὰ στάθμην καὶ γνώμονα τήνδε δικάσσαι,
Κύρνε, δίκην ἶσον τ' ἀμφοτέροισι δόμεν,
μάντεσί τ' οἰωνοῖς τε καὶ αἰθομένοισ' ἱεροῖσιν,
ὄφρα μὴ ἀμπλακίης αἰσχρὸν ὄνειδος ἔχω.   (543–6)

Unfortunately neither text nor interpretation is certain. In the first two lines it is at least clear that Theognis is concerned with giving fair treatment to contesting parties, and this suggests that he holds some public office, but after this the syntax is less tractable, and Bergk, Hartung, Diehl, and Edmonds have assumed that a couplet has fallen out between 544 and 545. This is not inevitable, and Carrière faces the situation fairly when he translates 545 'en recourant aux devins, aux oiseaux, et aux autels brûlants'. In this rendering the datives are instrumental and express the means by which Theognis will make his decisions as justly as he can. This seems too to be what D. Young means when he changes μάντεσί τ' to μάντεσί τ(οι) and keeps the punctuation as before. There is no serious difficulty in this instrumental use of the personal μάντεσι and parallels may be found at Soph. *Ant.* 164; *Phil.* 494; *Ajax*, 539; Eur. *Heraclid.* 392. This solution gives quite good sense but suffers from a stylistic flaw that cannot be ignored. μάντεσι is not on a par with οἰωνοῖς and αἰθομένοισ' ἱεροῖσι. Not merely is it personal, which they are not, but whereas they are specialized and clearly defined methods of discovering the divine will, the duties of a μάντις are general and include alike the examination of burned offerings (Pind. *O.* 8. 2; Hdt. 5. 44. 2; 7. 219. 1) and the flight of birds (Pind. *P.* 4. 190; Soph. *Ant.* 1034). To place seers, in this general sense, on the same level as burned offerings and birds is to introduce confusion where precision is essential, and it is unlikely that Theognis did it.

If we look at the MSS. tradition, we find that the reading μάντεσί τ', which occurs in the oldest MS., has in three good MSS. the variant μάντεσιν. This calls for attention, and if we give it a trial, we get, by a small change of punctuation, an entirely different sense:

> χρή με παρὰ στάθμην καὶ γνώμονα τήνδε δικάσσαι,
> Κύρνε, δίκην, ἶσον τ' ἀμφοτέροισι δόμεν
> μάντεσιν, οἰωνοῖς τε καὶ αἰθομένοισ' ἱεροῖσιν,
> ὄφρα μὴ ἀμπλακίης αἰσχρὸν ὄνειδος ἔχω.

I must judge this case by carpenter's rule and square, Cyrnus, and give equally to both seers, alike to birds and to burned offerings, that I may not have the shameful reproach of wrongdoing.

In this interpretation there is no need to assume that any words have fallen out, and the datives are perfectly normal. It looks as if Theognis were concerned with a decision between two seers, the one occupied with the flight of birds, the other with divination through burned sacrifice. Stylistically, the only unusual feature is the shift from the two seers to the two fields in which they work, but this is both effective and natural. It stresses Theognis' determination to deal fairly not only with the seers themselves but with their respective means of ascertaining the will of the gods. Just as it is possible to be fair to seers, so it is to birds and burned offerings.

If we take the poem in this sense, and it is certainly simpler than other ways of taking it, it looks as if Theognis were writing about his obligation to make a decision between two seers, of whom one is an οἰωνοσκόπος and the other a θυοσκόος. It is clearly an actual case, since otherwise Theognis would not speak of τήνδε . . . δίκην. Its exact nature is not revealed, but a dispute between two seers seems to turn on the respective merits of their different methods of divination. Watching birds and examining sacrifices are commonly associated as two main ways of exploring the future (Aesch. *P.V.* 487 ff.; Soph. *Ant.* 999 ff.; Eur. *Supp.* 211 ff., *Hel.* 744–8, *Phoen.* 954 ff.), but they do not seem always to have enjoyed the same authority. Though we do not find any very serious criticisms of the second, the first is treated more sceptically even in places where we might not expect it. Hector defies the discouraging auguries of Polydamas (*M* 243), and Plato's Socrates says that the augur should be put under the authority of the general (*Lach.* 198 e). It looks as if augury were held in less esteem than the examination of burned offerings, and the dispute to be settled by Theognis would turn on the relative merits of the two. His decision is that he must give ἴσον to both. This seems unlikely to mean 'what is just', since that usage is confined to persons and not applied to abstract matters. What Theognis means is that he will treat both forms of μαντική alike. We have no hint of how the dispute arose or of what issues were involved, but it looks as if Theognis had to decide a case in which two kinds of seer were at variance. Matters of this kind might well be entrusted to special judges, as at Athens disputed points on the Eleusinian mysteries were entrusted to the aristocratic clan of the Eumolpidae (*I.G.* i². 76). Theognis' principles are orthodox and traditional and stand in marked contrast to those of Xenophanes, who was not far from him in time but denied the validity of all divination (Cic. *de Div.* 1. 5; Aetius, 5. 1. 1).[1] To his task Theognis gives the same kind of seriousness that he gives to reporting an oracle from Delphi, feeling that it calls for the same degree of impeccable honesty and that any shortcoming in this is a grave fault.

The two poems, 805–10 and 543–6, are closely related in language, imagery, and temper. This suggests that there is a connection between them, and we may perhaps surmise what this was. The first poem indicates that Theognis was a θεωρός, who had the duty of consulting the Delphic Oracle. In Athens the word would mean no more than that at some time he went to Delphi on an official mission but did not, apart from this special duty, hold an official post. But elsewhere θεαροί are found as officials whose task is to look after matters which involve religious considerations. Their duties varied from place to place, but they seem always to have had some responsibility for seeing that certain public matters were carried out with due regard for religious forms. At Mantinea they take the oath for a treaty of peace (Thuc. 5. 47. 9). At Phocis the θεαρός receives a fee of one mina when asylum is given to some men from Tenos (Schwyzer, *D.G.E* 352. 16). At Pellana the θεαροί are responsible for seeing

[1] See also Eur. *El.* 399–400, *I.T.* 570–1, *Phoen.* 954–9, *I.A.* 955–9.

that sureties are given in a treaty with Delphi (ib. 328 I B 10). At Elis the θεαρός conducts purifications (ib. 412. 1) and sees that penalties are paid (ib. 417. 1). At Tegea θεαροί are associated with priests and ἱερομνάμονες in the conduct of purifications and the commemoration of the dead (*I.G.* v. ii. 4. 7). In Theognis' own city of Megara there were officers called θεαροί, whose duties were connected with Apollo, since at one place six of them, and at another seven, join with a flute-player in making a dedication to the god (*I.G.* vii. 39 and 40). It is true that this evidence comes from the third century B.C., but in Megara the titles of local officers seem to have survived from a distant past, since we find a βασιλεύς in the age of Hadrian (*I.G.* vii. 102). The name and the office of the θεαροί certainly look ancient, and we can hardly dispute that Theognis was one of them. The θεαροί at Megara may have resembled to some degree the four Πύθιοι at Sparta, who consulted the oracle, kept the record of its responses, and were held in such honour that they feasted with the kings, to whom they were in some sense attached (Hdt. 6. 57. 2; Xen. *Resp. Lac.* 15. 5; Cic. *de Div.* 1. 95). While Theognis' poem 805–10 shows that he consulted the oracle, 543–6 suggest that he had other official duties. Just as in other cities the θεαροί were responsible for the proper performance of certain religious rites which concerned public affairs, so at Megara one of their duties may have been to adjudicate between disputants on religious matters. Theognis seems to have been involved in some case concerned with the conflicting claims of οἰωνοπόλοι and θυοσκόοι, and he announces that he must act without favour or prejudice to either party. Hesychius defines θεωροί as οἱ φροντίζοντες περὶ τὰ θεῖα and indicates that they had a wide field of responsibility. If Theognis held such a post, it is understandable that he had more than one kind of task to perform, and that he gave to at least two kinds a serious spirit and pointed out to Cyrnus the gravity of his responsibilities.

X

XENOPHANES ON THE LUXURY OF COLOPHON[1]

ATHENAEUS, 12. 526 a, quotes three elegiac couplets of Xenophanes on the luxurious ways which the men of Colophon learned from the Lydians.[2] Since the lines lack theological or philosophical interest, they have not received so much attention as other fragments of Xenophanes, and few attempts have been made to unravel their exact significance.[3] But it is rash to overlook anything written by Xenophanes, and these lines are in their way as interesting as anything else that he wrote. For they show what he, a penetrating and serious critic, thought about one aspect of the impact of East on West, of barbarian on Greek, and they contain his only known judgement on historical events. They may be quoted as Diels–Kranz print them:

ἁβροσύνας δὲ μαθόντες ἀνωφελέας παρὰ Λυδῶν,
ὄφρα τυραννίης ἦσαν ἄνευ στυγερῆς,
ἤιεσαν εἰς ἀγορὴν παναλουργέα φάρε' ἔχοντες,
οὐ μείους ὥσπερ χίλιοι εἰς ἐπίπαν,
αὐχαλέοι, χαίτῃσιν ἀγάλμενοι εὐπρεπέεσσιν,
ἀσκητοῖσ' ὀδμὴν χρίμασι δευόμενοι.[4]

The text is not certain, and there are serious difficulties in lines 4 and 5, but they may best be discussed in their separate contexts.

We must first decide what period of Colophonian history Xenophanes is describing. For this there should be a clue in 2: it is a period when the Colophonians 'were free from hateful

---

[1] First published as 'Xenophanes, fragment 3' in *Classical Quarterly*, xl (1194) 119–26, slightly altered.
[2] Fr. 3, Diels–Kranz, Bergk, Hudson-Williams, Diehl, Edmonds.
[3] An exception is H. Fränkel, 'Xenophanesstudien', *Hermes*, lx (1925), 178–80. See G. L. Huxley, *The Early Ionians*, 53.
[4] In 5 I prefer ἀγαλλόμενοι εὐπρεπέεσσιν, despite the violent synecphonesis, which may be paralleled by B 651 'Ἐνυαλίῳ ἀνδρεϊφόντῃ.

tyranny', but the clue does not take us very far, since we know nothing about tyrants at Colophon in the seventh and sixth centuries. We do, however, know something about the most famous period of Colophonian luxury. Phylarchus (81 F 66 Jacoby), whom Athenaeus quotes just before he quotes Xenophanes, supplies an important fact when he says: Κολοφώνιοι τὴν ἀρχὴν ὄντες σκληροὶ ἐν ταῖς ἀγωγαῖς, ἐπεὶ εἰς τρυφὴν ἐξώκειλαν πρὸς Λυδοὺς φιλίαν καὶ συμμαχίαν ποιησάμενοι, προῄεσαν διηοκημένοι τὰς κόμας χρυσῷ κόσμῳ. Phylarchus seems to have drawn his information directly from Xenophanes. For not only does Athenaeus suggest that the actual words of Xenophanes were quoted by Phylarchus, but we may see echoes of Xenophanes' ἦσαν and ἀσκητοῖσ' in Phylarchus' προῄεσαν and διησκημένοι. Phylarchus must have known more of Xenophanes' poem than he quotes, and his statement that the period of luxury began when the Colophonians entered into friendship and alliance with the Lydians seems to be based on the text of Xenophanes where it is now lost. Such good relations had not always existed. Gyges attacked Colophon and τὸ ἄστυ εἷλε (Hdt. I. 14. 4), which must mean that, though he took the lower town, he did not take the citadel. The change from hostility to friendship may be explained by a passage in Polyaenus (7. 2. 2), which connects the alliance with Alyattes and explains its origin in an ingenious trick by which the Lydian king brought Colophon to terms by depriving it of its famous cavalry, which had in the past done splendid service against the Lydians (Mimnerm. fr. 13 D.). The story need not be trusted in all its details, but it gives ground for thinking that the alliance of Colophon and Lydia began in the reign of Alyattes, whose dates are usually given as 613–560 B.C., and was largely determined by the collapse of the famous cavalry, which was regarded by Strabo as one of the most noteworthy products of Colophon, ἀφ' οὗ καὶ τὴν παροιμίαν ἐκδοθῆναι τὴν λέγουσαν "τὸν Κολοφῶνα ἐπέθηκαν", ὅταν τέλος ἐπιτεθῇ βέβαιον τῷ πράγματι (643). The period of Lydian influence and luxury would seem to have been founded on what was a national failure for Colophon and would date from the years about 600 B.C. This gives a rough framework for the history of Colophon in the first half of the sixth century. First was the period of simplicity and independence based on the famous cavalry; second, the period of friendship with Lydia and of

Asiatic luxury; third, the period of tyranny. At the close was the Persian conquest of 546 B.C., but whether this was the period of tyranny or whether the tyranny preceded it we must discuss later.

The luxuries mentioned by Xenophanes are purple garments, elaborate coiffure, and fragrant scents. In picking these out he need not be suspected of exaggeration or satire; for other evidence shows that they were common among both Lydians and Asiatic Greeks. Purple garments were among the gifts sent by Croesus to Delphi (Hdt. 1. 50. 1), and their popularity on the Asiatic sea-board can be seen from Sappho's references to them (frs. 92. 8; 98 (a). 4 L.–P.) and from Herodotus' account of the Phocaean Pythermus at Sparta πορφύρεον εἷμα περιβαλόμενος (1. 152. 1). Elaborate hairdressing may be seen in the appearance of the Magnesian poet Magnes, who had a great success with Gyges and is handsomely described by Nicolaus of Damascus, ἤσκητο δὲ καὶ τὸ σῶμα διαπρεπεῖ κόσμῳ, ἁλουργῇ ἀμπεχόμενος καὶ κόμην τρέφων χρυσῷ στρόφῳ κεκορυμβωμένην (90 F 62 Jacoby). Long flowing hair was common among Ionians at the time, and Asius of Samos describes the Samians of an earlier time than his own in a friendly spirit of mockery (fr. 13. 4–5 Kinkel).[1] No less popular was the use of Lydian scents. Athenaeus (15. 690 ff.) devotes a chapter to passages about them from Hipponax, Semonides, and Ion of Chios, while echoes of them may be found in Sappho. For the βρένθειον to which she refers (fr. 94. 19 L.–P.) is said to be Lydian (Pollux 6. 104) and the 'royal' myrrh in the same poem may be named after the king of Lydia. The examples of luxury which Xenophanes gives are based on fact, and we need not suspect him of malicious exaggeration. His temper is entirely serious, and he feels strongly about this intrusion of Lydian luxury into an Ionian society.

To these three examples of luxury we may perhaps add two, of no great importance but enough to give more point to what Xenophanes has already said and to show that his strictures were perhaps more comprehensive than the surviving lines indicate. The first comes from Phylarchus, who says that the Colophonians decorated their hair with gold ornaments. We might expect a reference to this in line 5 of our piece, but neither the MS. reading ἀγαλλόμενοι εὐπρεπέεσσιν, which is possible, nor Wilamowitz's

[1] See *infra*, 122 ff.

correction ἀγάλμενοι εὐπρεπέεσσιν, adopted by Diels–Kranz, suggests anything about gold, but of course Phylarchus may have found it further on in his text of Xenophanes. A second detail comes from the same source. Immediately after quoting our lines Athenaeus goes on to say οὕτω δ' ἐξελύθησαν διὰ τὴν ἄκαιρον μέθην ὥστε τινὲς αὐτῶν οὔτε ἀνατέλλοντα τὸν ἥλιον οὔτε δυόμενον ἑωράκασιν. This looks like a paraphrase of actual words of Xenophanes, and J. M. Edmonds has ingeniously paraphrased it into verse:

οὐδέ τις ἥλιον εἶδεν ἀκαίριον οἰνοποτάζων
οὔτε ποτ' ἀντέλλοντ' οὔτ' ἄρα δυόμενον.[1]

It suggests that the Colophonians learned their habits of untimely drunkenness from the Lydians. We need not accept this too literally, but the Lydians were certainly fond of wine; for Herodotus makes the Lydian Sandanis tell Croesus that the Persians are a very strange people because they drink not wine but water (1. 71. 3), a characteristic as peculiar in his view as their abstention from figs. It is possible that the drunkenness which Xenophanes seems to have deplored in Colophon was influenced by Lydian example. These two small points supplement our picture of Colophonian luxury and confirm that Xenophanes was shocked by it.

In Xenophanes' indictment there is a special sting. The luxuries, bad enough in themselves, were displayed by the Colophonians when they went εἰς ἀγορήν. In antiquity this was taken to mean 'to the market-place'. So Theopompus took it in his paraphrase of Xenophanes, when he wrote χιλίους ἄνδρας αὐτῶν ἁλουργεῖς φοροῦντας στολὰς ἀστυπολεῖν, ὃ δὴ καὶ βασιλεῦσιν σπάνιον τότε ἦν καὶ περισπούδαστον (115 F 117 Jacoby), and so Cicero when he paraphrased *cotidiano in forum mille hominum cum palliis conchylio tinctis descenderent* (de Rep. 6. 2, p. 20. 11 Ziegler). This seems a reasonable explanation, since the agora was where members of a city saw each other, and such ostentation as this might well create a painful impression on the more modestly minded. This interpretation has, however, been questioned by H. Fränkel, who argues that the ἀγορή is not the market-place but 'the decisive gathering of the sovereign citizen-body'.[2] Such a meaning for ἀγορή is vouchsafed by Homer, who applies it

[1] *Elegy and Iambus*, i. 194. [2] *Hermes*, lx (1925), 180.

XENOPHANES ON THE LUXURY OF COLOPHON 113

to the Achaean princes (B 93), the council of Alcinous (θ 109), and the assembly on Ithaca (β 69), by Alcaeus (fr. 130. 18 L.-P.), by Herodotus to the councils of the Ionians at the time of their revolt from Persia (6. 11. 1), and by Theognis (268), who compares the absence of justice in the lawcourts with a similar absence in the ἀγορά and implies that this is a political institution. The word seems suitable enough for an assembly of aristocrats, such as Fränkel postulates, but he can hardly be right when he says 'these gatherings must belong to the time of tyranny'. For it is clear from Theopompus' paraphrase that the extravagant habits of the Colophonians were among the causes of tyranny and preceded it (115 F 117 Jacoby). In fact Fränkel's interpretation puts a considerable strain on the language. He has to take line 2 ὄφρα ... στυγερῆς as referring to line 1 and dependent on μαθόντες and to make line 3 describe a subsequent time when tyranny was already established. This might be possible if ὄφρα meant 'when', but since it means 'while' or 'so long as', it is unlikely to be dependent on the aorist participle μαθόντες, and this interpretation fails linguistically. It seems much better to take ὄφρα ... στυγερῆς with the whole sentence and to assume that Xenophanes writes of a time before tyranny was established and when such flaunting was possible. In that case there is no good reason to reject the view of Theopompus and Cicero that εἰς ἀγορήν means simply 'to the market-place'. This was the centre of Greek life, and when the rich Colophonians showed themselves off in it, they did very much the same as the offensive man in Theophrastus who goes to the public square wearing both tunic and cloak (*Char.* 19. 7). The detail, such as it is, draws attention to his insensitive character.

We cannot, however, dismiss Fränkel's interpretation of εἰς ἀγορήν simply on these grounds. For it is part of a theory, shared by him with Wilamowitz,[1] that Xenophanes refers explicitly to a time in Colophon when the government was in the hands of 'the Thousand', and it is to these that Xenophanes refers. In support of this contention they quote from Aristotle, who after discussing types of government which may be thought democracies but are not rightly so called, mentions a type in which the rule belongs to the rich because they exceed in number, οἷον ἐν Κολοφῶνι τὸ πάλαιον· ἐκεῖ γὰρ ἐκέκτηντο μακρὰν οὐσίαν οἱ πλείους πρὶν γενέσθαι τὸν

[1] *Sappho und Simonides*, 277.

πόλεμον τὸν πρὸς Λυδούς (Pol. 1290ᵇ16). But it seems impossible that Aristotle should refer to the same time and conditions as Xenophanes. The period 'before the war with the Lydians' cannot be identified with certainty. If it means the war with Gyges, it was long before the period described by Xenophanes; if it means the war with Alyattes, it preceded the period of luxury, for this followed the peace and alliance with him. There is in fact no reason to think that the state of affairs denounced by Xenophanes was one in which the majority was rich. On the contrary, it is more likely that the rich displayed their wealth before the rest of the population and were disliked for so doing.

The belief in a government of 'the Thousand' in Colophon deserves a rather more critical examination than it has received. The chief evidence for it is adduced from the words of Xenophanes

οὐ μείους ὥσπερ χίλιοι εἰς ἐπίπαν.

But before use can be made of this, the text and the grammar must be considered. Diehl puts οὐ μείους inside brackets, and J. M. Edmonds suggests a change to ἢ ὥσπερ.[1] But the text is good Greek as it stands. For as Hudson-Williams[2] and Kühner–Gerth[3] show, ὡς may be used in a comparison instead of ἤ, and examples such as Aesch. P.V. 629 μή μου προκήδου μᾶσσον ὡς ἐμοὶ γλυκύ, Lys. 7. 31 ἅπαντα προθυμότερον πεποίηκα ὡς ὑπὸ τῆς πόλεως ἠναγκαζόμην, Dem. 25. 53 τοῦτον ὑμεῖς ἀδικοῦντα λαβόντες οὐ μόνον οὐ τιμωρήσεσθε, ἀλλὰ καὶ μειζόνων ἀξιώσαντες δωρειῶν ἀφήσετε ὡς τοὺς εὐεργέτας, indicate that the text of Xenophanes is sound and means simply 'not less than a thousand'. Moreover, this is qualified by the words εἰς ἐπίπαν, which make quite a difference. Diels translates 'zumal' and Edmonds 'in all', but the meaning is more precise than either of these. The Ionic of Herodotus gives more than one example of ἐπίπαν in connection with recurring events, as in 2. 68. 5 ἔωθε γὰρ τοῦτο ὡς τὸ ἐπίπαν ποιέειν πρὸς τὸν ζέφυρον, 4. 86. 1 νηῦς ἐπίπαν μάλιστα κῃ κατανύει ἐν μακρημερίῃ ὀργυίας ἑπτακισμυρίας, 6. 46. 3 ἐκ μέν γε τῶν ἐκ Σκαπτῆς Ὕλης τῶν χρυσέων μετάλλων τὸ ἐπίπαν ὀγδώκοντα τάλαντα προσήιε. In these places the word means 'usually' or 'on an average'. Xenophanes, also an Ionian, surely uses the word in the

[1] *Elegy* and *Iambus*, i. 195.   [2] *Early Greek Elegy*, 103.
[3] *Ausf. gr. Gramm.* ii. 2. 304.

same way and means that usually or on an average a thousand Colophonians went to the public square in their full finery.

The point is relevant to Wilamowitz's interpretation of the passage. He thinks that the words refer to 'the oligarchy of a Thousand described by Aristotle',[1] but in this there is some confusion. Aristotle does not describe any governing class of 'the Thousand' at Colophon. In *Pol.* 1290^{b}15, no figure for the 'majority' is mentioned, while Heraclides' excerpt from Aristotle is equally uninforming when it says ἱπποτρόφοι δ' εἰσὶν ὃν τρόπον καὶ Κολοφώνιοι, πεδιάδα χώραν ἔχοντες (fr. 51 Rose). Nor is there any evidence that in the sixth century the government of Colophon was in the hands of an oligarchy of a thousand members. Such oligarchies existed at Locri (Polyb. 12. 16), Croton (Iambl. *Vit. Pyth.* 35. 260), and Rhegium (Heracl. Pont. fr. 55 Rose). All these are in the West and may have owed their existence to a single lawgiver like Charondas at Rhegium. But they seem also to have existed in the East. For at the Asiatic Cyme Prometheus limited the government to a class of a thousand (Her. Pont. fr. 39 Rose). If such a system existed at Cyme, it might also have existed at Colophon, but there is no evidence that it did, and it is unlikely that Xenophanes refers to it. For if he were really describing a display of wealth in public by the whole of a governing 'Thousand', he would not say 'not less than a thousand as a rule', for this implies that more could join in the display and sometimes did, nor would he omit the definite article which is necessary for any such class as is here believed to take part. He refers not to a class of 'the Thousand' but to a large number of rich Colophonians, and his point is that there was always a multitude of them. In such language he follows poetical tradition which often uses a thousand as a round figure for a large number, and there is no more need to take him literally than there is to take Homer's account of the thousand watch-fires before Troy (Θ 562) as an exact statement of fact.

Xenophanes aims his criticism not at a kind of government but at a class of persons, the rich of Colophon. Nor is he concerned with their political power, but with their behaviour in public. The main direction of his attack shows itself in the words ἀνωφελέας and αὐχαλέοι, in which he reveals an attitude towards luxurious living which is surprising in an Ionian Greek of the

[1] *Sappho und Simonides*, 28.

sixth century. Neither Homer nor Hesiod mentions ἁβροσύνη, nor does it seem to occupy any place in Greek thought until contact with the East brought new standards of comfort. Its oriental character may first be seen in Stesichorus, who uses the adverb ἁβρῶς in connection with Phrygian music (fr. 212/35. 2 P.). The Delphic Oracle calls Croesus Λυδὲ ποδαβρέ (Hdt. 1. 55. 2); Bacchylides applies ἁβροβάτας to an attendant of Croesus (3. 48), which may be derived from a Persian word but has been adapted to Greek views of Persians;[1] and no doubt Pindar had oriental luxury in mind when he spoke of the ἁβροτάς of Troy (*P.* 11. 34). So, more emphatically, Herodotus contrasts the older generation of Persians with those who came under Lydian influence, Πέρσησι γὰρ πρὶν Λυδοὺς καταστρέψασθαι ἦν οὔτε ἁβρὸν οὔτε ἀγαθὸν οὐδέν (1. 71. 4), and Aeschylus speaks of ἁβροδιαίτων Λυδῶν ὄχλος (*Pers.* 41).[2] This kind of ἁβροσύνη was especially connected with Lydia, and it is this which Xenophanes decries.

It was also common to ascribe such delicate living to the Asiatic Greeks and their neighbours on the islands. Bacchylides calls the Ionians ἁβρόβιοι (18. 2), and Antiphanes speaks of Ἰώνων ἁβρὸς ἡδυπαθὴς ὄχλος (fr. 91 K.). But in the sixth and fifth centuries words of this kind seldom carried any note of disapproval. For Bacchylides uses his phrase in a Dithyramb for Athenians about Athenians, while Herodotus significantly associates ἁβρὸν with ἀγαθόν. We can see from other writers that to claim ἁβροσύνη for oneself or for others was by no means a form of depreciation. Sappho uses the adjective of the Graces (fr. 128 L.–P.) and the adverb of Aphrodite (fr. 2. 14) and even seems to claim a personal love of luxury, ἐγὼ δὲ φίλημμ' ἁβροσύναν (fr. 58. 25). So Anacreon, who coined the word Λυδοπαθεῖς (fr. 481/136 P.) in full knowledge of its origin, uses the adverb ἁβρῶς of playing the lyre (fr. 373/28. 2 P.). Nor is the word confined to the more pleasure-loving poets. Solon speaks of his own comforts

γαστρί τε καὶ πλευρῇ καὶ ποσὶν ἁβρὰ παθεῖν

(fr. 14. 4 D.)

and since his whole passage reappears in the Theognidean

[1] So too does Aeschylus, *Pers.* 1072. Behind it may lie the Persian word **awrapata*, **ahura-pata*, 'protected by Ahura (Mazda)'. See B. Snell, *Bacchylides*[8], 10–11.
[2] See W. Kranz, *Stasimon*, 84.

XENOPHANES ON THE LUXURY OF COLOPHON

corpus (719–28), we may assume that its sentiments met with some approval, as we might guess from the appearance of the last two words at 474. There seems in fact to have been little serious opposition to oriental luxury or to ἁβροσύνη at all among Greeks before Xenophanes or among his contemporaries. Even after him it was regarded as one of life's good things. When Thucydides tells how the older generation of Athenians adopted Ionian ways διὰ τὸ ἁβροδίαιτον and changed ἐς τὸ τρυφερώτερον (1. 6. 3), he does not express any open disapproval. On this point Xenophanes was unusually and surprisingly puritanical.

For his disapproval Xenophanes has a reason—such luxuries are useless. In this judgement he shows the spirit in which he condemns rewards to athletes, because they do not enrich the city (fr. 2. 22 D.–K.), or songs 'in which there is nothing useful' (fr. 1. 23). All three cases are in his view unprofitable and perhaps worse. When he condemns ἁβροσύνας as ἀνωφελέας, the question for him is social and civic, and he judges it as a responsible citizen rather in the same spirit as that in which Aristophanes praises Homer ὅτι χρήστ' ἐδίδαξεν (Ran. 1035) or Plato condemns the oligarchic man because he despises moderation μετὰ πολλῶν καὶ ἀνωφελῶν ἐπιθυμιῶν (Rep. 8. 560 d). But whereas these later writers are concerned with broad principles of life and politics, Xenophanes is concerned with a particular historical fact. He deplores this Lydian luxury because it led to the rise of tyranny in Colophon. For, as Theopompus, after paraphrasing these lines, says, τοιγαροῦν διὰ τὴν τοιαύτην ἀγωγὴν ἐν τυραννίδι καὶ στάσεσι γενομένοι αὐτῇ πατρίδι διεφθάρησαν (115 F 117 Jacoby), and even without this testimony we might have guessed that Xenophanes pointed such a moral. Flaunting extravagance and hateful tyranny must have been connected in his argument, and he must have maintained that the first was the cause of the second.

That tyranny might be a fruit of unjust actions or a punishment for them is a doctrine familiar from Solon and Theognis. The first deplores the arrogance of the Athenian nobles and foresees that they will be subjected to a tyrant (fr. 3. 17–18 D.); the second anticipates that his city will give birth to a tyrant to chastise the prevalent ὕβρις (39–40). That the Colophonians were notorious for their arrogance is clear from the proverb Κολοφωνία ὕβρις, which was used ἐπὶ τῶν πλουσίων καὶ ὑβριστῶν

(Diogen. 5. 70). Xenophanes was concerned with such ὕβρις as his adjective αὐχαλέοι shows, but with a special form of it, the arrogant display of wealth. A similar disapproval appears in Solon's attack on the wanton feasting of the Athenian nobles:

> οὐ γὰρ ἐπίστανται κατέχειν κόρον οὐδὲ παρούσας
> εὐφροσύνας κοσμεῖν δαιτὸς ἐν ἡσυχίῃ.   (fr. 3. 9–10 D.)

On this point Solon and Xenophanes differed from most of their contemporaries. They saw that an insolent display of wealth might produce such hostility that it would create an opposition led by a future tyrant. This was different from the disapproval of τρυφή as such by Plato and later writers. It was based on sound political considerations, and in Xenophanes' experience such a display led to tyranny and the collapse of Colophon.

Xenophanes applies in his own way a doctrine of ὕβρις which is as old as Hesiod (*Op.* 238–41) to his own time and sees it as a real and actual problem. He seems to have known and described a sequence of events which followed the alliance with Lydia: first unbounded extravagance and display among the rich, then tyranny and στάσις, then the destruction of Colophon. That cities fall from pride and luxury was a belief as old as Callinus, who explained the fall of Magnesia on the Maeander διὰ τὸ πλέον ἀνεθῆναι (Athen. 12. 525 c). This made a great stir in the Greek world. Archilochus, on Thasos, knew of it and found it much less troubling than his own sorrows:

> κλαίω τὰ Θασίων, οὐ τὰ Μαγνήτων κακά.   (fr. 19 D.)

It was also celebrated in a Theognidean couplet as an outstanding case of its kind:

> τοιάδε καὶ Μάγνητας ἀπώλεσεν ἔργα καὶ ὕβρις,
> οἷα τὰ νῦν ἱερὴν τήνδε πόλιν κατέχει.   (603–4)

This seems to refer to the destruction of Magnesia by the Treres, of which Strabo says καὶ τὸ παλαιὸν συνέβη τοῖς Μάγνησιν ὑπὸ Τρηρῶν ἄρδην ἀναιρεθῆναι (647). Though this took place about the middle of the seventh century, it was long remembered as a classic case of catastrophe, and in due course two other cases were added to it as no less classic. Theognis says to Cyrnus:

> ὕβρις καὶ Μάγνητας ἀπώλεσε καὶ Κολοφῶνα
> καὶ Σμύρνην· πάντως, Κύρνε, καὶ ὔμμ' ἀπολεῖ.   (1103–4)

This was presumably written late in the sixth century, and by then the fall of Colophon and Smyrna was as notorious as that of Magnesia.

The fall of Smyrna cannot be its capture by Gyges, which seems to have been little more than a raid, and is probably its capture by Alyattes (Hdt. 1. 14. 4; 1. 16). After this the inhabitants deserted the ruined town and settled in villages without restoring their old homes or organization (Strab. 646). Relics of the siege have been found in the great siege-mound by the north-western walls of the city and in a cache of weapons and an oriental helmet found on the site.[1] This took place about 600 B.C. and is half a century later than the sack of Magnesia, with which in completeness it might well be compared. But what happened to Colophon that it should be classed with Magnesia and Smyrna? Theognis certainly suggests that it was a great disaster, and it is all the more remarkable that we have no independent evidence for it and must resort to conjecture. It must have come, as we have seen, later than the alliance with Alyattes. In this period the most likely enemies were first the Lydians under Croesus, and then the Persians under Cyrus and his generals. It seems unlikely that Croesus is the villain. For since he made the Ionians pay tribute (Hdt. 1. 27. 1), he can hardly have destroyed one of their richest cities, and Herodotus' silence about any attack by him on Colophon makes it unlikely that he did great harm to it. On the other hand, it is likely that Colophon was destroyed by the Persians. Herodotus passes rapidly over their conquest of Ionia, but it must have had its ugly chapters. The capture of Colophon certainly left its mark on Xenophanes as the end of an epoch in his life, for he makes it a means of dating men's ages 'when the Mede came' (fr. 22 D.-K.) The campaign is then that of Harpagus in 546–544 B.C. The actual destruction was presumably preceded and aided by the tyranny and intestinal troubles which followed the alliance with Alyattes, and may have been connected with the methods by which Croesus controlled his Ionian tributaries. It looks as if some Colophonians left Asia Minor at the time, and that Xenophanes, who is said to have taken part in the foundation of Elea (Clem. Alex. *Strom.* 1. 353 S.) was one of them. Xenophanes

[1] J. M. Cook, *P.B.S.A.* liii–liv (1958–1959), 23–7; J. K. Anderson, ibid. 148; G. L. Huxley, *The Early Ionians*, 77.

saw from the inside a catastrophe which startled Theognis, and analysed the fatal historical process which made the disaster inevitable.

These considerations, hypothetical though some of them are, show that Xenophanes applied to recent history the same seriousness and public sense that he applied to such contemporary customs as the payment of high rewards to Olympic victors and that he ranged himself on the side of such thinkers as Solon. His attitude to the irresponsible past of the Colophonian rich is critical, even hostile. His country has been conquered, and he feels that part of the blame belongs to the wealthy citizens who shirked their responsibilities and devoted themselves to an unprofitable and unpopular display of wealth. The Ionian temper which he deplores was no exceptional thing in the history of his age. The love of luxury and the dissensions which it bred were to be displayed half a century later in the Ionian revolt when the battle of Lade was lost because the Ionian seamen would not submit to discipline and ruined their cause by quarrels and disorder (Hdt. 6. 11–14). There the result was the restoration of Persian power. The brilliant Ionians of the sixth century lacked the will to withstand foreign strength and organization. Xenophanes saw this and passed judgement on those whom he thought to have ruined his country.

We do not know from what poem these lines come, nor even what kind of a poem it was. Elegiac poems varied much in scale and character, and the scanty remains which survive from most early elegists give little indication of what length their authors favoured. The other elegiac fragments of Xenophanes, certainly frs. 1 and 2, come from symposiac elegies and show to what serious themes these could be turned. From such a poem these lines too may come. But there was also a kind of historical poem written in elegiacs. That this could tell of a not too remote past is shown by the fragment of Mimnermus' *Smyrneis* which tells of the wars between Smyrna and Gyges.[1] Other such poems were the two books of elegiacs in which Semonides of Amorgos told the history of Samos (*Suda*, s.v. Σημωνίδης) and the *Ionica* of Panyassis, which told of Codrus, Neleus, and the Ionian migration and was surely written in elegiacs since the *Suda* (s.v. Πανύασις) speaks of it as ἐν πενταμέτρῳ. It is certain that

[1] *Antimachi Reliquiae*, ed. B. Wyss, 83.

XENOPHANES ON THE LUXURY OF COLOPHON

Xenophanes wrote narrative poems, since Diogenes Laertius credits him with a Κολοφῶνος κτίσις and ὁ εἰς Ἐλέαν τῆς Ἰταλίας ἀποικισμός in 2,000 ἔπη (9. 20). The last word is commonly used of the epic hexameter, but it can also be used of any line of poetry and may possibly refer to elegiacs. The account of the luxurious Colophonians may conceivably come from this poem or from another of the same kind, and belong to some passage which described the events which led to the migration from Asia Minor to Italy. If so, it would indicate that Xenophanes brought to historical narrative the same seriousness and ethical commitment that he brought to his discussion of theology.

XI

ASIUS AND THE OLD-FASHIONED SAMIANS[1]

LIKE other historians of his time, Duris of Samos (*c.* 340–*c.* 260 B.C.) was much concerned with τρυφή and liked to point morals from its prevalence in the past. His own countrymen were among his victims, and to prove that they ἐφόρουν χλιδῶνας περὶ τοῖς βραχίοσιν καὶ τὴν ἑορτὴν ἄγοντες τῶν Ἡραίων ἐβάδιζον κατεκτενισμένοι τὰς κόμας ἐπὶ τὸ μετάφρενον καὶ τοὺς ὤμους (76 F 60 Jacoby), he based his case on some lines of the Samian poet, Asius. The text preserved in the MSS. of Athenaeus (12. 525 f.) is incomplete, but, so far as it goes, presents no insuperable difficulties until the last line, and may be given in its usual form:

οἱ δ' αὔτως φοίτεσκον ὅπως πλοκάμους κτενίσαιντο
εἰς Ἥρας τέμενος, πεπυκασμένοι εἵμασι καλοῖς.
χιονέοισι χιτῶσι πέδον χθονὸς εὐρέος εἶχον·
χρύσειαι δὲ κορύμβαι ἐπ' αὐτῶν τέττιγες ὥς·
χαῖται δ' ἠωρεῦντ' ἀνέμῳ χρυσέοις ἐνὶ δεσμοῖς,
δαιδάλεοι δὲ χλιδῶνες ἄρ' ἀμφὶ βραχίοσιν ἦσαν,
. . . . τες ὑπασπίδιον πολεμιστήν.

In the same way, when they had combed their hair, they used to march to the precinct of Hera, wrapped closely in fine clothing, and filled the floor of the wide earth with their snowy garments. On them were golden fastenings like cicadas; their hair, in golden bands, was tossed by the winds, and round their arms were bracelets finely wrought . . . a warrior under his shield.

The word αὔτως suggests that Asius had just described some other occasion of festivity for which the Samians adorned themselves, but beyond that we know nothing about the context. We cannot be sure that the lines are continuous, and the lack of any connecting particle between 2 and 3 looks suspicious, but parallels to it may be found in the Homeric Hymn to Hermes, where there are nine cases. With these reservations we may

[1] First published in *Hermes*, lxxxv (1957), 391–401.

approach the lines in the hope that their meaning and implications may be unravelled.

We may first ask from what kind of a poem the lines come. In some respects they recall the passage about the Ionians in the Homeric Hymn to Apollo 147 ff., which also describes a festive occasion. This has led some scholars to think that they come from a Hymn to the Samian Hera,[1] and though this is not impossible, we must note that, while the Homeric rhapsode speaks in the present tense, Asius speaks in the imperfect. If the lines come from a Hymn, they do not describe a present occasion.[2] They might equally well come from a historical poem which told of the past, whether remote or recent, of Samos. But hexameters were put to so many different uses that a firm conclusion is impossible. A poet might well introduce some lines on his country's past into a poem which dealt with philosophy or religion or his own opinions, like the $\Sigma i\lambda\lambda o\iota$ of Xenophanes. What is clear is that Asius tells of the Samian past, though how remote this past was he does not say.

The intention and the tone of the poem call for close consideration. Even so acute a critic as F. Jacoby says that they 'contain a comparison of contemporary luxury with the warlike past'.[3] In fact they say nothing about the present, and any warlike suggestion, as we shall see, is at least questionable. Indeed suggestions of this kind seem to be based on an uncritical acceptance of Duris' notion that Asius here displayed a disapproval of $\tau \rho v \phi \acute{\eta}$, but a glance at Duris' historical methods will show how little he is to be trusted on such a matter. For instance, to prove that princes of old were given to drunkenness, he quotes (76 F 15 Jacoby) two passages from Homer. In the first Agamemnon calls Achilles $o \dot{\iota} v o \beta a \rho \acute{e} s$, $\kappa v v \grave{o} s$ $\ddot{o} \mu \mu a \tau$' $\ddot{e} \chi \omega v$ (A 225), and in the second Agamemnon's Ghost tells of his murder, $\dot{\omega} s$ $\dot{a} \mu \phi \grave{\iota}$ $\kappa \rho \eta \tau \hat{\eta} \rho a$ $\tau \rho a \pi \acute{e} \zeta a s$ $\tau \epsilon$ $\pi \lambda \eta \theta o \acute{v} \sigma a s$ $\kappa \epsilon \acute{\iota} \mu \epsilon \theta a$ (λ 419–20). The first proves no more than that Agamemnon in angry fury accuses Achilles of being drunk, and the second merely describes a feast on the return of Agamemnon from Troy. A man who could manipulate Homer in this way would think nothing of making a

---

[1] Schmid–Stählin, *Gesch. dr. gr. Lit.* I. i. 295.
[2] E. Bethe, *R.-E.* ii. 1606 is plainly at fault when he speaks of 'eine Schilderung der prunksüchtigen Samier seiner Zeit'.
[3] *Fr. Gr. Hist.* ii B 126.

passage of Asius prove the prevalence of τρυφή in Samos, even though Asius intended nothing of the kind. We have no right to assume that we must interpret Asius as Duris did, and indeed we may perhaps surmise why Duris took these lines to support his thesis. The word χλιδῶνες was too much for him; for not only did it suggest χλιδή, but in his time bracelets were hardly ever worn by men, and the mere suggestion of them would be enough to excite his disapproval. In treating this passage we must approach it without the ethical preoccupations of Hellenistic historians, especially since it says nothing about τρυφή or its consequences.

If we look at the lines without prepossessions, it is clear that they describe a perfectly possible state of affairs, splendid indeed but not exaggerated beyond credibility. The Samians naturally gathered at the great shrine of their national goddess on the southern coast of their island. For such gatherings they took much care with their appearance and put on their best clothes. For Asius there is something quaint and charming in this. He looks back to this past time and mentions certain features which were outmoded in his own day. His Samians dress themselves in the linen dress which lasted longer in Ionia than in Athens (Thuc. 1. 6. 3), and he speaks of its flowing folds and snowy whiteness as if they were no longer familiar. What he means can be illustrated by a marble statue of *c.* 550–540 B.C., found near Cape Phoneas on Samos, in which the garments fall over the wearer's heels and leave his feet only just showing in front.[1] It is ample and generous and cannot be far removed in style from the long garments of Homer's Ἴαονες ἑλκεχίτωνες (*N* 685) and the Homeric Hymn to Apollo 147. The latter passage, which is concerned with a festival, may well illustrate the kind of occasion which Asius has in mind. Since this manner of dress was normal in Ionian lands in the seventh and sixth centuries and did not pass out of use until the fifth, Asius need not necessarily refer to a distant past, and his reference to it does not give much help in fixing the date of what he describes. That he finds something unusual in it follows from the word πεπυκασμένοι, which suggests that these Samians were swathed in a mass of clothing unfamiliar to his own age, and when he follows this by saying πέδον χθονὸς εὐρέος εἶχον, he confirms the impression that he enjoys the scene because of its unfamiliarity and old-fashioned appeal.

[1] E. Buschor, *Altsamische Standbilder*, 46, and Taf. 160–2.

ASIUS AND THE OLD-FASHIONED SAMIANS 125

Asius' approach to his subject should help us to fix his date. On this external evidence is almost entirely lacking. The only clue is Athenaeus' description of him as τὸν Σάμιον ποιητὴν Ἄσιον τὸν παλαιὸν ἐκεῖνον (3. 125 b), but what παλαιόν means in this context we cannot say, though we may presume that it excludes a Hellenistic date. Nor do the remains of Asius' other works tell very much. The fragments of his Genealogies are indeed written in a style which recalls the Hesiodic school, but that such a style could exist in the fifth century is clear from Panyassis, while the allusive manner of Asius' elegiac quatrain suggests a date later than the sixth century.[1] That he did not in fact write before the fifth century follows with some certainty from his use of the form κτενίσαιντο. This, as J. Wackernagel has shown,[2] is an Attic form which makes its first appearance in the fifth century, and therefore Asius cannot have written before this date. It is true that the text can be emended, as by Kaibel, to οἱ δ' ὅτε φοίτεσκον ὀπίσω πλοκάμους κτενίσαντες, but there seems to be no good case for such a change, and the text is good enough, if not better, as it stands.[3] If Asius did not write earlier than the fifth century, he is not likely to have written later, since otherwise he would not deserve the adjective παλαιός. This date fits well with his attitude to the old Ionian manner of dress. He clearly regards this as something which has passed out of use and is interesting just for that reason. Though the style lasted longer in Samos than in Attica, where it was for the most part abandoned about 500 B.C., it disappeared early in the fifth century, and Asius looks back to it with a keen sense of its difference from the style of his own time.

From this standpoint Asius proceeds to speak of other features of dress and adornment, which have also passed out of use. The golden κορύμβαι, 'like cicadas', present a problem. We cannot but recall that Thucydides says of the old Athenian hair-style, which passed out of use with the linen chiton, χρυσῶν τεττίγων ἐνέρσει κρωβύλον ἀναδούμενοι τῶν ἐν τῇ κεφαλῇ τριχῶν (1. 6. 3). But this passage itself abounds in obscurities,[4] since even if we

[1] See Wilamowitz, Textg. d. gr. Lyr. 60–1.
[2] Sprachliche Untersuchungen zu Homer, 94.
[3] The use of ὅπως with an optative to mean 'whenever' in past time is an Ionic usage, and is found 49 times in Herodotus. See J. E. Powell, Lexicon to Herodotus, 263.
[4] A. W. Gomme, Commentary on Thucydides, i. 101 ff.

agree that the κρωβύλος was a 'bun' on the nape of the neck, it is not certain whether the τέττιγες were a sort of tiara or rings round the hair or merely ornaments. Nor does Thucydides mention κορύμβαι. The feminine form, used by Asius, is unique, and we cannot assume that it is an exact synonym for the masculine κόρυμβος, which is used by Heraclides Ponticus (fr. 55 Wehrli) and Aelian (*V.H.* 4. 22) as a substitute for the Thucydidean κρωβύλος. But for more than one reason we may doubt whether κορύμβαι can have this meaning for Asius. First, the words ἐπ' αὐτῶν are not easily taken of any word meaning 'hair'. Their natural connection is not with hair-style, since this follows and can hardly be anticipated, but with χιτῶσι in the preceding sentence, in the sense 'on them'. The omission of any verb meaning 'were' is not really troublesome, since it can be paralleled by Homeric usage at *K* 437, 457, *P* 43, ε 477.[1] Secondly, the κορύμβαι are said to be golden, and that does not square with their being some style of doing the hair. Thirdly, hair done in a 'bun' is not easily compared with cicadas. We must look for some other explanation.

The κορύμβαι look as if they were some kind of ornamental fastening. This makes sense of ἐπ' αὐτῶν and also suits the description of them as golden. With it we may compare the obviously cognate words κοσύμβη and κορυμβάδες, the first known from *Et. Mag.* 311 ἐγκόμβωμα· ὁ δεσμὸς τῶν χειρίδων, ὃ λέγεται παρ' Ἀθηναίοις ὄχθοιβος· ὑπὸ δὲ ἄλλων κοσύμβη, and the second from Hesychius, κορυμβάσι. περιδρόμοις δι' ὧν συσπᾶται γύργαθος καὶ κεκρύφαλος καὶ δεσμοί· The Samian robes seem to have been held in place by golden fastenings. The comparison of these with cicadas may mean either that they were shaped as cicadas or that something in their outline suggested cicadas. Gold and bronze images of cicadas have been found, and it is possible that they were worn on dresses. τέττιγες are mentioned in treasury-lists from the Parthenon (*I.G.* ii. 377) and the Asclepieum (ibid. 1533. 20), as well as from the temple of Hera on Samos, where they are called a κόσμος τῆς θεοῦ.[2] It is true that these cases are of relatively late date, the first being 400–399 B.C., the second 339–338 B.C., and the third 346–345 B.C., but an inventory of temple treasures may be expected to mention objects which have

---

[1] Kühner–Gerth, *Ausf. gr. Gramm.* ii. 2. 41–2.
[2] Gomme, 103.

been preserved for a long time, and there is no need to think that these τέττιγες were all as recent as the records of them.

If the κορύμβαι were dress-ornaments, it would be easier to understand why Asius takes his next step and speaks of the way in which the Samians wore their hair, which is tossed by the winds and bound with golden bands. That Samians in the sixth century wore their hair long is clear from the monuments. A bronze statuette of c. 600 B.C. from the Heraion shows a young man whose hair falls on his shoulders at the back and is dressed in front in two sausage-like ringlets,[1] while another statuette has two such ringlets on each side in front.[2] In general the Samians look as if they were still κάρη κομόωντες and maintained the Ionian custom of wearing long hair. This agrees with the story of the famous Samian boxer, Pythagoras, who won in the Olympian Games of 588 B.C. He wore his hair long and had a purple robe, and when he was excluded with contempt from the boys' contest, he went at once to the men's and won (Diog. Laert. 8. 47). If the purple robe was the chief objection to him, his long hair may have been thought unsuitable for a boy,[3] but that does not mean that it would be thought unsuitable for a man. The Samians of this time resembled the Colophonians, who in the middle of the sixth century delighted in their well-dressed hair and were reproved by the severe Xenophanes for doing so (fr. 3. 5 D.–K.). It was evidently the normal Ionian practice, and Asius looks back to it from a later age when the practice had changed. That this came about 500 B.C. seems to follow from the oracle which, according to Herodotus (6. 19. 2), was given by Delphi to the Milesians after the battle of Lade and marks out the Persians as long-haired, as if this were no longer usual among the Ionian Greeks:

σαὶ δ' ἄλοχοι πολλοῖσι πόδας νίψουσι κομήταις.[4]

The practice which Asius describes evidently belongs to the sixth and earlier centuries.

The hair of the festive Samians is held in δεσμοί of gold. That this was an ancient practice is clear from Homer, who tells how

[1] Buschor, 9; Taf. 5, 7, 8.   [2] Id. 11; Taf. 29, 31, 32.
[3] See Ps.-Phoc. 210–11:

μὴ μὲν ἐπ' ἄρσενι παιδὶ τρέφειν πλοκαμηίδα χαίτην,
μὴ κορυφὴν πλέξῃς μήθ' ἄμματα λοξὰ κορύμβον.

[4] I owe this suggestion to Professor A. Andrewes.

the Trojan Euphorbus kept his hair in place with rings of gold and silver,

πλοχμοί θ' οἳ χρυσῷ τε καὶ ἀργύρῳ ἐσφήκωντο,   (P 52)

and may refer to something of the same kind when he says of another Trojan, Amphimachus:

ὃς καὶ χρυσὸν ἔχων πόλεμόνδ' ἴεν ἠΰτε κούρη.   (B 872)

In the seventh century the Magnesian poet, Magnes, wore something of the same sort (Nic. Dam. 90 F 62 Jacoby), and at Colophon it was normal among the rich (Phylarchus, 81 F 66 Jacoby). Hardly less showy and extravagant was the head-dress of the oligarchical tyrants of Erythrae, who, according to Hippias of Erythrae, introduced a period of reckless display, κόμας δὲ ἔτρεφον καὶ πλοκαμῖδας ἔχειν ἤσκουν, διειλημμένοι τὰς κεφαλὰς διαδήμασι μηλίνοις καὶ πορφυροῖς· εἶχον δὲ κόσμον ὁλόχρυσον ὁμοίως ταῖς γυναιξίν (421 F 1 Jacoby). We do not know the date of this state of affairs, but it is unlikely to be later than the middle of the sixth century and may well be earlier. The monuments do not throw much light on head-bands, but one bronze statuette from Samos, of the sixth century, represents a young man wearing one,[1] and if the custom existed, there would be nothing unexpected in making the band as rich and elegant as possible.

The wearing of bracelets is less well authenticated. In the fifth century they were very seldom worn by Greek men, and though the Persians wore them, the Greeks thought it peculiar (Hdt. 3. 20. 1; 9. 80. 2; Xen. *Cyr.* 6. 4. 2). They are not, however, entirely absent from figures in Greek art. On the Tityus Cup, by the Penthesilea Painter, in Munich,[2] Apollo wears one, and so on the Darius Vase do both Zeus and the Greek treasurer, though the latter may perhaps have succumbed to oriental habits.[3] The κόσμος ὁλόχρυσος of the oligarchs of Erythrae may have included bracelets, since it is distinguished from their hair-ornaments and is said to be suitable for women. To a later generation the wearing of bracelets by Samians may have seemed effeminate, but there is no reason to assume that Asius thought so. His Samians lived

---

[1] Buschor, 13; Taf. 35, 37, 38.
[2] Furtwängler–Reichold, Taf. 55.
[3] Idem, Taf. 88. I am indebted for both these references to Sir John Beazley.

ASIUS AND THE OLD-FASHIONED SAMIANS 129

sufficiently close to Asia to adopt occasionally an Asiatic fashion, and the wearing of bracelets, like that of gold hair-bands, may have been due to Lydian or similar influences. That it had some prestige may be deduced from the belief that gods like Apollo and Zeus wore them, and it is possible that, though the practice had ceased in the fifth century, its attribution to gods means that it was once prevalent in human circles. Asius adds this detail as if it were on a level with what precedes it, and completes his picture of the Samians in their flaunting finery.

So far Asius describes how, at some date before his own, the Samians used to go to the temple of Hera, and nothing that he says looks untrue or improbable. He may exaggerate a little when he says that their robes filled the floor or that their hair fluttered in the wind, but such exaggeration is entirely legitimate for his purpose. Then unfortunately there is a gap in the text, and after it we come unexpectedly to the words ὑπασπίδιον πολεμιστήν, preceded by what looks like the end of a nominative plural participle. For those who see in the lines a contrast between luxury and warlike valour this presents no obstacle, since they assume that it stresses this contrast and puts the preceding lines in a proper perspective. It is no doubt for this reason that Jacoby suggests that the line should be completed into something like

⟨τὸν δεῖν' αἰσχύνον⟩τες ὑπασπίδιον πολεμιστήν

and indicate that the wearing of bracelets and other expensive ornaments brings shame to a man who ought to be a soldier under arms. But this is to treat Duris' comments too seriously. He quotes the passage to prove the τρυφή of the Samians, but there is no reason to think that Asius shared his view. He passes no comment on the Samians, and, if he had mentioned τρυφή, Duris would surely have made more of it. Nor can much be deduced from the proverb βαδίζειν ⟨εἰς⟩ Ἡραῖον ἐμπεπλεγμένον (Athen. 12. 525 f), which is not easy to unravel but seems to mean that it is right to go to the temple of Hera in full dress. But a more serious objection to Jacoby's suggestion is that the presumed transition is very abrupt and not very coherent, since the Samians who go to the temple are not at the moment concerned with war and can hardly be criticized for their unmartial dress. We should rather ask what connection can be intended between the frequenters of the goddess and a warrior. From a welter of possibilities the most sensible and most attractive is that of Naeke,—that in this line the Samians in their all-encompassing robes resemble Homeric warriors advancing under their shields, ὑπασπίδια προβιβῶντες.[1] They would hold up the ample folds of their dress as a warrior, marching to battle, holds up his shield and walks delicately behind it. This gives a neat and apt comparison, which catches the formality of the occasion. Asius, then, indulges an ingenious fancy and prepares the way to it by such words as φοίτεσκον, rather as Homer uses φοιτᾶν of warriors moving to battle (E 595; M 266; N 760; O 686) and πεπυκασμένοι, which the author of the Rhesus (90) uses of the arming of Aeneas. If so, the last line may have had some such meaning as

⟨ὣς ἴσαν εἰκάζον⟩τες ὑπασπίδιον πολεμιστήν,

and have suggested that the Samians, marching majestically in their encumbering garments, present the image of a warrior advancing under cover of his shield to battle.

If we read these lines without Duris' moralistic interpretation of them, we see that they were written by Asius in a mood of affectionate appreciation. He does not himself belong to this world, but from his own time he looks back to it and likes its style and its gaiety. He relates its details as one who savours its quality and dwells with pleasure on its picturesque appeal. Even if he finds something slightly absurd in it, that does not affect his liking. There is a vast difference of tone between him and Xenophanes. For the latter the political failure of Colophon was still a reality; for Asius the old habits of the Samians had passed into a romantic legend.

The temper in which Asius writes recalls the taste of the Old Comedy in Athens for references to a Golden Age. When Cratinus had set an example with his Πλοῦτοι (Athen. 6. 267 e), other poets in the thirties and twenties of the fifth century took pleasure in contrasting the miseries of the present with some idealized past.[2] This might be simply the Golden Age of Hesiod, as in the Πλοῦτοι of Cratinus or the Ἀμφικτύονες of Teleclides. But some poets found it much nearer to their own time. Athenaeus, who was well versed in the subject, makes this clear when

[1] Quoted by Kinkel, Fr. Ep. Gr. 206.
[2] A. W. Gomme, Commentary on Thucydides, i. 104–5.

he says καὶ τὸν ἐπὶ Θεμιστοκλέους δὲ βίον Τηλεκλείδης ἐν Πρυτάνεσιν ἁβρὸν ὄντα παραδίδωσι (12. 553 e). It was natural enough that in the Peloponnesian War Attic comedians should look back to the great past and glorify it in their imagination. We find this spirit more than once in Aristophanes. In the *Knights* the Sausage-seller promises that Demos will be restored to youth and appear as an Athenian of the Marathonian age:

Χο. ὦ ταὶ λιπαραὶ καὶ ἰοστέφανοι καὶ ἀριζήλωτοι Ἀθῆναι,
  δείξατε τὸν τῆς Ἑλλάδος ὑμῖν καὶ τῆς γῆς τῆσδε μόναρχον.
Ἀλ. ὅδ' ἐκεῖνος ὁρᾶν τεττιγοφόρας, ἀρχαίῳ σχήματι λαμπρός,
  οὐ χοιρινῶν ὄζων, ἀλλὰ σπονδῶν, σμύρνῃ κατάλειπτος.
Χο. χαῖρ', ὦ βασιλεῦ τῶν Ἑλλήνων· καί σοι ξυγχαίρομεν ἡμεῖς.
  τῆς γὰρ πόλεως ἄξια πράττεις καὶ τοῦ 'ν Μαραθῶνι τροπαίου.

(1329–34)

Again in the *Clouds*, when the Right Logic has spoken in praise of the decorous habits of the past, the Wrong Logic knows what he means and interrupts him, only to be put in his place:

Ἀδ. ἀρχαῖά γε καὶ Διπολιώδη καὶ τεττίγων ἀνάμεστα,
  καὶ Κηκείδου καὶ Βουφονίων. Δικ. ἀλλ' οὖν ταῦτ' ἐστὶν ἐκεῖνα
  ἐξ ὧν ἄνδρας Μαραθωνομάχους ἡμὴ παίδευσις ἔθρεψεν.

(984–6)

Aristophanes does not quite see the age of Marathon as a Golden Age, but he admires it greatly while he makes quiet fun of its old-fashioned ways. This is the spirit of Asius, and it is tempting to see some connection between him and this aspect of Attic comedy.

Asius resembles Aristophanes in his interest in the ornaments worn by a past generation and the belief that these symbolized a greater distinction of life. Both poets regard τέττιγες as a special and noteworthy feature of the old style of dress. That they were generally so regarded is clear from Thucydides, and though Asius may imply a different use of them, he certainly regards them as characteristic of the past. Aristophanes indeed points his paradox that the men who wore such finery were also the victors of Marathon, but Asius seems to have in mind nothing comparable to this and to have liked the past simply for its style and gaiety. It would be risky to claim that he learned directly from Aristophanes, still more that Aristophanes learned from him, but the similarities between them suggest that they both drew on current sentiments and ideas and must have been to some degree contemporaries and have moved in the same sort of society. Since Asius uses an Attic form in κτενίσαιντο, it is possible that he knew Athens, and the indications are that he could have written this poem in the latter part of the fifth century. This agrees with his point of view in looking back with admiration to the past and with his assumption that the old Ionian style of dress had passed out of use in his time.

This view receives support from the elegiac fragment which Athenaeus quotes and ascribes to Asius (3. 125 b):

χωλός, στιγματίης, πολυγήραος, ἶσος ἀλήτῃ
ἦλθε κνισοκόλαξ, εὖτε Μέλης ἐγάμει,
ἄκλητος, ζωμοῦ κεχρημένος, ἐν δὲ μέσοισιν
ἥρως εἰστήκει βορβόρου ἐξαναδύς.

Though the meaning is extremely obscure, the vocabulary looks real enough and, so far as it goes, confirms a date in the fifth century. It cannot be without significance that three of Asius' words are found elsewhere for the first time in Aristophanes,[1] στιγματίας at *Lysistrata*, 331, ζωμός at *Peace*, 716, and βόρβορος at *Wasps*, 259. There is no need to assume that Asius got the words direct from Aristophanes, but they indicate that he was acquainted with the language of Attic comedy and with the world from which it was derived. The coincidence is more impressive when we note that in our piece χλιδῶνες also has its earliest counterpart in a fragment of Aristophanes' second *Thesmophoriazusae* (fr. 320. 11 K.). The word occurs in an Attic inscription of after 397 B.C. (*I.G.* ii². 1388) and is almost certainly vernacular. Perhaps too χιονέοισι, in the sense of 'snow-white', is also Attic, since it appears in an Attic σκόλιον of an earlier date (no. 26 D.). If Asius lived in the latter part of the fifth century, there would be no difficulty in his being acquainted with Attic comedy and its language, and it is a reasonable supposition that he was influenced by it and picked up some words and ideas from it.

It remains to ask of what period Asius writes. The Marathonian age, beloved of Aristophanes, would mean very little to Samians, since in 490 B.C. Samos was under Persian rule. It is more likely that he refers to some period before the Persian conquest of

---

[1] L. A. Michelangeli, 'I frammenti di Asio', *Riv. stor. it.* (1898), 45 ff.

ASIUS AND THE OLD-FASHIONED SAMIANS

c. 517 B.C., when the Samians were able to indulge their love of finery in a free society. This may of course have been in the time of Polycrates, when the island was certainly rich and prosperous, but we may doubt whether a poet writing in the latter part of the fifth century, when tyranny had fallen into general disrepute, would look back to the rule of Polycrates as a Golden Age. Asius' Samians look rather as if they came from the same world as the young boxer Pythagoras with his long hair and his purple robe. This would put them about the eighties of the sixth century and, though we must not press the date too closely, Asius' lines would suit a period soon after 600 B.C., when the tyrant Demoteles was overthrown by the landowners or γεωμόροι (Plut. *Qu. Gr.* 57), and perhaps Asius described these as they were between the fall of one tyranny and the rise of another. This is no more than a speculation which we cannot hope to verify. What matters is that in this piece Asius seems to have shared the taste of the age of Aristophanes for idealizing the past and finding in it a charm which was in some ways a little absurd but none the less engaging.

XII

EURIPIDES' EPINICIAN FOR ALCIBIADES[1]

ALCIBIADES' sensational success in the chariot-race at the Olympian Games had sufficient political repercussions for Thucydides to pay attention to it. In his account of the debate at Athens before the Sicilian Expedition he puts as an opening gambit into the mouth of Alcibiades his pride in this achievement and his conviction that it greatly enhanced the prestige of Athens at a time when it was low: οἱ γὰρ Ἕλληνες καὶ ὑπὲρ δύναμιν μείζω ἡμῶν τὴν πόλιν ἐνόμισαν τῷ ἐμῷ διαπρεπεῖ τῆς Ὀλυμπίαζε θεωρίας, πρότερον ἐλπίζοντες αὐτὴν καταπεπολεμῆσθαι, διότι ἅρματα μὲν ἑπτὰ καθῆκα, ὅσα οὐδείς πω ἰδιώτης πρότερον, ἐνίκησα δὲ καὶ δεύτερος καὶ τέταρτος ἐγενόμην καὶ τἆλλα ἀξίως τῆς νίκης παρεσκευασάμην (6. 16. 2). What Thucydides says is supplemented by other sources. The speech *Against Alcibiades*, which is ascribed to Andocides but is certainly not by him and may be either the work of Phaeax or, much more probably, a rhetorical exercise based on a knowledge of him,[2] confirms the ill will and the disapproval which his victory won for Alcibiades in certain circles ('Andoc.' 4. 27). Isocrates, in a speech composed for the Younger Alcibiades, makes his client dwell on the lavish scale of his father's expenses (16. 34), and Diodorus specifies that the value of the horses was eight talents (13. 74), while Demosthenes praises the victory as characteristic of the benefits which the Alcmaeonids have brought to Athens (21. 145). But the most informative news comes from Plutarch, who consciously supplements Thucydides with independent information, of which the most important item is the news that Euripides wrote an ᾆσμα for the victory, from which he proceeds to quote (*Alcib.* 11). This poem he refers to in another context as τὸ ἐπὶ τῇ νίκῃ τῆς Ὀλυμπίασιν ἱπποδρομίας εἰς Ἀλκιβιάδην ἐγκώμιον (*Dem.* 1), but

---

[1] First published in *Historia*, ix (1960), 68–79.
[2] G. Dalmeyda, *Andocide*, 104 ff.; K. J. Maidment, *Minor Attic Orators*, i. 534 ff.

EURIPIDES' EPINICIAN FOR ALCIBIADES 135

we need not press the meaning of ἐγκώμιον too technically. Athenaeus, who knew about the poem but does not quote from it (1. 3 e), calls it an ἐπινίκιον, and such undoubtedly it was. When he calls the poem an ἐγκώμιον, Plutarch expresses some slight uncertainty about its authorship in the words εἴτ' Εὐριπίδης, ὡς ὁ πολὺς κρατεῖ λόγος, εἴθ' ἕτερός τις ἦν (Dem. 1). Athenaeus give no hint of such a doubt and may have known nothing about it. But Plutarch records the plain fact that there were two opinions, which is after all to be expected. Euripides is not known to have composed any other Epinicians, and it is not easy to imagine circumstances in which he might have done so. Though his plays were circulated in Athens in his own lifetime, there would be no place for an Epinician in a collection of them, and though it survived, it need not have been in common currency. Even if, as is not impossible in view of Alcibiades' love of publicity, it was inscribed in some public place, it might easily not have the author's name attached to it. Moreover, many students of Euripides who knew how his later plays were directed against such bellicose policies as those of Alcibiades may have doubted whether Euripides would ever have consented to write in praise of him. None the less there are good reasons for thinking that the poem is in fact the work of Euripides. First, as Plutarch says, the great majority of opinion was in favour of it, and he himself evidently is, since, when he quotes from it in his *Alcibiades*, he does not hint at any doubt. Secondly, as we shall see, the fragments which he quotes have some recognizably Euripidean traits in their language, and though the compass is so small that we must not make too much of them, they favour Euripidean authorship. Thirdly, it is quite likely that by 415 B.C. Euripides suffered a change of heart and took sides against the imperialist policy of Alcibiades, and if he did so, he might in later years be ashamed of the poem and neither include it in his works nor encourage its circulation. But at one time he felt differently and, failing to see in what direction Alcibiades would inevitably move, believed that he would further causes that he himself had at heart, and win the right kind of glory for Athens. In such a mood he was sufficiently impressed by Alcibiades to consent to write an Epinician for him.

The date of the poem calls for attention. Isocrates, 'Andocides', and Plutarch give no indication, while Diodorus seems to put it, impossibly, in 408 B.C. In Thucydides Alcibiades does not say when he competed at Olympia, and nothing can be deduced from the word ἐνόμισαν with which he refers to the effect of his chariot-victory on the Greeks at large (6. 16. 2). Our choice is restricted to three possibilities, 424, 420, and 416 B.C. In 424 Alcibiades could not have competed at Olympia, because he was on campaign and fought in the battle of Delion (Plut. *Alc.* 7). 420 B.C. might look more promising and was at one time accepted by Wilamowitz,[1] but it cannot be right, because in this year the chariot-race at Olympia was won by a Spartan, Lichas, son of Arcesilaus. It is true that the result was disallowed on the technical point that Lichas had no right to enter for the race and that the victory was announced as having been won by the Boeotian people (Thuc. 5. 50. 4), but in neither case can Alcibiades have been the victor. The words νικῶντος τοῦ ἑαυτοῦ ζεύγους leave no doubt that Lichas won not a heat but the race itself, and since the Boeotians came second and were awarded the first prize, there is no question of Alcibiades winning three of the first four places. This points by exclusion to 416 B.C., which fits the general situation well enough.[2] Alcibiades was in the Peloponnese at this time, since he sailed to Argos with twenty ships and seized 300 Argives whom he suspected of pro-Spartan leanings, and interned them on neighbouring islands (Thuc. 5. 84. 1; Diod. 12. 81. 2). From Argos he could easily have gone to Olympia, and that he did so gets confirmation from the story of his shabby treatment of Diomedes in buying a chariot-team which was the property of the Argive state (Plut. *Alcib.* 12). It is not even certain that he was in Melos later in the year, since the decision, for which he voted, to massacre the adult males and enslave the women and children, must have been taken at Athens, and even if he appropriated one of the women as a concubine, that too may have happened at Athens (Plut. *Alcib.* 16; 'Andoc.' 4. 22). In what is known of his movements in 416 B.C. there is nothing to prevent him from competing at Olympia, and this is perhaps why Nicias, as reported by Thucydides in the debate on the Sicilian Expedition, says that his motives are

---

[1] *Herakles*[2], ii. 135. In *Griechische Tragödien*, iii. 292, he puts the song in 416 B.C. but thinks that it is not the work of Euripides.

[2] H. Förster, *Die Sieger in den Olympischen Spielen* (Zwickau, 1891); L. Moretti, 'Olympionikai', *Atti Acc. Lincei*, s. viii, iii. 2 (1957), 109, no. 345.

ὅπως θαυμασθῇ μὲν ἀπὸ τῆς ἱπποτροφίας, διὰ δὲ πολυτέλειαν καὶ ὠφεληθῇ τι ἐκ τῆς ἀρχῆς (6. 12. 2). This indicates that Alcibiades' entry of seven chariot-teams in the Olympian Games and his extravagant behaviour at them were recent events and still fresh in men's minds. Since the words were aimed at Alcibiades in his own presence, they would be all the more effective if they recalled what had happened only a few months earlier. Moreover, in 416 B.C. it is understandable that the rest of the Greeks should think Athens καταπεπολεμῆσθαι (Thuc. 6. 16. 2), since she had recently suffered a humiliating defeat, with her new allies the Argives, at Mantinea, and it might still be thought that she had been exhausted by the Archidamian war. The only difficulty about this date is that at the festival of the Greater Dionysia in the following spring of 415 B.C. Euripides produced his triad of the *Alexander, Palamedes,* and *Trojan Women* (Ael. *V.H.* 2. 8), which are concerned with the causes, corruption, and brutality of war, and it might be thought difficult to reconcile this with an admiration for Alcibiades in the preceding summer. Yet in the summer of 416 B.C. the massacre and the enslavement of the Melians had not taken place, and it was these, and not the actual attack, that stirred Euripides so deeply. Nor need we assume that all three plays were written between the massacre and the spring, which would indeed have been a prodigious feat of composition. What we know of the *Alexander* and the *Palamedes* suggests that, though they are gravely concerned with serious issues, they have not the passionate urgency of the *Trojan Women*, and it looks as if they were written before the massacre, while the *Trojan Women* was written after it. In it Euripides has passed through an inner crisis, and there is no doubt of the violence of the revulsion which he felt against the newest barbarities inflicted on the defeated. The massacre must have turned him against Alcibiades, but in the summer of 416 B.C. he felt differently and may have seen in the actual attack on Melos no more than a legitimate act of war. When he yielded to Alcibiades' request to write an Epinician, he could have done so in all sincerity.

One of Plutarch's reasons for quoting from the poem is that it disagrees with Thucydides on the exact nature of Alcibiades' success. He is quite explicit on this and points out that, while according to Thucydides Alcibiades won first, second, and fourth places, according to Euripides he won first, second, and third (*Alcib.* 11). Though the discrepancy is of no importance to history, it is not without interest. Thucydides would not have taken the trouble to name the actual places taken by Alcibiades' chariots unless he meant implicitly to correct a version which he had found to be false, and this version, as Plutarch shows, came from no other than Euripides. Other authorities throw no light on the matter, since Athenaeus follows Thucydides, and Isocrates Euripides. Yet we cannot but ask why Euripides reported the victories incorrectly, and an answer may be forthcoming if we can settle where and when Euripides' Epinician was actually sung. At first sight Athenaeus might seem to suggest that it was at Olympia: Ἀλκιβιάδης δὲ ᾽Ολύμπια νικήσας ἅρματι πρῶτος καὶ δεύτερος καὶ τέταρτος, εἰς ἃς νίκας καὶ Εὐριπίδης ἔγραψεν ἐπινίκιον, θύσας ᾽Ολυμπίῳ Διὶ τὴν πανήγυριν πᾶσαν εἱστίασε (1. 3 e). But in fact this says nothing about the occasion. It merely says that it was for these victories that Euripides wrote the Epinician, and it leaves us in the dark about the place of its performance. Now Epinicians, as we know from Pindar, could either be performed immediately after the victory in the place where it had been won, or postponed till later when the victor came home and a song of honour could be sung at some local festival or feast for him. The first meant that, in view of the shortness of time available to the poet, at best only a short song could be written, and at the worst the victor might have to put up with the ancient Ἀρχιλόχου μέλος, as did Epharmostus of Opus (Pind. *O.* 11. 1–4). Examples of this class are relatively rare in Pindar, but to it belong *Pythian* 7 for Megacles the Alcmaeonid, *Olympian* 12 for Ergoteles of Himera, and *Olympian* 11 for Hagesidamus of Epizephyrian Locri. The first two of these were written for men exiled from their own countries, and that may explain why they were content with something performed immediately on the spot. The third case is that of a man who has not yet gone home, but when he does, receives praise at full length in *Olympian* 10.[1] Against these slim and scanty examples we may set the main bulk of Pindar's Epinicians, which were performed elsewhere than at the place of actual victory. We may fairly conclude that a full-scale Epinician, which took time to compose, was the normal form and that it was sung at some suitable occasion after the victor returned home. Unfortunately we do not know how

[1] A. B. Drachmann, *Moderne Pindarfortolkning*, 162 ff.

long Euripides' Epinician was, but there are reasons for thinking that it was performed not at Olympia but at Athens. Thucydides makes Alcibiades say of himself that τἆλλα ἀξίως τῆς νίκης παρεσκευασάμην (6. 16. 2), and though this certainly includes the feast which he gave at his own expense at Olympia (Plut. *Alcib.* 12; Athen. 1. 3 e), it may also include what he did on his return to Athens, and on this we have an illuminating piece of information. Satyrus, quoted by Athenaeus (12. 534 d) reports, ἀφικόμενος δ' Ἀθήνησιν ἐξ Ὀλυμπίας δύο πίνακας ἀνέθηκεν, Ἀγλαοφῶντος γραφήν, ὧν ὁ μὲν εἶχεν Ὀλυμπιάδα καὶ Πυθιάδα στεφανούσας αὐτόν, ἐν δὲ θατέρῳ Νεμέα ἦν καθημένη καὶ ἐπὶ τῶν γονάτων αὐτῆς Ἀλκιβιάδης καλλίων φαινόμενος τῶν γυναικείων προσώπων. Now Satyrus is not a scientific or even a serious historian, nor is he above reporting ridiculous tittle-tattle, as we can see from his 'Life' of Euripides (*Ox. Pap.* ix, 1912, no. 1176), but since he is here concerned with two pictures, which many people must have seen, he may be trusted on this point, especially as there is good external evidence for the second picture which he describes. Though we know nothing else about that of the Olympian victory, on the Nemean we have evidence both from Pausanias, who describes a picture in the library of the Propylaea at Athens and says that it showed Alcibiades and his horses 'as signs of his victory at Nemea' (1. 22. 6), and from Plutarch, who mentions a picture of Alcibiades in the arms of Nemea (*Alcib.* 16). The only discrepancy is that while Satyrus says that the painter was Aglaophon, Plutarch says that it was Aristophon. Since the two were closely related, the confusion is intelligible. Aglaophon was probably the nephew of Polygnotus, whose father bore the name (Plat. *Gorg.* 448 b; Harpocrat. s.v. Πολύγνωτος). Pliny knows of him as having flourished in the 90th Olympiad, 420–417 B.C., (*N.H.* 35. 9. 60), and Cicero classes him for accomplishment with Zeuxis and Apelles (*de Or.* 3. 7. 26). Aristophon would be a brother of Polygnotus, but he would probably be too old to be commissioned to paint a picture in 416 B.C. So perhaps Satyrus is right, and certainly Pliny's *floruit* for Aglaophon suits the date of Alcibiades' victory very nicely. There was also a statue of Alcibiades in his four-horsed chariot by Pyromachus (Plin. *N.H.* 34. 8. 80), and he may be the same as the Phyromachus mentioned in the accounts of the guardians of the Erechtheum, in which he appears at least three and probably five times as the sculptor of works paid for (*I.G.*² i. 374: 161, 169, 177; *S.E.G.* x. 283, 21; 294, 396). The date of these accounts is 408/7–407/6, and Phyromachus was plainly an established figure by this time. It is not impossible that Alcibiades employed him some eight years earlier to make a statue of himself in his chariot. The suitable time for ordering pictures and statue was after his return from Olympia, and this is where Satyrus places the pictures. If Alcibiades wanted an Epinician in honour of himself, it was the right time for that also, and we may assume that this was when the song was performed. This means that Euripides need not have gone to Olympia, and if he did not see the race with his own eyes but relied on talk about it, including that of Alcibiades himself and his household,[1] it is understandable that he did not report events with impeccable accuracy, while Thucydides, who liked to verify his references, took care to inquire, and found that Euripides was wrong.

Such text as survives from Euripides' Epinician is known only from Plutarch, and the more substantial part, which he quotes in *Alcibiades* 11, may first be set forth as Matritensis 55, known as N, presents it: σὲ δ᾽ ἄγαμε, ὦ Κλεινίου παῖ. καλὸν ἁ νίκα. κάλλιστον δ᾽, ὃ μηδεὶς ἄλλος Ἑλλάνων, ἅρματι πρῶτα δραμεῖν καὶ δεύτερα καὶ τρίτα, βῆναι δ᾽ ἀπονητὶ δὶς στεφθέντ᾽ ἐλαίᾳ κάρυκι βοὰν παραδοῦναι. If we compare this text with that of the *tripartiti generis libri* known as Y, there are two main discrepancies. First, instead of the worthless ἄγαμε we find ἀείσομαι, which looks impeccable and alluring. But in fact the middle voice of ἀείδειν with an accusative object of the person sung about is extremely rare and confined almost to Hom. Hymn 17. 1, Κάστορα καὶ Πολυδεύκε᾽ ἀείσεο (ἀείδεο Steph.), Μοῦσα λίγεια. It looks rather too simple and is a little suspect. On the other hand ἄγαμε is easily emended with Lindskog to ἄγαμαι. This gives excellent sense, and it is certainly more likely that some innovating scribe would correct the corrupt ἄγαμε to ἀείσομαι than that ἀείσομαι should degenerate into ἄγαμε. ἄγαμαι in the sense of amazement, not without admiration and awe, is suitable for an Olympian victor and has a place in Pindar's vocabulary (*P.* 4. 238; *Pae.* 8. 75 Sn.). It is also a good Euripidean word (*Alc.* 602, *Herc.* 846,

---

[1] H. W. Smyth, *Greek Melic Poets*, 44. When Isocrates (16. 34) says that Alcibiades won the first three places, he may be repeating what was said in Alcibiades' family, as the son retailed it to him.

Phoen. 1054). Secondly, after κάλλιστον the Y group omits δ' which N has, and here again N looks right, since it stresses the contrast between καλόν and κάλλιστον, which is clearly intended.

Since Plutarch is not always very accurate in his quotations, we cannot blame his copyists for what look like his mistakes, and certainly in this text there are a few which may be the fault of either. In correcting them we get help from the metre, which is dactylo-epitrite. First, after saying that victory is a beautiful thing, Euripides advances to the fresh point that Alcibiades has won the most beautiful victory possible; and for this it is right and necessary to insert τό, as Bergk does before κάλλιστον, since it singles out the occasion in its unique splendour and incidentally gives a needed short syllable. Secondly, something seems to have gone wrong with the next clause. A verb seems to be needed to show that Alcibiades has won a victory. Hermann supplied ἔλαχεν and Bergk ἔλαχες, and there is little to choose between them. If we take the first, it is perhaps rather more dramatic in drawing attention to the singular character of the victory. Thirdly, the MSS. give τρίτα, but Bergk's τρίτατα gives a better metre. Fourthly, the MSS. agree on δίς but victors did not go up to be crowned twice for the same event, and there were no second prizes. Hermann was certainly right to alter it to Διός, which makes excellent sense. Fifthly, βοάν of the MSS. may with some small advantage be altered, as by Bergk, to the infinitive βοᾶν on the analogy of νικῶν παραδιδοῖ Πεισιστράτῳ ἀνακηρυχθῆναι (Hdt. 6. 103. 2).

These small changes provide a reasonably intelligible text:

σέ δ' ἄγαμαι, ὦ Κλεινίου παῖ.
καλὸν ἁ νίκα, ⟨τὸ⟩ κάλλιστον δ', ὃ μηδεὶς
ἄλλος Ἑλλάνων ⟨ἔλαχεν⟩,
ἅρματι πρῶτα δραμεῖν καὶ δεύτερα καὶ τρίτατα,
βῆναί τ' ἀπονητὶ Διὸς στεφθέντ' ἐλαίᾳ
κάρυκι βοᾶν παραδοῦναι.[1]

I am amazed at you, son of Cleinias. Victory is a beautiful thing, but the most beautiful thing, which has been the lot of no other Hellene, is to be first and second and third in the chariot-race and to go without labour, crowned with the laurel of Zeus, to make the herald cry your name aloud.

[1] Page, *P.M.G.* 755, gives a rather different text.

The metre may be presented schematically according to current conventions:

⏑⏑⏑⏑ – e –
e – e – e –
e – d
D – D
– D – e –
– D –

In this only one point calls even for passing notice—the four short syllables with which the fragment begins— and this is paralleled by the fifth line in the epode of Pindar, *Olympian* 8. The rest is entirely straightforward and conforms to common practice.

Since Euripides is not known to have written any other Epinicians, and indeed this class of song does not seem to have been treated very seriously at this date, its composition must have fallen outside his usual scope, and he may well have asked himself how to write a poem of a kind which had such august precedents in the past. He could hardly be expected to copy Pindar's manner, but equally it must have been difficult to escape altogether from its influence or from making some concessions to certain conventional features expected in an Epinician. In fact Euripides makes such concessions and is well aware what the occasion demands. First, when he addresses Alcibiades as ὦ Κλεινίου παῖ, he follows Pindar's practice in mentioning the fathers of his victors, as when he calls Hagesidamus Ἀρχεστράτου παῖ (*O*. 11. 12), Hieron Δεινομένειε παῖ (*P*. 2. 18), Chromius Ἀγησιδάμου παῖ (*N*. 1. 29), and Hagesias ὦ παῖ Σωστράτου (*O*. 6. 80). Such a form of address was appropriate not merely because the song was sung in the presence of the victor's family, but because his success showed of what stock he was bred and asked that this should be mentioned. In the history of the Alcmaeonids Euripides had ample justification for doing the same with Alcibiades, especially as his father had been killed at Coronea in 447 B.C. (Isocr. 16. 28; 'Plat.' *Alcib. 1*, 112 C; Plut. *Alcib.* 1.). It is only a small touch, but it catches the aristocratic tone of the old Epinicians and would not be missed by Alcibiades. Secondly, Euripides makes a great point that the triumph of Alcibiades is something that no other Hellene has ever achieved. Since the Olympian Games were Panhellenic, a victory in them was regarded as a Hellenic event, which

EURIPIDES' EPINICIAN FOR ALCIBIADES 143

brought credit to a victor's city at the expense of other cities whose representatives he had defeated. Alcibiades was fully conscious of this and set himself to play a resplendent part on the Hellenic stage. Euripides adapts this to the notion that there is a special glory in defeating all other Greeks. So, in a rather general context which includes success in the Games, Pindar tells Hieron that he has won honour

οἵαν οὔτις Ἑλλάνων δρέπει, (P. 1. 49)

and more emphatically Bacchylides says of some young man, who may be Liparion of Ceos:

οὔτις ἀνθρώπων κ[αθ᾽ Ἑλλα-
νας σὺν ἅλικι χρόν[ῳ
παῖς ἐὼν ἀνήρ τε π[λεύ-
νας ἐδέξατο νίκας. (8. 22–5)

Since Alcibiades has really broken all records, Euripides honours his achievement in language which is both founded in tradition and entirely appropriate to the present. Thirdly, Euripides speaks of Alcibiades as στεφθέντ᾽ ἐλαίᾳ. This is right, since the crown of wild olive was regarded as a pre-eminent honour and would rightly deserve a mention. So Pindar speaks of it at *O.* 3. 14; 4. 14; 11. 13; *N.* 1. 17, and Bacchylides at 8. 30; 11. 28. The curious thing is that the crown was in fact not of ἐλαία, which is the domestic olive, but of κότινος, the wild olive, (Aristoph. *Plut.* 586; Paus. 5. 13. 3), and to call it ἐλαία must be a poetical convention, which Euripides, eager to do his task correctly, observes. But he does more than this. He adds the word Διός and is amply justified, since the crown was taken from an ancient tree which stood near the opisthodomos of the temple of Zeus at Olympia (Paus. 5. 15. 3) and was carefully walled off in its sanctity from other neighbouring trees (Phlegon, 257 F 1. 11 Jacoby). Neither Pindar nor Bacchylides goes out of his way to give this degree of sanctity to the olive-crown, but Euripides evidently does so because the Olympian Games are held in the precinct of Zeus, and he wishes to draw attention to this. This is fully in accord with tradition, since Pindar and Bacchylides are nearly always careful to mention the god at whose games the victor has won. We might think it a little out of character in Euripides, but after all he was much interested in local religious associations, and such a connection with Zeus might appeal to him. By these three tributes, paid in turn to the victor's family, to the Hellenic character of his achievements, and to the god at whose games he has won, Euripides conforms to traditional practice in the composition of Epinicians.

At the same time Euripides writes in his own manner, and even these few lines reveal characteristic traits. First, in καλὸν ἁ νίκα he uses a neuter adjective as a predicate to an abstract, feminine noun, and this is something that he often does. Typical examples are *Her.* 57 τοιοῦτον ἀνθρώποισιν ἡ δυσπραξία, ibid. 1292 αἱ μεταβολαὶ λυπηρόν, *Ion* 482 ἀλκά τε γὰρ ἐν κακοῖς σύν τ' εὐτυχίαις φίλον, *Phoen.* 374 ὡς δεινὸν ἔχθρα, μῆτερ, οἰκείων φίλων, *Or.* 234 μεταβολὴ πάντων γλυκύ, fr. 54 N. πενία δὲ δύστηνον. The device is as old as Homer, (B 204, T 235), but no poet uses it so frequently as Euripides, and its function in general statements is well suited to his gnomic propensities. Secondly, the rhetorical trope by which καλὸν ἁ νίκα is followed by κάλλιστον recalls various passages in which he combines the positive of an adjective with its comparative or superlative in order to give a special stress to some point. This is found at Sophocles, *Ant.* 33, where the positive δεινά prepares the way for the comparative δεινότερον, but Euripides uses the device more frequently and makes ingenious variations on it. The combination with the comparative can be seen in *Mel. Desm.* 33 (Page, *Gk. Lit. Pap.* i. 114) τῆς μὲν κακῆς κάκιον οὐδὲν γίγνεται γυναικός and *Hipp.* 610 τά τοι κάλ' ἐν πολλοῖσι κάλλιον λέγειν. The positive is combined with a superlative in *Andr.* 590 ὦ κάκιστε κἀκ κακῶν, but perhaps the most piquant parallel to our poem comes from another passage concerned with athletic games, in which Euripides comes down firmly on the other side:

κακῶν γὰρ ὄντων μυρίων καθ' Ἑλλάδα
οὐδὲν κάκιόν ἐστιν ἀθλητῶν γένους. (fr. 282 N)

This is a rhetorical device, especially suited to praise or blame and to such adjectives as καλός and κακός. In the Epinician this kind of emphasis shows that Alcibiades' victory is not only fine in itself but supreme in its class. Thirdly, the application of δραμεῖν to a man driving a chariot has no parallels in Pindar and Bacchylides. Pindar indeed uses ἱπποδρομία (*P.* 4. 67, *I.* 3. 13) and ἱπποδρόμιος as an epithet for Poseidon (*I.* 1. 54), but these

EURIPIDES' EPINICIAN FOR ALCIBIADES 145

are as straightforward as Homer's use of δραμέτην for horses in a chariot-race (Ψ 393) and quite different from applying δραμεῖν to a man who drives a chariot or, like Alcibiades, gets others to drive chariots for him. The word has lost some of its precision and purity, and we can see how Euripides, like Herodotus (7. 57. 1; 8. 102. 3; 9. 33. 2), is addicted to the metaphorical use of δραμεῖν (*Ion* 529; *Or.* 878, 959; *Alc.* 489; *El.* 1264; *I.A.* 1455), and for him the word has gathered associations beyond its primary meaning. When he says that Alcibiades δραμεῖν, he gives a general impression of racing without specifying of what kind it is.

Though he conforms to tradition in some main points, Euripides at one place goes directly against the Pindaric view of the games. His word ἀπονητί suggests beyond dispute that Alcibiades won his resounding victory without effort. This runs counter to a favourite tenet of Pindar that there is no real success without πόνος. He not only says so explicitly at *O.* 10. 22, but supports the view from different angles at *O.* 11. 4; *P.* 8. 73; *N.* 7. 74; *I.* 1. 42; 5. 25; 6. 11. In Pindar's view πόνος is an indispensable preliminary to success in the games and calls for praise on its own account. If we are right in thinking that Euripides wrote ἀπονητί, this is clearly not his view, and we can understand why some scholars have wished to emend it to ἐγκονητί on the model of Pindar *N.* 3. 36 καὶ ποντίαν Θέτιν κατέμαρψεν ἐγκονητί, which would refer to the vigour and enterprise of Alcibiades, or to ἀκονιτί which would refer to the apparently effortless character of the victory and get some support from an inscription on the statue-base of the famous athlete Theagenes of Thasos, who won a row of victories in 480 and 476 B.C.—Πυθοῖ πὺξ ἀκονιτί (*S.I.G.*4 36 A 14); but though ἀκονιτί is eminently suitable to an easy victory in boxing, it is not suitable for a chariot-race.[1] After all it is possible that Euripides wrote ἀπονητί and knew what he was doing. He must mean that Alcibiades' victory was so complete that it seemed to be won without trouble, and this is very much what Isocrates implies when he comments on it: κατέλυσε δὲ τὴν θεωρίαν, τὰς μὲν τῶν προτέρων εὐτυχίας μικρὰς πρὸς τὰς αὑτοῦ δόξαι ποιήσας, τοὺς δ' ἐφ' αὑτοῦ νικήσαντας παύσας ζηλουμένους (16. 34). It is not a point of view of which Pindar would have approved, but Euripides, impressed by the dazzling nature of the victory, felt otherwise.

[1] I owe this suggestion to Mr. T. C. W. Stinton.

This fragment may be supplemented in a small degree by another. In the opening sentence of his *Demosthenes* Plutarch says that the author of the poem φησὶ χρῆναι τῷ εὐδαίμονι πρῶτον ὑπάρξαι τὰν πόλιν εὐδόκιμον, and that this is a quotation is clear from the form τάν which is preserved by most of the MSS. Since the words have been grafted into Plutarch's argument, it is likely that he has adapted them to the syntactical needs of his own sentence, and we may feel that not only is χρῆναι due to the preceding φησί and that the original text was χρή or χρῆν but that τῷ εὐδαίμονι, which as τωὐδαίμονι would present a hideous crasis in verse, is much improved by the omission of the article. Without any great confidence we may suggest that the original words were something like

χρῆν εὐδαίμονι πρῶτον ὑπάρξαι
τὰν πόλιν εὐδόκιμον.

For a happy man the first need is that his country should have a noble renown.

In this we can surely see an echo of Alcibiades' claim that his victories brought fame to Athens. Thucydides makes the point firmly for him not only at the start of his speech but a little later when he claims that in after years even foreigners will be proud of his country because of him, καὶ ἧς ἂν ὦσι πατρίδος, ταύτῃ αὔχησιν ὡς οὐ περὶ ἀλλοτρίων οὐδ' ἁμαρτόντων, ἀλλ' ὡς σφετέρων τε καὶ καλὰ πραξάντων (6. 16. 5), and something of what he claimed can be deduced from Isocrates' words for the Younger Alcibiades concerning the same occasion: τὰς δ' εἰς ἐκείνην τὴν πανήγυριν ὑπὲρ τῆς πόλεως (λειτουργίας) εἰς ἅπασαν τὴν Ἑλλάδα γίγνεσθαι (16. 32). The belief that a man's victory in the games brought glory to his country is extremely common in Pindar, who implicitly suggests it when he refers to a man's home, and explicitly commends it at *O.* 4. 16; 8. 20; *P.* 1. 31; *N.* 3. 83; 9. 12, while similar sentiments are expressed by Bacchylides at 2. 9; 6. 16; 13. 70. No doubt this was traditional and seemly and expected, and Euripides did his duty as he understood it. But he gives to it a slightly new slant. His point is not merely that Alcibiades has brought glory to his city, but that his first thought is for it, with the implication that, if his city were not glorious, he himself would not be εὐδαίμων. The glory of a man's city is set forth as an essential part of his εὐδαιμονία, and though neither Pindar nor Bacchylides would in principle disapprove of this, they do not state it so obviously. It smacks of Athens and especially of Pericles' ideals and Alcibiades' professions.

The words τὰν πόλιν εὐδόκιμον have an authentically Euripidean ring, and there is a parallel to them in *Andromache*, 796–7:

Ἰλιάδα τε πόλιν ὅτε πάρος
εὐδόκιμον ὁ Διὸς ἶνις ἀμφέβαλε φόνῳ.

What Troy was in its heyday, 'before the sons of the Achaeans came', every man who wishes to be happy himself should wish his city to be. Renown of this kind may be won in many fields, and success in the games is certainly one of them, nor need we ask too closely what Euripides means in this context by the glory of a city. He saw Alcibiades as a man who, after fighting with distinction for his country, was now enhancing the glory of Athens through the tasks of peace. The victory in the Olympian Games was the latest manifestation of his will and capacity for this, and Euripides, who evidently still maintained that pride in his country which is so manifest in the *Suppliant Women* of 424 B.C.,[1] praised him. No doubt he paid no attention to the nasty story, which need not necessarily have been true, that Alcibiades made sure of his victory by cheating his fellow countryman Diomedes (Plut. *Alcib.* 12; Isocr. 16. 1; 'Andoc.' 14. 26; Diod. 13. 74. 3), but it would be interesting to know what Euripides thought of Aglaophon's picture of Alcibiades reclining in the lap of Nemea, which delighted some people but was regarded by the older generation as 'tyrannical and lawless' (Plut. *Alcib.* 16). For both adjectives there was some excuse. In placing the picture in a public place Alcibiades recalled the effrontery of the tyrants, and since the model for Nemea must have been a professional woman and it was forbidden by law to give the name of any of the quadriennial festivals to a slave-girl, prostitute, or flute-girl, (Harpocr. Νεμέας; Athen. 13. 587 c), it might be claimed that he had broken the law.[2] We may doubt whether either of these accusations would count for much with Euripides. His conception of a tyrant, as he displays it in Lycus in the *Heracles*, is much too penetrating and too serious to be troubled by so small a matter

---

[1] G. Zuntz, *The Political Plays of Euripides*, 88–96.
[2] J. G. Frazer, *Pausanias*, ii. 267.

as public display, and he might well argue that if Alcibiades had broken the law about names, he had done so only incidentally and almost by accident. What we know of Euripides at the time of his Epinician suggests that he still maintained the grave and considered patriotism of the *Suppliant Women*, and as yet he had not seen any reason to change his position. The reason came in the winter of 416–415 B.C., and the result in the following spring was the *Trojan Women*, in which he dramatized his horror and compassion at the brutal treatment of the vanquished in war. When he wrote it, he must have broken with Alcibiades, and the break must have come with the ugly events in Melos. In his last plays the patriotic spirit of the *Suppliant Women* is no longer present, and it is clear that Euripides found the policies of Athens increasingly distasteful. Of Alcibiades these plays say nothing by hint or implication, but perhaps Aristophanes conveyed Euripides' later feelings on the matter correctly when after his death he put him into the *Frogs* and made him say in an answer to a question about Alcibiades:

μισῶ πολίτην, ὅστις ὠφελεῖν πάτραν
βραδὺς πέφυκε, μεγάλα δὲ βλάπτειν ταχύς,
καὶ πόριμον αὑτῷ, τῇ πόλει δ' ἀμήχανον.   (1427–9)

This looks like a fair presentation of what on second thoughts Euripides must have felt about the man whom he had once regarded as bringing honour to Athens and celebrated in the high fashion of a more spacious age.

XIII

A LOVE-DUET[1]

IN his *Ecclesiazusae*, 952–75 Aristophanes makes a Young Woman and a Young Man sing an amoebaeic song, which falls into two pairs of parallel verses, nicely matched in manner, subject, and length. The Young Woman is either on the roof of a house or, less probably, looking through the window of an upstairs room,[2] while the Young Man is in the street at her door. Though the song is skilfully fitted into the dramatic action, it has its own interest for its form and contents and may be treated as a Greek love-poem of an unfamiliar kind. The remains of Greek literature provide no example of precisely this class of duet between lovers, and the literary critics say nothing about the type. This is a specimen of a kind of song which is common enough in most times and climes and the more interesting because it has survived so rarely in Greece. There is no need to assume that such songs were uncommon because of the comparative seclusion of women, since it is hard to believe that the Greeks denied themselves this immemorial means of courtship. It probably belonged to a low social level, at least so far as the woman was concerned, and indeed could hardly have been otherwise in a society where respectable young women were expected to observe a strict decorum. But Greek respectability had its limits and outside them there must have been many occasions for such songs. For the literary historian the song is of special interest because it is almost a unique example of its kind and because it illustrates the main characteristics which such songs must have had in Athens and elsewhere.

The form of the love-duet is not unique in Greek poetry. We should not perhaps quote as a parallel the poem which Aristotle claims to have been composed by Alcaeus and Sappho (*Rhet.* 1367ª9) and some scholars think to be a simple duet between

---
[1] First published in *American Journal of Philology*, lxxix (1958), 376–91.
[2] E. Fraenkel, in *Greek Poetry and Life*, 261–5.

lovers,[1] since this has been disputed.[2] More relevant is a poem inscribed on a tomb at Marisa, between Gaza and Jerusalem, of about 150 B.C., which contains a dispute between a man and a woman and ends more or less happily.[3] This is a late and humble specimen, but it is reasonable to think that the form played some part in more or less polite literature since Horace's *Donec gratus eram tibi* (*C*. 3. 9) looks as if it were based on a Greek original. It is a perfect example of an amoebaeic song which begins with expressions of disdain and ends with protestations of love. We can hardly doubt that there was a kind of song in which lovers began by quarrelling and then made it up, on the principle that 'amantium irae amoris integratio est'. With this the song of the *Ecclesiazusae* has something in common. It too is sung by a man and a woman; it ends in protestations of devotion; it is nicely balanced in four stanzas. On the other hand it contains no quarrel, however perfunctory; it has a more familiar, more vulgar tone than either of our other two examples; it is less formal than Horace's poem but more formal than the piece from Marisa, in which the male and female parts are unevenly divided through the two quatrains. Though it has relations with the tradition behind these two songs, it does not quite belong to it but shows traces of rather a different art because it has a different purpose.

In its context and its setting the song has some resemblance to the παρακλαυσίθυρα, of which examples survive both in Greek and in Latin,[4] and which are at least as old as Alcaeus (fr. 374 L.–P.). They were sung by young men, who had usually feasted more well than wisely, outside the houses of girls whose morals were presumably easy. Such a song was intended to make the beloved aware of her lover's presence outside. Conversely, women could sing similar songs to their hard-hearted lovers. Of such the so-called 'Alexandrian erotic fragment'[5] is a notable example, and something akin to it can be seen in a papyrus from Tebtunis (*Teb. Pap.* i. 6 ff.), while another papyrus contains a song of a girl who bewails her lover's absence (*Ryl. Pap.* 1, 15).[6] Our song

---

[1] Wilamowitz, *Sappho und Simonides*, 41.
[2] D. L. Page, *Sappho and Alcaeus*, 107–9; but see C. M. Bowra, *Greek Lyric Poetry*[2], 224–7.
[3] J. U. Powell, *Coll. Alex.* 184; Wilamowitz, *Griechische Verskunst*, 345.
[4] The evidence is collected by Headlam–Knox, *Herodas*, 83, and Gow, *Theocritus*, ii. 66. See also F. O. Copley, *Exclusus Amator*.
[5] Powell, op. cit. 177–8.   [6] Id. 200.

has something in common with both these kinds. In it the Young Man is in the street and sings from there in the manner of παρακλαυσίθυρα. If the Young Woman sings in a like strain, her song is akin to the erotic songs of her sex, and it is worth noting that it is not he but she who begins. On the other hand our song differs from these examples in that it is not a monody like them, but a duet, and there is no hint that either the Young Woman or the Young Man is treating the other badly.

Though our song recalls the structure of the formal love-duet and the manner and the situation of the παρακλαυσίθυρα, there is no reason to think that it is derived from either. Its subject has enough in common with both to explain its employment of some of their devices, but a love-duet is too usual and too indispensable a form to have grown up in so artificial a way. There are many ways of singing about love, and the Greeks certainly knew some of them. Our song may well owe something to other kinds of love-song, but in effect it belongs to a slightly different species and displays peculiar characteristics. The questions before us are what kind of poem Aristophanes aimed at writing, what models he had in mind, what temper and style he gave to it, how far he intended to make fun of a standard form. He was so great a *virtuoso* in more than one kind of poetry that his decision to write a piece of this kind should throw some light on the whole class which it represents.

Aristophanes loved Greek song, carried much of it in his head, and was himself a most accomplished practitioner of it. There are times when he writes songs of an exquisite lightness and ease, which may perhaps owe something to the example of Phrynichus, whom he greatly admired (*Av.* 749; *Thesm.* 164; *Ran.* 910, 1299), but he keeps his own enchanting, airy manner, which is among the glories of Greek lyric poetry. He was fully conscious of the claims of tradition and of the need to make a song conform to the characteristics expected of its kind. The song of the *Clouds*, 563–74, 595–606, is an authentic hymn; the songs of the Athenian and Laconian choruses in the *Lysistrata* (1247–70, 1279–94, 1296–1321) are another kind of hymn, less formal and sung by women but none the less noble and dignified; the marriage-song in the *Birds* (1731–42) is a true marriage-song worthy of a high occasion; the hymns of the Initiates in the *Frogs* reflect with unfailing grace another aspect of Greek religion. We cannot doubt that when Aristophanes wrote songs of this kind, he followed good precedents and allowed his own genius to refashion an old form without letting it lose any of its traditional dignity. The song of the *Ecclesiazusae* is not in this class. It comes from a much lower order of things and breathes a different air. It is not nearly so dignified or so stylish or so graceful. None the less we may assume that in it Aristophanes conformed in some degree to his practice of writing a song true to type, that even in this love-duet he followed certain examples and precedents. This is his idea of such a song, and, though there is mischief in his presentation of it, its presence in the *Ecclesiazusae* fills a gap in the history of Greek poetry.

Songs of this kind were born naturally and inevitably from the pursuit of pleasure by young κωμασταί after an evening's wine. They would then roam the town singing and shouting as they visited its looser quarters.[1] If such songs had an element of improvisation in them, they would soon attain a more or less stable form and be sung whenever young men had with them girls, whether ὀρχηστρίδες or αὐλητρίδες or others whose functions were less specialized. Since the girls were trained to music and expected to perform, they would be able to take their part in songs with their young hosts or visitors. This was the ancient counterpart of the music-hall song, which is easily learned and readily available for any festive occasion. It could hardly have been sung unless women were present, and the women were not likely to be of a kind to appeal to the official ideal of Athenian womanhood. We must not expect such songs to have the true spirit or the fine style of serious lyrical poetry, but they are its poor relations, its disreputable parasites. They do not live in a self-sufficient world of their own, but draw much of their art, such as it is, from a grander order, and if they debase this, that is after all what songs of this kind do whenever they occur. Our song shows the characteristics of its kind and is for that reason an illuminating example of what happens to Greek poetry when it abandons its formal occasions and descends to the lure of convivial abandonment.

The song combines obviously popular elements with others which are more pretentious and more sophisticated, and this combination is perhaps due to such a song's having its first beginnings

[1] Plat. *Symp.* 212 d; Xen. *Symp.* 2. 1; Theognis, 1046; Eubulus, fr. 94 K.

A LOVE-DUET 153

in a tour of the streets, when only something very simple and standardized would be needed, and later being developed for performance at feasts and parties. The most obviously popular element is the refrain. In truly primitive songs the refrain is the most important thing, passed from poet to poet and supplemented by each as he thinks fit. It need not come at the end of the verse, and in some literatures commonly comes at the beginning. In high Greek poetry also the refrain is to be found, but is not used as Aristophanes uses it here. In Aeschylus or Euripides it has a formal dignity which suggests a ceremonial occasion and is closely related to its context. In our song it plays a different part. Each of the first two stanzas begins with the same line, and each ends with the same three lines except for the necessary substitution of τήνδ' for τόνδ' in the second case. So too the second pair of stanzas is balanced by each ending with the same two lines. The change of refrain between the first and the second pair of stanzas is unusual in Greek poetry, though the practice of Aeschylus at *Supp.* 141–3 and 151–3 and at *Eum.* 328–33 and 341–6 suggests that a refrain need not appear throughout a poem and can be placed only at selected places in it. Since serious Greek poetry did not often use refrains, it is likely that there was no consistent practice for them, and our poem may well follow its own models in treating them as it does.

An interesting feature of these refrains is that they have the ease and the simplicity of a well-tried formula and, as often happens with refrains, may be exploited in different situations. Just because they are popular and perhaps traditional, they are not very exact or ideally suited to their place. The opening words δεῦρο δή, δεῦρο δή would be appropriate to any invitation to love, and such was surely their origin in this kind of poetry. They smack of common speech and recall *Lysistrata* 930, when Cinesias says to Myrrhine δεῦρό νυν, ὦ χρύσιον, or Herodas' Bawd, when he summons a girl to show her charms (2. 65), δεῦρο, Μυρτάλη, καὶ σύ. The words are admirably suited to an erotic invitation, but in our song they are not absolutely apt. When the Young Woman and the Young Man invite each other, their words have no very practical significance since the only course is for her to come down and unlock the door for him. They have a formalized, conventional air as if they came from a stock of popular refrains. They belong to the language of courtship and set the tone for what follows. That is why it does not matter if they are not absolutely to the point. The language of love abounds in such inexactitudes, but nobody misunderstands them.

The third refrain (971–2, 974–5) is no less pointed and no less ambiguous:

ἄνοιξον, ἀσπάζου με·
διά τοι σὲ πόνους ἔχω.

That the Young Man should ask the Young Woman to open the door and let him in is natural and easy, but that she should say the same to him is almost pointless, since he cannot do what she asks. She has the key, and he must wait for her to use it. That is why emendations have been suggested for ἄνοιξον in her part of the song, and we may take our choice between von Velsen's ἄνελθε κἀσπάζου με, and Hermann's ἄρηξον, ἀσπάζου με. But neither is really necessary. The words suit, more or less, any occasion when lovers are separated by a locked door, and since this is the situation here, they are applied to it. Like the other formulaic phrases in the song, they would not be expected to be very exact, but their intention is clear enough. The whole refrain has a concentration which suggests that it has been matured and proved by hard work. It has even its touch of emotion in διά τοι σὲ πόνους ἔχω, which is indeed far removed from the noble pathos in which Simonides' Danaë says οἶον ἔχω πόνον (fr. 543/38. 7 P), but, though it has come a long way down in the world, it still keeps an echo of its old power.

These formulaic refrains look as if they came from popular usage and belonged originally to real serenades, in which they could be used without difficulty by either party. But the manner in which they are incorporated in a greater whole suggests that a complete song of this kind arose from somewhat different circumstances and was intended to be learned and sung by men and women on convivial occasions. To this need it owes some of its other characteristics, which show that, although it is in no sense an accomplished art, it has its own technique and style and licences. Its somewhat humble rank may help to explain the vexed question of its metre. Despite heroic efforts to secure a reasonably close correspondence between the first strophe and antistrophe, no solution has been found, and we can understand why Wilamowitz, after starting in a confident mood,[1] was later

[1] *Griechische Verskunst*, 478.

compelled to admit defeat.[1] It is, of course, possible to rewrite the lines so that a correspondence is procured, but it demands drastic changes, and we have little reason to think that any result will be what Aristophanes wrote. It is also possible to blame the manuscripts, which are far from good, and to assume that the fault lies with them. But the lines otherwise are not blatantly corrupt. They betray no defects of sense or syntax which would justify emendation, and this should make us beware of it for purely metrical reasons. It is at least possible that the strophe and the antistrophe were never intended to correspond exactly, and that what the manuscripts record is reasonably close to what Aristophanes wrote. For this the best argument is that this is not the only song in the *Ecclesiazusae* in which metrical correspondence is inexact. It is equally deficient between 900–5 and 906–10 and between 911–17 and 918–24. Since this other song is also of a popular character, the comparison suggests that at this level correspondence was not always demanded. Nor is it hard to see why. In a truly popular song, which relies to some extent on traditional refrains, the rest may often have entailed some improvisation, and then exact correspondence presented serious difficulties. This is not to say that each of the first two strophes is metrically independent of the other. There is plainly a close balance between them; they are not μέλη ἀπολελυμένα. But the balance is not so precise as it would be in more formal and more dignified song. The beginnings match neatly, and so do the ends, but the rest goes more or less its own way. Thus, though we cannot be certain that our manuscripts record the song rightly, we may assume that they are not so far wrong as has sometimes been thought. We find something of the same sort in the amoebaeic song from Marisa, in which the correspondence between the first four lines and the second four is certainly rough and seems to depend mainly on the maintenance of a trochaic rhythm. It can indeed be altered to secure a closer correspondence, but since there is no question here of a manuscript tradition in which the text has been corrupted, and the text itself is of the second century B.C., we have probably got very much what the poet wrote. He too secures balance between his two stanzas, but it is not at all exact.

The popular character of our duet and its suitability for

[1] *Aristophanes: Lysistrata*, 216.

performance at unrestrained festivities appears also in its free speech on physical matters. Since it belongs to the world of the κῶμος and the wine-party, we must not expect it to be decorous or even decent. It belongs to a more earthy order than the lovesongs of Ibycus and Anacreon, which were controlled by the decorum and elegance of court-life, or than the convivial elegiacs of Theognis, which have a certain pedagogic restraint. Just as the refrains leave no doubt of their intention, so the Young Man must be well within his artistic rights when he says that he wishes πληκτίζεσθαι μετὰ τῆς σῆς πυγῆς (965). Freed from the restraints of orderly company and conscious of the songs which they might sing in the streets, Greek young men would not be shy of exposing their appetites in this candid manner, and it is not difficult to imagine that songs, which otherwise had some literary pretensions, might admit less respectable elements. The whole song hangs together, as we should expect from the circumstances in which songs of its kind were born. Prudery had no place in them, and Greek forthrightness on sexual matters does not mince its words.

This outspokenness is combined with something more pretentious and more complex. The singers oscillate between complete frankness and ideas which recall, however distantly and perversely, the language of serious poetry. This is just what we might expect in a song composed for wine and women. The songs of the music-hall have their touches of attempted poetry, and that is what we find here. The imagery has certain similarities with that of serious poetry and must owe something to it. It looks as if some devices, canonized by famous writers, had passed into common currency and popular usage without quite losing all their original appeal. This is to be expected in songs which are popular in the sense not of being folk-songs but of being sung in circles and on occasions when no great art is demanded and the emotions expressed are not of an exalted order. Images and metaphors which have caught the general fancy and been divorced from their original context are used again, often with some lowering of tone, until a style emerges which is not truly poetical but aims at being literary and speaks fairly for the frame of mind which it represents.

The adaptation of traditional imagery can be seen in 956, where the Young Woman speaks of the longing ὅς με διακναίσας ἔχει, 'which has lacerated me'. The word διακναίειν has a respectable place in high poetry, as when Aeschylus uses it of Prometheus, διακναιόμενος, (P.V. 94), and Euripides of anguish of spirit, ψυχὴν διακναῖσαι (Heraclid. 296) or of what ἄτη has done to Electra and Orestes (El. 1307). These are lyrical passages, and no doubt the word has a lyrical aptness. But it passed into comedy, and may have done so by way of conversation, to speak of suffering or disaster. So at *Clouds* 120 Phidippides says that he would look διακεκναισμένος if he followed the counsels of Socrates, and at *Peace* 251 Trygaeus uses διακναισθήσεται of what will happen to Athens. So too Pherecrates makes his Muse tell of what Timotheus has done to her, διακέκναικ' αἴσχιστα (fr. 145. 20 K.). The word has a double life, partly lyrical and exalted, partly conversational and comic. No doubt Aristophanes was aware of this and profited by it. His Young Woman speaks in her own *argot* and conjures up literary associations of intense suffering. The combination of associations suits her position, since it is exaggerated and overstated and has the right ring for a song which tries to make out that there is more in its themes than there really is.

The ambiguous character of such imagery comes out more clearly in 962, when the Young Man tells the Young Woman that, if she does not open the door, καταπεσὼν κείσομαι. The image comes from wrestling and means that the excluded lover is like the wrestler who, after being thrown, gives up the fight. It is a confession of defeat and despair. That it belonged to the world of serenades is clear from its appearance in Theocritus, whose love-lorn shepherd closes his song to Amaryllis with the words:

ἀλγέω τὰν κεφαλάν, τὶν δ' οὐ μέλει. οὐκέτ' ἀείδω,
κεισεῦμαι δὲ πεσών, καὶ τοὶ λύκοι ὧδέ μ' ἔδονται.   (3. 52–3)

But behind this lies a more dignified past. In Aeschylus the image is used by the Chorus to Orestes:

Χο. ἓν μὲν τόδ' ἤδη τῶν τριῶν παλαισμάτων.
Ὀρ. οὐ κειμένῳ πω τόνδε κομπάζεις λόγον.

(Eum. 589–90)

But, no doubt because wrestling was a common topic of conversation, the notion passes into a different circulation, as when Thucydides, son of Melesias, said of Pericles: ὅταν ἐγὼ καταβάλω παλαίων, ἐκεῖνος ἀντιλέγων ὡς οὐ πέπτωκε, νικᾷ καὶ μεταπείθει τοὺς ὁρῶντας (Plut. *Per.* 8). If this still maintains a certain style and dignity, we have only to look at Aristophanes, whose Strepsiades uses the image to show his contempt for his son, when, in defiance of paternal orders, he goes into the φροντιστήριον:

ἀλλ' οὐδ' ἐγὼ μέντοι πεσών γε κείσομαι.   (*Nub.* 126)

The wrestler who accepts defeat is a good parallel to the lover who gives up hope, or indeed to anyone who surrenders in a struggle. So in our song the word fits because it catches the mood of the despairing Young Man, who uses language which is at once appropriate to high poetry and to ordinary conversation.

Imagery which percolates into the vernacular loses some of its power and intensity. What was once a noble and austere phrase is applied to less dignified circumstances and creates a different impression. So when the Young Woman says:

πάνυ γάρ τις ἔρως με δονεῖ
τῶνδε τῶν σῶν βοστρύχων,   (954–5)

she may remind us uncomfortably of some lines of Sappho:

Ἔρος δηὖτε μ' ὁ λυσιμέλης δόνει
γλυκύπικρον ἀμάχανον ὄρπετον.   (fr. 130 L.–P.)

The difference between the two passages is immeasurable. While Sappho makes a formidable divinity the subject of δόνει, Aristophanes reduces it to ἔρως τῶν σῶν βοστρύχων, and the word has lost much of its old punch and flavour. In the older poetry it still kept this, as when Pindar applies it to Medea's longing for Hellas (*P.* 4. 219) or Bacchylides to the heart troubled by vain thoughts (1. 179). Later the word seems to have declined in significance and to have done service for less powerful emotions, as when Bion speaks of the lover as one whom the Muses favour:

ἢν δὲ νόον τις Ἔρωτι δονεύμενος ἁδὺ μελίσδῃ.   (9. 5)

Here δονεύμενος still shows some traces of its lineage, but has begun to waste its strength on a relatively unimportant task. So Aristophanes, by limiting its scope to strictly physical desire, also in some way degrades it. Behind it we hear faint echoes of an earlier poetry, and feel that we are moved in a decayed and different order of things.

So again when the Young Woman says

ἄτοπος δ' ἔγκειται μοί τις
πόθος,   (956)

A LOVE-DUET 159

the image comes ultimately from high poetry. ἔγκειται means 'presses hard on' and presents πόθος in the role of an attacker, rather as Sophocles does when he says

μέγα τι σθένος ἁ Κύπρις ἐκφέρεται
νίκας ἀεί, (*Tr.* 497–8)

or

ἔρως γὰρ ἄνδρας οὐ μόνους ἐπέρχεται. (fr. 684. 1 P.)

When Aristophanes transfers the idea of attack from Κύπρις or ἔρως to πόθος, he does not necessarily lower its dignity, but he certainly does so both by the epithet ἄτοπος, which is not found in Aeschylus, Sophocles, or Pindar, and is in the main a prosaic word which Euripides took up now and again to secure a dramatic realism (*Ion* 690; *I.T.* 842), and by ἔγκειται itself, which is almost entirely confined to prose in this sense. The old notion of a god sweeping irresistibly to the attack is made more commonplace and reduced to a more familiar level. In this case Aristophanes uses imagery which is indeed of good ancestry but which he so tempers and assimilates to ordinary speech that its implications are blurred and almost lost.

At one point Aristophanes goes further than this and applies a famous image to a highly undignified purpose. Among the many metaphors which the Greeks derived from sport, they chose some from boxing to convey a struggle with love. So Anacreon calls for water and wine and garlands.

ὡς δὴ πρὸς Ἔρωτα πυκταλίζω. (fr. 396/51. 2 P.)[1]

So Sophocles makes Deianira speak of the difficulty of opposing love:

Ἔρωτι μέν νυν ὅστις ἀντανίσταται
πύκτης ὅπως ἐς χεῖρας, οὐ καλῶς φρονεῖ. (*Tr.* 441–2)

The association of boxing with the trials of love is natural enough and suits both lyric and tragic poetry. But Aristophanes applies it in a different spirit, when his Young Man sings:

φίλον, ἀλλ' ἐν τῷ σῷ
βούλομαι κόλπῳ πληκτίζεσθαι
μετὰ τῆς σῆς πυγῆς. (964–5)

[1] The same image evidently occurs again, χα]λεπῶι δ' ἐπυκτάλιζο[ν (fr. 346/1. 4. 1 P.)

The word πληκτίζεσθαι, which Homer uses of bandying blows (Φ 499), is drawn from boxing, and is here transferred to amorous struggles not in a metaphorical but in an almost literal sense, as when in the Middle Comedy a character of Timocles says what a pleasure it is

τὸ μὴ σφόδρ' εἶναι πάνθ' ἕτοιμα, δεῖν δέ τι
ἀγωνιᾶσαι καὶ ῥαπισθῆναι τε καὶ
πληγὰς λαβεῖν ἁπαλαῖσι χερσίν,   (fr. 22. 4–6 K.)

or an epigram of Strato enumerates as desirable preliminaries of love πληκτισμοί, κνίσμα, φίλημα, λόγος (A.P. 12. 209. 4). The image has been debased and passed into disreputable currency.

The tendency of this kind of poetry to lower the nobility of language and to accommodate it to ambiguous uses is matched by a parallel tendency to overstate its case and to wish to be grander than the actual occasion allows. Having indulged the first tendency in the earlier part of the song, Aristophanes, knowing full well what he is doing, makes the language take a new direction and stir different associations. When the Young Man says:

ὦ χρυσοδαίδαλτον ἐμὸν μέλημα, Κύπριδος ἔρνος,
μέλιττα Μούσης, Χαρίτων θρέμμα, Τρυφῆς πρόσωπον,   (972–3)

we are reminded not indeed of Sappho and Anacreon, but of Ibycus, when he writes:

Εὐρύαλε γλαυκέων Χαρίτων θάλος, ⟨Ὡρῶν⟩
καλλικόμων μελέδημα, σέ μὲν Κύπρις
ἅ τ' ἀγανοβλέφαρος Πει-
θὼ ῥοδέοισιν ἐν ἄνθεσι θρέψαν.   (fr. 288/7 P.)

After keeping the theme of love at a physical level, Aristophanes now introduces its canonical divinities, when the Young Man celebrates his beloved as the incarnation of celestial graces. This is the crisis and the climax of the song and prepares the way for the hideous frustration which is to come after it. The change of tone is manifestly deliberate and brings the song to an excited and effective finish.

In this part Aristophanes picks up in a different way images and words from lyric poetry and turns them to a comic purpose. He no longer relates them ambiguously to common speech but leaves it behind in an obviously factitious grandeur. We can hardly claim that the misuse of high language was characteristic of this kind of song, and our task is rather to see how by deft exaggeration Aristophanes makes fun of such a style. Obviously it aims at being highflown but falls short because it attempts too much, and this is what Aristophanes derides, as he accumulates the hallowed phrases and somehow makes them absurd. At the start μέλημα is a good lyrical word known from Alcman (fr. 73. 4 P.), Sappho (fr. 163 L.–P.), Pindar, who calls Pan Χαρίτων μέλημα (fr. 85. 3 Bo.; 95 Sn.) and Hippocleas of Thessaly νέαισίν τε παρθένοισι μέλημα (P. 10. 59), and a hymn to Pan at Epidaurus, in which he is Ναΐδων μέλημα (fr. 936. 2 P.). In our song it is combined with χρυσοδαίδαλτον, and though this is suitable enough for a girl who has put on all her finery, and it may be significant that Euripides applies the word to horses (I.A. 219), yet the combination with μέλημα is a little too fruity for a pure taste and suggests burlesque.

We feel the same in much that follows. The Young Woman is first called Κύπριδος ἔρνος, which recalls the passage from Ibycus already quoted and Alcman's description of Astymeloisa as χρύσιον ἔρνος (fr. 3. 68 P.). These are natural extensions from the Homeric ὁ δ᾽ ἀνέδραμεν ἔρνεϊ ἶσος (Σ 56, 437) and have parallels enough in the sense of 'offspring' (Pindar, N. 6. 37; Bacch. 5. 87; Aesch. Ag. 1525). When the Young Woman is called μέλιττα Μούσης, it pays tribute to her song and recalls the application of this image to poets, as when Pindar compares himself with a bee (P. 10. 54), or Bacchylides calls himself νασιῶτιν λιγύφθογγον μέλισσαν (9. 10), or Aristophanes speaks of Phrynichus as gathering the fruit of celestial songs like a bee (Av. 748–9), or an anonymous epigram praises Erinna as μέλισσαν μουσῶν ἄνθεα δρεπτομέναν (A.P. 7. 13. 1–2). Χαρίτων θρέμμα is no less traditional and recalls Ibycus on Euryalus and Pindar's praise of Theoxenus as one whom Χάρις has nursed in Tenedos (fr. 108. 10 Bo.; 123 Sn.), while Theocritus describes Nicias as Χαρίτων ἱμεροφώνων ἱερὸν φυτόν (28. 7). The Graces and the Muses were commonly associated with Aphrodite, and it is natural enough to place them after Κύπριδος ἔρνος. The three phrases hang together, and though they are quite in character for the Young Man as he throws all his resources into his amorous campaign, their total effect is ludicrous because they attempt too much. Aristophanes has struck a weakness in this kind of song, which is that it overreaches itself, and he takes advantage of this as he piles up the time-honoured images until they become absurd. Though each in isolation might ring more or less true, yet, when they are combined, they lose their authentic appeal and sound hollow.

The next phrase, Τρυφῆς πρόσωπον, presents a special case. The personification of τρυφή seems not to occur elsewhere before Alexis (fr. 230. 3 K), but that is no serious difficulty, since in our context such a personification comes without great trouble after the Cyprian, the Muse, and the Graces. The question is rather what shade of meaning to give to it. It is a rare word in poetry and below the level of the preceding abstracts. Though Euripides uses it, it seems to be in a derogatory sense as referring to effeminate luxury (*Phoen.* 1491; *Bacch.* 970; fr. 54. 2 N.). The Young Man plainly does not mean it to be derogatory. For him it suggests the readiness of the Young Woman to comply with his desires, as when in the *Lysistrata* the Magistrate asks:

ἆρ' ἐξέλαμψε τῶν γυναικῶν ἡ τρυφή;   (*Lys.* 387)

For the Young Man τρυφή is an engaging quality, and that is why he sets it in such august company and boldly attaches to it the word πρόσωπον, which recalls Pindar's description of a chariot-victory as φάει πρόσωπον ἐν καθαρῷ (*P.* 6. 14) and is intended to convey a bright embodiment of some abstract quality. Just as a beautiful face shines with a special light, so here τρυφή is given a visible form and credited with an alluring brilliance. Yet because τρυφή is below the level of the powers which precede it, the effect, plainly intentional, is comic bathos. The Young Man exalts his appetites too ambitiously, and the result is not so much an anticlimax as a climax which fails because it aims too high. So the song ends with an unsuccessful attempt to do more than the form allows, before it falls back into its final refrain, which is much more suitable to the occasion than any highflown attempts at personification.

That Aristophanes makes fun of this kind of song we cannot doubt, especially in the contrast between the frank declarations of physical desire and the heavily loaded imagery which accompanies them. In giving a ludicrous bathos through this contrast Aristophanes passes judgement on this kind of song, presenting it as a specimen of an undignified class. The essence of parody, in the hands of a master like Aristophanes, is to exploit to the full something that already exists and to make it absurd by adroit exaggeration. Behind Aristophanes' duet we can discern a class of song which was both outspoken and pretentious, and it is this mixture which he catches. From him we may deduce that such songs embellished their crude intentions with attempts at a high style and dressed them up partly with images which had once been dignified but had now been largely acclimatized to common speech, partly with mythological abstractions which were at home in grand choral song but not suited to uninhibited, erotic outbursts. Though Aristophanes' duet pokes fun at this kind of song, it is still good evidence for what young Greeks might sing in moments of alcoholic or sexual excitement. There are so many gaps in our remnants of Greek lyric poetry that we must recognize with gratitude this unruly and disreputable member of a large family. In Athens, as in many other places, there existed a second-rate and largely second-hand type of song, which, despite its lack of authentic poetry, might still have some human or social interest. Aristophanes knew and enjoyed this sort also. His duet is, of course, a parody, but when parody is written with real understanding and insight, it provides an illuminating commentary on the originals which it copies and mocks.

XIV

ARION AND THE DOLPHIN[1]

THE story of Arion and the Dolphin is known in the first place from Herodotus (1. 23–4), and most other versions of it can, despite additions and embellishments, be traced back to him,[2] but information outside the common round comes from Aelian, who, in discussing the predilection of dolphins for song and the music of the flute (*N.A.* 12. 45), refers to a monument of Arion on Cape Taenarum and proceeds to quote first an epigram inscribed on it and then a song which, he claims, Arion composed on being delivered from the sea. Aelian is deplorably unreliable and uncritical, but what he says is sufficiently provocative to call for examination. It may not in the end tell us anything about Arion, but it should throw light on his legend and the way in which it was kept alive. The monument to which Aelian refers must be that of which Herodotus, at the end of his account of Arion, says καὶ Ἀρίονος ἔστι ἀνάθημα χάλκεον οὐ μέγα ἐπὶ Ταινάρῳ, ἐπὶ δελφῖνος ἐπεὼν ἄνθρωπος (1. 24. 8). The statue was extant in the time of Pausanias (3. 25. 7, cf. 9. 30. 2), and may still have been in position in the time of Aelian, but, even if it was not, he would have been able to get his information from good sources and reckon that, when he spoke of it, his audience would not be entirely ignorant. Herodotus certainly speaks as if he himself had seen the statue and carefully places his mention of it after the story of the dolphin which he claims to have been told by Corinthians and Lesbians. The statue, then, existed in the fifth century, but Herodotus gives no hint of the date of its erection. Aelian does not explicitly say that it was erected by Arion, and indeed his words, τὸ τῶν δελφίνων φῦλον ὥς εἰσι φιλῳδοί τε καὶ φίλαυλοι τεκμηριῶσαι ἱκανὸς καὶ Ἀρίων ὁ Μηθυμναῖος ἔκ τε τοῦ ἀγάλματος τοῦ ἐπὶ Ταινάρῳ, might seem to do no more than quote as testimony to Arion's adventure the actual

---

[1] First published in *Museum Helveticum*, xx (1963), 121–34.
[2] See O. Crusius, *R.-E.* ii. 837 ff.

figure of him on a dolphin. But since in the next sentence he says that the epigram on the monument was written by Arion, he suggests that both are of the same date. A bronze statue of a man on a dolphin before 600 B.C. is not easy to accept. Arion's date is given by the *Suda*, s.v. Ἀρίων, in the 38th Olympiad (628–625 B.C.) and by Eusebius–Jerome in the fourth year of the 40th Olympiad (617 B.C.), and we are asked to believe that at this date a bronze statue demanding considerable skill could have been made. Much may depend on what Herodotus means by saying that it was οὐ μέγα. At least it cannot have been life-size, and it may conceivably not have been beyond the powers of such Corinthian artists as those who made for Cypselus the famous χρυσοῦς σφυρήλατος Ζεύς at Olympia (Strab. 353, 378; Paus. 5. 2. 3; Plat. *Phaedr.* 236 b; Diog. Laert. 1. 96). None the less, since the earliest extant bronze statue of any size is not earlier than the third quarter of the sixth century, the existence of such a monument of Arion in the time of Periander seems highly questionable. What matters is that it existed in the time of Herodotus and that to it Aelian relates two documents.

The first of these is an elegiac distich which Aelian claims to have been written by Arion. He more or less explicitly states that it was on the base of the statue, and we may assume that this was the right place for it, while the word ἐπίγραμμα confirms that it was inscribed. Aelian quotes it as evidence for the music-loving habits of dolphins:

ἀθανάτων πομπαῖσιν Ἀρίονα, Κυκλέος υἱόν,
ἐκ Σικελοῦ πελάγους σῶσεν ὄχημα τόδε.

Herodotus says nothing of any inscription, but his mention of the statue is no more than a brief note, and there was no reason for him to expand on the subject. So we must try to assess the worth of Aelian's account by internal evidence, and at once doubts arise. First, the name Κυκλεύς given to Arion's father is uncomfortably close to the κύκλιοι χόροι which Hellanicus relates that Arion founded (4 F 86 Jacoby; cf. Procl. *Chrest.* ap. Phot. *Bibl.*, p. 320 Bekker). The name is too patently aetiological to be convincing and though it was known to the *Suda*, s.v. Ἀρίων, that proves no more than that with the passage of years it had come to be accepted as part of the tradition about Arion. It is as obvious an invention as Homer's ascription of a father called

Τερπιάδης to the bard Phemius (χ 330). Secondly, though an elegiac epigram for a dedication is perfectly feasible about 600 B.C. and the remains of one have been found on the rim of a clay kettle in the Heraion at Samos and dated to the seventh century,[1] the epigram quoted by Aelian uses words in a manner which smacks of a rather later age. The plural πομπαῖσιν is alien to the epic, which uses in much the same sense the singular πομπῇ (Z 171, ε 32, η 193), but we find the plural in Hom. Hymn, 15. 5, which cannot be dated with any assurance but could be of the fifth century, in an Aeschylean chorus (*Pers*. 58), and in Euripides (*Her*. 580; *Hel*. 1121), while Pindar has Ζεφύροιο πομπαί (*N*. 7. 29). The use of the plural seems to be a feature of mature poetry rather than of the age of Periander. A similar point arises with the epigram's use of ὄχημα. Originally this means no more than 'carriage', but it can, by the addition of a suitable epithet, be applied to a ship (Aesch. *P.V*. 468; Soph. *Trach*. 656; Eur. *I.T*. 410). The epigram applies it in the different sense of 'mount', for which the closest parallel is when Aristophanes makes Trygaeus speak of his dung-beetle as ὄχημα κανθάρου (*Pax* 866), though it is possible that a similar meaning should be given to ὄχῳ πτερωτῷ for the mounts of the Oceanids at *P.V*. 135. The application of the word to Arion's dolphin does not look archaic, but though neither it nor πομπαῖσιν suggests a pupil of Alcman (*Suda*, s.v. Ἀρίων), whatever that may mean, or the end of the seventh century, there is no difficulty about their being at home in the fifth.

A different question is raised by the way in which the epigram is composed. If we compare it with other dedicatory epigrams of almost any period from archaic to Graeco–Roman, we find obvious differences. First, the dedicator normally names himself, but here no dedicator is mentioned. Secondly, the god to whom the dedication is made is normally named, but here nothing is said of him. Thirdly, a dedication normally proclaims its character by some such word as ἄγαλμα, μνῆμα, ἀπαρχήν and the like, but here the character of the dedication is specified indirectly by σῶσεν ὄχημα τόδε. These divagations from common form might suggest that the couplet is a literary exercise of a late date. Such exercises are common as imitations both of dedicatory epigrams and of epitaphs, but this couplet lacks their conscious literary

[1] P. Friedländer and H. B. Hoffleit, *Epigrammata*, no. 94.

ARION AND THE DOLPHIN

flavour and sticks more closely than they usually do to its central theme. An alternative is that it is not, strictly speaking, a dedication at all, but an inscription to explain what the statue represents, and for this there is something to be said. A good example of such an inscription is that on the base of the statue of Harmodius and Aristogeiton at Athens.[1] Such inscriptions have something in common with dedications, and Arion's dolphin may be illustrated by a parallel from the last years of the sixth century. Probably before 506 B.C., a horse called Aura, which belonged to Pheidolas of Corinth, lost its rider in the horse-race at Olympia, but none the less won the race and was awarded the prize (Paus. 6. 13. 19). A couplet celebrates this victory and would be appropriately inscribed on the pedestal of the horse's statue:

οὗτος Φειδόλα ἵππος ἀπ' εὐρυχόροιο Κορίνθου
ἄγκειται Κρονίδᾳ μνᾶμα ποδῶν ἀρετᾶς. (*A.P.* 6. 135)

The lemma in the Palatine Anthology ascribes the lines to Anacreon, but such an ascription, like all ascriptions of unsigned verses on monuments, is open to grave doubts, and in this case the forms εὐρυχόροιο, μνᾶμα, ἄγκειται, ἀρετᾶς are alien to his manner.[2] But this need not mean that the couplet is not of respectable age. Though Pausanias does not mention it, he may have known it, for he says that the Eleans told Pheidolas ἀναθεῖναι τὴν ἵππον ταύτην (6. 13. 9), and this echoes the ἄγκειται of the couplet. It looks authentic, and has something in common with our lines. First, negatively, it does not give the name of the dedicator directly but suggests him in Φειδόλα; and second, positively, it says what the subject of the statue is and why it is there. It is possible that the couplet on the statue of Arion served a somewhat similar purpose in explaining an unusual subject. The manner is sufficiently terse and factual for a date in the fifth century, though perhaps in the later part of it, when the lines could have been composed for the actual statue known to Herodotus. So far Aelian's information is not worthless in its main substance and tends to confirm what we might surmise from Herodotus, that the statue of Arion was an object of general interest and known beyond its immediate vicinity.

[1] Friedländer–Hoffleit, no. 150.
[2] L. Weber, *Anacreontea*, 31; R. Reitzenstein, *Epigramm und Skolion*, 107.

Having quoted the epigram Aelian proceeds to quote what he calls a ὕμνος, which he says that Arion wrote as a χαριστήριον to Poseidon for his delivery from the sea and as his ζωάγρια to the dolphins who saved his life. The text may be presented as follows:[1]

    ὕψιστε θεῶν,
    πόντιε χρυσοτρίαινε Πόσειδον,
    γαιάοχ' ἐγκύμον' ἀν' ἅλμαν·
    βραγχίοις δὲ περί σε πλωτοὶ
5 θῆρες χορεύουσι κύκλῳ
    κούφοισι ποδῶν ῥίμμασιν
    ἐλάφρ' ἀναπαλλόμενοι, σιμοὶ
    φριξαύχενες ὠκύδρομοι σκύλακες, φιλόμουσοι
    δελφῖνες, ἔναλα θρέμματα
10 κουρᾶν Νηρεΐδων θεᾶν,
    ἃς ἐγείνατ' Ἀμφιτρίτα·
    οἵ μ' εἰς Πέλοπος γᾶν
    ἐπὶ Ταιναρίαν ἀκτὰν ἐπορεύσατε
    πλαζόμενον Σικελῷ ἐνὶ πόντῳ
15 κυρτοῖς νώτοισι φορεῦντες,
    ἄλοκα Νηρείας πλακὸς
    τέμνοντες, ἀστιβῆ πόρον,
    φῶτες δόλιοί μ' ὡς ἀφ' ἁλιπλόου γλαφυρᾶς νεὼς
    εἰς οἶδμ' ἁλιπόρφυρον λίμνας ἔριψαν.

Aelian professes to believe, and expects others to believe with him, that this is a Hymn composed by Arion, who first pays a tribute to Poseidon as lord of the sea and then, by an easy transition, tells his own tale in the first person and indirectly gives thanks to the dolphins who have saved his life. The poem seems to be complete, since it is hard to imagine what could have preceded or followed the surviving words, and Aelian certainly suggests that it is when he introduces it, καὶ ἔστιν ὁ ὕμνος οὗτος. Nothing in it contradicts Herodotus' story of Arion. The poem is no masterpiece, but it is not without interest as a relatively rare specimen. We ought to be able to find a place for it in the scope of Greek literature and relate it to what we know of Arion.

As van der Hardt saw in 1723[2] and Boeckh argued in 1836,[3]

[1] The latest and best text, especially in punctuation and division of lines, is that of D. L. Page, *Poetae Melici Graeci*, 506–7. I have in the main followed this, but I have adopted Hermann's correction in 3 and Page's own proposal in his apparatus in 15.   [2] Quoted by H. W. Smyth, *Greek Melic Poets*, 207.
[3] *Sitz. Berl. Akad.* 1836, 74.

ARION AND THE DOLPHIN

a poem of this kind cannot conceivably have been composed in the time of Periander. We must ask what it is and how it arose, and it is natural to claim that it is a forgery fashioned for whatever obscure reasons impel forgers to fill gaps in the works of famous authors. It has indeed been claimed that Aelian himself wrote it,[1] but though Aelian has many faults, there is no reason to think that he was a conscious swindler, still less that with his meagre gifts he was capable of writing even such a poem as this. A superficially more attractive candidate is Lobon of Argos, who has in modern times been credited with a formidable array of works ascribed to famous authors,[2] and, if he was guilty of it, must have been quite a gifted cheat. But in fact nothing is known about him except that he wrote a book Περὶ ποιητῶν (Diog. Laert. 1. 112) and said that Thales' writings ran to about two hundred lines (1. 34). This is hardly enough to brand him as an energetic and successful swindler, and he may be ruled out of account. The poem might still be a forgery by someone else, and, when the *Suda* says that Arion ἔγραψε ᾄσματα, προοίμια εἰς ἔπη β΄, there may have been among these pieces some deliberate forgeries planted with dishonest intent. Yet the poem may in its own way be authentic, written by some poet whose name is lost, and ascribed, ignorantly but not fraudulently, to Arion because of its obvious connection with him. It has the appearance of having been composed in the period when reforms in music had prompted reforms in language[3] and especially it recalls the experiments of the dithyrambic poets which found their culmination in the *Persae* of Timotheus. Premonitions of this style may be found in Pratinas, but he probably intended them to create a comic or satirical effect, as later Philoxenus of Leucas did in his Δεῖπνον, but Timotheus is in deadly earnest. His new style may owe something to Aeschylus, whose ὄγκος it tries to imitate, but it aims at too much and fails. In our poem we can see something of this spirit, not indeed sensationally but still purposefully, at work. It has been thought that this change in language was due to the growing predominance of music over words, which meant that the words had to fit the tune instead of

[1] K. Lehrs, *Populäre Aufsätze*, 204.
[2] W. Kroll, *R.-E.* xiii. 931 ff.
[3] See among others H. Flach, *Gesch. d. gr. Lyr.* 351 ff.; G. S. Farnell, *Greek Lyric Poetry*, 397; H. W. Smyth, *Greek Melic Poets*, 205 ff. An important pioneering article is that of F. G. Welcker, *Kleine Schriften*, i. 89 ff.

being chosen for their own sake,¹ but this does not explain why the change in words took the strange direction that it did. The poets of this school tend to load every word with an equal weight, and this in the end destroys variety and balance. We can see such influences at work in our piece.

First, as Aristophanes notes, the new dithyramb likes compound words (*Pax*, 827 ff.), and his view is shared by Plato (*Crat.* 409 c–d) and Aristotle (*Poet.* 1459ᵃ10), while Demetrius, in recommending the use of compound words, makes an exception for τὰ διθυραμβικῶς συγκείμενα (*Eloc.* 91). The point of his criticism is that the compound words of the new style tended to be neologisms of an almost brutal ingenuity, and are well exemplified by a sample from Timotheus' *Persae*, which offers such oddities as ὀξυπαραυδήτῳ (66), ὀριγόνοισιν (77), κλυσιδρομάδος (81), μακραυχενόπλους (89), μαρμαροφέγγεις (92), δενδροέθειραι (106), μελαμπεταλοχίτωνα (123), σιδαρόκωπος (143), μουσοπαλαιολύμας (216), and many other words formed on similar lines. Our poem offers nothing so bizarre as these, but it has a liking for compound words, and in its short compass produces χρυσοτρίαινε (2), γαιάοχε (3), φριξαύχενες, ὠκύδρομοι, φιλόμουσοι (8), ἁλιπλόου (18), ἁλιπόρφυρον (19). But there is an obvious difference. These words are not new inventions but come from the language of earlier poetry. χρυσοτρίαινε is to be found at Aristoph. *Equ.* 559, γαιάοχε at Aesch. *Sept.* 310, as well as commonly in Homer, φριξαύχενες in an anonymous fragment about a boar (Trag. Ad. fr. 383. 1 N.), ὠκύδρομοι at Eur. *Bacch.* 872, φιλόμουσοι at Aristoph. *Nub.* 358, ἁλιπλόου at M 26, ἁλιπόρφυρον at Alcman fr. 26. 4 P. Our poet is certainly much less reckless than Timotheus and finds his compounds in highly respectable places. At the same time the dithyrambic style liked to pile up adjectives, especially compounds. So Philoxenus makes his Cyclops address Galatea

ὦ καλλιπρόσωπε χρυσεοβόστρυχε
χαριτόφωνε θάλος Ἐρώτων, (fr. 821/8 P.)

and Timotheus achieves even more astonishing effects, such as ἐπ' ἰχθυοστέφεσι μαρμαροπτύχοις κόλποισιν Ἀμφιτρίτας (38–9), μάχιμον δάϊον πλόϊμον Ἕλλαν (112–13), κατακυμοτακεῖς ναυσιφθόροι αὖραι (132–3), παλίμπορον φυγὴν ταχύπορον (162–3); and much the same kind of thing is to be found in Telestes,

¹ A. W. Pickard-Cambridge, *Dithyramb, Tragedy, Comedy*², 56.

νυμφαγενεῖ χειροκτύπῳ φηρὶ Μαρσύᾳ (fr. 805/1a 4 P.), ἀερὸν πνεῦμ' αἰολοπτέρυγον (ibid. c 2 P.). Our poet tries this on a generous scale when he calls the dolphins σιμοὶ φριξαύχενες ὠκύδρομοι σκύλακες, φιλόμουσοι δελφῖνες. Yet even this is not comparable with most of Timotheus' effects and is far milder and less startling. We are left with the impression that for some reason or other our poet uses this mannerism, as he uses compound adjectives, with more caution and less confidence than do more boisterous dithyrambic poets.

Secondly, the dithyrambic style was condemned as being inflated and having, as Philostratus says, λόγων ἰδέαν ... φλεγμαίνουσαν ποιητικοῖς ὀνόμασι (Vit. Apollon. 1. 17), which the scholiast explains διθυραμβώδη συνθέτοις ὀνόμασι σεμνυνομένην καὶ ἐκτοπωτάτοις πλάσμασι ποικιλλομένην. The desire to get more out of words by stretching their meaning to serve new purposes is not necessarily a fault, and though our poet takes risks in this direction, they are not all unsuccessful. At 5 he calls dolphins θῆρες, and this certainly they are not; for we can see from Homer (ω 291), Hesiod (Op. 277), and Archilochus (fr. 74. 7 D.) that θῆρες are contrasted, as animals on land, with fish in the sea and birds in the air. But by giving them the adjective πλωτοί our poet suggests that they are like animals in the sea, and he is justified in this because, when he says that they dance, he has behind him precedents in Pindar (fr. 125. 69–71 Bo.; 140b 15–17 Sn.), Sophocles (fr. 762 P.), and Euripides (Hel. 1454). We can see why he takes a risk with θῆρες, and the result is quite happy. Again, when he calls the dolphins σκύλακες (8), we might find an excuse for it in Euripides, who speaks of φύσιν ὀρεσκόων σκυλάκων πελαγίων τε (Hipp. 1276), but the text has been questioned and σκύμνων suggested as a substitute.[1] In any case our poet uses the word in a more specific sense. In origin it means 'puppy' and, when it is applied to dolphins, it suggests that they gambol like puppies over the sea. In 7 they are called σιμοί, which means 'snub-nosed', and is applied variously to human beings, whether Ethiopians (Xenophanes, fr. 16. 1 D.–K.) or Scythians (Hdt. 4. 23. 2), to dogs (Xen. Cyn. 4. 1), to hippopotami (Hdt. 2. 71. 1) and to ponies (id. 5. 9. 2). It is not obviously appropriate to dolphins, who have a long snout rather than any feature that can be called snub, but in so far as this tapers off at

[1] See W. S. Barrett, Euripides: Hippolytos, 394.

ARION AND THE DOLPHIN

the end, the word is permissible. Its special point is that it anticipates the comparison with puppies in the next line. In 16 the words ἄλοκα Νηρείας πλακός apply the language of the land to the sea, and there is some affinity with Timotheus' much more pretentious σμαραγδοχαίτας δὲ πόντος ἄλοκα ναΐοις ἐφοινίσσετο σταλάγ[μασι (32–4), but our poet treats the trope with less violence and accommodates it to his picture of dolphins as racing and leaping animals. He practises the dithyrambic device of extending the meaning of words, but with much less bravado than Timotheus, and this indicates either that he was of a less adventurous temperament or that he wrote when the new style had not yet permeated all ranks of writers.

With this in our mind we may look at the metrical structure of the poem, recognizing that any analysis of it may be disputable at some points. None the less a main pattern emerges:

```
        – – ⏑ ⏑ –                     anapaests
        – ⏑ ⏑ – ⏑ ⏑ – ⏑ ⏑ – –         4 dactyls
        – – ⏑ – | – ⏑ ⏑ – –           iambic, adonius
        – ⏑ – ⏑ ⏑⏑ ⏑ – –              trochaic dimeter
  5     – – ⏑ – | – ⏑ – –             iambic, trochaic
        – – ⏑ ⏑ – | – ⏑ ⏑             anapaests, cretic¹
        ⏑ – ⏑ ⏑ – ⏑ ⏑ – – –           anapaestic dimeter
        – – ⏑ ⏑ – ⏑ ⏑ – ⏑ ⏑ – ⏑ ⏑ – – anapaestic trimeter catalectic
        – – ⏑ ⏑⏑ ⏑ – ⏑ ⏑              iambic dimeter
 10     – – – ⏑ ⏑ – ⏑ –               glyconic
        – ⏑ – ⏑ – ⏑ – ⏑               trochaic dimeter
        – – ⏑ ⏑ – –                   reizianum,
        ⏑ ⏑ – ⏑ ⏑ – | – – ⏑ ⏑ – ⏑ ⏒   anapaests, telesillean
        – ⏑ ⏑ – ⏑ ⏑ – ⏑ ⏑ – –         4 dactyls
 15     – – – – ⏑ ⏑ – –               paroemiac
        ⏑ ⏑ ⏑ – ⏑ ⏑ – ⏑ –             glyconic
        – – ⏑ – ⏑ – ⏑ –               iambic dimeter
        – – ⏑ ⏑ – – | ⏑ ⏑ – ⏑ – ⏑ ⏑ – ⏑ –  reizianum, ⏑ ⏑ glyconic²
        – – ⏑ ⏑ – ⏑ – | – – ⏑ – –     telesillean, iambic penthimimer
```

In this there is nothing unusual. Most of the metrical elements are to be found in the *Persae* of Timotheus, and so far there is

---

¹ This line could conceivably be analysed as two major ionics, but their rarity in choral verse makes this unlikely.

² The glyconic preceded by two short syllables in what A. M. Dale, *Lyric Metres of Greek Drama*, calls a blunt choriambic enneasyllable with the first long resolved.

ARION AND THE DOLPHIN

no reason why our poem should not belong to more or less the same period. But it uses three metra which do not appear in the *Persae*, notably anapaests at 1, 6, 7, 8, and 13; reiziana at 12 and 18; and an adonius at 3. We cannot argue too much from this, since these metra may well have been in common currency in the time of Timotheus, but it is perhaps significant that not only the other metra of the poem but these three also are found in Euripides[1]—the anapaestic sequences at *Hec.* 154, 177, *Ion* 144, 859, *Tro.* 153, *Andr.* 841, *Her.* 1190; the reiziana at *Her.* 1049, *I.T.* 894, *Tro.* 1086; the adonius at *Cyc.* 661, *Med.* 855, *Her.* 786. Euripides was certainly touched by the new style, and a not very adventurous poet who felt that he must conform to fashion might take him as in some respects a model. The metre suggests that the poem may have been written when the influence of Euripides was still strong and had not been finally displaced by that of the dithyrambic poets. This does not give a firm date, but it suggests that some period about 400 B.C. may not be far out.

The ascription of the poem to Arion can be explained simply by the part which he plays in it in telling of his adventure, and if the *Suda* is right in reporting the existence of ᾄσματα in his name, this may conceivably have been one of them,[2] especially if it is unlikely that any authentic poems by him survived into later times.[3] The poem is a genuine production in its own kind, but this kind is unfamiliar and calls for attention. We cannot doubt that this is a solo song performed by a single actor who takes the part of Arion. This is clear from the use of μ' in 12 and 18, which must refer to a single person, who is the chief actor. But secondly there are undeniable signs that he is supported by a chorus which acts the role of dolphins. This is most obvious when the song says that they χορεύουσι κύκλῳ (5), which indicates that they form a κύκλιος χορός and dance round the actor in their midst. This is clear from κούφοισι ποδῶν ῥίμμασιν ἐλάφρ' ἀναπαλλόμενοι (6–7). The last word recalls Homer's ἀναπάλλεται ἰχθύς (Ψ 692), and is perfectly applicable to dolphins, since the notion that they leap is well established in Greek thought. But to ascribe πόδες to them is by any calculation extremely odd. Euripides may seem to do something of the same kind for ships (*Hec.* 940, 1020), but he is

---
[1] I am much indebted to O. Schroeder, *Euripides, Cantica*, 198 ff.
[2] I assume that the ᾄσματα are different from the προοίμια.
[3] Wilamowitz, *Textg. d. gr. Lyr.* 8.

simply exploiting the familiar image of a journey, and though Timotheus calls oars ὀρείους πόδας ναός (*Pers.* 90), it is an extension of the same notion. But to ascribe feet to fish is unexampled and would be absurd if there were not a good excuse for it. What the poet means is that the dancers who enact the dolphins leap into the air and throw their feet about, no doubt imitating the way in which dolphins leap out of the sea. The singer has his eye more on the actors than on any actual fish, and this determines his language. The movements of the chorus imitate those of fish in their leaps and their speed, ὠκύδρομοι (8), and this is an idea familiar from Pindar (*P.* 2. 51; *N.* 6. 64–5; fr. 220 Bo.; 234 Sn.). We can form a picture of dancers leaping and running as they take the part of dolphins, while the actor, who takes the part of Arion, describes their actions in appropriate words.

A performance of this kind, conducted by a soloist who sings and a chorus which dances, is not the formal Greek choral μολπή. Before it could come into existence two steps had to be taken. First came the introduction of solo songs. This is ascribed by Aristotle to Melanippides (*Rhet.* 1409^{b}26), but it seems to have been extended by Philoxenus of Cythera; for we hear that Aristophanes referred to him in this context, καὶ Ἀριστοφάνης ὁ κωμικὸς μνημονεύει τοῦ Φιλοξένου, καί φησιν ὅτι εἰς τοὺς κυκλίους χοροὺς μέλη εἰσηνέγκατο (Ps.-Plut. *Mus.* 30), and the contrasted collocation of κυκλίους χοροὺς and μέλη suggests that the latter are solo songs. It does not much matter for our purpose whether they were introduced by Melanippides or Philoxenus, but it is important that they belonged to the new dithyramb, and this would explain the part played by the soloist in our song. This change was followed by another no less decisive, when the chorus, instead of singing, played a part which called for too much action to allow them also to sing. This follows from the Aristotelian *Problemata*, 918^b. 23, where, in answer to the question why nomes are not arranged in strophes and antistrophes like other songs, it is said that it is because they are delivered by professional artists, ἀγωνισταί, whose function is to imitate actions, and this means that the music is varied to suit the various actions. Then follows the important information that the same is true of dithyrambs, which used to be performed by amateurs, ἐλεύθεροι, but are now performed by professionals—μεταβάλλειν γὰρ πολλὰς μεταβολὰς τῷ ἑνὶ ῥᾷον ἢ τοῖς πολλοῖς καὶ τῷ ἀγωνιστῇ ἢ τοῖς τὸ ἦθος φυλάττουσιν, 'for it is easier for a single person to make many changes than for a number of persons, and for a professional actor than for those who keep the character of the music'. This puts beyond doubt the conclusion that the single actor has assumed a new prominence and performs duties which are beyond the capacity of the actual chorus. His separation from them is clear from the *Cyclops* of Philoxenus, who made the lovelorn Polyphemus play a harp and sing a solo to Galatea (frs. 819–821/6–8 P.), and it is possible that his chorus took the part of sheep and goats, since the chorus in Aristophanes' *Plutus*, 296 ff. seems to imitate them in this role. By about 400 B.C. the soloist's duties were different from those of the chorus and called for a more professional handling. This indicates that our song is a solo sung by a professional while the chorus dances to it. Once the solo-part gained this prominence, the role of the chorus might be limited to dancing and miming. In our song they play the part of dolphins, and it is tempting to think that, when they are spoken of as κυρτοῖς νώτοισι φορεῦντες, they mimic what happened to Arion by making some of their number leap on the backs of others, as still happens in some traditional Greek dances.

That the chorus should take the part of fish is unusual but not unprecedented. Soon after 403 B.C. Archippus produced his comedy 'Ἰχθύες,[1] and though its main purpose was political, it took its name from the chorus who were presented as fish or, more specifically, as θρᾷτται (Ath. 7. 329 c), and must have been dressed with some degree of verisimilitude. But though Archippus may have been encouraged to desert the human race for his chorus by such examples as the *Birds* of Aristophanes and the Θηρία of Crates,[2] yet, like them, he may have had earlier dances in mind. Just as the *Birds* recalls a black-figure oenochoe of the sixth century which depicts men decked with feathers to look like birds as they dance to a flute-player,[3] so a black-figure skyphos of about the same date shows men dressed as warriors riding on dolphins and seems to reflect a similar kind of dance.[4] This indicates that in the not too distant background of our song

---

[1] A. von Mess, *Rh. Mus.* lxvi (1911), 382 ff.; H. Swoboda, *R.-E.* iA. 842.
[2] Schmid–Stählin, *Gesch. d. gr. Lit.* I. 4. 156.
[3] M. Bieber, *History of the Greek and Roman Theater*², fig. 123.
[4] Ibid., fig. 125.

there existed dances in which men took the part of fish and even of dolphins. A dance of this kind need not necessarily have been accompanied by a song, but it provided a precedent first for Archippus and then for our poem. There may well have been other dances of a like kind, and in that case the decision to make the chorus act as dolphins might not be so unusual as we might think. We cannot be sure how the dancers would be made to look like dolphins, but perhaps something may be deduced from a 'Pontic' vase, which shows three elderly figures, each with the hind-quarters of a fish attached to his waist, advancing towards four Nereids.[1] This has been thought to be a mythological scene,[2] but if it were, surely the figures would have been modelled on the usual fashion of Tritons and not merely have had fish-like quarters added to them. It looks more like a dance in which fish and Nereids take a part, and it is perhaps worth noting that our song mentions both Nereids (10) and Nereus (16), and even goes out of its way to make the Nereids daughters of Amphitrite, though Doris is usually regarded as their mother (Hes. *Theog.* 240; Apollodor. *Bibl.* 1. 2. 2 and 7; Ovid. *Met.* 2. 269; 13. 742). This may be because earlier forms of such dances sometimes contained Nereids. In any case fish were sufficiently represented in dances for our author to have no difficulty in making his chorus play the part of the dolphins who rescued Arion. We may also assume that the music was played by a flute-player, since not only was this the regular practice for κύκλιοι χοροί but the flute was especially associated with Dolphins, and when here they are called φιλόμουσοι (8), it has the backing of Pindar (fr. 125. 69–70 Bo.; 140 b 12 Sn.) and Euripides (*El.* 435 φίλαυλος; cf. Aristoph. *Ran.* 1317–18), to say nothing of actual fact.

Our poem is unusual in not drawing its subject from the repertory of ancient myth. It is true that special circumstances allowed this for outstanding events of recent years, as when Phrynichus wrote his *Capture of Miletus* and *Phoenissae* and Aeschylus his *Persae*, and it may have been with such examples in mind that Timotheus wrote his *Persae*. Anything to do with the Persian Wars was sufficiently heroic to deserve a place in serious song. Arion, however, falls between two stools. On the one hand he does not belong to the heroic past; on the other, he

[1] A. Lesky, *Thalatta*, 111, fig. 29.
[2] E. Buschor, *Sitz. Bay. Akad.* 1941, 2. 11.

is not connected with recent events of glorious memory. That he was honoured at Corinth is likely enough from Pindar's reference to the dithyramb as a Corinthian invention (*O.* 13. 18–19), but there is no sign that heroic rites were offered to him. If he was sufficiently important to receive a song about himself, it calls for explanation. At the start we need not doubt that the Corinthians believed the story, which they told to Herodotus, about Arion and the Dolphin. Such a thing is by no means impossible, and we have no reason to disbelieve the story of the dolphin which carried a boy on its back in the bay of Hippo Zarytus, as it is told soberly by the Elder Pliny (*N.H.* 9. 8. 26), more elaborately by his nephew (*Ep.* 9. 33), and more fancifully by Oppian (*Hal.* 5. 452–518). A similar story is told about a boy from Iasus in Caria (Plut. *Soll. Anim.* 35; Ael. *N.A.* 6. 15).[1] Details may be added to make the tales more interesting, but that a basis of fact is possible is clear from a very similar adventure reported on unimpeachable authority in recent years from New Zealand.[2] Yet for the story of Arion such stories are perhaps irrelevant, and we need not ask whether he actually rode on a dolphin or not. What is told of him is so similar to what is told of certain other characters that it must be related to them and assessed by comparison with them.

What concern us are not folktales but myths, that is stories told to explain religious monuments or rites or names, and we may look at some examples:

1. Telemachus. The people of Zacynthus said that as a boy he fell into the sea and was rescued by dolphins, and that is why Odysseus has a dolphin emblazoned on his shield (Plut. *Soll. Anim.* 36). This looks like an aetiological explanation of Odysseus' blazon, which had been described by Stesichorus (fr. 225/45 P.) and was known in later times to Euphorion (fr. 67 Powell) and Lycophron (*Alex.* 658). The blazon called for an explanation, and this was found in the popular belief in the benevolent services of dolphins. The connection with Telemachus is late, for it is difficult to fit any such episode into the career of Odysseus as Homer tells it, since this leaves almost no time when Odysseus could have been with his son in his childhood.[3]

[1] A. W. Mair, *Oppian, Colluthus, Tryphiodorus*, 487 ff.
[2] T. F. Higham, *Greece & Rome*, n.s. vii (1960), 82–6.
[3] A. Tümpel, *R.-E.* v. 2545–7.

2. Koiranos of Paros. He was shipwrecked between Paros and Naxos or off Mykonos, and brought by dolphins to the island of Sikinos, south of Paros (Plut. *Soll. Anim.* 35) or to Miletus (Phylarchus, 81 F 26 Jacoby). When after a long life he died, dolphins attended his funeral (Ael. *N.A.* 8. 3). His special interest is his shipwreck, in which all his companions perished. It is mentioned by Archilochus (fr. 117 D.), but we do not know whether Archilochus regarded him as a mythical figure or a more recent historical character, but at least he says that he was saved by Poseidon.

3. Enalos of Lesbos. He was a Penthilid, one of the first colonists of the island. He leapt into the sea after his beloved, and both were brought to land by dolphins and landed in a place where later a temple of Poseidon was built by them with the help of the dolphins, and the god himself was worshipped as Enalos (Plut. *Sept. Sap. Conv.* 20; *Soll. Anim.* 36; Athen. 11. 466 c–d).

4. Melicertes of Corinth.[1] After being cast into the sea, he was brought to land, either dead or alive, by a dolphin (Lucian. *Dial. Mar.* 8. 1; Paus. 1. 44. 11; Philostrat. *Im.* 2. 16) and was connected with the foundation of the Isthmian Games, over which Poseidon presided (Pind. Hypoth. *Isthm.*, p. 192. 7 Dr.).

5. Palaemon of Corinth.[2] On the road from Corinth to Lechaion were statues of Poseidon and Leucothea and between them Palaemon on a dolphin (Paus. 2. 3. 4). On Corinthian coins he is depicted as standing on a dolphin,[3] and has naturally been identified with Melicertes.

6. Taras and Phalanthus of Tarentum. At Tarentum coins which show a figure riding on a dolphin have the inscription ΤΑΡΑΣ, and this has been thought to be the figure of the eponymous hero, especially as Aristotle ἐν τῇ Ταραντίνων πολιτείᾳ καλεῖσθαί φησι νόμισμα παρ' αὐτοῖς νοῦμμον, ἐφ' οὗ ἐντετυπῶσθαι Τάραντα τὸν Ποσειδῶνος δελφῖνι ἐποχούμενον (fr. 590 R.). But he seems to have been misled by the inscription, which refers not to the figure but to the place, and it is more likely that the figure is of Phalanthus than of Taras.[4] Phalanthus was said to have been

---
[1] A. Lesky, *R.-E.* xv. 514–19.
[2] P. Weizsäcker, in Roscher, *Lex. Myth.* iii. 1. 1255–62.
[3] Imhood–Blumer, *Arch. Jahrb.* 1888, fig. 9. 14.
[4] F. Studniczka, *Kyrene*, 175 ff.; V. Ehrenberg, *R.-E.* xix. 1623 ff.

wrecked on his way to the west and to have been saved by a dolphin, and that is why near his statue at Delphi there was an image of it (Paus. 10. 13. 10). The distinction between Taras and Phalanthus does not matter very much for the present discussion, since both were closely connected with Tarentum, and Taras was the son of Poseidon (Paus. 10. 10. 8). All these cases are familiar and have often been discussed,[1] but they are relevant to our enquiry because they provide a background for the story of Arion.

In every case, except that of Telemachus, whose story looks like a late, literary invention not very dissimilar from that which Euphorion tells about a girl called Apriate who leaps into the sea from an unwanted lover and is saved by a dolphin (Page, *Gr. Lit. Pap.* i. 495), the man saved is connected with Poseidon, and there is good reason to think that these heroes are in some sense substitutes for him.[2] Aristophanes addresses him as δελφίνων μεδέων (*Equ.* 560), and in the market-place at Corinth he had a dolphin under his feet (Paus. 2. 2. 7). Moreover, it is clear that at times he was thought to ride on a dolphin. It may be he who is so depicted on a gold strip in Leningrad,[3] and Lucian makes him say to Triton σὺ δὲ ἀλλὰ δελφῖνά τινα τῶν ὠκέων παράστησον· ἐφιππάσομαι γὰρ ἐπ' αὐτοῦ τάχιστα (*Dial. Mar.* 6. 2). The cult of a male figure on a dolphin is essentially the cult of a sea-god, who may not yet be fully differentiated as Poseidon, or may be called by a different name, or have taken over some of his attributes, such as the dolphin. The curious thing is that Arion should have been added to this company. He was a historical figure known to Solon (ap. Ioh. Diakonos, *Rh. Mus.* lxiii (1908), 150) and to Hellanicus (4 F 66 Jacoby). His fame was that of a singer and an organizer and producer of dithyrambs, and neither of these suggests any connection with Poseidon or any reason why he should be treated as a hero. On the other hand at two points he touches the legends of the other dolphin-riders. First, Herodotus says that he got his information on Arion from Corinthians and Lesbians (1. 23. 1), and Arion was closely connected with both, being born at Methymna in Lesbos and spending much of his life at Corinth under Periander. It happens

[1] Notably by H. Usener, *Sintflutsagen*, 154 ff. and K. Klement, *Arion*, *passim*.
[2] J. Ilberg in Roscher, *Lex. Myth.* iii. 2239.
[3] J. Overbeck, *Kunstmaterialien*, iii. 319.

also that among the riders Enalos belongs to Lesbos, and Melicertes and Palaemon to Corinth. Secondly, though Herodotus does not mention any connection between Arion and Poseidon, our poem emphatically does, and there must be a reason for it. It looks as if the story of the dolphin had been attached to the historical Arion because he was connected with rites in which a god and his dolphin took a central place.

How this happened we can only guess, but even a guess may help to clarify the nature of the question. Dolphin-dances, held in honour of a sea-god, who need not necessarily have had a name or, if he had, could be variously Poseidon or Melicertes or Palaemon, would be held from an early date in Corinth among the κύκλιοι χοροί, which Arion found in existence and put in order and organized. Such a dance would be performed by a chorus imitating dolphins in its movements to a flute-accompaniment. Since Poseidon was held in high honour at Corinth, which Pindar calls 'Ἰσθμίου πρόθυρον Ποτειδᾶνος (O. 13. 3–4), a dance of this kind would be prominent in local celebrations and come to be connected with the name of Arion who had turned it into a formal ceremony. In the course of time, as often happens with rites, the original meaning or purpose of the dance would be forgotten, and its remembered connection with Arion would lead to his being credited with riding on a dolphin in such a way as the dance imitated. Though the original sea-god was displaced from the chief part, he would still, as Poseidon, keep some vague association with the dance just because he was god of the sea and through his dolphins responsible for such a deliverance. The statue at Taenarum, originally erected to a sea-god, would inspire some poet to write an epigram on it saying, as he may well have believed, that it represented Arion on a dolphin. The story, thus started and set on its course, gained enough credence to spread to Arion's original home on Lesbos, from whose people, as well as from the Corinthians, Herodotus heard it, and where it accorded sufficiently with local traditions to gain acceptance. Then, in the musical and poetical revolution of the late fifth century, an unknown poet, who knew something about the dance and the legend of Arion associated with it, and was acquainted with the work of Euripides and Philoxenus, took advantage of the new conditions to compose a song which could be sung by a single actor in the part of Arion, while the chorus, dressed as dolphins, ran and leapt around him. Much of this is mere supposition and must not be accepted as anything more. The song may not be very distinguished, but it has some small merits, and it shows not only what a minor poet might do in a time of literary change but how the Greeks were able to keep some relics of an ancient ritual even when they thought that they had reformed it out of existence.

XV

A CRETAN HYMN[1]

THE Hymn, of which the fragments, inscribed on stone, were found in May 1904 near Palaikastro, the ancient Heleia, in eastern Crete, was fortunate in its first publication[2] and has subsequently received distinguished attention.[3] There are still large gaps in the text unlikely to be filled by fresh discoveries, but this need not deter us from looking again at what we have. Though the existing text comes from the second or third century A.D., we cannot doubt that it is copied from a much earlier original, thought by some to have been composed in the fourth or even the fifth century B.C.[4] Both as a document from Crete, where poetical texts are rare, and as an example of an authentic Hymn, it invites further examination.

The Hymn is in the first place noteworthy for its refrain, which both starts it and is repeated after each of the six strophes. No other Greek refrain does this, and the only even partial parallel is Archilochus' song for Heracles, which begins with ὦ καλλίνικε and repeats τήνελλα καλλίνικε after each line (fr. 120 D.). The unusual space occupied by the refrain calls for explanation, which is that it embodies what matters most in the rite—the summons to the god to come to his worshippers. Once the refrain was established, the actual strophes could be shaped to suit and amplify it, and

---

[1] First published in *For Service for Classical Studies*, edited by Maurice Kelly (F. W. Cheshire, Melbourne, 1966), 31–46.
[2] R. C. Bosanquet, *A.B.S.A.* xv (1908–9), 339–56; G. Murray, ibid. 357–65; J. E. Harrison, ibid. 308–38; *Themis*, 1 ff.; *Inscriptiones Creticae*, III. ii. 2.
[3] K. Latte, *Rel.–gesch. Versuch. u. Vorarb.* xiii. 43 ff.; W. Aly, *Philol.* lxxi (1912), 469 ff.; K. Guarducci *S.M.S.R.* 1939, 1–22; M. P. Nilsson, *Minoan–Mycenaean Religion*, 546 ff.; A. B. Cook, *Zeus*, i. 15 ff., ii. 931 ff.; W. K. C. Guthrie, *The Greeks and their Gods*, 46 ff.; W. E. Willetts, *Cretan Cults and Festivals*, 198 ff.; U. von Wilamowitz–Moellendorff, *Griechische Verskunst*, 499–501, whose division into lines I follow. The text is presented with short commentaries by E. Diehl, *Anth. Lyr.* ii. 279–81, and J. U. Powell, *Collectanea Alexandrina*, 160–2. My article went to press before the appearance of M. L. West, *J.H.S.* lxxxv (1965), 149 ff.
[4] Murray, 365, 'not earlier than 400'; Wilamowitz, 502, 'ein Dichter des 5. Jahrhunderts'.

new strophes could be added, but the refrain expresses the main purpose of the Hymn and imposes its character on the rest. Moreover, whereas normally the metrical scheme of a refrain is closely related to that of the rest of a poem, in the Hymn it is notably different. It may be set out as follows:

ἰώ, μέγιστε κοῦρε, χαῖρέ μοι Κρόνειε,
παγκρατὲς γάνος, βέβακες δαιμόνων ἀγώμενος·
Δίκταν εἰς ἐνιαυτὸν ἕρπε καὶ γέγαθι μολπᾷ.

∪ – ∪ – ∪ – ∪ – | ∪ – ∪ – ∪   iambic dimeter, iambic penthimimer
– ∪ – ∪ – ∪ – – – ∪ – – – – ∪ –   trochaic tetrameter catalectic
– – – ∪ ∪ – ∪ – | ∪ – ∪ – ∪ – –   glyconic, iambic dimeter catalectic

This is a simple, easily intelligible scheme, which provides a lively rhythm and indicates some degree of accomplishment. The opening iambs pass without trouble into the following trochees, and the insertion of a glyconic in 3 varies the metre without distorting it, very much as Aeschylus inserts a glyconic between trochaic elements in *Eum.* 321 ff.[1] But when we turn from the refrain to the strophes, we find a different scheme, which is by no means so neat. The strophes consist each of two lines, which have a break after the eighth syllable but are in principle fifteen syllables long. In theory they are constructed in a falling rhythm from major Ionics, and the pure form of the lines is

– – ∪ ∪ | – – ∪ ∪ | – – ∪ ∪ | – – – .

This gives three major Ionics followed by a molossus.[2] Ionics may be connected with religious songs, since Sappho's two lines on the death of Adonis consist of three minor Ionics preceded by a molossus (fr. 140 L.–P.). Moreover, the final molossus in the Hymn is paralleled by the end of choral sections in Eur. *Cyc.* 502, *Med.* 159, *Bacch.* 71, *Hipp.* 734. But though this fundamental form is suitable for a Hymn, here it is in practice subjected to remarkable variations. Though the first line of the first strophe follows the scheme in its proper shape, no other extant line does. Every

---

[1] Wilamowitz, 501, says 'in ἐνιαυτόν wird das Iota verschluckt sein', but the parallel in Aeschylus makes such a hypothesis unnecessary.
[2] That this is the metre in both lines of the strophe and not merely in the second is clear from αὐλοῖσιν in 4, which sets the correct form at the start and cannot be explained, as by Powell, as a form of syncope.

strophe has examples of the pure Ionic being replaced by the anaclastic form – ∪ – ∪ or by – ∪ – –, while at 29 it is replaced by a minor Ionic ∪ ∪ – – and at 30 by ∪ ∪ – ∪, and the final molossus becomes a trochaic dipody at 19 and a minor Ionic at 29. The state of the text at other places makes it impossible to discover the practice of the incomplete lines, but even so the degree of aberration is abnormally high for a formal poem. We might of course argue that the Hymn is not a literary work of art and must not be expected to display a classical formality, but the refrain shows that Cretans could write with some elegance and distinction, and the difference between it and the actual strophes is notable. The former could well have been written in the classical age of choral song, but the latter shows a freedom which recalls that of the minor Ionics in the Paean of Isyllus,[1] where they are subjected to anaclasis (49 twice), catalexis (42, 51, 57), and resolutions (39, 42, 43, 46, 51).[2] The Paean is probably to be dated to the third quarter of the fourth century, and its method indicates that at this date Greek lyric metres had begun to lose much of their elegant formality. Our Hymn displays similar symptoms, but since the refrain shows some understanding of metrical structure, it is possible that the variety in the strophes is due to the needs of improvisation for which an easy metre would be extremely helpful. It is the refrain that really matters, and the strophes are not composed with a similar care.

The Hymn is a true ὕμνος, not merely because it is sung εἰς θεούς (Menander, p. 33. 17 Spengel), but more specifically because it conforms to the definition ὁ δὲ κυρίως ὕμνος πρὸς κιθάραν ᾔδετο ἑστώτων (Procl. Bibl. Phot. 320ᵃ18 ff. Bekker). The choir tell how they sing it:

> τάν τοι κρέκομεν πακτίσι μείξαντες ἅμ᾽ αὐλοίσιν,
> καὶ στάντες ἀείδομεν τεὸν ἀμφὶ βωμὸν οὐερκῆ. (4–5)

The performance takes place round the altar of the god at Dikte, whither he is summoned (3). Dikte must once have been connected with the Dictaean Cave where Zeus spent his childhood (Ap. Rhod. 1. 508–9; Lucian. Dial. Mort. 15. 3). Though the original cave has not been identified with certainty, there is a probability

---

[1] Powell, 133–6.
[2] Wilamowitz, *Isyllos von Epidauros*, 19 ff.; J. W. White, *The Verse of Greek Comedy*, 144 ff.

that it is above Psychro, overlooking the Lasithia plain in central Crete,[1] and though claims have been made for other caves at Arkalochori and Phaneromeni, they are less substantial. The Psychro Cave has a past dating to Minoan times, and excavations have unearthed a rich supply of ritual offerings. But the Dictaean Cave cannot be the same as Dikte itself, for it is clear that this had a well-built altar around which the choir sang, and for this there is no place in the Cave. In early days the god must have been summoned to an altar near it, and that is easy enough, but the Cave itself is at some distance from Palaikastro, and was clearly deserted and probably forgotten after the seventh century B.C.[2] The cult continued at Heleia in eastern Crete and must have been transferred there. This explains Strabo's statement (479) that Dikte lay 1,000 stades to the east of Ida and only 100 stades from Cape Salmonion, which is near Praisos. By the time that the Hymn was composed the Cave, which is not mentioned in it, must have ceased to count. What is remembered is the connection with Dikte, which is now a different place, but has appropriated the connection with the childhood of Zeus (9).[3]

The Hymn is not only a ὕμνος but a ὕμνος κλητικός (Menander, p. 333. 2 Spengel). The purpose of such a Hymn is to summon a god to a place where a rite awaits him. Sometimes the summons indicates the place from which he is asked to come, but this is not indispensable and is not the case in our Hymn, perhaps because in the loss of knowledge of the Cave the god is not thought to have any specific dwelling-place. What matters is that he must come to Dikte. But who is he? The vocative Κρόνειε gives a clue. It is a patronymic, like Ἰνάχειος (Aesch. P.V. 590, 705) for Io as 'daughter of Inachus', and, somewhat differently, like Κρόνιος for Zeus as 'son of Kronos' in such phrases as ὦ Κρόνιε παῖ (Aesch. P.V. 577; Pind. O. 2. 12). In the Hymn it should have this meaning and refer to Zeus as son of Kronos, but this is qualified by the address to him as μέγιστε κοῦρε which presents him in a very unusual light. He can be no other god but Zeus, but he is not the usual Zeus. When here he is uniquely called κοῦρος, it is a peculiarly Cretan usage, connected with the

[1] J. Boardman, *The Cretan Collection in Oxford*, 1–2.
[2] Ibid., 5.
[3] There remains the possibility that the Cave has not been discovered and is much nearer to Keleia; so Willetts, 215–16. See also Faure, *B.C.H.* lxxxiv. 183–4. But since the Cave is not mentioned in the Hymn, it is not very relevant to it.

legend that he was born in Crete and spent his childhood there. Apollonius gives a general notion of this:

ὄφρα Ζεὺς ἔτι κοῦρος, ἔτι φρεσὶ νήπια εἰδώς,
Δικταῖον ναίεσκεν ὑπὸ σπέος. (1. 508–9)

and Callimachus a more forcible hint:

ἀλλ' ἔτι παιδνὸς ἐὼν ἐφράσσαο πάντα τέλεια. (H. 1. 56)

But neither mentions any specific cult of Zeus as κοῦρος, still less as the greatest of κοῦροι. But this he certainly was at Dikte, where there was a statue of him without a beard (*Et. Mag.* 276. 18 Δίκτη· ἐνταῦθα δὲ Διὸς ἄγαλμα ἀγένειον ἵσταται) and this can only mean that he was worshipped as a youthful god who could properly be called κοῦρος. Nor was this cult unique. The coins of Phaistos show a beardless male figure, with a hen on his lap, sitting in a tree, with the inscription Ϝέλχανος.[1] As such he had a temple on the ruins of the Minoan palace at Hagia Triada, where the bricks were inscribed Ϝεύχανος.[2] At Lyttos[3] and at Gortyn[4] there was a festival called Ϝελχάνια, and at Knossos a month Ἐλχάνιος.[5] Ϝέλχανος is without doubt a pre-Greek name, and its antiquity is confirmed by the appearance, on a stone from Golgoi in Cyprus, of the proper name *wa-la-ka-ni-o* i.e. Ϝαλχάνιος, which is modelled on the god's name.[6] That the cult had some dispersion in Greece follows from Hesychius, s.v. Γελχάνος· ὁ Ζεὺς παρὰ Κρησίν, but it differed from other cults of Zeus in Crete, since even Zeus Κρηταγενής was no longer a youth but bearded.[7] It is with this youthful Zeus, Δίκταιος and Ϝέλχανος, that the Hymn is concerned.

At 2 Zeus is called παγκρατές followed by a word which appears three times on the stone as γανους, once as γανος, and once as γανοις. Murray took παγκρατὲς γάνους to mean 'Lord of all this gleaming', but, though this gives an intelligible sense, there is no good parallel to such a genitive after παγκρατής, and it seems more prudent to follow Wilamowitz in reading γάνος in the vocative. To address a god with a vocative abstraction is not impossible, since Melanippides invokes Zeus as θαῦμα βροτῶν

[1] B. V. Head, *Hist. Num.*[2] 473; Cook, ii. 946.
[2] L. Banti, *Culti di H. Triada*, 70.   [3] *Inscr. Cret.* 1. xviii. 11. 2.
[4] Ibid. iv. 3. 1.   [5] Ibid. 1. xvi. 3. 2.
[6] O. Masson, *Les Inscriptions chypriotes*, 298–9.
[7] L. R. Farnell, *Cults of the Greek States*, i. 109.

(fr. 726/6 L.–P.), and Aratus as μέγα θαῦμα (*Phaen.* 15).[1] To call him παγκρατὲς γάνος means that he has associations with all things bright and reviving, such as water and wine, and this suits the young god who in his celestial radiance revives life on the earth, rather as, if Porson's correction is right, Aeschylus speaks of the corn-crop rejoicing διοσδότῳ γάνει (*Ag.* 1392).[2] Such an address is indeed unusual, but it is clear and impressive and fits a young god associated, as the coins of Phaistos show, with physical nature. He is summoned to Dikte in the word ἕρπε, which we might suppose to be poetical or hieratic, but which is in fact vernacular in central and eastern Crete, found on inscriptions at Hierapytna (*G.D.I.* 5040. 33. 35; 5041. 3), Knossos (ibid. 5073. 7), Lyttos (ibid. 5100. 8) and Itanos (Schwyzer, *D.G.E.* 197. 18), and means simply 'come' with no ritual overtones. It is preceded by βέβακες, and we might feel that this involves some contradiction, since there is no point in summoning a god who has already arrived, but it means no more than that the god has 'set out', and this is the moment to summon him specifically to Dikte.

That the time for this is the spring follows from εἰς ἐνιαυτόν, and what this means we can see from an inscription of the third century B.C. from Thera, which also deals with the arrival of divine beings and says Ἡρῶσαι καρπὸν νέον εἰς ἐνιαυτὸν ἄγουσιν (*I.G.* XIII. iii. 1340). The god is asked to come to Dikte 'for the year', and his arrival is in the spring, probably in his month Ἐλχάνιος.[3] As the first editors saw, this yearly visit is highly remarkable, and though the phrase ἐνιαυτὸς δαίμων is not Greek but the invention of Jane Harrison, there is no doubt that this is a year-god, whose arrival is the cause and the sign of renewal and rebirth in natural things. In his own sphere he does what Dionysus and Adonis do in theirs, and that is why, like them, he is a κοῦρος. He differs, however, in not dying yearly. He must once have done so, but the Hymn says nothing of it, and implicitly denies it by calling him παῖδ' ἄμβροτον at 9. Yet there was a belief that Zeus died and was buried in Crete,[4] and when Callimachus denies that Zeus was born there, he does so on the

---

[1] Wilamowitz, 501.
[2] West ingeniously emends to γᾶν ὅς, but this creates the impression that the god normally dwells in the sky, and this seems out of character.
[3] Willetts, 501.
[4] Willetts, 219, gives a full list of references.

ground that the Cretans, who say so, claim that he also died there, which on his view is absurd:

"Κρῆτες ἀεὶ ψεῦσται"· καὶ γὰρ τάφον, ὦ ἄνα, σεῖο
Κρῆτες ἐτεκτήναντο· σὺ δ' οὐ θάνες, ἐσσὶ γὰρ αἰεί.

(H. 1. 8–9)

It is likely that in the far past the year-god was believed to die and to be born again, but in the Hymn what counts is not his death nor even his birth, but his yearly renewal of youthfulness, implicitly in himself and explicitly in much else. When the original year-god was identified with Zeus, he lost much of his old character, but in Crete, and nowhere else, he kept his importance as a spirit of the spring. This is a survival from Minoan times,[1] and that is why it is found only in Crete and in that part of it which kept in closest touch with the past.

The god sets out δαιμόνων ἀγώμενος, and this might receive some illumination from three inscriptions,[2] which come from the district where the Hymn was found. The first, from Itanos, and the second, from Hierapytna, record oaths in which Zeus Diktaios is mentioned first before other gods ($S.I.G.^4$ 526. 1 ff.; $G.D.I.$ 5039), while the third, from Praisos, records a grant of lands in a similar fashion ($S.I.G.^4$ 524. 16). We might therefore conclude that, when the Hymn summons the young god, it means that he is to be followed by a like assembly of gods and goddesses.[3] Yet this is doubtful for more than one reason. First, would the θεοί, as the inscriptions call them, be called δαίμονες in the Hymn? There are certainly times when the word is used in this sense, but more commonly it implies something vaguer and less specific than θεοί, which stands for the gods in their individual character, and this surely would be the case here. Secondly, though both the Hymn and the inscriptions are late and might admit almost any mixture of gods and goddesses, in the Hymn the young god is much more obviously pre-eminent than is Zeus Diktaios in the inscriptions, and seems to call for a less exalted and more specialized following. Thirdly, the god in the Hymn is summoned εἰς ἐνιαυτόν for an unusual task, which implies functions that do not belong to the ordinary Olympians.

[1] Nilsson, 532 ff.
[2] Bosanquet, 350; Willetts, 208.
[3] That Zeus can have a retinue of gods is clear from Plat. *Phaedr.* 266 e but, despite Wilamowitz, 501, he seldom does.

A CRETAN HYMN

We may therefore try to find some more suitable candidates for the δαίμονες whom the young Zeus leads.

The inscription from Hierapytna gives a hint when, after more famous gods and before a general inclusive reference, it mentions 'Kouretes and Nymphs and Korybantes'. They do not look at home in this august company, and we cannot but suspect that they are mentioned because they have a special place in Hierapytna, and for this reason cannot be omitted from an oath. Of these the Kouretes have a peculiar claim to attention; for it is they who protect Zeus after his birth in Crete, and in legend hide him from Kronos by making such a din with their weapons that his cries cannot be heard. A clear account of this comes from Callimachus:

οὖλα δὲ Κούρητές σε περὶ πρύλιν ὠρχήσαντο
τεύχεα πεπλήγοντες, ἵνα Κρόνος οὔασιν ἠχὴν
ἀσπίδος εἰσαΐοι καὶ μή σεο κουρίζοντος.   (H. 1. 52–4)

The Kouretes are closely connected with Zeus, and Strabo compares their attachment to him with that of the Satyrs to Dionysus (468) while Hesiod calls them θεοὶ φιλοπαίγμονες ὀρχηστῆρες (fr. 123. 3 M.–W.). They were honoured in central and eastern Crete, where oaths were taken in their name at Lato (*G.D.I.* 5075), Hierapytna (ibid. 5039), and Lyttos (ibid. 5041), while their original position as guardians of herds is to be seen near Gortyn in a thankoffering, Κωρῆσι τοῖς πρὸ καρταιπόδων ἀρὰν καὶ [χα]ριστ[ή]ιον (Schwyzer, *D.G.E.* 192).[1] They are not merely suitable companions of the young Zeus; they are intimately connected with the κοῦρος, whom they follow and whose title is reflected in their own. Their role, now as always, is to assist him in a special task, even if he has assumed other tasks with which they have no connection.

That the Kouretes are the δαίμονες of the refrain follows from strophes 2–4 of the Hymn, which must be taken separately, since each presents problems of text and interpretation. On the stone strophe 2 gives

ἔνθα γάρ σε παῖδ' ἄμβροτον ἀσπιδ[
πὰρ 'Ρέας λαβόντες πόδα κ[

The 'immortal child' can only be Zeus, and the agents who took him from Rhea are the Kouretes (Diod. 5. 65. 4; Apollodor.

---

[1] Similar inscriptions are recorded in *Inscr. Cret.* 1. xxxi. 7 and 8.

Bibl. 1. 1. 6; Dion. Hal. *Ant. Rom.* 2. 61), and then protected him with the din of their weapon-dance (Callim. *H.* 1. 52–4; Strab. 468; Eur. *Bacch.* 119 ff.; Lucr. 2. 632–9). The Hymn not only speaks of people in the plural taking the child from Rhea but in ἀσπιδ[suggests something to do with shields. Murray fills the gap with ἀσπίδ[ηφόροι τροφῆες, but this is perhaps a little too allusive in a context where plain facts are needed. Wilamowitz's ἀσπίδ[εσσι Κωρῆτες introduces the Kouretes by name where they are almost indispensable and pulls the sentence together. In the next line we want a main verb and something to govern the accusative πόδα. Wilamowitz's κ[υκλῶντες, on the analogy of Eur. *Or.* 632 Μενέλαε, ποῖ σὸν πόδ' ἐπὶ συννοίᾳ κυκλεῖς, does not yield a very precise sense, but Murray's κ[ρούοντες meets most needs and is well backed by Eur. *El.* 180 κρούσω πόδ' ἐμόν. Add his ἀπέκρυψαν and we get

ἔνθα γάρ σε παῖδ' ἄμβροτον ἀσπίδ[εσσι Κωρῆτες
πὰρ ʿΡέας λαβόντες πόδα κ[ρούοντες ἀπέκρυψαν. (9–10)

This sets out the essential elements of the legend. The Kouretes are remembered for their protection of Zeus in his childhood, and this comes with the more force if they are the δαίμονες of the refrain.

Of the third strophe nothing remains except the words τᾶ]ς καλᾶς ἀός at the end of 15, and though it is tempting to speculate that this refers to a time before the sun and moon had regular movements[1] there is no prospect of reaching any secure conclusion. The fourth strophe, 19–20, is more promising:

]ύον κατῆτος καὶ βροτὸς Δίκα κατῆχε
]πε ζῷ' ἁ φίλολβος εἰρήνα.

In the past Justice governed men, and Peace, bringer of prosperity, did something for animals. That this lasted for some time follows from κατῆτος which must mean 'year by year'. Murray[2] connected the lines with a passage in Diodorus (5. 65. 1–2), who tells how after living in woods and wild places without proper shelter the Kouretes introduced momentous changes, such as tending flocks and domesticating animals, organizing the production of honey and introducing archery and hunting. This is

[1] So Bosanquet, 354–5, quoting some lines ascribed to Empedoclēs (fr. 154 D.-K.), Diod. 3. 56, and Ovid. *Met.* 1. 116–18.
[2] 360.

not a Golden Age like Hesiod's (*Op.* 111–26), nor is it, as the first editors thought, a Pythagorean version of a past time when men did not eat meat and animals did not eat one another (Plat. *Politic.* 271 e; *Legg.* 6. 782 c); for the Kouretes used the bow and practised hunting. It is a Cretan version of the past, and if it has parallels, they are to be found rather in Aeschylus' account of what Prometheus did for men (*P.V.* 462 ff.), which includes the provision of proper dwellings and the taming of animals, and is followed by Sophocles (fr. 432 P.) and Euripides (*Supp.* 201–13; fr. 578 N.), who ascribe some of these innovations to Palamedes.[1] A new point in the same tradition is made by Critias, when in his *Sipylus* he explains with paradoxical ingenuity the beginning of law and religion (fr. 1 N.)[2] and by Moschion, when he tells how men have advanced from cannibalism and lawlessness either through the teaching of Prometheus or by ἀνάγκη and μακρὰ τριβή (fr. 6 N.). These different accounts associate progress in material welfare with the growth of a social order, and though they do not assume that such an order is never broken, they do not believe in a progressive degeneration like that of Hesiod. They reflect the spirit of the fifth century with its conviction that man has fought his way forward by experiment and discovery. Diodorus owes something to this general outlook, even if he ascribes man's progress to the divine Kouretes. Theirs was an age of ὁμιλία, συμβίωσις, ὁμόνοια, εὐταξία, and in this the Hymn agrees with him when it ascribes an important role to Justice in the government of men (19) and to Peace, who is called φίλολβος, presumably because she prevents domestic animals from being eaten by wild beasts (20). Moreover the leading part taken by the Kouretes in the past accounts for their present importance. They no longer live on the earth but as divine beings they have something in common with the men of Hesiod's Golden Age, who after death survive as δαίμονες and look after men (*Op.* 122 ff.). If the Kouretes are now in such a position, there is good reason to tell of their beneficent actions in the past and to summon them to the present ceremony.

These considerations should help us to regain the sense of 19–20. Bosanquet began the lines with ῟Ωραι δὲ βρ]ύον and certainly βρ]ύον consorts well with abundance on earth, but it is

[1] They may have owed something to Stesichorus, see fr. 213/36 P.
[2] W. Jaeger, *The Theology of the Early Greek Philosophers*, 186 ff.

not clear that *Ὧραι should be the subject. It is true that both Justice and Peace are *Ὧραι (Hes. *Theog.* 902), but since in the Hymn they are mentioned immediately afterwards, there is no need to anticipate them here, and though Himerius says *Ὧραι δὲ λειμῶνας βρύουσι, 'the seasons swell the meadows', (*Or.* 9. 19 Colonna), it does not follow that the seasons themselves swell intransitively. Since animals are mentioned in the next line, and this must refer to their domestication by men, we should first expect something referring to vegetable nature, and perhaps a simple word like ἄγροι is all that we need. In 20 there must be a reference to the domestication of animals, which is one of the achievements of the Kouretes. When Wilamowitz suggests the completion of the fragmentary]πε by καὶ πάντα διῆ]πε ζώ⟨ι⟩', the verb, which means 'managed', falls a little short of an adequate sense, and we may doubt whether even in this free-and-easy metre a major Ionic can be replaced by − − − ∪, while Murray's πάντα δ' ἄγρι' ἄμφε]πε ζῴ' suggests that domestic animals are not in question.[1] Perhaps we can restore on the following plan:

ἄγροι δὲ βρ]ύον κατῆτος καὶ βρότος Δίκα κατῆχε,
καὶ παντοδάπ' ἄμφε]πε ζῴ' ἁ φίλολβος Εἰρήνα. (19–20)

The Hymn, then, at this point reflects the Cretan legend known to Diodorus that in the past the Kouretes brought justice to men and peace to animals. Its tribute to the Kouretes is well suited to them as guardians of oaths and flocks. This is rather a special version of the past, but since it refers to the time of Kronos, it is appropriate to the young god as Κρόνειος.

When three strophes have told of the Kouretes and their beneficent actions in the past, the Hymn returns to its chief purpose and in the last two strophes makes its explicit supplications to the god. For 24–5 the stone shows

α[   ]μνια καὶ θόρ' εὔποκ' ἐ[
       ]α καρπῶν θόρε κὲς τελεσ[

The god is asked to leap into what seem to be flocks and fruits. Since the adjective εὔποκος is applied to sheep (Aesch. *Ag.* 1416), the line is adequately completed by Wilamowitz's ἐ[ς πώεα in the

---

[1] Wilamowitz's claim, 500, that ἄμφε]πε is against the traces on the stone does not seem to be justified, nor his assertion that ζῴ' must be wrong because the Ionic is always replaced by a pure 'Ditrochäus'. It is not in 19. Incidentally he seems to think that the last syllable of his διῆ]πε can be short before ζ.

A CRETAN HYMN

Homeric manner (λ 402), and the contraction of the two final syllables into a single long presents no difficulties. But the incomplete]μνια responds less easily to treatment. Xanthoudides' δέ]μνια is not specific enough to make a clear impact, and if it refers to human beings, it anticipates what is coming later. Murray's στά]μνία is attractive with its bold image of the god leaping into the wine-jars, but we should expect him rather to leap into the vines. Wilamowitz felt that the sheep needed to be balanced by oxen and restored the beginning of the line as ἀλλὰ βῶν θόρ' ἐς ποί]μνια, which gives a neat balance but suffers from the defect that ποί]μνια is used invariably not of oxen but of sheep or goats, except in the Septuagint, 1 Kings 25 : 2, where it means head of cattle. It could just conceivably be applied to cattle in the Hymn, but surely not when sheep are mentioned immediately after it. The two lines cover a wide range, and it is tempting to think that what is missing is some reference to the meres and marshes from which Heleia gets its name and which give water for its fields. Such a word can be found in λί]μνια and then the physical setting of Heleia, with its obvious advantages in a dry district, precedes the sheep which pasture about it.[1] In the next line καρπῶν calls for an accusative before it, and the remains suggest a neuter plural. Bosanquet's κὲς λάϊ]α makes good sense, if καρπῶν is used, as it often is, with a general meaning of 'crops', including corn. The end of the line has been brilliantly restored by Wilamowitz, who, quoting Hesychius s.v. τελεσφόρος· οἶκος· τοῦ γεγαμηκότος καὶ τεκνώσαντος, proposes τελεσ[φόρος οἶκος. The final result is by no means certain, but a tolerable sense is secured if we read

ἁ[μῶν δὲ θόρ' ἐς λί]μνια, καὶ θόρ' εὔποκ' ἐ[ς πώεα,
κὲς λάϊ]α καρπῶν θόρε κὲς τελεσ[φόρος οἶκος. (24–5)

The god is asked to leap successively into the meres, the sheep, the crops in the fields, and human families. It is rational and orderly and leaves no doubt of what is required of him.

In this strophe and the next the repeated θόρε plays a leading part in specifying what the god is to do, and it is important to fix its exact meaning. The repetition suggests that the act of leaping is necessary and beneficial, and the repeated θόρε shows that the

[1] The god's association with water is perhaps implied in γάνος, as in Aesch. Pers. 483, Eur. Suppl. 1150, Hyps. fr. 60. 60 Bond.

god leaps not 'for' things but 'into' them, and this means an intimate relation. It is therefore reasonable to connect θόρε with those passages where it has a sexual connotation, as in Aeschylus' ὁ θρῴσκων for 'sire' (*Eum.* 660) and θρῴσκων κνώδαλα (fr. 15 N.).[1] If θόρ' ἐς means something like 'impregnate', then its repetition reveals its significance. The god is asked to impregnate flocks and fields and human families, and this is precisely what we should expect from such a god as he is.[2] When he comes in the spring, he gives life to all natural and human things, and the leap is the way in which he fulfils his task. This idea is almost without parallel in Greece. The Olympians do not behave in this manner, but some of their representatives do, and this seems to be specially true of the Kouretes, since Dionysius of Halicarnassus associates them closely with the Roman Salii, who were renowned for their leaping (*Ant. Rom.* 2. 70). In that case just as the Salii leap for Mars, the god of the fields, so the Kouretes leap for their Kouros, who is also a god of vegetation, and just as the Arval Brothers call upon their god 'Limen sali', so the singers of the Hymn call upon theirs "θόρε". This leaping god has predecessors in the Minoan past,[3] and though then he may have leapt with his followers, now he is called to leap alone. It is in this that virtue for the earth lies, and that is why he is summoned so emphatically to it.

The sixth and final strophe, 29–30, presents no serious difficulties of text and may be presented without trouble:

θόρε κὲς] πόληας ἁμῶν, θόρε κὲς ποντοφόρος νᾶας,
θόρε κὲς ν[έος πολ]είτας, θόρε κὲς Θέμιν κλ[είταν.   (29–30)

The only doubt is the last word. Murray's καλάν does not suit the remains on the stone, and Wilamowitz's κληνάν might perhaps be accepted in the sense of 'beloved', which it had in Crete (Strab. 484; Athen. 11. 782 c), and now seems to have in a text of Alcman (fr. 4. 1. 11 P.), but we may doubt whether such a word, normal for ordinary human love, is entirely suitable to Themis, and it is perhaps wiser to accept Bosanquet's κλείταν. It is then clear that in this strophe the god is asked to do something different almost in kind from before. The repeated θόρε κὲς has had its meaning extended and made less literal. The god is to

---
[1] The same use may perhaps be found in Callimachus, fr. 43. 123 Pf.
[2] Latte, 49; Nilsson, 272; Willetts, 214.
[3] Nilsson, 267–8; Willetts, 214.

give life to cities, ships, young citizens, and Themis. The cities are probably those which still worshipped Zeus Diktaios, notably Itanos, Hierapytna, Praisos, and Heleia. The sea-borne ships[1] present the other side of the picture for a people which lived as much from the sea as from the land. The young citizens are those who are most in need of the god if the race is to flourish, and pick up the notion of τελεσ[φόρος οἶκος in 25. Finally comes Themis, who looks a little out of place in this company. She may of course reflect Δίκα in 19, and then what the Kouretes gave in the past, the god is asked to give in the present. But Themis seems too remote and too august to be prayed for in this way, and it is tempting to think that the Hymn views her in quite another light—as Γαῖα, with whom Aeschylus' Prometheus identifies her (P.V. 210) and who was recognized as such by a seat in the theatre at Athens reserved for the priestess of Γῆ Θέμις.[2] The final request to the god would then be that he should leap with his life-giving powers not into this or that particular thing but into the earth itself. Mythologically this would be admirably appropriate, since it was Gaia who received the child Zeus in Crete and saw to his safety (Hes. *Theog.* 479 ff.).

Who sang the Hymn? The first editors called it a 'Hymn of the Curetes' and assumed that it was sung by a choir who took their part and identified themselves with them. That this is possible in principle is clear from the existence of an ἀρχεῖον Κουρήτων at Ephesus, who held yearly συμπόσια and μυστικαὶ θυσίαι, while priests were called Κουρῆτες εὐσεβεῖς (Strab. 640).[3] But to this view there are serious objections. First, the Kouretes were renowned for their vigorous weapon-dance, which was said to have been derived from the time when they protected the young Zeus with the din of it, but here such a dance is out of the question. Not only the steady procession of strophes and refrains but the word στάντες rule out any possibility of it. Nor does the Hymn at any point refer to weapons other than the shield with which the Kouretes once protected the young Zeus. These belong to the past and have no place in the present. Secondly, the Hymn summons the Kouretes as δαίμονες, and this means that the

[1] I have kept the ποντοφόρος of the stone. It is easy to change to ποντοπόρος, especially as ποντοφόρος is not found elsewhere, but it is a possible form and may well be right.
[2] L. Weniger, in Roscher, *Lex. Myth.* v. 583.
[3] F. Schwenn, *R-.E.* xi. 2205.

singers cannot see themselves as Kouretes. Nor, if they did, would they refer to their past activities in the third person. There is in fact no reason to think that the choir see themselves as anything else than worshippers, and this is our only clue to their identification. It is clear that they belong to Dikte and are connected with the cult of Zeus Diktaios. They may be priests of the temple or, more probably, young men specially appointed for this task, and that would explain why towards the end of the Hymn they ask the god to leap κὲς ν[έος πολ]είτας (30). The words come with a special emphasis because the singers who take part in the rite are themselves young men and appropriately represent all such in the participating cities.

The Hymn has both a pre-history and a history. Its origins lie in the Minoan cult of a young god who is responsible for fertility in human beings and natural things and, like other gods of animals and vegetation, was once thought to be born yearly and to die yearly. He was then connected with the Dictaean Cave, and Hesiod may have known something about him when he told how Rhea brought the unborn Zeus to Lyttos in Crete and hid him:

ἄντρῳ ἐν ἠλιβάτῳ ζαθέης ὑπὸ κεύθεσι γαίης,
Αἰγαίῳ ἐν ὄρει πεπυκασμένῳ ὑλήεντι.   (*Theog.* 483–4)[1]

When the cave fell into disuse and oblivion, the rite continued near Heleia. Because the god has lost his old seat, he is summoned to the new, which is called by the same name. But the Hymn itself still reflects a very ancient side of his character. The absence of the name Zeus means that the κοῦρος, though a son of Kronos and identifiable with Zeus, is addressed not by his name but by a more ancient, less personal, and more specific title, and this is a tribute to the peculiarity of his role. With him the Kouretes, who have kept a place in local worship, are closely associated, and this too is a survival from the distant past. In some respects the Hymn reflects a diminished conception of the god. His yearly birth and death, even the existence of his cave, are forgotten, but at the same time his old functions as a fertility-god have been extended from physical activities to social. None the less the Hymn remains true to him as a giver and renewer of

[1] Since Mount Aigaion is near Lyttos, it cannot be Mount Ida, and may conceivably be the mountain above Psychro which contains the cave. See M. L. West, *Hesiod: Theogony*, 297–300.

life, and its first, almost its only function, is to ask him to perform his immemorial tasks in this character.

The refrain was probably composed first. It contains everything needed for the essential purpose of the ceremony, and the strophes do no more than amplify and illustrate it. It looks like the work of a good period, and though we know too little about Cretan poetry to date it with any exactness, it could perhaps have been composed in the fifth century. Though the form βέβακες comes from the Hellenistic κοινή and has parallels in the Septuagint,[1] it has simply replaced βέβακας, while ἀγώμενος is a correct Cretan formation,[2] and ἕρπε, as we have seen, is authentic vernacular. γάνος raises a more difficult question. It may be a literary word of no great antiquity, picked up from poetry, but the absence of any close parallels leaves open the possibility that it is almost a cult-word such as we might expect at the beginning of a Hymn. More significant is the special use of κοῦρε. The word is of ancient lineage, being found in the form *ko-wo* in Linear B tablets from Knossos and Pylos,[3] where it seems to mean 'youth'. In later Greek it usually means 'child' or 'boy', but in some districts it has kept its Mycenaean meaning and passed into Dorian parlance (Eustath. 1535. 49 κῶρος . . . ἅμα καὶ Δωρικὸς ὁ νέος). That it existed in Crete may be deduced from the use there of the diminutive κωράλισκος in the sense of μειράκιον (Phot. Lex. κωράλισκος). In the Hymn κοῦρε means 'youth' and must have belonged to the rite almost from the first days, when it was transferred from Minoan to Greek, and round it almost everything else gathers. Κρόνειε is no less remarkable. It occurs nowhere else,[4] and since the common alternative Κρονίων would have been metrically just as satisfactory, we must assume that Κρόνειε had ancient local associations which could not be disregarded. The refrain shows early elements, and, since it seems to be free of later literary influences, it may be placed in the fifth century, though there may have been earlier, less polished versions before it reached its present shape.

Once the refrain was composed and accepted and incorporated into the rite, strophes could be added at will to widen the scope

[1] Jannaris, *Historical Greek Grammar*, s. 798, quoted by Powell, 162.
[2] C. D. Buck, *Greek Dialects*[2], 42.
[3] Ventris–Chadwick, *Documents in Mycenaean Greek*, 398.
[4] The word is not given by Liddell–Scott–Jones.

and increase the significance of the whole occasion. So far as the vocabulary of the Hymn is concerned, it is in the main a poetical κοινή varied by one or two specifically Cretan features. οὐερκῆ (5) is paralleled by οὐεργέταυς (*G.D.I.* 5148. 10); κατῆτος (19) is probably to be explained as a contraction of κατὰ ϝέτος, and though the elimination of the digamma indicates that it cannot be early, its unusual character suggests that it is at least authentic. The treatment of ναᾶς as a monosyllable in 29 has a precedent in the Homeric treatment of νέα in ι 283, and the similar treatment of τεόν in 5 has a parallel in Praxilla (fr. 748/2 P.). Yet the strophes look later than the refrain. Strophes 2–4, which tell of the past activities of the Kouretes, come indeed from indigenous legend, but 4 has surely been touched by later influences when it gives leading parts to such abstractions as Justice and Peace. The free and easy metre of the strophes suggests the fourth century at the earliest, but they need not all have been composed at the same time, and it is tempting to think that strophe 6, with its wide generalities and its shift in the meaning of θόρε, is later than strophe 5, which deals with the primary activities of the young god. A Hymn of this character could easily pass through several stages as it was adapted to incorporate new notions, and if it lost some of its first precision on the nature of the god, it extended his activities in new directions. If from one angle we regard the Hymn as a provincial composition from the fourth and later centuries, from another angle it is seen to reach back to a remote past and contain relics of a religion which flourished in Crete before the first Greeks came.

XVI

MELINNO'S HYMN TO ROME[1]

IN his collection of passages περὶ ἀνδρείας Stobaeus (*Ecl.* 3. 7. 12) quotes a poem in five Sapphic stanzas and, in introducing it with the words Μελιννοῦς Λεσβίας εἰς ῥώμην, blunders. The poem, as Grotius saw long ago,[2] is addressed not εἰς ῥώμην, to physical strength, but εἰς ῾Ρώμην, to Rome, and has in fact nothing to do with ἀνδρεία. Nor is there any good reason to think that the authoress came from Lesbos. Though she uses the Sapphic stanza, she does not use the Lesbian dialect, and such faint echoes of it as can be detected like κάρτος in 7 and ὑπὰ σδεύγλᾳ in 9 are countered by demonstrably non-Lesbian forms like κρατερῶν in 9 and κρατίστους in 17. The poem is written not in the vernacular of Sappho and Alcaeus but in the mixed, artificial language familiar from choral poetry. The text may be presented as Diehl gives it:[3]

χαῖρέ μοι ῾Ρώμα, θυγάτηρ Ἄρηος,
χρυσεομίτρα δαΐφρων ἄνασσα,
σεμνὸν ἃ ναίεις ἐπὶ γᾶς Ὄλυμπον
4   αἰὲν ἄθραυστον.

σοὶ μόνᾳ, πρέσβιστα, δέδωκε Μοῖρα
κῦδος ἀρρήκτω βασιλῆον ἀρχᾶς,
ὄφρα κοιρανῆον ἔχοισα κάρτος
8   ἀγεμονεύῃς.

σᾷ δ' ὑπὰ σδεύγλᾳ κρατερῶν λεπάδνων
στέρνα γαίας καὶ πολίας θαλάσσας
σφίγγεται· σὺ δ' ἀσφαλέως κυβερνᾷς
12   ἄστεα λαῶν.

πάντα δὲ σφάλλων ὁ μέγιστος αἰὼν
καὶ μεταπλάσσων βίον ἄλλοτ' ἄλλως
σοὶ μόνᾳ πλησίστιον οὖρον ἀρχᾶς
16   οὐ μεταβάλλει.

[1] First published in *Journal of Roman Studies*, xlvii (1957), 21–8.
[2] *Dict. Poet.* 522, putavit haud dubie Stobaeus ῾Ρώμην hic esse ἀνδρείαν.
[3] *Anth. Lyr. Graec.* ii². 315–16.

ἦ γὰρ ἐκ πάντων σὺ μόνα κρατίστους
ἄνδρας αἰχματὰς μεγάλους λοχεύεις
εὔστοχον Δάματρος ὅπως ἀνεῖσα
20 καρπὸν ἀπ' ἀνδρῶν.

Some details are uncertain.[1] There is no good reason for reading εὔστοχον instead of εὔσταχυν in 19, and surely ἀπ' ἀνδρῶν at the end cannot be right, and we ought to read something like Bergk's ἀπ' ἀγρῶν or Buecheler's ἄρουρα. But the main sense is clear enough, and the problems are rather of character, contents, and date. The poem is an oddity which calls for attention.

The poem is obviously a ὕμνος in honour of Rome, who is treated as a goddess, as *dea Roma*. She is addressed formally with χαῖρε at the start, as Alcaeus addresses Hermes (fr. 308 L.–P.) or Pindar Delos (fr. 78. 1 Bo.; 87 Sn.). In using the Sapphic stanza for such a purpose Melinno follows the precedent of Sappho, who uses it for Aphrodite (fr. 1 L.–P.) and the Nereids (fr. 5), and of Alcaeus, who uses it for Hermes (fr. 308 L.–P.), Zeus (fr. 69), and the Dioscuri (fr. 34). It is remarkable that this poem, which cannot have been written before the third century B.C. at the earliest, should go back to the sixth for its metre. Between Sappho and Alcaeus on the one hand and Melinno on the other we have only a single Sapphic stanza in Greek, and that is a forgery designed to prove that Sappho was in love with Anacreon, and used by Chamaeleon for his book on Sappho. Athenaeus, who quotes it (13. 599 c), rightly says that it is clear to everyone that it is not the work of Sappho, but since it is our only surviving specimen of the stanza in the intervening period, it is interesting because it shows how a Greek of the fourth century handled the form and how unable he was to catch its essential melody and ease of movement:

κεῖνον, ὦ χρυσόθρονε Μοῦσ', ἔνισπες
ὕμνον, ἐκ τᾶς καλλιγύναικος ἐσθλᾶς
Τήϊος χώρας ὃν ἄειδε τερπνῶς
πρέσβυς ἀγανός.

Like Melinno's poem, this has a slow, cumbrous progress, quite unlike that of Sappho or Alcaeus. The adjectives are too weighty for their place, and the order of words is too contorted for the old style. These considerations suggest that after the heyday of

[1] The latest discussions known to me are by H. Hommel, *Die Antike*, xviii (1942), 155–8, and W. Schubart, *Philologus*, xcvii (1948), 319–20.

Lesbian song the Sapphic stanza was not much used, and that, when it was, poets had no real feeling for it. We do not know why Melinno chose it for her hymn. Perhaps it had been revived in her time; perhaps she admired the Lesbian poets. In either case the poem is metrically a unique specimen for its date, and shows what unexpected things could happen to Greek poetry in the Hellenistic or Graeco-Roman age.

The five stanzas of the poem are sharply separated from one another. Each is complete in itself and ends with a full stop. This is not the practice of Sappho or Alcaeus, or of Catullus and Horace in poems whose technique is largely taken from Lesbian models. But it is the practice of Statius in *Siluae*, 4. 7, where each of the fourteen stanzas ends with a full stop or something equally decisive. This has led some scholars to think that Melinno wrote in the period between Horace and Statius and was influenced by Roman metrical practice.[1] This is highly disputable, since Greek poets took surprisingly little notice of Latin poetry at any time and shaped their technique without reference to its methods, which were governed by different linguistic needs and capacities. Just as the later Greek hexameter and elegiac owe nothing to Latin models, so there is no reason to think that the Greek Sapphic was less independent. None the less, Melinno's method of construction is worthy of notice, since it is contrary to the usage not merely of Greek Sapphics but of much Greek lyrical poetry, which in general likes its sentences to break through the confines of strophes and overflow from one to another. We may conjecture that Melinno adopted this strict isolation of strophes for a ritual reason, that the song was sung, as it were, at five stations, and that is why it is divided in this rigorous way. So *Olympian* 5, whether it is the work of Pindar or of a Sicilian imitator, moves through three stages of a ceremony, each of which is marked by a self-contained triad. If Melinno's hymn was performed in this way, it helps to explain why Horace used Sapphics for his *Carmen Saeculare*, which is plainly ceremonial and planned on a neatly balanced scheme. It is possible that he found his model in Greek hymns, like that of Melinno,[2] which met not entirely dissimilar needs.

[1] H. Usener, *Rh. Mus.* lv (1900), 290; T. Birt, *Ind. Lect. Marb.* 1887, xii, and *Horaz' Lieder*, 145.
[2] L. P. Wilkinson, *Horace and his Lyric Poetry*, 11, says that Melinno and Catullus

The composition of a Greek hymn to Rome presented special problems, because the subject had very little tradition behind it and was not easily adapted to the usual technique of mythological illustration. Old Greek ideas and images must be turned to this new purpose, and the result must be impressive and convincing. Whatever we may think of Melinno's purely poetical gifts, we cannot deny that she faces her task with invention and ingenuity. She begins by making Rome a daughter of Ares. Rome had long been connected with Mars, and it was simple for Ovid (*Trist.* 3. 7. 52), the author of the *Consolatio ad Liuiam* (246), and Martial (5. 19. 5) to speak of *Martia Roma*. For them the alleged parentage of Romulus and Remus would justify some not very precise connection between Rome and Mars. But Melinno goes her own way, and we may appreciate her reasons. So new a deity as Rome had to have a suitable parent, and Ares was excellent in every respect for so belligerent a daughter. We can even see how Melinno's ascription of parentage arose. Ares was the father of the Amazon Penthesilea, as we know from the *Aethiopis*:

Ἄρηος θυγάτηρ μεγαλήτορος ἀνδροφόνοιο,   (fr. 1 Allen)

and from what Quintus of Smyrna makes Penthesilea say:

καὶ γάρ μευ γένος ἐστὶν ἀρήϊον, οὐδέ με θνητὸς
γείνατ' ἀνήρ, ἀλλ' αὐτὸς Ἄρης ἀκόρητος ὁμοκλῆς.
(1. 560–1)[1]

He was, also, according to Apollonius Rhodius, father of all the Amazons:

ἀλλ' ὕβρις στονόεσσα καὶ Ἄρεος ἔργα μεμήλει·
δὴ γὰρ καὶ γενεὴν ἔσαν Ἄρεος Ἁρμονίης τε
νύμφης, ἥ τ' Ἄρηϊ φιλοπτολέμους τέκε κούρας.
(*Arg.* 2. 989–91)

Though Ares is credited with a large number of children (Hygin. *Fab.* 159), the Amazons are his only known daughters, and it

'both show as marked tendencies what Horace later established as rules'. This seems to be true of (1) the break after the fifth syllable, which Melinno uses nine times in a possible fifteen; and (2) the preference for a long syllable in the fourth place in the line, which she keeps in every place but two. In neither of these need we see Latin influence, but it is just conceivable that Horace, who went further in both directions, found precedent in Hellenistic Sapphics for this usage which suited the Latin language better than did the practice of Sappho and Alcaeus.

[1] The same account is stated or implied by Diod. 2. 46. 5; Apollodor. *Epit.* 5. 1; Quint. Smyrn. 1. 5; Hyg. *Fab.* 12; Serv. *Aen.* 1. 491; Verg. *Aen.* 11. 661.

would be easy for a Greek to take Melinno's hint that Rome, as a daughter of Ares, belongs to the same breed as the Amazons and shares their warlike propensities.

This view gets some support from two small points. Melinno calls Rome χρυσεομίτρα. The word might mean no more than 'with a diadem of gold'; for this is a familiar use of μίτρα in Hellenistic times (Plut. *Demetr.* 41; Theocr. 17. 19; Call. *H.* 4. 166; Athen. 12. 536 a), but when it is applied to Amazons, it may refer to their girdle or ζωστήρ. Nonnus (*Dion.* 25. 250) uses the word in this sense, but the idea is much older. Originally the girdle seems to have been regarded as the seat of an Amazon's strength or superiority, and Apollodorus speaks of the girdle of Hippolyte, which Herakles takes from her, as the σύμβολον τοῦ πρωτεύειν ἁπασῶν (*Bibl.* 2. 5. 9). When Rome is given a golden girdle it is a sign of her unusual and special strength. Secondly, Melinno's adjective δαΐφρων may be significant in the same connection. It means 'warlike' and is applied by Quintus of Smyrna to Penthesilea δαΐφρονι Πενθεσιλείῃ (1. 47). He surely got it from some ancient source like the *Aethiopis*, and when Melinno uses it, she adds another small touch to her portrait of Rome as resembling an Amazon.

The association of Rome with Ares may have served other purposes than to emphasize how warlike she is. It was natural to associate her, as a newly arrived divinity, with some other god of more august antecedents and to combine her worship with his. Marianus (fr. 1 Morel) makes her a daughter of Aesculapius, and no doubt she shared his rites and was through him connected with Apollo. At Athens Rome was worshipped with Demos and the Charites (*I.G.* iii. 63). In 163 B.C. the Rhodians set up a colossal statue of the Roman people in the temple of Athene (Polyb. 31. 4). When Quintus Lutatius Catulus restored the Capitol, he had a small figure of Rome set in the hand of Jupiter (Dio Cass. 40. 2. 3). But the most illuminating testimony of the association of Rome with other divinities can be seen in the Paean which the girls of Chalcis sang in honour of Titus Flamininus:

πίστιν δὲ 'Ρωμαίων σέβομεν
τὰν μεγαλειοτάταν ὅρκοις φυλάσσειν.
μέλπετε, κοῦραι,
Ζῆνα μέγαν 'Ρώμαν τε
Τίτον θ' ἅμα 'Ρωμαίων τε

πίστιν· ἰὴ ἰέ Παιάν·
ὦ Τίτε σῶτερ.[1]

Here Rome and the Roman *fides* are asssociated with Zeus on the one hand and with Titus Flamininus on the other. The company is more mixed than in Melinno's hymn, but both poems follow the principle that Rome should be brought into a close relation with a powerful god whose antecedents are beyond question.

Having established Rome as a warrior-goddess, Melinno then says that 'upon earth she has for dwelling-place Olympus for ever unshaken'. Behind this lies the ancient conception that the gods have an everlasting abode on Olympus. This is the θεῶν ἕδος ἀσφαλὲς αἰεί of Homer (ζ 42) and the ἀσφαλὲς αἰὲν ἕδος of Pindar (*N.* 6. 3), but Melinno differs from them by moving her goddess from the sky to earth and settling Olympus firmly ἐπὶ γᾶς. Her idea is that Olympus, as the abode of the gods, is not a physical place on the top of a mountain or in the sky but a spiritual situation on earth, where those who have earned divinity receive their honours. This conception of Olympus is to be found, in a similar connection, in Virgil, when he says:

> illa incluta Roma
> imperium terris, animos aequabit Olympo,
> *(Aen.* 6. 781–2)

and not very differently in Manilius:

> Italia in summa, quam rerum maxima Roma
> imposuit terris caeloque adiungitur ipsa.[2]   (4. 694–5)

The notion was current in the Greek East, as we can see from an oracle, probably of Jewish origin *(Or. Sib.* 7. 108–13), which presents the same idea from a hostile point of view:

> Ῥώμη καρτερόθυμε, Μακεδονίην μετὰ λόγχην
> ἀστράπτεις ἐς Ὄλυμπον· θεὸς δέ σε πάμπαν ἄπυστον
> ποιήσει, ὁπόταν δοκέῃς πολὺ κρεῖσσον ἐς ὄμμα
> ἑδραίη μίμνειν· τότε σοι τοιαῦτα βοήσω·
> ὀλλυμένη . . .

In these cases Olympus stands for a certain magnificence or glory and is applied to Rome. But the idea, in other applications, was already familiar in the Hellenistic age. It can be seen in

[1] J. U. Powell, *Coll. Alex.* 173.
[2] D. R. Shackleton-Bailey, *C.Q.* n.s. vi (1956), 85, changes *ipsa* to *ipsi*. Housman ad loc. compares Rutil. Nam. 1. 48–50.

the lines on Zeno, which Diogenes Laertius (7. 29) assigns to Antipater of Sidon:

τῆνος ὅδε Ζήνων Κιτίῳ φίλος, ὅς ποτ' Ὄλυμπον
ἔδραμεν, οὐκ Ὄσσῃ Πήλιον ἀνθέμενος,
οὐδὲ τά γ' Ἡρακλῆος ἀέθλεε· τὰν δέ ποτ' ἄστρα
ἀτραπιτὸν μούνας εὗρε σαοφροσύνας.

The same notion is implicit in the remark which a Laconian is said to have made to the great Rhodian athlete Diagoras, κάτθανε, Διαγόρα, οὐκ εἰς τὸν Ὄλυμπον ἀναβήσῃ (Plut. *Pelop*. 34), meaning that Diagoras could never again hope for such felicity as he enjoyed at this moment. Nor was the idea confined to individuals, as we can see from the Athenian demagogues, who in the Chremonidean War, which ended in 263/2 B.C. said: τἆλλα μὲν πάντα εἶναι κοινὰ τῶν Ἑλλήνων, τὴν δ' ἐπὶ τὸν οὐρανὸν ἀνθρώπους φέρουσαν ὁδὸν Ἀθηναίους εἰδέναι μόνους (Athen. 6. 250 f.). Melinno differs only in fixing Rome more firmly on the earth and having a clearer picture of what such a nation can be.

This power, Melinno continues, has been given to Rome by μοῖρα or Fate. Her reduction of the three Fates to one, and the powerful part which she gives to it, might suggest that here Melinno is influenced by some Roman notion that Fate has given to Rome power that cannot be broken. We recall Jupiter's words in the *Aeneid*, when, after saying that he is revealing *fatorum arcana* (1. 262), he goes on the explain what this means to Rome:

his ego nec metas rerum nec tempora pono:
imperium sine fine dedi. (1. 278–9)

The parallel is certainly close, but there is no need to conclude that Melinno got her idea from Augustan Rome. Ideas of this kind were in the air some time earlier and percolated to Greek historians. The notion that Rome was guided by an irresistible destiny was at least as old as Polybius, who at the beginning of his history says: ἡ τύχη σχεδὸν ἅπαντα τὰ τῆς οἰκουμένης πράγματα πρὸς ἓν ἔκλινε μέρος· καὶ πάντα νεύειν ἠνάγκασε πρὸς ἕνα καὶ τὸν αὐτὸν σκοπόν (1. 4. 4). It is true that τύχη is not quite the same as μοῖρα and that Melinno implies a more embracing determinism than Polybius, but in this passage at least, despite somewhat different views elsewhere (1. 63. 9; 2. 38. 5),[1] he goes far in

[1] J. B. Bury, *The Ancient Greek Historians*, 202 ff.; F. W. Walbank, *Commentary on Polybius*, 1. 16–25.

ascribing the growth of Rome to superhuman agency and expresses it in terms not unlike Melinno's; for he stresses the singleness of purpose in τύχη and makes it so like μοῖρα that it is virtually impossible to distinguish between them. His words show that in the second century B.C. it was possible to anticipate views held later in the *Aeneid*.

Melinno attributes to Rome that rule over land and sea which had for some time been a commonplace of Hellenistic rhetoric and was applied to Ptolemy Philadelphus (Theocr. 17. 91–2), Philip of Macedon (*A.P.* 9. 518), and the Rhodians (ib. 6. 171).[1] The same notion was applied to Rome and makes a mysterious appearance in the text of Lycophron:

γένους δὲ πάππων τῶν ἐμῶν αὖθις κλέος
μέγιστον αὐξήσουσιν ἄμναμοί ποτε,
αἰχμαῖς τὸ πρωτόλειον ἄραντες στέφος,
γῆς καὶ θαλάσσης σκῆπτρα καὶ μοναρχίαν
λαβόντες.   (*Alex.* 1226–30)

Melinno was well acquainted with this idea and builds it into an elaborate image. In her third stanza, 9–12, her metaphor is of a team yoked and held in strict control. The yoke, σδεύγλα, and its straps, λέπαδνα, are fastened on the breasts of land and sea. The word στέρνα, used by Homer of horses (Ψ 365, 508), adds to the picture of a team, and σφίγγεται emphasizes the firm control which Rome has of land and sea as she drives them. Behind this imagery lies the use of such adjectives as βαθύστερνος for both land (Pind. *N.* 9. 25; *Cypr.* fr. 1. 2) and sea (*Orph. Hymn*, 17. 3) and of parallel phrases like νῶτα θαλάσσης (*B* 159) and νῶτα γαίης (Pind. *P.* 4. 26). The way to Melinno's picture of Rome has been prepared by earlier poetry, and indeed she presupposes more than this. When Rome is presented as driving a chariot, it is an extension of a familiar, well-attested image. So Simonides, addressing himself, says:

τοσσάκι δ' ἱμερόεντα διδαξάμενος χορὸν ἀνδρῶν
εὐδόξου Νίκης ἀγλαὸν ἅρμ' ἐπέβης.   (fr. 79. 3–4 D.)

So, too, Cratisthenes of Cyrene erected at Delphi a bronze chariot which contained a figure of himself and another of Victory at his side (Paus. 6. 18. 1). A chariot was traditionally a symbol of victory and glory and is well fitted to Melinno's

[1] A. Momigliano, 'Terra Marique', *J.R.S.* xxxii (1942), 53–64.

conception of Rome. Nor are the following words inconsistent with it. Though at first sight κυβερνᾷς suggests the different imagery of a ship, it could be used for chariots (Plat. *Theag.* 123 b) and applied to government (Pind. *P.* 10. 72; Eur. *Supp.* 880). So the whole stanza gives a picture, not indeed precise but still coherent, in which Rome, like Victory, drives Earth and Sea in her chariot-team. It is instructive to compare this with Virgil's simile which likens Rome to Cybele:

> qualis Berecyntia mater
> inuehitur curru Phrygiae turrita per urbes
> laeta deum partu, centum complexa nepotes,
> omnis caelicolas, omnis supera alta tenentes.
>
> (*Aen.* 6. 784–7)

Both for Melinno and for Virgil Rome rides triumphantly in a chariot and dominates the world from it, but while Virgil suggests the role of Rome as the mother and the nurse of peoples, for Melinno she is first and foremost the conqueror and the ruler. No hint is given of blessings brought by the *pax Romana*; Rome is praised simply for her power.

The phrase ἄστεα λαῶν, with which Melinno ends the third stanza, has been thought to have a more technical and more precise meaning than we might at first see in it, and these 'cannot be the great lands, kingdoms, and peoples' conquered in the extension of the empire but must be the 'separate cities of south Italy and Etruria'.[1] But we may doubt whether Melinno's language, which employs so much traditional material, can be pressed on such a matter. Surely she has in mind what Homer says of Odysseus.

> πολλῶν δ' ἀνθρώπων ἴδεν ἄστεα καὶ νόον ἔγνω. (α 3)

Her ἄστεα λαῶν are no more than Homer's ἀνθρώπων ἄστεα. This use of λαῶν in the plural to mean 'men' is common in Homer and survives in Pindar (*O.* 9. 46), Aeschylus (*Supp.* 90), and Euripides (*Hec.* 553; *Hel.* 1329; *Supp.* 669). Melinno speaks of the 'cities of men' in the sense of the known world which is governed by Rome.

The notion that Rome's dominion is everlasting appears in the first three stanzas in αἰὲν ἄθραυστον in 4, ἀρρήκτω ἀρχᾶς in 6, and ἀσφαλέως in 11, but in the fourth stanza it is stressed by answering, as it were, an imaginary objection that, since all things change,

[1] W. Oldfather, *R.-E.* ix. 168.

so will this also, by the assertion that to this general rule Rome provides a singular and surprising exception. Melinno starts the theme by repeating the old notion that time destroys or changes everything. For this she has precedents in Aeschylus (*Eum.* 286), Sophocles (*Ai.* 714; *O.C.* 609; fr. 954 P.), and Theodectes (fr. 9. 3–4 N.). She then proclaims that Rome alone will not be changed by time,[1] and in this she assumes another related notion, familiar from funeral speeches and epitaphs, that glory won by great deeds is alone immune from time. Melinno extends this beyond posthumous renown to the manifest embodiment of lasting power. She expresses her belief in the unalterable destiny of Rome through the image of a ship sailing before a favourable wind. Her words πλησίστιον οὖρον come from Homer, who applies them to the wind sent by Circe to carry Odysseus on his journeys (λ 7, μ 149),[2] but Melinno turns them to a symbolical purpose. The notion that fortune, whether for individuals or for cities, resembles a wind is at least as old as Pindar, who applies it to Hagesias of Syracuse (*O.* 6. 103 ff.), Diagoras of Rhodes (*O.* 7. 94 ff.), and Aegina (*P.* 8. 98 ff.). In each case, the wind, whether foul or fair, is but a temporary phenomenon in a world of change and uncertainty. But Melinno, who associates time closely with fate, imagines a wind which blows for ever. She takes the old idea and displays the unique character of the Roman destiny by claiming that from an otherwise universal law Rome alone is exempt.

In the last stanza Melinno compares the never-failing generations of Romans with the fruits of the earth sent forth by Demeter. It is surely going too far to take κρατίστους ἄνδρας αἰχματὰς μεγάλους of the Roman oligarchy and to read a political reference into it.[3] The phrase is traditional and has behind it such combinations as Homer's κρατερὸς αἰχμητής (Γ 179) and Pindar's ἀνδράσιν αἰχματαῖσι (*O.* 6. 86). It would hardly convey to a Greek the specific notion of aristocrats in power, and would

---

[1] Melinno's association of αἰών with μοῖρα is clear enough. αἰών gives power, and μοῖρα does not take it away. For the connection of the two cf. Eur. *Heracl.* 898–900:

πολλὰ γὰρ
τίκτει Μοῖρα τελεσσιδώ-
τειρ' Αἰών τε Χρόνου παῖς.

[2] Eur., *I.T.* 430, also refers to πλησιστίοισι πνοαῖς.

[3] Wilamowitz, *Timotheos ; die Perser*, 91, punctuating after ἄνδρας and μεγάλους.

MELINNO'S HYMN TO ROME

more probably suggest mighty soldiers like the heroes of the past. Indeed in the word εὔσταχυν Melinno seems to compare the Romans with the Σπαρτοί, the warriors who sprang from the Dragon's teeth, and are called σταχύς by Euripides (*Phoen.* 939; *Her.* 5; *Bacch.* 264), and whose rapid growth is vividly described by Apollonius Rhodius:

οἱ δ' ἤδη κατὰ πᾶσαν ἀνασταχύεσκον ἄρουραν
γηγενέες· φρῖξεν δὲ περὶ στιβαροῖς σακέεσσιν
δούρασί τ' ἀμφιγύοις κορύθεσσί τε λαμπομένῃσιν
Ἄρηος τέμενος φθισιμβρότου, ἵκετο δ' αἴγλη
νειόθεν Οὔλυμπόνδε δι' ἠέρος ἀστράπτοισα.

(*Arg.* 3. 1354–8)

Melinno's metaphor of a rich crop reveals its full range when we set it against this background of legend. There is an implicit note of praise in the suggestion that the Romans are like the Σπαρτοί, whom Pindar calls Σπαρτῶν ἱερὸν γένος ἀνδρῶν (fr. 9. 2 Bo.) and Σπαρτῶν ἀκαμαντολογχᾶν (*I.* 7. 10). Both classes are mighty warriors and progenitors of a mighty breed.

In 20 ἀπ' ἀνδρῶν is very difficult, not only because it is clumsy after ἄνδρας in 18 but because it yields a feeble sense, 'as if from men you brought forth the rich crop of Demeter's fruit'. It spoils the otherwise clear comparison between the progeny of Rome and the fruits of the earth. But even if we keep it and reject either ἀπ' ἀγρῶν or ἄρουρα, is is clear that the poem ends with this comparison. The mention of Demeter would easily suggest Gê, or Earth, with whom she is identified by Euripides (*Bacch.* 275).[1] and with whose cult her own was associated at Athens, where they had a common shrine (Paus. 1. 22. 3), and at Patrai, where in the shrine of Demeter there was an image of Gê (id. 7. 21. 11). The close connection between the two goddesses would justify the notion of Demeter as the mother of men, just as the Homeric Hymn to Earth calls her παμμήτειρα (30. 1). So, too, Demeter was sometimes identified with Cybele, notably by Euripides (*Hel.* 1301 ff.) and Melanippides (fr. 764/8 P). Melinno may not have distinguished Demeter very carefully from either of these similar goddesses. In her view Rome breeds warriors as the earth breeds crops, and the mention of Demeter serves to show that this is a divinely appointed process.

[1] E. R. Dodds *ad loc.* quotes Diod. 1. 12. 4, Sext. Emp. *Adv. Math.* 9. 189, Cic. *N.D.* 2. 67, as examples of the belief that the name Demeter meant 'Earth Mother'.

The analysis of Melinno's hymn shows that, despite its unusual structure and complex imagery, it is based on an ancient tradition of Greek poetry. It borrows freely from the past and turns its loans to elaborate new purposes. The phenomenon of Roman power is presented through an outlook steeped in literary and legendary allusion. If Melinno's imagery sometimes lacks precision, that is partly because she is attempting something new, for which the traditional technique of Greek poetry is not very well suited. But her poem belongs to a Greek tradition, and there is no evidence that she is influenced by Roman example. Though she recalls some famous effects of Virgil, the ideas behind them were already current in the Hellenistic world. So far as the literary and stylistic evidence goes, the poem looks as if it were written in the Hellenistic age, and such likeness as it may have to Roman poetry is more likely to be due to Roman imitation of Greek models than to Greek imitation of Roman. The poem is notably lacking in local or personal references, and this may be due to Melinno's desire to write in a high, detached manner worthy of her subject. The poem is a hymn to Rome composed by a Greek at a time when Rome was regarded with awe and admiration because of her power. Melinno does not celebrate the πίστις 'Ρώμης proclaimed by the coins of Locri.[1] Her attitude towards Rome is more like that of Alpheus of Mytilene, who at the end of the first century B.C. wrote:

κλεῖε, θεός, μεγάλοιο πύλας ἀκμῆτας 'Ολύμπου·
φρούρει, Ζεῦ, ζαθέαν αἰθέρος ἀκρόπολιν.
ἤδη γὰρ καὶ πόντος ὑπέζευκται δορὶ 'Ρώμης,
καὶ χθών· οὐρανίη δ' οἶμος ἔτ' ἔστ' ἄβατος.

(*A.P.* 9. 526)

No doubt many Greeks felt something like this at the unexampled rise of Rome, and Melinno gave voice to their feelings.

Of Melinno herself we know nothing. The appearance of the name Αὐτομέλιννα in an epigram of Nossis[2] may possibly suggest that the name Melinno comes from Epizephyrian Locri, but

[1] *B.M.C. Italy*, 375, nos. 15 ff.
[2] Αὐτομέλιννα τέτυκται· ἴδ' ὡς ἀγανὸν τὸ πρόσωπον
ἁμὲ ποτοπτάζειν μειλιχίως δοκέει.
ὡς ἐτύμως θυγάτηρ τᾷ ματέρι πάντα ποτῴκει.
ἦ καλὸν ὄκκα πέλῃ τέκνα γονεῦσιν ἴσα. (*A.P.* 6. 353)

Cf. F. G. Weleker, *Kleine Schriften*, 2. 163; L. Winniczuk, *Twórczość poetek greckich*, 116.

there is no reason to think that it was confined to this region, or that this reference has any connection with the poetess. The date of her poem has been much disputed. Welcker argues for soon after 295 B.C.;[1] Oldfather puts it in the heyday of the Republic between 340 and 201;[2] Wilamowitz prefers the era of senatorial ascendancy over the Greek cities before the Mithridatic wars;[3] Schmid–Stählin suggest the first century B.C.;[4] Usener and Birt are for the period between Horace and Statius. At the start we may rule out the imperial age, since a poem in praise of *dea Roma* would be almost bound to mention the Princeps, and Melinno's failure to do so suggests that she wrote under the Republic. On the other hand the third century B.C. seems a little too early. It was indeed a time of Roman expansion, but there is no indication that Rome had begun to be worshipped in Greek cities, and such a rite is presupposed in Melinno's hymn. This cult seems to have become fashionable in the first half of the second century B.C. The 'goddess Rome' was worshipped at Smyrna in 195 B.C. (Tac. *Ann.* 4. 56) and at Alabanda in 170 B.C. (Liv. 43. 6), and before long a similar worship had been established at Erythrae, Miletus, Elaea, and elsewhere.[5] In 161 B.C. Ariarathes V of Cappadocia sent a 'crown' of 10,000 gold pieces to the goddess Rome (Polyb. 32. 3. 3), and in 160 B.C. his example was followed by Demetrius I of Syria (id. 32. 6. 1). The same period saw the foundation of festivals called Ῥωμαῖα in honour of Rome, of which that at Delphi, started in 189 B.C., is the earliest known (*S.I.G.*[4] 611.3), and at least twelve others are recorded.[6] The worship of the goddess Rome and the institution of Ῥωμαῖα seem to have become less popular after the middle of the second century B.C., as might be expected after the behaviour of Mummius. Though we cannot date Melinno's hymn with any assurance, the first half of the second century is at least an appropriate time, since the cult of the goddess Rome was then lively in Greek cities and may have inspired Melinno. With this

[1] Op. cit. 160 ff.
[2] *R.-E.* ix. 168.
[3] *Timotheos: die Perser*, 71; in *Griechische Verskunst*, 128 he places it in 'die Zeit der Senatsherrschaft... vermutlich nach 133, vor Sulla'. So too U. Lisi, *Poetesse Greche*, 223.
[4] *Gesch. d. gr. Lit.* ii. 1. 326.
[5] W. W. Tarn and G. T. Griffith, *Hellenistic Civilisation*[3], 55; M. Nilsson, *Gesch. d. griech. Rel.* ii. 167 ff.
[6] Tarn–Griffith, 114; C. Pfister, *R.-E.* iA, 1061 ff.

date the literary evidence is quite consistent. Melinno s manner, learned, associative, and rich in literary echoes and mythological references, is what we expect from the second century, and even if she learned her art in some local school, there is no reason why she should not write in a special version of the general Alexandrian manner.

Melinno's hymn is something of a sport, to which the extant remains of Greek poetry present no parallel. If we compare it with the hymns of Sappho and Alcaeus, from which it is remotely and insecurely descended, it looks stiff and stilted; and indeed it lacks their ease and grace of movement and their immediate response to the calls of the heart. Its strict division into self-contained stanzas forbids the old flow and unity; each step is taken with some effort and demands a like effort of appreciation from us. Nor are its elaborate, synthetic images comparable with the simple symbols of an accepted faith on which the older poets throve. Rome may be a goddess, but she is not so vivid as the Olympians and cannot be approached in so intimate and personal a spirit. Melinno is not a distinguished poet, but she did something. She composed a hymn with its own character and conviction, which shows what impression the emergence of a new world-power made on the awestruck Greeks of the disintegrating Hellenistic world.

XVII

ORPHEUS AND EURYDICE[1]

THE story of Orpheus and Eurydice, as we normally think of it, comes from Latin poets, especially Virgil, *Georgics*, 4. 454–503 and Ovid, *Metamorphoses*, 10. 1–73, to which may be added shorter versions in *Culex*, 268–95, Seneca, *Hercules Furens*, 569–91 and *Hercules Oetaeus*, 569–91. No doubt Lucan dealt with it in his lost *Orpheus*, but the scanty fragments tell very little. The same story was known to mythographers, notably Conon, *Narrationes*, 45. 2 and Apollodorus, *Bibliotheca*, 1. 3. 3, and is presupposed alike in the rationalistic version of Pausanias 9. 30. 6 and the allegorical interpretation of Fulgentius, *Mitologiae*, 3. 10. This form of the story does not survive in Greek poetry, but we cannot doubt that it was told before Virgil, who deals with it allusively as if it were already familiar, and we may assume that it is derived from a Greek poem. We may first try to recover the main outline of the story as this poem told it.

Ovid certainly knew Virgil's treatment, but since his debt is not very striking, while some of his divergences are, we can hardly dispute that he knew the Greek original and drew directly from it. This may be demonstrated by a small and otherwise unimportant point. In Virgil the command given to Orpheus against looking back comes from Proserpina:

namque hanc dederat Proserpina legem.   (487)

On the other hand Apollodorus says that it was given by Pluto. Behind this variation we can discern the original point—that it was given by both Proserpina and Pluto; and this is in fact what Conon says and Ovid implies:

nec regia coniunx
sustinet oranti nec qui regit ima negare.   (46–7)

This missing step is provided by the *Culex*, which says that

[1] First published in *Classical Quarterly*, N.S. ii (1952), 113–26, slightly altered.

Proserpina persuaded her husband (286–7). From this we can surmise what the lost version was: Proserpina, moved by Orpheus' appeal, asks her husband to grant the release, and he consents, but adds the restriction about not looking back, which Proserpina delivers. The detail is trivial but indicates that, if on this point Ovid moved independently of Virgil and got his information direct from the Greek poem, he is likely to have done so on other points also.

Something about this lost poem may be deduced from other divergences between Virgil and Ovid. First, they differ about the occasion of Eurydice's death. While Virgil says that she was running away from Aristaeus when the snake bit her, Ovid says that it was soon after her wedding when she was wandering with some Naiads. The discrepancy cannot really be harmonized, and either Virgil or Ovid must have forsaken the original for a new situation. Of the two Virgil is the more likely innovator, since his introduction of Aristaeus is needed to connect the episode with what precedes it. The association of Orpheus with Aristaeus is flimsy and uncanonical, and Virgil may perhaps have based it on the legend that Aristaeus was born of a nymph on a Mount Orpheus (Nigidius Figulus ap. schol. Germanic. 154. 12 Breys). On the other hand, Ovid's association of Eurydice's death with her marriage is in the true Hellenistic taste which liked to dwell on the pathos of death in the newly wedded, as Erinna's epitaphs on Baucis show (*A.P.* 7. 710 and 712).[1] From this we may conclude that the Greek original told this part of the story very much as Ovid does, and that he drew straight from it instead of relying upon Virgil.

Secondly, Virgil and Ovid differ about Eurydice's behaviour after Orpheus has looked back. Virgil exercises a characteristic pathos when he makes her lament her fate and chide Orpheus for it:

> illa 'quis et me' inquit 'miseram et te perdidit, Orpheu,
> quis tantus furor? en iterum crudelia retro
> fata uocant, conditque natantia lumina somnus.
> iamque uale: feror ingenti circumdata nocte
> inualidasque tibi tendens, heu non tua, palmas.'   (494–8)

[1] See also Meleager, *A.P.* 7. 182. 7 ff.; Antonius Thalles, ib. 184, 4 ff.; Antipater of Thessalonica, ib. 185. 5, and 367. 5 ff.; *Carm. Lat. Epigr.*, ed. Buecheler, i. 383. 1 ff.

Ovid is more restrained, but not less dramatic nor less moving:

> iamque iterum moriens non est de coniuge quicquam
> questa suo (quid enim nisi se quereretur amatam?)
> supremumque 'uale', quod iam uix auribus ille
> acciperet, dixit revolutaque rursus eodem est.   (60–2)

Both poets may have improved upon the Greek original, but again Ovid seems closer to it.[1] The note of despairing lamentation is so typical of Virgil, and his elaboration of it is so little what we expect from a Greek poet, that it looks as if he had seized the chance to indulge one of his favourite effects. Ovid eschews anything of the kind, perhaps because his Greek original also eschewed it. Moreover, even at this point he keeps firmly to the theme of love. His Eurydice does not complain, since her only cause of complaint would be that she is loved too much. This is thoroughly Ovidian, but it is not alien to the spirit of a Hellenistic poem on the failure of a love which seemed to be stronger than death. So perhaps here too we may through Ovid see how the Greek poet handled the situation. For him, it seems, what counted was the suddenness of the disaster and its immediate effect on Eurydice, who dies a second death,[2] utters an all but inaudible farewell, and returns whence she came.

A third point of difference may be seen in two passages in which Virgil and Ovid tell how physical nature laments for a death. In Virgil it is for Eurydice:

> at chorus aequalis Dryadum clamore supremos
> implerunt montis; flerunt Rhodopeiae arces
> altaque Pangaea et Rhesi Mauortia tellus
> atque Getae atque Hebrus et Actias Orithyia: (460–3)

in Ovid for Orpheus:

> te maestae uolucres, Orpheu, te turba ferarum,
> te rigidi silices, tua carmina saepe secutae

---

[1] E. Norden, *S.P.A.W.* 1934, 54 ff., plausibly connects the triple *fragor* which in Virgil greets Orpheus' look with a summons from the underworld, but we cannot say whether it comes from the Greek poem or from some older source, though it would hardly be, as he suggests, a poem about Orpheus' descent to Hades. The theme seems to have been elaborated, if misunderstood, by Lucan:

> gaudent a luce relictam
> Eurydicen iterum sperantes Orphea Manes,   (fr. 3 Morel)

but of course he may have taken it from Virgil.

[2] Ovid repeated this idea of a double death in a lost poem: *bis rapitur uixitque semel* (fr. 7. Morel). Cf. Seneca, *H.O.* 1089, *quae nata est iterum perit*.

fleuerunt siluae; positis te frondibus arbor
tonsa comas luxit; lacrimis quoque flumina dicunt
increuisse suis obstrusaque carbasa pullo
Naiades et Dryades passosque habuere capillos. (11. 44–8)

Verbally the two passages have little in common, but their main theme is the same and suggests that the Greek poet used it, since not only is it sufficiently striking but Ovid in his own ways repeats Virgil's main points. He too mentions the Dryads; his Naiads do duty for Orithyia, his rigid rocks for Rhodope and Pangaea, his swollen rivers for Hebrus. But assuming that the Greek original contained such a theme, did it apply to Orpheus or to Eurydice? Is Virgil's version or Ovid's the more faithful? On the whole, Virgil's seems to be. His opening mention of the Dryads is much more apt for Eurydice than for Orpheus, since, as Servius correctly infers (ad *G.* 4. 460), she was a Dryad, and the Vatican Mythographer (2. 44) and Fulgentius (3. 10) pick up a hint from Virgil in calling her a Nymph. Virgil's resounding proper names and Greek prosody suggest that he kept fairly close to a Greek model, which must surely have been concerned with a Dryad in a Thracian setting, while Ovid's lack of precision indicates that he found the Greek passage not quite apt for the death of Orpheus and therefore reduced it to more general terms. Finally in Virgil the lamentation of nature is followed easily and naturally by the lamentation of Orpheus, which Ovid seems to find a little inconvenient and dismisses rather summarily, though we may detect a Greek echo when he calls Orpheus 'Rhodopeius' (10. 50). It looks as if here Virgil followed the original and gave to weeping nature a similar place in his scheme.

A fourth point of comparison comes not between Virgil and Ovid but between them and the *Culex*. While Virgil and Ovid make Orpheus' fault lie simply in turning round to look at Eurydice, the *Culex* advances a different explanation:

illa quidem nimium manes experta seueros
praeceptum signabat iter nec rettulit intus
lumina nec diuae corrupit munera lingua;
sed tu crudelis, crudelis tu magis, Orpheu,
oscula cara petens rupisti iussa deorum. (289–93)

Here are three points of divergence. First, the command is given

ORPHEUS AND EURYDICE 217

to Eurydice as well as to Orpheus, and she obeys, while he disobeys. Secondly, when he turns round, it is with a desire to kiss her. Thirdly, the command is not only against looking round but against speaking. The poet's fancy has clearly been at work, and we may surmise what the original command was—that Orpheus was not so much forbidden to look back at Eurydice as to look back at all, and this was not a test of his patience or his obedience, but an application of the old rule that the living should keep their eyes averted from the dead.

From Virgil and Ovid, with some help from the *Culex*, we can reconstruct the main features of the lost poem. In so far as they agree, they probably reproduce its episodes, and their minor points of disagreement help to fill in the picture by suggesting what the lost details were. Of course it is likely that they added their own touches, as when Ovid says that Eurydice is still limping from her wound (49). None the less the agreement is substantial and gives a coherent story. This evidence may be supplemented on a few points by other authorities. We have seen that Conon states that the command was given by both Pluto and Persephone, and we may assume that he got this from the lost poem. According to Apollodorus, Orpheus was told not to turn round till he got home. This is not quite consistent with not turning round before leaving Hades, and may reflect the Greek version, especially as Apollodorus, who ignores Roman literature, is unlikely to have drawn on Virgil and Ovid. The evidence from Seneca is harder to assess. He agrees with Ovid on several points, and may have got them from him, and in that case we cannot be sure that Ovid did not invent them. If, however, Seneca derives points from the Greek poem, that not only makes him an additional witness, but affords some assurance that points made both by him and Ovid but not by Virgil are also of Greek origin. On the whole it looks as if Seneca knew the Greek text, since not only does his account of Charon's boat coming to Orpheus *nullo remigio* (*H.O.* 1072) seem unlikely to be his own invention, but his statement that the Parcae begin to spin again the thread of Eurydice's life (ib. 1083–4) has the support of Statius (*Theb.* 8. 58) and is sufficiently unlike Ovid's allusive reference (31) to look independent. The joint contribution of Seneca and Ovid is mainly confined to the effect of Orpheus' song on the torments of the three great sinners, Tantalus,

Sisyphus, and Tityus, and, since it is reasonably certain that the Greek poem told of a similar effect on Ixion, there is no good reason to doubt that it did the same for the three others also.

We may now try to recover the outline of the lost poem as far as the loss of Eurydice on the assumption that it was known to Virgil, Ovid, the *Culex*, Conon, and Apollodorus, and perhaps to Seneca and Statius. Orpheus marries Eurydice, but at his wedding the omens are bad, and soon afterwards, when she is out with some Naiads, she is bitten by a snake and dies. Nature laments her, and Orpheus, unable to console his grief, goes down through the cavern of Taenarum (Virgil, Ovid) to Hades. He makes his way by the power of song, which astounds the Eumenides into impotence or tears (Virgil, Ovid, Statius), draws Charon's boat to him (Seneca), quietens Cerberus (Virgil, Ovid), gathers the ghosts round him (Virgil, Ovid), halts Ixion's wheel (Virgil, Ovid, Seneca), makes Tantalus forget his thirst, stops Sisyphus from rolling his stone and the vulture from tearing the liver of Tityus (Ovid, Seneca). Orpheus then charms Proserpina and Pluto with song, with the result that Proserpina persuades Dis to release Eurydice, but the condition is added that Orpheus is not to look back until he reaches his home. The Parcae then begin to spin again the thread of Eurydice's life (Ovid, Seneca, Statius), and Orpheus departs, followed by her, but when he is almost at the entrance to the upper world (Virgil, Ovid, Seneca), he looks back and at once, with a faint cry of farewell, she dies again and fades among the shadows, while Orpheus vainly tries to embrace her. He begins to go back for her, but is prevented by Charon (Virgil, Ovid), and returns to the upper world in despair.[1]

This lost poem was surely written in the Hellenistic Age. In the first place it was emphatically a tale of tragic love, a subject not dear to earlier times but eminently dear to the centuries which produced Philetas, Euphorion, and other poets epitomized by Parthenius. To this theme our poem seems to have sacrificed any didactic or theological elements which might have been found in earlier poems on Orpheus but are lacking in Virgil and Ovid. Secondly, it told how nature laments the death of

[1] It is not certain, and perhaps not even probable, that the poem ended at this point. It may well have continued to the death of Orpheus and the miraculous fate of his severed head.

Eurydice, and in this it exploited the 'pathetic fallacy'. This does indeed make a remarkable appearance in Aeschylus (*P.V.* 431 ff.), but it was much favoured in Hellenistic times. The spontaneous demonstration of grief by mountains, trees, rivers, and animals is treated by Theocritus (1. 71; 7. 74), Bion (1. 31), *Lament for Bion* (1 ff.), and possibly by Antipater of Sidon (*A.P.* 7. 10), and bears no relation to earlier scenes in Pindar (fr. 61. 18 Bo.; 70b Sn.) and Euripides (*Bacch.* 727), where nature is stirred to ecstatic movement by a god, since there is a fundamental difference between miracles worked by a god and the unsolicited outburst of grief in natural things. Thirdly, if Virgil's proper names in this context are derived from a Greek original, it is surely from a Hellenistic poet who shared the taste of his time for this kind of learned sonority. That Virgil was not above borrowing such lines is clear from the statement of Macrobius (*Sat.* 5. 18) that

Glauco et Panopeae et Inoo Melicertae   (*G.* 1. 437)

is taken from Parthenius,

Γλαύκῳ καὶ Νηρῆϊ καὶ Ἰνώῳ Μελικέρτῃ.[1]

(fr. 20 Diehl)

This was a world in which Virgil and Ovid were equally at home, and it is as certain as such things can ever be that in telling of Orpheus and Eurydice both poets used a Hellenistic poem which had the characteristics of its kind.

The poem made the loss of Eurydice a cardinal point and was because of it a tale of love twice lost, the second time through a tragic fault. As such it has become the classic version of the story for the modern world. But though it was in the main accepted by poets and mythographers of the Roman age, there are some who seem not to take it quite as we do or at least do not pay so much attention to its fatal climax. In the *Thebaid* of Statius, Dis, complaining of the sensational intrusion of Amphiaraus into his realm, says that he regrets that he ever allowed Pirithous,

---

[1] Aulus Gellius, 13. 27, quotes the line as

Γλαύκῳ καὶ Νηρῆϊ καὶ εἰναλίῳ Μελικέρτῃ,

but Ἰνώῳ seems superior to εἰναλίῳ both because it is more likely to have been corrupted and because Lucian (or Lucillius) has it when he incorporates the line into an elegiac poem in *A.P.* 6. 164. 1.

Theseus, and Hercules to enter it, and is ashamed of his weakness in letting Orpheus persuade him to release Eurydice:

> Odrysiis etiam pudet heu! patuisse querelis
> Tartara: vidi egomet blanda inter carmina turpis
> Eumenidum lacrimas iterataque pensa Sororum.
> (*Theb.* 8. 57–9)

It is tempting to exaggerate the significance of these lines and to claim that Statius implies another version of the story, in which Eurydice came home safely; for otherwise Dis would not regret his weakness with Orpheus as he regrets it with the three heroes whom he mentions in the same context. But there is no need to make this assumption, since Dis is concerned simply with the question of unwelcome visitors from the upper world, of whom Orpheus is one, and confines himself to this theme and its disturbing consequences on his otherwise well-regulated dominion. None the less, if in fact Dis triumphed soon enough over Orpheus, he surely makes a little too much of his yielding to these entreaties and shows an unwarranted disregard of what really happened. More serious is the passage in which Manilius says:

> Oeagrius Orpheus
> et sensus scopulis et siluis addidit aures
> et Diti lacrimas et morti denique finem.
> (5. 326–8)[1]

From this we may be tempted to conclude that, since the last words contain no qualification and imply a decisive defeat of death by Orpheus, he actually succeeded in bringing Eurydice back. Of course we might argue that, since Manilius is speaking of the constellation of the Lyre, his immediate purpose is limited to the power of song. Even so he could easily have confined himself to Orpheus' persuasion of Dis and avoided the last three words. Even for a poet so fond of point and paradox as Manilius this is a curious way to speak of a man who may have conquered death temporarily but failed to enjoy his victory, and that in a peculiarly tragic way. Neither passage proves that Statius or Manilius refers to a happy ending, but both suggest that they

---

[1] No problem is raised by Manilius' other reference to Orpheus and his lyre:
> qua quondam ceperat Orpheus
> omne quod attigerat cantu, manesque per ipsos
> fecit iter domuitque infernas carmine leges. (1. 325–7)

may have known something of the kind, and just because there was more than one conclusion to Orpheus' quest, refrained from committing themselves too definitely about it.[1]

That another version existed becomes more probable when we look at some Greek authors who are less likely to have been influenced by Virgil or Ovid. First, Plutarch says: εἰ δή πού τι καὶ μύθων πρὸς πίστιν ὄφελός ἐστι, δηλοῖ τὰ περὶ Ἄλκηστιν καὶ Πρωτεσίλεων καὶ Εὐρυδίκην τὴν Ὀρφέως, ὅτι μόνῳ θεῶν ὁ Ἅιδης Ἔρωτι ποιεῖ τὸ προσταττόμενον (*Amatorius*, 17). Here Eurydice is associated with Alcestis and Protesilaus, who were by common consent restored to life; and Plutarch, with a neat allusion to the notion that alone of gods Death is inexorable,[2] adds that 'for Love alone of the gods Death does what he is told'. Eurydice's place among those whom love has brought back to life would be almost absurd if in fact she was not brought back but actually lost through an excess of love. Secondly, in his *Dialogues of the Dead* Lucian makes Protesilaus approach Pluto with a request to be allowed to return to life because of his love for his wife and argues from two precedents: ἀναμνήσω σε, ὦ Πλούτων· Ὀρφεῖ γὰρ δι' αὐτὴν ταύτην τὴν αἰτίαν τὴν Εὐρυδίκην παρέδοτε καὶ τὴν ὁμογενῆ μου Ἄλκηστιν παρεπέμψατε Ἡρακλεῖ χαριζόμενοι (*Dial. Mort.* 23. 3). Protesilaus classes Eurydice with Alcestis, and Plutarch implicitly classes her with Protesilaus. The appeal would be at least feeble if her release were a disastrous failure. Thirdly, the scholiast on Euripides, *Alcestis*, 357 (ed. E. Schwartz, ii. 227) says: 'Ὀρφέως γυνὴ Εὐρυδίκη, ἧς ἀποθανούσης ὑπὸ ὄφεως κατελθὼν καὶ τῇ μουσικῇ θέλξας τὸν Πλούτωνα καὶ τὴν Κόρην ἀνήγαγεν ἐξ ᾅδου. The aorist ἀνήγαγεν does not clinch the matter but at least suggests that Eurydice was on the edge of being brought back. These three passages do not prove that there was a version of the story which differed from the Virgilian in not ending with a tragic catastrophe, but at least they say nothing about such a catastrophe and concentrate on occasions when the dead have been brought back to life. If they do not confirm the happy ending, they equally do not confirm the unhappy.

So far we have confined ourselves to the story as it was presented in the Graeco-Roman age, but it had a considerable career

---
[1] *Aen.* 6. 119 ff. is of course concerned only with Orpheus' descent and not relevant to our question.
[2] Aesch. fr. 161 N.; Soph. fr. 770 P.; Propert. 4. 11. 2.

before Virgil took it up. In the *Alcestis*, produced in 438 B.C., Admetus says to Alcestis just before her death:

εἰ δ' Ὀρφέως μοι γλῶσσα καὶ μέλος παρῆν,
ὥστ' ἢ Κόρην Δήμητρος ἢ κείνης πόσιν
ὕμνοισι κηλήσαντά σ' ἐξ Ἅιδου λαβεῖν,
κατῆλθον ἄν, καὶ μ' οὔθ' ὁ Πλούτωνος κύων
οὔθ' οὑπὶ κώπῃ ψυχοπομπὸς ἂν Χάρων
ἔσχον, πρὶν ἐς φῶς σὸν καταστῆσαι βίον.   (357–62)

In her commentary on the play Miss A. M. Dale says 'there is nothing in this passage to indicate that Euripides is referring to such a version (in which Orpheus succeeded in bringing back Eurydice); still less can the lines be taken as evidence that a later tragic ending was not yet current in 438 B.C.'[1] This implies that the tragic version was current at this time and that Euripides knew it, but confined himself to the 'miraculous potency of Orpheus' music'. This would be admirable if we knew that the tragic version was current at this time, but there is no evidence that it was. In that case these lines of Euripides are equally and indeed more applicable to something like a happy ending. If for the moment we assume this, and Admetus suggests the possibility of success, his point is more forcible. Indeed if he knew that Orpheus failed, he would surely refer not to Cerberus and Charon, whom Orpheus subdued, but to the disobedience which ruined him, and claim that he himself would not be so feeble. Since Admetus does not say this, it is at least tenable that he thought Orpheus, in some sense, to have succeeded, and was certainly not obsessed by his story as one of total disaster.

Something of the same kind may be recognized in other passages from centuries after the fifth. In his *Busiris* Isocrates criticizes Polycrates for his praise of the brutal Busiris, and draws two contrasts: the one between Busiris, who used to eat shipwrecked mariners, and Aeolus, who used to send them away safely on ships; the other between Busiris, who used to kill men before their time, and Orpheus who used to bring back the dead τοὺς τεθνεῶτας ἀνῆγεν (11. 8). The imperfect ἀνῆγεν and the plural τοὺς τεθνεῶτας might seem to suggest that Orpheus made a habit of this, and in that case the recovery of Eurydice would be only one case among several. But this is to assume also that

[1] *Euripides: Alcestis*, 80.

Aeolus often sent men safely away, and since Odysseus is the only case in which he is known to have done this, we may conclude that the imperfects ἀπέστελλεν and ἀνῆγεν indicate not a series of actions but a habit of conduct and mean that Aeolus and Orpheus were the sort of men to behave in this way. Despite his exaggeration Isocrates clearly knows the story that Orpheus brought back someone from the underworld, and this was presumably his wife.

In the beginning of the third century the story appears in Book III of the *Leontion* of Hermesianax, which begins with Orpheus:

οἵην μὲν φίλος υἱὸς ἀνήγαγεν Οἰάγροιο
Ἀγριόπην Θρῇσσαν στειλάμενος κιθάρην
Ἀιδόθεν. (fr. 7. 1–3 Powell)

Then after a few lines on the perils through which Orpheus passes on his journey through Hades, we hear:

ἔνθεν ἀοιδιάων μεγάλους ἀνέπαισεν ἄνακτας
Ἀγριόπην μαλακοῦ πνεῦμα λαβεῖν βιότου. (13–14)

Hermesianax gives no hint of a tragic failure, and both his ἀνήγαγεν at the start and his final couplet suggest that Orpheus' wife was restored to life. It is true that he calls her Agriope, and on that we shall have something to say later, but none the less there is no essential disagreement between him and Euripides or Isocrates. Finally, at the beginning of the first century B.C. the *Lament for Bion* closes with the poet's saying that he will sing to Kore a song which will bring back Bion as Orpheus brought back Eurydice:

οὐκ ἀγέραστος
ἐσσεῖθ' ἁ μολπά· χὼς 'Ορφέϊ πρόσθεν ἔδωκεν
ἁδέα φορμίζοντι παλίσσυτον Εὐρυδίκειαν
καὶ σέ, Βίων, πέμψει τοῖς ὤρεσιν. (122–5)

So from the fifth to the first century we have a series of passages which testify that Orpheus brought his wife back from the dead but do not hint that his mission ended in disaster.[1]

[1] For what it is worth, Tzetzes, *Chil.* 2. 843 ff., seems to imply that Eurydice was brought safely back to life:

ἡ Εὐριδίκη σύζυγος ὑπῆρχε τοῦ 'Ορφέως.
ταύτην ὑπ' ὄφεως φασὶ δηχθεῖσαν τεθνηκέναι,
ἀνενεχθῆναι δὲ πρὸς φῶς πάλιν ἐκ τῶν νερτέρων
'Ορφέως Ἅιδην θέλξαντος καὶ Κόρην μουσουργίαις.

This, however, is not the end of the question. In Plato's *Symposium* Phaedrus argues that in a few cases the gods have sent back souls from the dead as a reward for great love, and gives Alcestis as an example. He then continues: Ὀρφέα δὲ τὸν Οἰάγρου ἀτελῆ ἀπέπεμψαν ἐξ Ἅιδου, φάσμα δείξαντες τῆς γυναικὸς ἐφ᾽ ἣν ἧκεν, αὐτὴν δ᾽ οὐ δόντες, ὅτι μαλθακίζεσθαι ἐδόκει, ἅτε ὢν κιθαρῳδός, καὶ οὐ τολμᾶν ἕνεκα τοῦ ἔρωτος ἀποθνῄσκειν ὥσπερ Ἄλκηστις, ἀλλὰ διαμηχανᾶσθαι ζῶν εἰσιέναι εἰς Ἅιδου (179 d). This is the version neither of Virgil nor of some happier tale, but a third, in which Orpheus neither wins back his wife alive nor loses her in trying to do so, but brings a phantom. This is partly, no doubt, Plato's invention, modelled on stories like that of the phantom Helen who went to Troy. But it must presuppose some recognizable and accepted story, if only to show its difference from it, and here a difficulty arises. Plato makes it clear that Orpheus' quest was a failure—the gods sent him back ἀτελῆ— not, however, in the Virgilian sense but in that he brought not a wife but a phantom, and this he deserved because he relied not on courage but on song. The contrast with Alcestis, who was truly and fully restored to life, is obvious, and it is clear that Eurydice's case is not like hers. The conception of such a failure is consistent with neither the accounts of success nor with the accounts of failure. It follows that the version which Plato builds is one which we have not considered. It stands halfway between two marked alternatives in its assumption that Orpheus failed, not in any heart-breaking way, but none the less sufficiently for Phaedrus to be able to say that, being after all a mere musician, he deserved it.

A clue to the story which Plato presupposes may perhaps be found in copies of an Attic relief from the last part of the fifth century.[1] On the best example, in Naples, are inscribed the names of Orpheus, Eurydice, and Hermes, and even if they are not copied from the original stone, there is no reason to dispute what they say. On the relief are three standing figures, of whom the man on the right, with a lyre and a Thracian cap, is obviously

[1] See Frontispiece. Of the copies, three—in the Museo Nazionale at Naples, the Louvre at Paris, and the Villa Albani at Rome—are complete. The other two, in the Palatine Museum at Rome and the University Collection at Oxford, Mississippi, show little more than the figure of Hermes. See D. M. Robinson in *Hommages à Joseph Bidez*, 303-11. Sir John Beazley tells me that, since we have only copies, the original relief cannot be more closely dated than between c. 430 and 400 B.C.

ORPHEUS AND EURYDICE 225

Orpheus. With his right hand he turns back the veil from the face of Eurydice, who looks at him and lays her left hand on his shoulder. Behind her is Hermes, who is about to take her right hand with his left. Attempts have been made to fit this scene into the Virgilian story, which is assumed to be the standard form.[1] First, it is suggested that this is the moment of Eurydice's death, when Hermes comes to take her to Hades. This is hard to accept, since there is no hint of the snake-wound, from which she dies and which may not perhaps matter, but, more importantly, Orpheus' calm air of resignation does not suit the wild anguish which the poets report that he suffered. A second suggestion is that it is the moment when Orpheus, having regained Eurydice, looks round and loses her. Against this it is perhaps not sufficient to argue that the scene is very unlike what Virgil and Ovid describe. They do not mention Hermes, and treat the crisis in a very different spirit. Both the disappearance in Virgil,

ceu fumus in auras
commixtus tenuis, (499–500)

and the frantic gestures of Orpheus in Ovid,

bracchiaque intendens prendique et prendere certans
nil nisi cedentes infelix adripit auras, (58–9)

are at variance with the quiet restrained figures on the relief. We need not necessarily press this, since the Hellenistic age liked the violent display of emotion as the fifth century did not, but the decisive objection remains that the relief shows far too little distress for such a catastrophe and indeed displays no distress at all.

There remains a third possibility that the relief portrays a version different from that of Virgil or Ovid and catches the moment when Eurydice, having been brought successfully to the upper world, has to return to Hades under the guidance of Hermes. This suits the action of Hermes, who lays a controlling hand on her; the resigned air of Orpheus, who may be presumed to know that this must happen; and the gentle gesture of Eurydice, who takes a calm and affectionate farewell of her husband. This is only a hypothesis, but it suits the spirit and the action of the relief. What is more, it suits Plato, who implies frustration at

[1] O. Grüppe, in Roscher, *Lex. Myth.* iii. 1194–7.

some point, and this would be that, though Orpheus regains Eurydice, it is only for a short time, at the end of which he has to give her back to Hermes. If this is correct, the story would resemble that told by Euripides in his *Protesilaus* (schol. Aristid. 671 ff.; Hygin. *Fab.* 103 and 104), in which the dead hero persuades the gods of the underworld to let him return to his wife but is allowed to do so for only a single day or less. It is true that there is no evidence that this happens to Eurydice, but that is not surprising in view of the paucity of early references to her. But it explains why Plutarch associates her with Protesilaus, and it fits the spirit and gestures of the relief. It makes it easier to understand how the Hellenistic poet was able to transform a successful recovery into a tragic failure: someone had already taken the first step by limiting the success of Orpheus. If Euripides, Isocrates, Hermesianax, and the *Lament for Bion* leave the conclusion vague, it is because there was more than one version of it. That implied by the relief gives a special twist to it, and looks as if it were the invention of an Attic tragedian whose new conception appealed to the sculptor of the relief and was known to Plato, who made his own use of it.

We may now consider the name of Orpheus' wife. Neither Euripides nor Plato nor Isocrates mentions it, while Hermesianax calls her Agriope, 'wild-eyed', which sounds suitable for a Thracian nymph, though some prefer Zoëga's emendation of Ἀργιόπη, since it is less unusual. On the other hand the name of Eurydice is carved on the Naples relief and may be derived from the fifth-century original; it is used by Plutarch and Lucian, who seem to draw on early sources; it is inscribed above a female figure in Hades on an Apulian vase of the late fourth century in Karlsruhe,[1] though she is not certainly Orpheus' wife; and it appears in the *Lament for Bion*. With this problem it is tempting to be too ingenious. We might, for instance, postulate two versions, in one of which the wife is called Agriope, because it is the name of a nymph, who went to Thrace, became the mother of Thamyris (Apollodor. *Bibl.* 1. 3. 3; Paus. 4. 33. 4; Schol. *Il.* 2. 595), and as such would be a suitable wife for Orpheus;[2] in the other she is called Eurydice because in the *Cypria* that is the name of Aeneas' wife (fr. 22 Allen), whose spectre fades away from her husband

[1] Hartwig, *Arch. Ztg.* 1884, 263, Taf. 19 b.
[2] K. Ziegler, *R.-E.* xviii. 227.

as Eurydice does from Orpheus.[1] But there is no need for such ingenuity. The Greeks were never too consistent with proper names in legends, and there is no difficulty in Orpheus' wife having one name in this poem and another in that. But at least the variation shows that at quite an early stage there were two names and therefore at least two poems, while in the later stage the name of Eurydice holds the field.

It seems then that in the fifth and fourth centuries more than one poem was known about Orpheus' descent to Hades and told how, after charming Cerberus and Charon, as Euripides and Hermesianax report, he regained his dead wife with or without the restriction that it was only for a short time. The general character of these poems may perhaps be deduced from some lines in the Orphic *Argonautica*, which seem to be derived from an early original known also to Virgil and used by him in *Aeneid* 6.[2] Speaking of the revelations contained in his sacred books, Orpheus says:

ἄλλα δέ σοι κατέλεξ' ἅπερ εἴσιδον ἠδ' ἐνόησα,
Ταίναρον ἡνίκ' ἔβην σκοτίην ὁδὸν Ἄϊδος εἴσω,
ἡμετέρῃ πίσυνος κιθάρῃ δι' ἔρωτ' ἀλόχοιο.   (40–2 p. 65 Kern.)

It is clear from this that, though Orpheus' visit to Hades was inspired by love for his dead wife, it resulted in his acquiring knowledge about the afterworld, and from this we may deduce that his descent was connected with Orphic mysteries and that the recovery of his wife did not necessarily have pride of place in it. He was already a subject of poetry in the sixth century, as Ibycus' tantalizing reference to ὀνομάκλυτον Ὀρφήν (fr. 305/25 P.) shows, but at this time his main interest seems to have lain in his gift of song and a little later in his hideous death. As a singer he took part in the voyage of the 'Argo' and is so depicted on a metope of the Sicyonian Treasury at Delphi; such he was to Simonides (fr. 567/62 P.) and, a little later, to Pindar (*P.* 4. 166–7); and such he may be on an Attic black-figured oenochoe of about 500 B.C.[3] His death was treated by a number of Attic red-figure vase-painters in the first half of the fifth century[4] and

[1] O. Grüppe in Roscher, *Lex. Myth.* iii. 1162.
[2] See E. Norden, *S.P.A.W.* 1934, 1162; *Aeneis Buch VI*, 158–9.
[3] J. D. Beazley, *Attic Black-figure Vase-Painters*, 432.
[4] J. D. Beazley, *Attic Red-figure Vase-Painters*², iii. 1729, records thirty-three instances.

by Aeschylus in his *Bassarae*. But the descent to Hades does not appear in the extant art and literature of this period, and its first emergence is hard to date. It was certainly known about 450 B.C. when Polygnotus painted his Νέκυια in the Cnidian Lesche at Delphi, since there Orpheus was depicted with his lyre in the underworld (Paus. 10. 30. 6–8). It has been argued that since Polygnotus is said by Pausanias (10. 28. 2) to have followed the *Minyas*, and the *Minyas* is attributed to Prodicus of Phocaea (id. 4. 33. 7), the story of Orpheus' descent is a creation of Prodicus, especially as Clement attributes a Κατάβασις εἰς Ἅιδου to a Prodicus of Samos (*Strom.* 1. 21). The theory is that a man called Prodicus wrote a *Descent to Hades*, also called *Minyas*, which was known to Polygnotus and contained the story of Orpheus' attempt to recover his wife from the dead. But despite Wilamowitz's advocacy,[1] this is open to a fatal objection. There is no reason to think that Polygnotus' Orpheus was in search of his wife. Pausanias does not mention her in his careful account of the painting, and, what is more important, Orpheus was depicted not as playing his lyre, an essential element in the story, but as holding it in his right hand and touching a willow-tree with his left. Polygnotus' subject was Orpheus after death and provides no evidence about his descent to Hades when alive.

The earliest known evidence for this descent is the *Alcestis*. That the story was reasonably familiar before 438 B.C. may be deduced from Euripides' words, which presuppose some knowledge in his audience. It may even have been popularized before this by references in dramas like Aeschylus' *Bassarae* and Aristias' *Orpheus*, but we have no evidence that it was. Normally such a story would be treated in narrative poetry, nor are names of poets who wrote such καταβάσεις lacking, though very little is known of them. Clement's Prodicus of Samos need not be the same as Prodicus of Phocaea, nor his Κατάβασις as the *Minyas*, and in that case nothing remains of him but a name. Clement also records that the Alexandrian scholar Epigenes, who seems to have been earlier than Callimachus, listed among Orphic works a *Descent into Hades*, which he attributed to Cercops the Pythagorean (*Strom.* 1. 21), and this was the *Orphicum carmen* known to Cicero (*N.D.* 1. 107). It is true that a poet called Cercops of Miletus was connected with Hesiod (Diog. Laert. 2. 46) and

[1] *Homerische Untersuchungen* 223–6.

was said to have written about Aegimius (Athen. 11. 503 c), but it is highly improbable that he was a Pythagorean, and in that case the Cercops who told of Orpheus is another man, of whom almost nothing is known. To these faint candidates we may add others even fainter, whose names were known to the *Suda* (s.v. 'Ορφεύς), such as Herodicus of Perinthus and Orpheus of Camarina, each of whom is credited with a *Descent of Orpheus*, and Orpheus of Croton, who is not, but is said to have been an epic poet associated with Peisistratus. These names prove very little, but they confirm the suspicion that there was more than one poem on the subject and suggest that some of the poets called themselves Orpheus because they claimed a special authority and may even have spoken in the first person, as in the later Orphic *Argonautica*, on the assumption that Orpheus himself, or his severed head, speaks.[1] All that we can say is that more than one poem on the subject was known in the middle of the fifth century. That such poems existed much earlier is unlikely, but they may have taken shape in the time of Peisistratus, when the spread of Orphic beliefs would encourage the use of Orpheus' quest for his dead wife as a means to explain why he visited the underworld and was thereby able to reveal its mysteries.

Such poems would resemble others which told of descents to Hades by heroes like Theseus and Heracles or by gods like Dionysus. Norden has shown that a *Descent of Heracles* may have provided themes in *Georgic* 4 and *Aeneid* 6, such as the comparison of the dead with birds which is used in connection with Orpheus.[2] We may also note that the whole subject has something in common with the descent of Dionysus to fetch Semele. Euripides, Hermesianax, Virgil, and Ovid all speak of the charming of Cerberus by Orpheus, and so too does Horace (*C*. 3. 11. 15–16), but Horace also makes it clear that Dionysus had a similar skill and a similar success:

> te uidit insons Cerberus aureo
> cornu decorum leniter atterens
> caudam et recedentis trilingui
> ore pedes tetigitque crura.
>
> (*C*. 2. 19. 29–32)

When Orpheus went to fetch Eurydice, he behaved as Diodorus

[1] I. Linforth, *The Arts of Orpheus*, 123 ff.
[2] *S.P.A.W.* 1934, 36–9; *Aeneis Buch vi*, 223–4.

says, παραπλησίως τῷ Διονύσῳ (4. 23. 4). No doubt the theme was interchangeable between god and man, though it would not be suitable for heroes like Heracles and Theseus.

We may, then, postulate three main stages in the story of Orpheus and Eurydice. The first may belong to the sixth century, when more than one poem told of Orpheus' descent to Hades and no doubt dealt, among other themes, with the power of song which enabled him to bring back his wife from the dead, though they did not make much of what happened to her after her recovery. Such poems would use themes familiar from the old class of καταβάσεις εἰς Ἅιδου and one or more of them survived to the time of Hermesianax and even of Virgil, both of whom seem to draw on them, when, for instance, they speak of the reeds by Acheron (fr. 7. 5–9 Powell; *G*. 4. 478–9). In the second stage, which may be due to an Attic tragedian, the theme of Eurydice's return is emphasized and elaborated in such a way that it is only for a short time, at the end of which she is reclaimed by Hermes. This version was followed by the sculptor of the relief and adapted by Plato. The third stage is represented by a lost Hellenistic poem, on which Virgil and Ovid drew freely. No doubt it owed elements to earlier poems, but it made a vitally important change by emphasizing what happened to Eurydice after her release by Pluto and turning her recovery into a tragic loss. The poet took up an ancient idea that, when gods or ghosts of the underworld are summoned, men should avert their eyes. This belief was known to Homer (κ 528), Aeschylus (*Cho.* 99), and Sophocles (*O.C.* 490; fr. 534 P.) and in the Alexandrian age to Theocritus (24. 96) and Apollonius, who shows how well he understands it when he makes Medea tell Jason that, after sacrificing to Hecate, he must on no account look round:

μή πως τὰ ἕκαστα κολούσας
οὐδ' αὐτὸς κατὰ κόσμον ἑοῖς ἑτάροισι πελάσσῃς.

(3. 1040–1)

The assumption is that, if on such an occasion a man looks round, he both frustrates his purpose and brings harm to himself. The brilliant idea of our Hellenistic poet was to apply this notion, with precisely these implications, to the story of Orpheus, who is made to lose his half-regained Eurydice by doing what no man should to the inhabitants of the underworld.

ORPHEUS AND EURYDICE

We do not know who wrote the Hellenistic poem, and though names of candidates can be put forward, their claims are very flimsy. Philetas, for instance, wrote poems of tragic love, and in his *Hermes* told of a descent to Hades (fr. 6 Powell), but it was that of Odysseus. Nicander, as the author of a Γεωργικά and a Ἑτεροιούμενα, seems to have done something for Virgil's *Georgics* and Ovid's *Metamorphoses*, but there is no hint that he told of Orpheus and Eurydice. Though Euphorion also favoured tales of tragic love and described a visit of Heracles to Hades (fr. 51 Powell), his claims are equally unsubstantial. Parthenius wrote a *Metamorphoses*, but nothing is known of it except that it told of Nisus and Scylla and was doubtless used by the pseudo-Virgilian *Ciris*. We do not know who our poet was. Nor do we know the date of his poem. A *terminus ad quem* may be set by Conon's short abstract, which explicitly mentions the loss of Eurydice. Since he dedicated his work to Archelaus Philopator (Phot. *Bibl.* 186. 330^{b}25), who became king of Cappadocia in 36 B.C., it is possible that his account is earlier than that in *Georgic* 4, which Virgil seems to have read to Octavian in the summer of 29 B.C.,[1] especially as Conon differs from Virgil in his account both of the command given to Orpheus and of his death and may be presumed to derive his information direct from a Greek source. We could place the appearance of the Greek poem earlier if we were certain that the *Culex*, or at least that part of it which tells of Orpheus, was really Virgil's youthful work, published when he was twenty-one in 48 B.C.,[2] but on this there are too many legitimate doubts for any conclusions to be based on it. A *terminus a quo* is equally uncertain, but since the *Lament for Bion* implies the earlier version of the story, it is possible that this still held sway at the beginning of the first century B.C. In that case the lost poem may be the work of this century, possibly of its middle years. Nor is this inconceivable. That its subject was to the taste of the time is clear from the thirty-six plots of love-tales which Parthenius composed for Cornelius Gallus. It is therefore surprising that it seems to have made very little impression on Greek poetry or scholarship, and that even Parthenius says nothing about it. Perhaps, apart from its new and magnificent

---

[1] Donat.–Suet. 27 (42).
[2] T. Frank, *Vergil: a Biography*, 24.
[3] See E. Fraenkel, 'The Culex', *J.R.S.* xlii (1952), 1–9.

idea of making Orpheus lose Eurydice by looking back, it was not very distinguished; or perhaps it was composed so soon before Virgil found it and made it his own that it was superseded by his version and largely neglected or forgotten. In either case it looks as if here, as elsewhere, the best composers of Hellenistic *epyllia* were Romans.

XVIII

ΕΙΠΑΤΕ ΤΩΙ ΒΑΣΙΛΗΙ[1]

No Greek poem of late antiquity has won so great a renown in modern times as three hexameter lines, which were, according to tradition, delivered by the Delphic Oracle to Julian's quaestor, the famous physician Oribasius:

εἴπατε τῷ βασιλῆι· χαμαὶ πέσε δαίδαλος αὐλά.
οὐκέτι Φοῖβος ἔχει καλύβαν, οὐ μάντιδα δάφναν,
οὐ παγὰν λαλέουσαν. ἀπέσβετο καὶ λάλον ὕδωρ.

Their modern fame, which owes much to romantic notions of the twilight of the Olympian gods, far exceeds their ancient vogue, which was, so far as we can see, small. They are quoted, with no serious variants, by the *Artemii Passio*, 35 (Philostorg. *Hist. Eccl.* 7. 77) and by Georgius Cedrenus (*Hist. Comp.* 1. 532 Bekker). Each gives an account of their delivery and provides a relative date for them. In the *Passio* Artemius, who is on trial for his life, quotes them to the emperor:

γίνωσκε τοίνυν ὡς ἡ τοῦ Χριστοῦ ἀνίκητος καὶ ἀήττητος ὑπάρχει ἰσχύς τε καὶ δύναμις· πάντως δὲ καὶ αὐτὸς πεπληροφόρησαι ἐξ ὧν σοι χρησμῶν Ὀριβάσιος ὁ ἰατρὸς καὶ κουαίστωρ παρὰ τοῦ ἐν Δελφοῖς Ἀπόλλωνος ἄρτι κεκόμικεν· ἐγὼ δέ σοι καὶ τὸν χρησμόν, κἂν μὴ βούλῃ, ἐπαναγνώσομαι· εἴπατε κ.τ.λ.

The appropriate date for this would be 362, when Artemius was summoned from Alexandria, tried, and beheaded (Amm. Mar. 22. 11. 2; Iulian. *Ep.* 10; Theodoret. *Hist. Eccl.* 3. 14; *Chron. Pasch.* 363), and the word ἄρτι suggests that the oracle had recently been given. We cannot, of course, trust the pious author's account of Artemius' speech, but we can at least note the approximate date which he gives to the oracle. Cedrenus is vaguer than this, but suggests, without drawing much attention to it, that the oracle was given to Julian soon after he became sole emperor and began to disclose his intention of reviving the pagan religion:

οὗτος μονοκράτωρ γενόμενος ἀναιδῶς ἑλλήνιζεν, αἵματι θυσιῶν τὸ ἅγιον

[1] First published in *Hermes*, lxxxvii (1959), 426–35.

ΕΙΠΑΤΕ ΤΩΙ ΒΑΣΙΛΗΙ

βάπτισμα ἀποπλυνάμενος καὶ πάντα ποιῶν οἷς οἱ δαίμονες θεραπεύονται. πέμπει οὖν 'Οριβάσιον τὸν ἰατρὸν καὶ κουαίστωρα ἐν Δελφοῖς ἀνεγεῖραι τὸν ναὸν τοῦ Ἀπόλλωνος· ἀπελθὼν οὖν αὐτὸς καὶ τοῦ ἔργου ἁψάμενος λαμβάνει χρησμὸν παρὰ τοῦ δαίμονος· εἴπατε κ.τ.λ.

This adds the point that the oracle was given when Julian was trying to revive or restore the temple of Apollo at Delphi, and seems to place it early in his reign. But perhaps we should not give too much weight to this, since the words about the temple are an easy deduction from the text of the oracle. In so far as Cedrenus suggests a date, it is not inconsistent with that suggested by the *Passio*.

This chronology is not in itself unthinkable. In the latter part of 362 Julian was at Antioch, preparing for his Parthian expedition. It is therefore natural to connect his consultation of the Delphic Oracle with his plans for war and to assume that he sent Oribasius to Delphi because he wished to find out Apollo's intentions.[1] This is not explicitly stated by either of the authorities who quote the lines, but is a reasonable deduction from them, since at this time Julian was certainly much interested in the shrine of Apollo at Daphne near Antioch (Amm. Marc. 21. 12. 8) and might easily turn his thoughts to the parent shrine at Delphi. Yet it is hard to believe that such an oracle was given at Delphi in 362. It tells Oribasius that the shrine of Apollo has fallen down and that the ancient apparatus of divination no longer exists. Who announced this from the holy place, and how, we are not told, but it presupposes the desolation of Delphi, of which Julian must have been ignorant when he sent Oribasius on his mission. Some scholars have indeed accepted the lines as an authentic utterance of the Oracle,[2] but it is hard to agree that they can be. It is true that by 362 Delphi must have lost much of its former splendour and influence. Constantine had looted some of its chief treasures, including the famous Plataean memorial, to adorn his new capital at Constantinople (Zosim. 2. 31. 1; Eus. *Vit. Constant.* 3. 54), but it kept remnants of its old prestige and had not fallen into ruins. It is significant that statues of Constantine, Constans, and Julian were erected there,[3]

[1] Hiller von Gaertringen, *R.-E.* iv. 2583.
[2] H. G. Schröder, *R.-E.* Supp.-Bd. vii. 800; H. W. Parke and D. E. W. Wormell, *The Delphic Oracle*², i. 290; W. S. Wright, *Julian*, iii. lvii; T. Dempsey, *The Delphic Oracle*, 180; F. W. H. Myers, *Classical Essays*, 100.
[3] E. Homolle, *B.C.H.* (1896), 728 ff.; Hiller von Gaertringen, *R.-E.* iv. 2582.

ΕΙΠΑΤΕ ΤΩΙ ΒΑΣΙΛΗΙ 235

since this indicates that the main buildings were extant and that the place was still held in some regard. It is moreover clear from Himerius that rites were still conducted in the temple; for in addressing Flavianus, who was proconsul of Africa in 361 (*Cod. Theod.* 11. 36. 14) and seems at the time to have been setting out for this post,[1] Himerius says Δελφοὶ δὲ ἄρα, ἱερὰ πόλις Ἀπόλλωνος, λατρεύουσι μὲν ἀεὶ τῷ θεῷ καὶ περιχορεύουσι μετὰ παιάνων τὸν τρίποδα (*Or.* 12. 6 Colonna). The speech comes from early in Julian's reign before he had had time to carry out his religious reforms, and indicates that the temple of Apollo was then intact. On the other hand its oracular activities had been declining for some time. The oracle given to the Nicaeans, which Eusebius (*Praep. Ev.* 5. 16) reports from Porphyry, indicates that in the third century it had lost its old skill and confidence,[2] and all such activities must have been brought to an abrupt conclusion when Constantius in 357 forbade the consultation of Oracles, *sileat omnibus perpetuo diuinandi curiositas* (*Cod. Theod.* 9. 16. 4). It is therefore not surprising that Julian should himself speak of the decay of divination (*Contr. Gal.* 198 c). The evidence suggests that, while Delphi itself survived in 362, its oracular activities had been discontinued for some years. This is a different picture from that implied in our 'oracle', in which the shrine itself is in ruins, but an oracle can still be given. This forces us to ask whether the lines can really have been delivered to Oribasius when he consulted the Oracle.

Even if the Oracle had fallen on evil times, it might for that very reason attract Julian's attention and inspire him to a wish to revive it by his own personal patronage. On this possibility E. A. Thompson has made an important contribution.[3] He argues that Julian did in fact consult the Delphic Oracle before setting out for the East, but the reply which he received was quite different from the lines quoted by the *Artemii Passio* and Cedrenus. He gets his information from Theodoretus, *Hist. Eccl.* 3. 21 (200 Parmentier) and Cedrenus, i. 538 Bekker. The two quotations are almost identical except that Cedrenus inserts μέν as the second word. What they give is not a metrical text but its substance, which betrays its origin not only by what look like fragments of hexameters but by a neat attempt to catch the oracular style by

[1] O. Seeck, *R.-E.* vi. 2506. [2] Parke and Wormell, i. 287.
[3] *C.Q.* xl (1946), 35–6.

using Θῆρι for Τίγριδι with reference to the river Tigris. The text runs νῦν πάντες ὡρμήθημεν νίκης τρόπαια κομίσασθαι παρὰ Θῆρι ποταμῷ· τῶν δ' ἐγὼ ἡγεμονεύσω θοῦρος πολεμόκλονος Ἄρης. Cedrenus quotes Agathias as his authority, and if we can believe him, Agathias could have got his information from Theodoretus, who lived from 393 to *c*. 465 and was in a good position to gather material for his *Ecclesiastical History*, in which among other matters he was concerned with Julian's opposition to Christianity. But Cedrenus seems to have made a mistake. The information is not to be found in the existing text of Agathias, and nothing is gained by supposing either that there is a lacuna or that Cedrenus has some other, unknown work of Agathias in mind.[1] Whatever Cedrenus' source is, he agrees with Theodoretus in connecting the consultation of the Oracle with Julian's preparations for the Parthian War, and both draw the lesson that he was deceived by Apollo. This lesson was drawn by other critics of Julian and is not only emphasized by Philostorgius τοῖς πανταχόθεν χρησμοῖς τῶν Ἑλλήνων ὁ παραβάτης ἀναπεισθεὶς ὡς ἄμαχον ἕξει τὸ κράτος κατὰ Περσῶν ἐκστρατεύει (*Hist. Eccl.* 7. 15, p. 100 Bidez), but is evidently in the mind of Gregory of Nazianzus, when he describes the superstitious spirit in which Julian sets out against the Parthians, ἀλλ' οὖν ἔδοξε ταῦτα, καὶ τῆς ὁρμῆς ἦν πᾶσαν μαντείας καὶ γοητείας, ῥητῆς τε καὶ ἀρρήτου θυσίας τερατείαν εἰς ἓν ἀγαγών, ἵν' ἐν βραχεῖ πᾶσα καταλυθῇ (*Or*. 5. 9, Migne, *P.G.* 35. 674). It was obviously common knowledge that before setting out Julian consulted a number of Oracles, and we should expect Delphi to be among them, since he speaks of Apollo as ὁ τῆς Ἑλλάδος κοινὸς ἡγεμὼν καὶ νομοθέτης καὶ βασιλεύς, ὁ ἐν Δελφοῖς θεός (*Or*. 6. 188 a). The text of the oracle was clearly a promise of success in the forthcoming campaign, and it is certainly a far more probable answer than the three lines about the fallen shrine.

All would be clear if we were certain that on the occasion mentioned in different ways by Theodoretus, Cedrenus, Philostorgius, and Gregory of Nazianzus Julian really consulted Delphi. In defence of his case for this Thompson quotes from Theodoretus (*Graec. Affect. Curat.*, Migne, *P.G.* 83. 1069) some words which look much to the point. Theodoretus is speaking of the deceitful answers given by Apollo and, after quoting the notorious case of Croesus, says that the god did very much the

[1] A. M. Cameron, *J.R.S.* liii (1963), 91–4.

same thing to Julian, παραπλήσιον δέ τι δέδρακε καὶ ἐπὶ 'Ιουλιανοῦ τὴν ὁρμὴν ἔχοντος κατὰ τῶν Ἀσσυρίων, and then quotes the substance of the oracle. This certainly suggests Delphi, since it was from there that Croesus received his answer, but since the passage is not in all the MSS. and has been suspected of being an interpolation, it is argued that the reference is not to Delphi at all but to some other Oracle, probably in Asia.[1] But this objection is not fatal, for, as Thompson shows, when Theodoretus quotes the same oracle at *Hist. Eccl.* 3. 21, he says immediately afterwards τὸ μὲν οὖν τῶν ἐπῶν καταγέλαστον κωμῳδείτωσαν οἱ λόγιον θεὸν καὶ τῶν Μουσῶν ἀρχηγέτην τὸν Πύθιον ὀνομάζοντες,[2] and this is too obvious a reference to the Pythian Apollo for the oracle to have been given by any other god. We may therefore accept with confidence the view that this second oracle was given at Delphi in the winter of 362–3 and that the god's failure to keep his promise was known and noted soon enough. This can only mean that by this date the Delphic Oracle had resumed its old functions and that Julian consulted it on a matter of the greatest importance to himself and accepted its answer in the assurance that it must be right.

The conclusion compels us to look again at our first oracle with rather more critical attention. It was evidently not given at Delphi in answer to an enquiry about the Parthian expedition, but it might conceivably have been given to Oribasius at some other time, as for instance at the beginning of Julian's sole *imperium* when he disclosed his religious policy, and this is where Cedrenus may be taken to place it. Yet this too is impossible. Delphi was not, as the lines declare, in ruins, and though the Oracle was practically defunct, it was capable of reviving its prophetic activities if it were encouraged to do so, and this Julian evidently did. We must therefore try to discover the credentials of the 'oracle' in the hope of establishing what its original purpose and occasion were. Of the two authorities who quote it Cedrenus is so late that he can only have copied it from some earlier historian, but the *Artemii Passio* is another matter. In its present form it is the work of John of Rhodes, and though it is not later than the tenth century, it is not likely to be much

---

[1] Parke and Wormell, ii. 232.
[2] This looks like a hint at Julian, who at *Or.* 6. 188 b quotes with approval Iamblichus' description of Apollo as τὸν ἀρχηγέτην τῆς φιλοσοφίας.

earlier,[1] but it incorporates much older material from Philostorgius, who lived from c. 388 to c. 426 and was sufficiently close to Julian's time to be well informed about him. Philostorgius is responsible for the appearance of the 'oracle' in the *Artemii Passio*, and this means that it is within two generations of Julian's death and possibly less. We do not know where Cedrenus found it, but if his remarks about reviving the temple are no more than his own deduction from the poetical text, he may have derived all that he says from Philostorgius. The question is what such a poem really is, what interests or party or faith it represents, and what purpose it is meant to serve.

It is impossible to believe that the lines really are an oracle. They suit neither Delphic procedure nor the spirit of Julian's attempt to revive pagan cults. Despite their undeniable power, they are a forgery—a poem masquerading as an oracle but meant in fact to meet some other need. But who wrote them? Was he a Pagan who had regrets about the decay of the old religion, or a Christian who wished to expose the futility of the Olympian gods? Both views have been held, and each has something to be said for it. It is understandable that after the triumph of the Church some adherent of the ancient faith, conscious that it had been mortally stricken but unwilling to abandon his affection for it, should dramatize his feelings in this form and ascribe the words to an occasion in the career of Julian.[2] Yet though we ourselves easily read such a spirit into the lines, it is doubtful whether it is really there, since they contain no word of regret or sorrow or affection for the vanished rite. Such signs as they give point in an opposite direction. In λαλέουσαν and λάλον there is a hint of irony, and the repetition of λαλ- gives the impression that the utterances of the Oracle have ceased to count for religion.[3] This is confirmed by the way in which the *Passio* makes Artemius quote them to prove the uselessness of Apollo to Julian. Philostorgius saw them in a hostile spirit, and if we look at them without preconceptions, we see that they sound a note of mocking triumph over an emperor, and were composed by a Christian to show the futility of Julian's belief in the

[1] G. Geutz, *R.-E.* xx. 120.
[2] E. R. Bevan, *Christianity*, 106.
[3] For the use of the word in the 4th century see Himer. *Or.* 39. 4 Colonna, οὐ γὰρ Ἀττικὸν τὸ σιγᾶν οὐδὲ τῆς λάλου πόλεως ἄξιον.

ΕΙΠΑΤΕ ΤΩΙ ΒΑΣΙΛΗΙ 239

Oracle.[1] Nor would a Christian of this time have felt any qualms or difficulty about presenting the Oracle in this way; for though he would think Apollo a demon, he would not deny his existence, and to make him confess his own defeat would present certain attractions. It looks as if the 'oracle' were a Christian fabrication, intended to put into convincing, dramatic form a situation which most Christians would accept as real. What gives it such distinction is not a melancholy regret for the irrecoverable past but a sharp impulse to expose the futility of Delphic pretensions as Julian in his credulity had believed and fostered them.

In our search for the origins of the 'oracle' we have an important clue in Gregory of Nazianzus, who lived from 329 to 390. As a youth he had been with Julian in Athens in 356 when they were both students. Even in Julian's lifetime he composed *Or.* 2 against him, and after his death followed it with *Or.* 5. In these λόγοι στηλιτευτικοί he denounces the vacuity and folly of Julian's religious beliefs, and at one place, in a comparison between them and the Christian revelation, he points with scorn to the futility and the collapse of oracles. After mentioning the now speechless oaks and the silent cauldrons of Dodona, he goes on to say: οὐκέτι ἡ Πυθία πληροῦται, οὐκ οἶδ' ὧντινων πλὴν μύθων καὶ ληρημάτων. πάλιν ἡ Κασταλία σεσίγηται καὶ σιγᾷ, καὶ ὕδωρ ἐστὶν οὐ μαντευόμενον ἀλλὰ γελώμενον. ἄφωνος δ' Ἀπόλλων. πάλιν ἡ Δάφνη φυτόν ἐστι μύθῳ θρηνούμενον (*Or.* 5. 32, Migne, *P.G.* 35. 704). The parallels between this and the 'oracle' are striking and instructive. Both speak of Delphi as if it had recently ceased its oracular activities and refer to them in the spirit of 'no longer', and both make play with the Castalian spring, the prophetic water, and the laurel-tree of Apollo. The theme is well chosen by Gregory, who knows how highly divination was valued by the dead man, whom he execrates and derides, and he is determined to show that it is over and done with. By an ingenious device of controversy he elaborates and uses against Julian some words from his own work against the Galilaeans, which he wrote in the winter of 362–3 (Liban, *Or.* 17. 18; 18. 167. 178). This work had a large circulation after Julian's death, and its influence may be gauged from the care which Cyril of Alexandria took, about 433, to refute it in his book Ὑπὲρ τῆς τῶν Χριστιανῶν εὐαγοῦς

[1] This was first suggested by G. Wolff, *De novissimorum oraculorum aetate*, Berlin, 1854.

θρησκείας πρὸς τὰ τοῦ ἐν ἀθέοις Ἰουλιανοῦ. In his attack on Christian doctrine and ethics Julian surprisingly asserts that, just as the prophetic spirit has vanished from the Hebrews and the Egyptians, so it has waned among the Greeks: φαίνεται δὲ καὶ τὰ αὐτοφυῆ χρηστήρια σιγῆσαι ταῖς τῶν χρόνων εἴκοντα περιόδοις (*Contr. Gal.* 198 c). This remarkable admission does credit to Julian's candour and courage and explains his desire to restore the fallen fortunes of ancient shrines, but it played into the hands of such adversaries as Gregory, who was quick to take advantage of it. If Julian put such views into a controversial book, he is likely to have expressed them in talk, and gossip would pass them round malcontent circles of Christians. It is not surprising that Gregory, for whom almost any stick was good enough to beat the dead apostate, picked on the point after Julian's death and turned it against him.

The main theme, then, of our 'oracle' can be traced back through Gregory of Nazianzus to Julian himself, but the question remains: who put this theme into verse and passed off his work as the utterance of a voice from Delphi? This had already been done by the time when Philostorgius brought the lines into his account of Artemius in his *Ecclesiastical History*, which must have been completed before his death c. 426. It has been suggested that the poem is the work of Gregory himself,[1] and if he circulated it with some note saying that it was an oracle given to Oribasius, we can understand why Philostorgius makes such use of it as he does. Gregory wrote a great deal of poetry, and though many of his 17,000 lines are rather sad stuff, it is conceivable that he might have been inspired by detestation of Julian and by joy in his discomfiture to write lines so good as these. They are indeed much shorter than his usual scale of composition, but oracles tended to be short, and if it is to deceive the public, a forgery must resemble the genuine article as closely as possible. If he wrote the lines, Gregory would presumably be responsible also for the circumstantial story of their delivery and could comfort himself for his fraudulence with the thought that after all this was very much what Julian himself had said. Yet for more than one reason we may doubt whether Gregory wrote the lines. First, though he hated Julian and all his works, it is hard to believe that he would resort to so circuitous a method of discrediting

[1] O. Lampsides, *Platon* ix (1957), 133–5.

him. His favourite tactic was open onslaught, especially after Julian's death, and it is difficult to see why he should abandon it for something devious and underhand. Secondly, if Gregory really wrote the lines and wished them to be accepted as evidence for the betrayal of Julian by his gods, he would surely have used them in *Or.* 5 instead of giving something which is very like them in its contents but lacks their concentrated, dramatic power. Conversely, if he composed them after the speech, he would surely have used them somewhere else, since he did not cease his attacks on the dead emperor, and a quotation of this calibre might have been unusually effective in winning the kind of support which he wanted. Thirdly, though the 'oracle' and the speech have much in common, their substance is not identical. The 'oracle' starts with the sensational announcement that the temple at Delphi has fallen to the ground and that Apollo no longer has a shrine, but the speech says nothing at all about this. If Gregory had entertained such an idea, he would surely have exploited it, and his failure to do so confirms that he did not write the lines. We may conclude that they reflect a situation different from that which he himself knew, for the good reason that in his time the temple of Apollo was still standing at Delphi. To claim that it had fallen down would be to tax too far the credulity of his public, and he is unlikely to have thought of it.

The 'oracle' presupposes the ruin of the temple and is addressed to a public which would take this for granted, even though it did not know how or when it happened. The collapse of the temple is the *terminus a quo* for the date of the 'oracle'. Although Claudian is not a good witness, he may perhaps be trusted when, addressing Honorius in 398, he refers to the emperor's birth in 384 and says:

> qui uatum discursus erat? tibi corniger Hammon
> et dudum taciti rupere silentia Delphi.   (8. 143–4)

This suggests that, though in 384 the Oracle had been silent for some years, Delphi was sufficiently intact to be capable of reviving it. This same year saw the beginning of the process of destruction, for it was then that Theodosius instructed a special commission under Cynegius to stop all pagan ceremonies and close all temples, with the result that all which were not converted into Christian churches fell sooner or later into ruins. But the ruins of the temple of Apollo at Delphi suggest that it did not decay gradually but was destroyed by the violent hands of men, who razed it to its base and left only the main platform and the steps. An entirely suitable time for this would be in 396–7 when the invading forces of Alaric devastated large parts of Greece, and were, according to Eunapius, helped in the work of destruction by Christian monks: τοιαύτας αὐτῷ τὰς πύλας ἀπέδειξε τῆς Ἑλλάδος ἥ τε τῶν φαιὰ ἱμάτια ἐχόντων ἀκωλύτως προσπαρεισελθόντων ἀσέβεια, καὶ ὁ τῶν ἱεροφαντικῶν θεσμῶν παραρραγεὶς νόμος καὶ σύνδεσμος (*Vit. Soph.* 476). That the destruction was general and accepted by the authorities is clear from a edict of Theodosius in November 397, which orders that material obtained from the destruction of temples shall be used to repair roads, bridges, aqueducts, and walls (*Cod. Theod.* 15. 1. 36). By 399 such destruction has become imperial policy, for another edict lays down that any temples in the country districts shall be torn down, *his enim deiectis atque sublatis omnis superstitioni materia consumetur* (16. 10. 16). So important a shrine as Apollo's at Delphi would be a first object of attack, and we may with some assurance conclude that it was destroyed in 396–7. Once the temple had lost its roof and its walls, it was easy to speak of it as the 'oracle' does, and we may conclude that this was composed between the demolition of the temple and the death of Philostorgius *c.* 426, and nearer to the first than to the second.

We cannot seriously doubt that the author of these lines derived his original idea from Gregory of Nazianzus and may have known Julian's own views on the decay of divination, but he brought the situation up to date by an eloquent anachronism and made the desolation of Delphi his opening gambit. We do not know who he was, but he was clearly a well-educated man with a real talent for poetry and a taste for Christian polemic against Julian's memory. He was moreover sufficiently acquainted with the old religion to know the precise nature of the oracular rites at Delphi. His δαίδαλος αὐλά is the temple of Apollo, and his καλύβα, in its later meaning of 'chamber' (Hesych. καλύβη· παστάς), is the inner sanctuary. The prophetic bay-tree must be that which was said to have grown inside the temple (Aristoph. *Plut.* 213 cum scholl.). The παγὰ λαλέουσα and the λάλον ὕδωρ are correctly distinguished, the first being the Castalian spring and the second the stream of Cassotis near the temple (Paus. 10. 24. 7). In naming these different elements in the oracular procedure our author is probably stressing those parts of it to which Julian gave particular attention when he restored the rite. They were not always equally important and it looks as if Julian insisted on restoring both earlier and later features of the rites to make sure that nothing was lacking. The bay-tree was as ancient as the Homeric Hymn to Apollo, 386, where the god speaks ἐκ δάφνης, but before long its duties were adapted to ceremonies in the temple, and it played a considerable part in them, as we can see from Callimachus:

καὶ Πυθία γὰρ ἐν δάφνῃ μὲν ἵδρυται,
δάφνην δ' ἀείδει καὶ δάφνην ὑπέστρωται.

(fr. 194. 26–7 Pf.)

In the second and third centuries A.D. its functions seem to have been reduced to the provision of leaves which the Pythia ate in order to establish contact with the god (Eus. *Praep. Ev.* 5. 224; Lucian. *Bis Acc.* 1; *Hes.* 8; Tzetz. in Lyc. *Alex.* 6).[1] On the other hand the Castalian spring and the Cassotis seem originally to have been used not for oracular but for purifying purposes (Simon. fr. 577/23 P.), and the notion that the Pythia drew inspiration from Castalia (Lucian. *Herm.* 60; Clem. Alex. *Protr.* 1. 11. 2) and that the Cassotis made women prophetic (Paus. 10. 24. 7) is not, so far as we know, earlier than the second century B.C. In resuscitating the Oracle Julian seems to have been meticulously conscientious about restoring the rites in their full range and to have included in them both older elements, which may have fallen into desuetude, and newer elements, which had gained some importance before the Oracle fell into decay. The realistic air which this inside information gives to the 'oracle' would help it to look authentic, and the author enhanced its verisimilitude by connecting it with Oribasius. Since it is more than likely that Oribasius was Julian's agent in dealing with Delphi, he was an obvious figure to introduce into the story. Indeed in making use of him our author shows insight and ingenuity; for Oribasius was not only execrated as a friend of Julian but had after Julian's death been banished by Valens and Valentinian to live among barbarians. In his exile he was in no position to

---

[1] Parke and Wormell, i. 26–8. For the connection with the god see *Pap. Mag. Gr.* i. 26 δάφνη . . . ἧς ποτε γευσάμενος πετάλων ἀνέφηνεν ἀοιδὰς | αὐτὸς ἄναξ σκηπτοῦχος.

contradict stories told about him in the Eastern Empire, and though he was back and alive in 396 (Eunap. *Vit. Soph.* 499), he was probably dead when the 'oracle' was composed and passed off as a historical record, and any danger of a denial from him had disappeared.

This forgery of a Delphic oracle to suit the purposes of Christian polemic is not unique. Eusebius, who died about 340, quotes an alleged oracle given by the Pythia to Augustus, in which the god announces that at the command of a 'Hebrew boy' he must go back to Hades (Cedr. 1. 320). Since oracles about emperors were forged by Pagans, it is not surprising that Christians should do the same. The 'oracle' to Augustus is a poor affair compared with ours and betrays more obviously the literary tradition from which it arose. This is the Sibylline Prophecies, which contain Christian passages, notably in Book 7, with its forecasts of ruin to the heathen, and Book 8, 1–126, with its curses on Rome. These make a direct assault on their victims, and to this degree the 'oracles' to Augustus and Julian, with their circumstantial detail, differ from them. But the 'oracles' maintain the same policy and something of the old manner and method in denouncing the great even when they are dead. Our lines are much more accomplished than any Sibylline prophecy or the 'oracle' to Augustus, and show how, when Christianity triumphed, some of its adherents were able to maintain the literary standards of pagan culture. But otherwise our author is truly representative of those Christians who pursued the phantom of Julian with obloquy and derision. His distinction among them is that he is much more skilful than most and, by creating not only a memorable story but an impressive text to support it, makes Julian in retrospect look foolish and futile for trusting in gods who, when he sought their help, had already forsaken him.

XIX

PALLADAS AND THE CONVERTED OLYMPIANS[1]

PALLADAS refers only once to Christians by name, in three hexameter lines which present no difficulty of text or translation:

Χριστιανοὶ γεγαῶτες 'Ολύμπια δώματ' ἔχοντες
ἐνθάδε ναιετάουσιν ἀπήμονες· οὐδὲ γὰρ αὐτοὺς
χώνη φόλλιν ἄγουσα φερέσβιον ἐν πυρὶ θήσει. (A.P. 9. 528)

Owners of halls on Olympus, having become Christians, dwell here unharmed; for not even them will the melting-pot which provides life-giving small change put in the fire.

The main drift is clear. Metal images of Olympian gods, which would otherwise have been melted down to make small coins (Eustath. 136. 13 φόλλεις· ὀβολοί. ἤγουν εὐτελῆ τινα νομίσματα), have unexpectedly found safety in some place which Palladas calls simply ἐνθάδε, as if his readers would know where it was. The lemma is ready with an identification, εἰς τὸν οἶκον Μαρίνης, and this has generally been accepted as independent and reliable information. There are two candidates for the name of Marina. The first is the first wife of Valentinian I and the mother of Gratian.[2] She was born in 359 and survived the death of her husband in 375 (Malal. 341. 89 ff.; Chron. Pasch. 560. 17 ff.). The difficulty about her is that her life was spent mostly in the west, first with Valentinian and then with Gratian, and she is unlikely to have been connected with any 'house of Marina' which could have been well enough known to Palladas for him to speak of it in this way. Most scholars prefer to identify Marina with the youngest daughter of Arcadius,[3] who was born 11 February 403, (Marcell. Com. Chron. 2. 67. 403. 1) and died 3 August 449 (ibid.

---
[1] First published in Byzantinische Zeitschrift, liii (1960), 1–7, slightly altered.
[2] L. A. Stella, Cinque Poeti dell'Antologia Palatina, 382.
[3] A. Franke, De Pallada Epigrammatographo, 38 ff.; W. Peek, R.-E. xviii. 3. 158; Christ–Schmid–Stählin, Gesch. gr. Lit. ii. 2. 979, n. 2.

2. 83. 449. 1). Her claim is that she was credited with having built an οἶκος τῶν Μαρίνης (*Chron. Pasch.* 1. 566. 13), and this looks as if it suited very nicely what the lemmatist has in mind. She was noted for her piety, and not only did Cyril of Alexandria dedicate to her a work on orthodox belief (Migne, *P.G.* 76. 1201 ff.), but she was persuaded by her sister Pulcheria to remain a virgin (Theophan. 1. p. 81. 5 de Boor). If Palladas' poem is really connected with her, it cannot have been written much before 425, when she might be old enough to have her own palace, but since he lived to be at least seventy-two years old (*A.P.* 10. 97) it is thought that he was still alive at this time. At first sight the lemma looks as if it provided a useful date in the life of Palladas and incidentally cast an illuminating side-light on what could happen to the Olympian gods after the triumph of the Church and the legislation of Theodosius and Arcadius against Pagan rites.

Yet the more closely we examine the lemma, the less confidence it inspires. The scanty lemmata on Palladas' poems seldom go beyond what may be deduced from the text, and even on this they are sometimes demonstrably wrong. 9. 169 is indeed about Palladas' wife, but not ὅτι κερατᾶς ἦν παράξενος; 9. 171 is about the sale of books but not διὰ τὸ καταφρονεῖσθαι τὴν παιδείαν; 10. 94 is not concerned εἰς τὴν κρίσιν; 9. 489 makes a nasty point but not ἐπὶ βρέφεσι δύο ἅμα τεχθεῖσι καὶ παραχρῆμα ἀποθανοῦσιν. A similar untrustworthiness is obvious in other lemmata which claim to give external information not contained in the actual text. 9. 400 is neither the work of Palladas nor addressed to Hypatia the daughter of Theon;[1] 9. 501 has nothing to do with Berytus, and the lemma εἰς τὴν Βήρυτον is derived from the preceding poem, which is by an anonymous poet on the destruction wrought by the earthquake of 529 (Agath. *Hist.* 2. 6); in 9. 168 the attribution of the name Andromache to Palladas' wife is a false deduction from 11. 378. 5 ἀλόχου τῆς ἀνδρομάχης; in 11. 204 the lemma εἰς Αἰγύπτιον ῥήτορα is an obvious misinterpretation of the personal name Μαῦρον in the text, and if Maurus was the man known to Ammianus (20. 4. 18; 31. 10. 21), he was not an Egyptian in any relevant sense of the word; 11. 291 does not look as if it were really directed εἰς Νίκανδρον, if he is the man to whom Synesius wrote *Epp.* 1 and 75. Even more

[1] G. Luck, *H.S.C.P.* lxiii (1958), 462–6.

PALLADAS AND THE CONVERTED OLYMPIANS 247

respectable looking cases have their shady side. 11. 292 may well be directed at Themistius for becoming Prefect of Constantinople in 384,[1] but the actual lemma says εἴς τινα φιλόσοφον γενόμενον ὕπαρχον πόλεως ἐπὶ Βαλεντιανοῦ καὶ Βάλεντος, which gives a date that is demonstrably wrong, and the right information comes from the Planudean scholiast, who gives Θεμίστιον for τινα and Κωνσταντινουπόλεως for πόλεως. Almost the only case left is 11. 283 εἰς Δαμόνικον, and though this may be the man known to Libanius (*Epp.* 1054 and 1055 F.), we cannot be sure that it is. The lemmata are clearly not infallible, and reveal far too much stupidity, ignorance, and guesswork. We should indeed be unwise if we accepted the lemma εἰς τὸν οἶκον Μαρίνης as reliable information simply because it is in the MSS.

In considering our poem this general doubt is reinforced by others. First, it is clear that the House of Marina was not her private palace but some sort of foundation or institution. This follows from the words of *Chronicon Paschale*, 1. 566. 3, Μαρῖνα δὲ ἔκτισε τὸν οἶκον τῶν Μαρίνης, where τῶν Μαρίνης indicates that the foundation was not a dwelling for Marina herself but for some persons or purposes in which she was interested, and as such it resembled the foundation made by Marina's sister, Arcadia, mentioned in the next sentence but one, ἡ δὲ Ἀρκαδία ἔκτισε καὶ τὸν οἶκον τοῦ ἁγίου Ἀνδρέου. This explains why the House of Marina survived and kept its name after her death, and also why it had a curator in 533 (Theophan. 1. 235. 2), received the περιουσία of Belisarius' possessions in 557 (ibid. 240. 26), and so late as the time of Phocas was used for the celebration of his daughter's marriage (ibid. 284. 13). It is conceivable that at some time such an institution received statues of pagan gods, though it is unlikely that the pious Marina herself introduced them. Secondly, the lemma, instead of calling Palladas Ἀλεξανδρέως, as in nine other places, mysteriously calls him τοῦ μετεώρου. The only other poet so called in the *Anthology* is Julianus Scholasticus at 9. 481. Though Stadtmueller identified him with Julianus of Egypt, the case for this is flimsy, and we know nothing about him. The lemmatist seems to have been in a like case, and on seeing the name Julianus confused him with the Apostate, and added the words τοῦ μετεώρου as suitable to the Emperor. μετέωρος has not the same meaning as παραβάτης, but it has derogatory associations,

[1] H. Scholze, *De temporibus Themistii*, 58 ff.

as we can see from Hesych. μετέωρος· κοῦφος, ἐνέος, and conveys a meaning similar to other words used of Julian by his detractors, such as ἐμβρόντητος (Theodoret. *Hist. Eccl.* 3. 25; Anon. ap. Eunap. fr. 23 D.), κενόδοξος (Socr. *Hist. Eccl.* 3. 21), μάταιος (Greg. Naz. *Or.* 4. 23), and even μανίαις οἰστρηλατούμενος καὶ δονούμενος (id. *Or.* 5. 7). When the lemmatist applies μετέωρος to Palladas, it must surely be because he regards him as resembling the Apostate in vanity and folly. To form such an opinion he need not have known anything more than the three lines of the poem, in which the suggestion that Olympian gods could become Christians would shock him into using such an epithet. Its appearance can only increase our distrust and make us wary of accepting what he says. Thirdly, Palladas' words indicate that the images of the gods are unexpectedly fortunate in not being melted down. This is stressed by οὐδέ, which suggests that they would normally be the first to go to the pot. This would be a natural observation in 391 when Theophilus and his mob were destroying temples and images of the gods, but it would have little point *c.* 425, when it was accepted in principle that such images would be preserved if only for their intrinsic merit as works of art. Fourthly, when Palladas says that the images survive ἐνθάδε, it is unlikely that he refers to some special location like a palace, since this would diminish the intelligibility of his poem and restrict its currency and be alien to his usual emphatic clarity. ἐνθάδε looks as if it meant no more than 'in Alexandria', which is the only place where we know that Palladas lived. It is true that attempts have been made to show that he visited Constantinople,[1] but the poems quoted in support of this do not prove it. 9. 180–3, which tell of a temple of Tyche transformed into a wine-shop, may easily refer to the Τυχεῖον of Alexandria described by Libanius (*Progymnas.* 12. 25. 6). In 16. 282 the statues of Victory would be quite as much at home in Alexandria as in Constantinople. 6. 85 is likely to have been composed in Alexandria, since the Timotheus whom it mentions looks like the bishop of that name who died 20 July 385 (Socr. *Hist. Eccl.* 4. 37. 2; Sozom. *Hist. Eccl.* 8. 7. 30). It is of course possible that Palladas went to Constantinople, but there is no sure evidence that he did, and for this Alexandrian poet the natural meaning for ἐνθάδε is Alexandria. These considerations suggest that the lemma εἰς τὸν

[1] Stella, op. cit. 381.

PALLADAS AND THE CONVERTED OLYMPIANS 249

οἶκον Μαρίνης is unworthy of serious trust and no more than the guess of an ignorant commentator. We do not know how the 130 or so poems of Palladas came into the collection of Cephalas, but it looks as if they formed a single book, a *Sylloge Palladana*, which may have been put together by the poet himself and had no explanatory introductions or notes. When these were added at a later date, they were usually feeble and often false.

Even so we must ask why the lemmatist connected this poem with the House of Marina. The evidence for the House is too scanty to allow a confident answer, and anyhow the errors of the lemmatist need not always be susceptible of a rational explanation. But it is possible that in the House of Marina images of gods were placed and converted to Christian purposes, rather as Constantine took an image of Apollo and, after substituting his own head for the god's, placed it on a high pillar in the oval forum at Constantinople (Hes. Mil. 4. 41). Such a process need not have taken place in Marina's own time, and it is unlikely that it did, but an institution which could receive such benefactions as the estate of Belisarius might well find itself inheriting images which were suitably disposed of by some sort of adaptation to Christian usage. The lemmatist, who evidently lived at Constantinople, and knew the House of Marina either from personal observation or from hearsay, guessed that it was the subject of Palladas' poem. This is the kind of spirit in which he seems to have worked, and his guess about this poem is no more soundly based than his guesses about some other poems on which he had in fact no independent information, but relied on his own fancy.

We must then start again and ask when Palladas is likely to have written such a poem as this, and we may begin with the highly relevant passage of Socrates, in which he tells of the destruction wrought by Theophilus and his Christian mob in 391:

τὰ μὲν οὖν ἱερὰ κατεστρέφετο, τὰ δὲ ἀγάλματα τῶν θεῶν μετεχωνεύετο εἰς λεβήτια καὶ ἄλλας χρείας τῆς Ἀλεξανδρείας ἐκκλησίας, τοῦ βασιλέως χαρισαμένου τοὺς θεοὺς εἰς δαπανήματα τῶν θεῶν (*Hist. Eccl.* 5. 16). That Palladas knew of this and did not treat it too seriously is clear from his epigram on an image of Eros which has suffered in the process:

χαλκότυπος τὸν Ἔρωτα μεταλλάξας ἐπόησε
τήγανον, οὐκ ἀλόγως, ὅττι καὶ αὐτὸ φλέγει,

(9. 773)

while another, anonymous epigram on the theme is surely from his hand:

χάλκειόν τις "Ερωτα μετήγαγεν ἐκ πυρὸς εἰς πῦρ
τήγανον ἁρμόζων τῇ κολάσει κόλασιν.   (16. 194)

It is against this background that we must set Palladas' references to images of gods which have escaped the melting-pot. His poem presupposes these events, and the question is how near he was to them at the time of writing our poem.

In his account of this crisis Socrates goes on to tell that the destruction of images was complete except for one which Theophilus insisted on keeping that in future the Hellenes, by whom he means the adherents of the old cults, might not deny that they had once worshipped such gods. He insists, on the authority of Ammonius, who was an eyewitness, that this was a unique case, but we may presume that Ammonius based his story on the Serapeum and that the destruction of images was not universal. Palladas evidently refers to some survivors, and we must ask how they came to be saved. It might be argued that they were preserved for use in some Christian church, and that just as the Serapeum itself was turned into a church by Arcadius (Sozom. 7. 15), so images might be adapted to represent saints and martyrs. This might have happened in 391, if the authority which commanded it was high enough. But the trouble with this view is that statues of heathen gods could not be brought into Christian service without a good deal of refashioning and refurbishing, and this is surely excluded by Palladas' use of ἀπήμονες. A god or a goddess who has been deprived of essential emblems or been reshaped to represent some quite different character would hardly qualify for this adjective. Nor would they aptly be called Χριστιανοὶ γεγαῶτες, for the change would be not only in their status and associations but in their function and appearance. Palladas suggests that the gods still maintain their identity in their earthly dwelling-places, and this rules out any notion that they have been substantially transformed. It looks as if something rather different were in his mind, and we may perhaps surmise what it is.

Theodosius' policy in dealing with images of Pagan gods was not free of inconsistency and ambiguity. His law of 391 lays down that they must not be worshipped, *nemo . . . mortali opere*

PALLADAS AND THE CONVERTED OLYMPIANS 251

formata simulacra suspiciat (*Cod. Theod.* 16. 10. 10), and no doubt this helped to justify Theophilus in his work of destruction and may even have forced Theodosius to approve the work when it was done. Yet such destruction does not seem to have been essential to his policy. When in 382 he initiated his attack on pagan rites, he commanded the preservation of images for artistic reasons, *artis pretio quam diuinitate metienda* (*Cod. Theod.* 16. 10. 8). In Libanius' *Or.* 30 πρὸς Θεοδόσιον βασιλέα ὑπὲρ τῶν ἱερῶν, which is in fact an open letter to the emperor, written probably in 388,[1] he pleads at length the case for preserving temples and their contents for aesthetic considerations, and he would hardly have done this if he had not thought that such a policy might appeal to Theodosius. The desirability of preservation was restated in 399, when Honorius insisted that *uolumus publicorum operum ornamenta seruari* (*Cod. Theod.* 16. 10. 15) and though the actual enactment refers to Spain, it seems to be part of a general policy, since Prudentius writing in 404–5 says:

O proceres! liceat statuas consistere puras,
artificum magnorum opera: haec pulcherrima nostrae
ornamenta fiant patriae, nec decolor usus
in uitium uersae monumenta coinquinet artis.
(*Contr. Symm.* 1. 502–5)

It looks as if the legal position were that images should be kept intact, and though there were exceptions to this and in the crisis of 391 Theodosius gave his support and approval to destruction, the rule was enforced at intervals, and we may surmise that after the wasteful treatment of the Serapeum imperial authority intervened to see that this kind of thing was not repeated. It is evidently such a situation that Palladas has in mind. Quite recently images had been melted down, but now they have unexpectedly become safe. It looks as if the poem came very soon after the riots under Theophilus and was not likely to be much later than 391.

When then exactly does Palladas mean? And in what sense does he label the gods as Χριστιανοὶ γεγαῶτες? At the least he must mean that they have been saved through Christian intervention and survive under Christian protection. That this could happen in the reign of Theodosius is clear from a remarkable

[1] R. van Loy, *Byz. Zeits.* xxii (1913), 313–18.

case, the collection of famous statues, including the Cnidian Aphrodite of Praxiteles, the Zeus of Pheidias, and the Samian Hera of Lysippus, in the building known as τὸ Λαυσεῖον or τὰ Λαύσου at Constantinople (Cedr. *Hist. Comp.* 1, p. 564 Bekker; Theophan. 239. 10). Lausus was *cubicularius* first to Arcadius and then to Theodosius II, but his famous collection seems to have been established towards the end of Theodosius' reign, since Cedrenus tells of it in the middle of his account of Arbogastes and Eugenius in 392–4, and it looks as if it were formed at this time. If it was, it would indicate that Theodosius allowed high officials of his court to preserve images of heathen gods and may have given his personal approval to their doing so. At a time when Palladas had become accustomed to the melting of images and assumed that it was their inevitable fate, he was confronted by a changed situation in which they were preserved, and this is what excites his interest. What Theodosius allowed to Lausus, he may have allowed in a similar manner to other men in other places than Constantinople, notably ἐνθάδε in Alexandria.

The point of Χριστιανοὶ γεγαῶτες is sharp and clear. When Palladas says that the Olympian gods have become Christians, he compares them implicitly with human beings who have saved themselves by changing their religious status and allegiance. Instead of dwelling in splendour on Olympus, the gods have a diminished existence in Christian surroundings under Christian protection. This is the kind of gibe that Palladas likes to make against the figures of pagan belief. Though he has nothing good to say for Christians or Christianity, he is not much better disposed towards the elder gods. When the temple of Tyche is turned into a wine-shop, he mocks her for getting what she deserves (9. 180–3), and when he sees a figure of Heracles flung down where the road divides, he makes the god say that he too has learned to be a time-server (9. 441). So when he speaks of the gods as Χριστιανοὶ γεγαῶτες, he suggests that they have survived by joining the winning side. He cannot have believed at all seriously in them, but he was sufficiently trained in the old literature to speak of them in anthropomorphic language and to judge them by the same standards as they were supposed to apply to men.

XX

PALLADAS AND CHRISTIANITY[1]

THE question whether Palladas was a Christian is not new,[2] and recent attempts to settle it one way or the other have not advanced the subject very much. The case that he was turns on too many vague assumptions,[3] and the case that he was not is insecure because we know so little about him,[4] but we can track down certain passages in his poems which are concerned with the conflict between Pagans and Christians in the last twenty years of the fourth century A.D., and from them we can deduce conclusions about his response to some dramatic events which he witnessed and about changes in his own life. In such an inquiry a certain amount of surmise is inevitable, but since Palladas is an important and independent witness to the last days of paganism, it is worth while attempting to see what light he throws on it, even if he does so from a highly personal angle.

The first sign of a change for the worse for Pagans came with the law of Theodosius in 381 which forbade the use of sacrifices as a means of consulting the gods and stigmatized anyone who did so as 'uelut insanus ac sacrilegus' (*Cod. Theod.* 16. 10. 7). The injunction against divination can scarcely have troubled Palladas, whose only references to oracles, at *A.P.* 7. 687 and 688, show that he had no respect for them. The far-sighted might have seen in the law the signs of a wrath to come, but the first overt trouble came from the monks. In his *Or.* 30. 8, probably composed in 388 as an open letter to Theodosius,[5] Libanius speaks indignantly of what they do:

οἱ δὲ μελανειμοῦντες οὗτοι καὶ πλείω μὲν τῶν ἐλεφάντων ἐσθίοντες πόνον δὲ παρέχοντες τῷ πλήθει τῶν ἐκπωμάτων τοῖς δι' ᾀσμάτων αὐτοῖς

---

[1] First published in *Proceedings of the British Academy*, xlv (1959), 91–5, slightly altered.
[2] A. Franke, *De Pallada epigrammatographo* (Diss. Leipzig, 1899), 45–7.
[3] P. Waltz, *R.E.G.* lix–lx (1946–7), 209, answered by G. Luck, *H.S.C.P.* lxiii (1958), 457–8.
[4] One aspect of the case is well put by R. Keydell, *Byz. Zeits.* l (1957), 1–3.
[5] R. van Loy, *Byz. Zeits.* xxii (1913), 313–19.

παραπέμπουσι τὸ ποτόν, συγκρύπτοντες δὲ ταῦτα ὠχρότητι τῇ διὰ τέχνης
αὐτοῖς πεπορισμένῃ μένοντος, ὦ βασιλεῦ, καὶ κρατοῦντος τοῦ νόμου
θέουσιν ἐφ' ἱερὰ ξύλα φέροντες καὶ λίθους καὶ σίδηρον, οἱ δὲ καὶ ἄνευ
τούτων χεῖρας καὶ πόδας. ἔπειτα Μυσῶν λεία καθαιρουμένων ὀροφῶν,
κατασκαπτομένων τοίχων, κατασπωμένων ἀγαλμάτων, ἀνασπωμένων
βωμῶν, τοὺς ἱερεῖς δὲ ἢ σιγᾶν ἢ τεθνάναι δεῖ.

It may have been in answer to complaints such as this that
Gregory of Nazianzus composed his poem εἰς τοὺς διαβάλλοντας
τοὺς μοναχούς (*Carm.* 2. 1. 44) before his death in 390. The monks
caused such havoc that even Theodosius issued a short-lived law
against them in 390: 'quicunque sub professione monachi
repperiuntur, deserta loca et uastas solitudines sequi adque
habitare iubeantur' (*Cod. Theod.* 16. 3. 1). A poem of Palladas on
the same topic must come from this period and displays his usual
love of point and calculated double meanings:

εἰ μοναχοί, τί τοσοίδε; τοσοίδε δέ, πῶς πάλι μοῦνοι;
ὦ πληθὺς μοναχῶν ψευσαμένη μονάδα.   (*A.P.* 11. 384)

Palladas mocks the monks, as he mocks prominent men such as
Themistius (11. 292), for the inconsistency between their claims
and their behaviour, but there is nothing very savage in what
he says. He certainly does not compete in condemnation with
what another Pagan, Eunapius, says a little later about these
same monks when Theophilus of Alexandria and his allies, the
prefect Evagrius and the military commander Romanus, εἶτα
ἐπεισῆγον τοῖς ἱεροῖς τόποις τοὺς καλουμένους μοναχούς, ἀνθρώπους
μὲν κατὰ τὸ εἶδος, ὁ δὲ βίος αὐτοῖς συώδης, καὶ εἰς τὸ ἐμφανὲς
ἔπασχον τε καὶ ἐποίουν μυρία κακὰ καὶ ἄφραστα (*Vit. Soph.* 472).
Even if Palladas wrote this couplet, as he probably did, before
the monks committed their worst excesses, he is still relatively
kind to them, and his words have no very obvious bias against
Christianity or for Paganism. He keeps his usual detachment, and
if he has a position, it is not far from that of Theodosius, since
the play between μοναχῶν and μονάδα reflects in an ironical
spirit the emperor's insistence that the *monachi* must retire into
deserta loca.

The real crisis came in 391, when Theodosius issued two laws
(*Cod. Theod.* 16. 10. 10 and 11) which almost completely forbade
the practice of the old religion. His injunctions, and especially
his condemnation of the worship of idols, 'nemo . . . mortali

opere formata simulacra suspiciat', were taken more than literally by the enthusiastic Christians of Alexandria, who under the leadership of Theophilus proceeded to destroy the temples of Serapis, Mithras, and Dionysus (Socr. 5. 16. 1; Sozom. 7. 15. 2–3; Zosim. 5. 23. 3; Eunap. *Vit. Soph.* 472). In some matters connected with this catastrophe Palladas kept his old ironical detachment. When the images of gods were melted down, he wrote two epigrams in which he makes the point that the image of Eros deserves its fate of being turned into a frying-pan because he himself played with fire (9. 773; 16. 184). Yet this spirit was more than Palladas could sustain. Events caught him unawares in his desire to stand alone, and were too strong for him to do so. We cannot say in what order his other poems connected with the crisis were written, but we can distinguish different strands in them, and from these we can see the strain to which he was subjected.

Palladas was a Ἕλλην in the sense in which the word was used from at least Julian onwards for almost anyone who was not a Christian.[1] He might have no respect for the Olympian gods, but as a schoolmaster he taught the literature in which they figured so centrally, and was committed by his livelihood, miserable though it was, to other Ἕλληνες for its continuance. Financially and professionally, if not by intellectual conviction, he was of the anti-Christian party, and no desire for personal independence could save him from being classed with it by its enemies. The legislation of Theodosius struck not only at what the Hellenes believed but at sources of livelihood connected with it, and among these was that of a schoolteacher. So Palladas, who was capable of taking the situation quite lightly, found himself dangerously menaced by it. It caught him off his guard and almost knocked him off his feet. His reaction to it can be seen in four lines in which his usual irony gives place to amazement and anxiety and a feeling that the whole order of things has been overturned, so that he does not know what he is or what is happening:

ἆρα μὴ θανόντες τῷ δοκεῖν ζῶμεν μόνον,
Ἕλληνες ἄνδρες, συμφορᾷ πεπτωκότες,
ὄνειρον εἰκάζοντες εἶναι τὸν βίον;
ἢ ζῶμεν ἡμεῖς τοῦ βίου τεθνηκότος; (10. 82)

---

[1] A. D. Nock, *Sallustius*, xlvii.

In this there is a characteristic love of point and antithesis but there is no note of mockery or derision. Palladas is caught in a dilemma and unable to make up his mind about what has happened. His first thought is that the Pagan cause is dead, and for this he had ample justification in reality. The alternative is that he and others of his kind are indeed still alive, but life itself, the whole system which they have taken for granted, has come to an end and may justly be described as dead. The alternatives are not mutually exclusive at every point, and in both Palladas exploits the ancient notion, familiar from Attic tragedians, that in times of disaster the unreality of existence is revealed and men know that they are no more than dreams and shadows. Palladas may have had no great love for the classical authors whose work he had to teach, but in this moment of crisis he found their imagery useful for describing his predicament.[1]

Another couplet, which is commonly taken to speak for the normal conditions of human life and to reflect Palladas' black pessimism, may have been inspired by the bloodshed of the riots:

πάντες τῷ θανάτῳ τηρούμεθα καὶ τρεφόμεσθα
ὡς ἀγέλη χοίρων σφαζομένων ἀλόγως. (10. 85)

The words are so brutal and so savage that they look as if they reflected some actual occasion, and the absence of any elaboration or playfulness indicates that Palladas is deeply moved. The Pagans, who have hitherto been sustained and tolerated by the Christians, suddenly find themselves being slaughtered. Palladas feels the whole unexpected horror of it.

Palladas' love of ingenious tropes and his own kind of mythological wit arise from some conflict in him between a desire for rational order and a conviction that in this world nothing and nobody are what they claim to be. Just as he derides men for their inconsistencies, so he derides gods, and though there is no cause to think that he believes at all seriously in them, he knows that others do and that his comments will be noticed in certain quarters. In 391 and the following years many images of gods were cast down, and as Theodoretus says about Theophilus, οὗτος τὴν Ἀλεξάνδρου πόλιν τῆς εἰδωλικῆς ἠλευθέρωσε πλάνης (*Eccl. Hist.* 5. 22). One such case inspired Palladas to six lines:

---

[1] Keydell, op. cit. 3, puts this poem in 394, but it seems rather to reflect the shocked surprise that Palladas must have felt earlier, and 391 suits this.

τὸν Διὸς ἐν τριόδοισιν ἐθαύμασα χάλκεον υἷα,
τὸν πρὶν ἐν εὐχωλαῖς, νῦν παραριπτόμενον.
ὀχθήσας δ' ἄρα εἶπον· "Ἀλεξίκακε, τρισέληνε,
μηδέποθ' ἡττηθεὶς σήμερον ἐξετάθης."
νυκτὶ δὲ μειδόων με θεὸς προσέειπε παραστάς·
"Καιρῷ δουλεύειν καὶ θεὸς ὢν ἔμαθον." (9. 441)

The first four lines build up a contrast between Heracles, the honoured and unconquered figure, and the present fallen idol. That is why Palladas calls him not by his name but 'son of Zeus', and though χάλκεον means that the image is of bronze, it cannot fail to evoke such associations as χάλκεος Ἄρης in Homer (E 704, 859, H 146) or the use of Χαλκοῦς for a nickname (Din. ap. Did. in Dem. 9. 57; Plut. Dem. 11). The image stood ἐν τριόδοισιν, which was where vulgar idlers and hucksters used to gather (Theophr. Ch. 16. 4; Aristid. Or. 22. 10; Gal. 9. 823; 10. 57; Lucian. Hist. Conscr. 16). This formidable figure used to be in everyone's prayers, and we have only to recall how characters of Aristophanes, in moments of surprise or anger or disgust, exclaim ὦ Ἡράκλεις (Ach. 284; Nub. 184; Pax, 180; Ran. 298).[1] Palladas notes that the great figure, upon whom everyone used to call in need, is now παραριπτόμενον, cast aside (cf. 9. 174. 6), and the implication is not so much violence as contumely. The god's present situation is in sharp contrast with his former glory when he stood in a frequented place and his name was on everyone's lips.

Palladas then addresses the fallen god in anger, ὀχθήσας, a word which echoes Homer (Λ 403, P 90, Σ 5, Υ 343, Φ 53, 552, Χ 14), and its air of being a quotation indicates that he does not expect it to be taken very literally or seriously. He suggests, without intending to be believed, that his first reaction is of outraged propriety, but this is no more than a means to make fun of the god who till recently was the embodiment of power. In speaking of Heracles Palladas chooses his words with care. He first calls him ἀλεξίκακε, which is a familiar epithet for him (Schol. Aristoph. Nub. 1372; Pax, 422; Ach. 284; Ran. 298; Schol. Ap. Rhod. 1. 1218; Varro, de Ling. Lat. 7. 82; Alciphr. 3. 47; Lucian. Alex. 4; Hellanic. 4 F 109 Jacoby; I.G. iv. 1. 1092). It is a cult-title, similar to ἄλεξις at Cos (Aristid. Or. 40. 15) and

---

[1] Stadtmueller ad. loc. quotes Aristid. Or. 40. 14; Schol. Lucian. Iup. Tr. 32; Phot. Lex., s.v. Ἡράκλεις, to which we can add Hesych., s.v. Ἡράκλεις.

ἀπαλεξίκακος at Chaeronea (*I.G.* vii. 3416). It presents Heracles as the protector of mankind, which invokes him in its troubles. Palladas supplements this with τρισέληνε, which is not a cult-title but a personal epithet derived from the length of Heracles' conception, which took three days and three nights (Lycophr. *Alex.* 33; Lucan, fr. 8 Morel; Alciphr. 3. 38; Apollodor. *Bibl.* 3. 4. 8; Diod. 4. 9. 2; Lucian, *Somn.* 17). The relevance of the epithet can be seen from Nonnus

Ἡρακλῆος, ὃν ἤροσεν ἀθάνατος Ζεὺς
Ἀλκμήνης τρισέληνον ἔχων παιδοσπόρον εὐνήν,

(*Dion.* 25. 242–3)

from Lucian *Dial. Deor.* 10. 1, where Helios is told by Hermes not to take out his chariot for three days, τεχθῆναι γάρ τινα δεῖ ἐκ τῆς ὁμιλίας ταύτης μέγαν καὶ πολύαθλον θεόν, and from Aristides *Or.* 40. 2, who ascribes the event to Zeus' care for his latest son. The adjective is a tribute to the heroic nature of Heracles, who from the start shows his prodigious character, and in this way it supplements from a more personal angle the implications of ἀλεξίκακε. Heracles is a fit protector of others because he has always had to fight for himself and show his surpassing strength and endurance.

This hero has never before been conquered, μηδέποθ' ἡττηθείς, and Heracles was in fact honoured as ἀνίκητος at Priene (*Inschr. v. Pri.* 194) and Dorylaion (*C.I.G.* 3817), but now he has been laid low, ἐξετάθης, and whether we take this in the affirmative, or with A. D. Nock[1] in the interrogative, it is clear that Palladas makes the most of the contrast between Heracles' invincible past and defeated present. The language comes from wrestling and means that the great champion has been thrown and counted out.

In the last two lines Palladas springs a surprise. The god, who has been so humbled, appears to him in a dream and shows that he is not troubled by his fall, since he too, though a god, has learned Καιρῷ δουλεύειν. In this there is an elegant *double entendre*. Its primary meaning is that Heracles is the slave of Kairos, and this makes excellent sense, since in the fourth century A.D. Kairos was still worshipped as a god (Himer. 13. 1 Colonna; Ausonius, *Ep.* 3; Paulinus, *Ep.* 38. 346; Tzetz. *Chil.* 8. 428; 10.

---

[1] Quoted by Luck, op. cit. 469.

PALLADAS AND CHRISTIANITY 259

270), and indeed at one place Palladas himself, speaking of the excellence of unpremeditated thoughts, says:

εὖγε λέγων τὸν Καιρὸν ἔφης θεόν, εὖγε, Μένανδρε.
(10. 52. 1)

This is the superficial meaning, but the words also mean that Heracles is a time-server, and this is the real point of the poem. It is tempting to think that Palladas makes use of a phrase which some manuscripts give to St. Paul at Rom. 12: 11 τῷ καιρῷ δουλεύοντες, and this would certainly be neat if the statue was thrown down, as it surely must have been, by Christians. But unfortunately the best manuscripts read not καιρῷ but κυρίῳ, and we must take their word. Nor is the notion of being a slave to Kairos a specifically Christian notion. Pagans also use it, as we can see from Dio Cass. 63. 5 τῷ τε καιρῷ καὶ τῇ χρείᾳ ἐδούλευσε, Plut. *Arat.* 42 τὸν καιρὸν ᾧ δουλεύουσιν οἱ δοκοῦντες ἄρχειν, Liban. *Epist.* 1567 ἀνάγκη παρέπεσθαι καὶ δουλεύειν τῇ χρείᾳ καὶ πείθεσθαι τῷ καιρῷ.[1] Palladas ends with this joke, and it shows that he does not treat the fall of Heracles at all solemnly. Yet though the joke is good enough so far as it goes, there is more in it than the desire to raise a laugh. Palladas suggests that, in being thrown from his old prominent position without complaint and even with humorous resignation, Heracles pays homage to the new regime in religion. Here are no angry cries of Olympian gods retiring to Hades such as we hear of in the alleged Delphic Oracle to Augustus (Cedren. 1. 320 Bekker), but a smiling acceptance of the situation. Palladas treats the god's apostasy as an expedient policy, and we begin to suspect that this may have been his own position.

We may begin our examination of Palladas' own views with a poem which concerns the troubles of the Pagans in these troubled years from 391 onwards:

ὦ τῆς μεγίστης τοῦ φθόνου πονηρίας·
τὸν εὐτυχῆ μισεῖ τις, ὃν θεὸς φιλεῖ.
οὕτως ἀνόητοι τῷ φθόνῳ πλανώμεθα,
οὕτως ἑτοίμως μωρίᾳ δουλεύομεν.
Ἕλληνές ἐσμεν ἄνδρες ἐσποδωμένοι
νεκρῶν ἔχοντες ἐλπίδας τεθαμμένας·
ἀνεστράφη γὰρ πάντα νῦν τὰ πράγματα. (10. 90)

[1] W. Headlam, *J.Ph.* lx (1907), 300.

In this Palladas still suffers from the shock of the Christian reversal of his familiar world. He regards the Pagans as defeated and no better than dead, but he precedes this with a denunciation of the wickedness of φθόνος, and we must ask what precisely he means by this. A clue lies in the second line with its reference to the hatred felt for the fortunate man ὃν θεὸς φιλεῖ. Now the phrase 'friend of God' is common enough in Christian writings from Alexandria with reference to martyrs,[1] and this suggests that Palladas is using Christian language. But he uses it for a special purpose; for we can hardly doubt that he refers to a single recognizable person, and this can be none other than the bishop of Alexandria, Theophilus, who played a leading part in the troubles of 391.[2] If we accept this, all is clear. When Palladas denounces the φθόνος of his fellow Hellenes, it is their hatred for Theophilus, who is called τὸν εὐτυχῆ because he is successful and has defeated them. In their hatred of him they have lost their senses and become the slaves of μωρία, and by this Palladas refers to the behaviour of the Pagans to the Christians.[3] They had indeed been provoked by the public display of intimate symbols from the Serapeum, but they retaliated by attacking the Christians and fortifying themselves in the temple (Socr. 5. 16). Palladas regarded their action as folly. They failed, and their failure was followed by even more stringent ordinances in 392 (*Cod. Theod.* 16. 10. 12).

This poem is followed by another of a similar character in which the 'friend of God' is again mentioned and may again be identified with Theophilus:

> ὅταν στυγῇ τις ἄνδρα, τὸν θεὸς φιλεῖ,
> οὗτος μεγίστην μωρίαν κατεισάγει·
> φανερῶς γὰρ αὐτῷ τῷ θεῷ κορύσσεται
> χόλον μέγιστον ἐκ φθόνου δεδεγμένος,
> δεῖ γὰρ φιλεῖν ἐκεῖνον ὃν θεὸς φιλεῖ.   (10. 91)

This goes further than the preceding poem in that it regards the resistance to the man whom God loves as a fight against God himself. It is hard to believe that there is any irony in the words,

[1] R. Bultmann, *Das Evangelium des Johannes*, 419, n. 3.
[2] See L. Stella, *Cinque poeti dell'Antologia palatina*, 380, on 9. 175; Keydell, op. cit. 2.
[3] L. Sternbach, *Festschrift. Th. Gomperz* (1902), 398, n. 2, sees in μωρίαν a reference to 1 Cor. 1: 23 'Ἰουδαίοις μὲν σκάνδαλον, ἔθνεσιν δὲ μωρίαν, but if there is a reference, it is very oblique and the text is fully intelligible without it.

and in them we must surely see Palladas' conviction that resistance to Theophilus is an impious folly. In new circumstances he asserts the worth of the old rule that χρὴ δὲ πρὸς θεὸν οὐκ ἐρίζειν (Pind. P. 2. 88) and pleads the need to love the man by whom he himself and his fellow Pagans have been defeated. If we take this poem with the preceding, it looks as if Palladas saw in the triumph of Christianity a manifestation of some divine will which it was wicked and foolish to resist. If he felt like this, it is not surprising that he took the fall of the old gods so lightly. They had the wisdom not to resist and were saved by this from the worst disasters.

In this situation Palladas was himself involved through his profession. He was probably forbidden to pursue it, and in any case it would have been dangerous to continue public instruction in the old literature which was the stronghold of Pagan beliefs. Whatever his reasons were, he gave up his profession and sold his books, and two poems on this theme throw light on his personal position. The first comes from the crucial moment of a professional and financial crisis:

Καλλίμαχον πωλῶ καὶ Πίνδαρον, ἠδὲ καὶ αὐτὰς
πτώσεις γραμματικῆς πτῶσιν ἔχων πενίης.
Δωρόθεος γὰρ ἐμὴν τροφιμὴν σύνταξιν ἔλυσε
πρεσβείην κατ' ἐμοῦ τὴν ἀσεβῆ τελέσας.
ἀλλὰ σὺ μὲν πρόστηθι, θεῷ φίλε, μηδέ μ' ἐάσῃς
συνδέσμῳ πενίης τὸν βίον ἐξανύσαι. (9. 175)

In three calculated ambiguities derived from his teaching, πτώσεις, σύνταξιν, and συνδέσμῳ, Palladas reverts to his familiar manner, but the situation is none the less serious. His source of livelihood has been cut off by Dorotheus, who is otherwise unknown to us but has evidently informed against Palladas, who regards his behaviour as impious. Having lost his job, Palladas sells his books, but this suffices only for the moment, and he must get other work. For this he appeals to someone whom the manuscripts agree in presenting as θεῷ φίλε, and we cannot doubt that this is the nearest that restrictions of metre will allow Palladas to get to Θεόφιλε. The bishop would surely have power to help him, and Palladas follows his own decision that we must love the man whom God loves, even if love means no more than an anticipation of benefits. Palladas would hardly have made such a request unless he thought that he had deserved well of Theophilus, and perhaps his attempt to restrain his fellow Pagans was what he counted on.

A second poem on a similar subject is certainly connected with the same situation and shows that Palladas may have succeeded in getting other employment:

ὄργανα Μουσάων, τὰ πολύστονα βιβλία πωλῶ
εἰς ἑτέρας τέχνης ἔργα μετερχόμενος.
Πιερίδες, σῴζοισθε· λόγοι, συντάσσομαι ὑμῖν·
σύνταξις γὰρ ἐμοὶ καὶ θάνατον παρέχει.   (9. 171)

Here too Palladas plays with double meanings in συντάσσομαι and σύνταξις, but he makes two new points which help to complete the picture of his position. First, it is clear that his profession as a teacher of literature brings danger even to life. This is the obvious meaning of the last line, and it is perfectly appropriate to a time of persecution. Secondly, it is clear that Palladas' new post has nothing to do with teaching, for after the reference to books the words ἑτέρας τέχνης ἔργα exclude this. On the other hand there is no need to assume that, when he says farewell to the Pierides, he gives up writing poetry.[1] They are the same as the Muses already mentioned and stand for the subjects of his syllabus in teaching.

Palladas' new τέχνη must surely be connected with the λιμήν which he claims to have found in 9. 172, when he says that he no longer cares for Ἐλπίς or Τύχη and welcomes what he regards as an important change in his life. He does not specify what the λιμήν is, and though 9. 49 also refers to it, we are reduced to guessing. The least we can say is that Palladas seems to be content with it, and this is so uncommon with him that we cannot neglect it. It looks as if his new employment coincided with some change in his outlook, and this must be that he came to some sort of terms with Christianity. His adherence to it was presumably dictated by expediency and prudence, as with some of his gods (9. 441, 528), and he was happy enough about it. But the stern fact remains that he gives hardly any indication of Christian belief. Those poems which have been thought to reflect Christian sentiments do not unquestionably do so. For instance, we may well be surprised that Palladas should write such a poem as this:

[1] Luck, op. cit. 458. For the situation see also 11. 378.

PALLADAS AND CHRISTIANITY 263

σῶμα πάθος ψυχῆς, ᾄδης, μοῖρ', ἄχθος, ἀνάγκη
καὶ δεσμὸς κρατερὸς καὶ κόλασις βασανῶν.
ἀλλ' ὅταν ἐξέλθῃ τοῦ σώματος ὡς ἀπὸ δεσμῶν
τοῦ θανάτου, φεύγει πρὸς θεὸν ἀθάνατον. (10. 88)

and it is tempting to think that it is due to Christian influence, but in fact the sentiments are equally Platonic and Pythagorean, and Becky quotes appositely from the Pythagorean *Carmen Aureum*:

ἢν δ' ἀπολείψας σῶμα ἐς αἰθέρ' ἐλεύθερον ἔλθῃς,
ἔσσεαι ἀθάνατος θεὸς ἄμβροτος, οὐκέτι θνητός. (70–1)

Similarly we might think that we hear an echo of 1 Tim. 6 : 7 in

γῆς ἐπέβην γυμνός, γυμνὸς δ' ὑπὸ γαῖαν ἄπειμι·
καὶ τί μάτην μοχθῶ γυμνὸν ὁρῶν τὸ τέλος; (10. 58)

but it has been demonstrated that the sentiment may equally have come from a classical source.[1] If Palladas became a Christian, it does not seem to have affected his general view of things at all deeply, and we may suspect that in his conformity he was more *pratiquant* than *croyant*.

This would mean that, while he was regarded as a Christian and may have conformed outwardly, he still kept some of his old ties and associations with Paganism. Such a position would explain an otherwise elusive couplet, which the lemma quite wrongly connects with the destruction of Berytus by an earthquake:

τὴν πόλιν οἱ νέκυες πρότερον ζῶσαν κατέλειψαν,
ἡμεῖς δὲ ζῶντες τὴν πόλιν ἐκφέρομεν. (9. 501)

The city is Alexandria, from which in the troubles of 391 and later many Pagans departed, πράξαντες γὰρ ἃ ἐδόκει αὐτοῖς καὶ ταῖς μιαιφονίαις τὸν θυμὸν ἀποσβέσαντες, ἄλλος ἀλλαχῇ κατεκρύπτοντο· πολλοὶ δὲ καὶ ἐκ τῆς Ἀλεξανδρείας ἔφυγον κατὰ τὰς πόλεις μεριζόμενοι (Socr. 5. 16). If we set these words against Palladas' couplet, they are plainly relevant to it, but we must first decide what exactly he means by his distinction between the living and the dead. It has been argued that the 'dead' are the Pagan gods, and for this there is certainly good evidence.[2] They were often called νεκροί, and as νέκυες is merely a synonym for this, then the first line of the couplet means that the old gods have left Alexandria. But surely Palladas means more than this and in effect

[1] Luck, op. cit. 461–2; W. Schmid, *Gnomon*, xxvii (1955), 409, n. 1.
[2] A. D. E. Cameron, *J.H.S.* lxxxiv (1964), 61.

says that the city is dead because not merely its gods but its inhabitants have left it. In other words, when he speaks of νεκροί, he means both the gods and their adherents, the whole apparatus of Paganism. This is implied in 10. 90 when Palladas speaks of himself and the Hellenes in general as νεκρῶν ἔχοντες ἐλπίδας τεθαμμένας, where νεκρῶν refers to themselves and not to their gods. It is also implied in 10. 82. 4 τοῦ βίου τεθνηκότος, where the life that has perished is that of the Hellenes. This notion that the triumph of Christianity brought a kind of death to Pagans was not new. Soon after the death of Julian, Libanius wrote ἀτεχνῶς ἔτι ζῶντες τεθνήκαμεν (*Ep*. 1187), and when Valentinian forbade Pagans to celebrate nocturnal rites Vettius Agorius Praetextatus said that it would ἀβίωτον τοῖς Ἕλλησι καταστήσειν τὸν βίον (Zosim. 4. 3).[1] The notion of death applied both to the gods and their worshippers. So in the couplet about the desertion of Alexandria, the 'dead' who leave it are the Pagan element, the living who stay behind and bury the city are the Christians, and among these Palladas belongs. He has evidently joined the Christian side, but he misses his old associations and laments what has happened.

A similar feeling for the defeated cause may be seen in another poem, which has with good reason been placed in 394,[2] when, for the last time, it looked as if Paganism might be revived by Eugenius and Arbogastes. The events which settled the issue took place in the west far from Alexandria, but since Theodosius took the lead in them and eventually triumphed at the battle of the Frigidus, they would be watched and noted in the east. Palladas seems to have shared this excitement at a time when rumours were rife, and the result is a poem on the deceitfulness of Rumour:

εἰ θεὸς ἡ Φήμη, κεχολωμένη ἐστὶ καὶ αὐτὴ
Ἕλλησι, σφαλεροῖς ἐξαπατῶσα λόγοις.
Φήμη δ', ἄν τι πάθῃς, ἀναφαίνεται εὐθὺς ἀληθής·
πολλάκι καὶ Φήμην ἔφθασεν ἡ ταχύτης. (10. 89)

The word Ἕλλησι shows that Palladas speaks of the fate of the Pagans, who have had their spirits first raised by Rumour and then cast down, only to find that the reality has already outstripped it. This would suit a situation in which Eugenius was

---
[1] A. D. E. Cameron, *C.Q.* n.s. xv (1965), 219.
[2] Keydell, op. cit. 3.

PALLADAS AND CHRISTIANITY 265

first reported to be winning and then known to have lost. Palladas speaks with inside knowledge and understanding of the inside situation, and to this degree he is still with them, but his ascription of deity to Rumour is characteristically countered by his statement that she is a liar.

This is the last poem of Palladas to which we can give a date. Though 11. 293 has been connected with the year 405 through a letter of Synesius,[1] the connection breaks down because the horse which is thought to provide a link between them is in one case given to Palladas and in the other to Synesius.[2] So far as Palladas' poems can be dated, none is later than 394, while others are demonstrably earlier, notably 11. 292 on Themistius in 384,[3] 7. 681–8 on Gessius in 393,[4] 11. 204 and 16. 20 on Maurus before 394 (Amm. Marc. 31. 10. 21). Though we have no information about the date of Palladas' birth or how old he was when the events of 391 struck him, it has hitherto been assumed that he was born about 360[5] and would be in his thirties at this time.

This raises an important question. What we do know about Palladas is that he lived to be at least seventy-two years old. This is the one clear point in an otherwise elusive epigram:

λίτραν ἐτῶν ζήσας μετὰ γραμματικῆς βαρυμόχθου,
βουλευτὴς νεκύων πέμπομαι εἰς Ἀίδην. (10. 97)

There were seventy-two *solidi* to the gold pound of Constantine, and Palladas compares his span of life to date with this. But after this, if we accept the ordinary view of Palladas' chronology, the difficulties begin. First, though he abandoned his schoolmaster's work under Christian pressure, he must have returned to it later. This is difficult to believe, since he would not be allowed to teach his old subjects, and it is to these that he refers in γραμματικῆς, nor does he hint that his career has ever been interrupted. Secondly, the second line has defeated the commentators. If we are to understand it, we must look at it without presuppositions.

If we do this, we find that the couplet would fit very well into

[1] N. Rubensohn, *Berl. phil. Woch.* 1903, 1032.
[2] W. Peek, *R.-E.* xviii. 381.
[3] H. Scholze, *De temporibus librorum Themistii*, 58 ff.
[4] O. Seeck, *R.-E.* vii. 1325.
[5] Franke, op. cit. 39.

the years of crisis 391–4 and that it must have been written before Palladas ceased to be a γραμματικός. It then means that after a long and wearisome life of teaching, he finds himself being sent to death; that is to say, threatened either with starvation or quite literally with persecution. The only point left to decide is the meaning of βουλευτὴς νεκύων. νεκύων can refer either to the Pagan gods or to their adherents or, less clearly, to both. In the first case it might mean that Palladas belongs to some council which deals with religious matters, such as the government of a temple or ceremony. In the second case it might mean that he is the member of some council which consists of Pagans and may even deal with their specific interests. The two meanings are very close, and we do not know enough to decide between them. In either case Palladas fears that his participation may cost him his life. That he had some authority in Pagan circles seems to follow from 10. 90 and 91, but, though they have not taken his advice, he is still associated with them through some office, perhaps municipal, which he has held. This ambiguous position fits into what we have established about his standing in these fateful years. The only objection is that it rejects the conventional chronology and puts back his birth to about 319. Yet this objection is not serious. The late dates in the chronology of Palladas are based on false assumptions,[1] and once we have got rid of them, we are free to construct it anew. That he was already old in 391 may follow from 9. 175, where he asks Theophilus that he may not τὸν βίον ἐξανύσαι in poverty and suggests that he has not many years before him. If we accept this date for 10. 97, the different pieces fall into a single pattern. For many years Palladas was a schoolmaster, and no doubt to this period belong some of his brighter and more irresponsible poems, but in 391–4 he was struck hard by the religious strife at Alexandria and, on losing his work as a teacher, compromised with the Christians and received some other work which seems for the moment to have kept him content. However specious his outer conformity may have been, it does not seem to have been matched by any inner conviction, and his last poems show that at heart he still had some sneaking interest in the lost Pagan cause.

---

[1] See supra 246–7. The main sources of error are 9. 400, which would give a date not long before 415, but is not the work of Palladas, and the lemma on 9. 528, which we have already found to be worthless.

INDEX VERBORVM

ἁβροσύνη, 116, 117.
ἄγαμαι, 140, 141.
ἀγλαός, 29, 38, 44.
ἀγορή, ἀγορά, 112–13.
ἀγωνισταί, 174.
ἀῆται, 28, 42.
αἰπεινή, 5, 6, 12.
αἰπή, 5, 6.
αἰπύ, 5, 6.
αἶσα, 28, 34.
αἰχμή, 28, 39.
αἶψα, 28, 37.
ἀλεξίκακος, 257, 258.
ἅλις, 28, 36.
ἀμπλακίη, 101, 102, 105.
ἄνδρες, 76, 77.
ἄνθος, 75, 83.
ἄορ, 28, 36.
ᾆσμα, 52.
ἄστυ μεγά, 4, 5.
ἄτοπος, 159.
αὐδή, 28, 42, 100.

βρένθειον, 111.

γάνος, 197.
γνώμων, 104, 105.
γόος, 28, 37.

δέπας, 28, 40.
διακναίειν, 156, 157.
δονεῖ, 158.
δραμεῖν, 144, 145.
δῶμα, 28, 36.

ἔγκειται, 159.
ἐγκώμιον, 134, 135.
ἐκβάλλειν, 81, 82.
ἐλαία, 143.
ἐλεύθερα, 56, 57.
ἔλπομαι, 28, 44.
ἔμαρψεν, 28, 43.
ἐν, 68, 69.
ἔντεα, 28, 40.
ἔπη, 47.
ἐπίγραμμα, 165.
ἐπινίκιον, 134, 135, 138.

ἐπίπαν, 114, 115.
ἔπλετο, 51, 54.
ἐρατεινή, 2, 3, 12.
ἐριβώλαξ, 2, 12.
ἐρίβωλος, 2, 12.
ἕρπε, 187, 197.
εὐ-, 11.
ἐΰδμητος, 3, 11.
εὐθύ, 103, 104.
ἐϋκνήμις, 14 f.
ἐϋκτίμενος, 2, 12 twice.
εὖ ναιόμενον, 8, 11.
εὔπυργος, 4, 11.
εὔπωλος, 5, 11.
εὔρεια, 3, 12.
εὐρυάγυια, 7–8, 11, 12.
εὐτείχεος, 3, 4, 11.
ἔχοισα, 46, 51.

ἡμεῖς, ἡμέτερος, 78, 79.
ἠνεμόεσσα, 7, 11.

θεαρός, θεωρός, 99, 100, 101, 102, 105, 107, 108.
θῆρες, 171.
θυοσκόος, 105.

Ἰθωμάτας, 51.
ἰός, 28, 44.
ἱππόδαμοι, 5, 25.
ἱρή, 3, 12.

καθαρά, 51, 55.
κασσίτερος, 20, 21.
κατα-, 52.
καταθύμιος, 51, 52, 54.
κλίνεσθαι, 71.
κορύμβαι, 125, 126, 127.
κότινος, 143.
κοῦρος, 28, 41, 185, 186, 187, 189.
κρωβύλος, 126.
κῶμος, 156.

λᾶς, 28, 34, 40.
λάσιος, 83.
λάτρις, 28, 37, 38.
λεύσει, 28, 34, 35.

μᾶζα, 70.
μάντις, 105, 106.
μέθου, 28, 35.
μείων, 28, 34, 40.
μέλημα, 161.
μετέωρος, 247, 248.
μῆλα, 28, 36.
μίτρα, 203.
μοῖρα, 205, 206, 208.
μοῖσα, 46, 51.
μολπή, 174.
μόχθος, 28, 43, 263.

ναίει, 29, 37.
νέκυς, 28, 38.

ὀθνεῖος, 28, 35.
οἷος, 28, 35, 36.
οἰωνοσκόπος, 105 f.
ὀμφή, 100.
ὄφρα, 113.
ὀφρυσόεσσα, 4, 11.
ὄχημα, 166.

πανοῦργος, 60, 61, 161.
παρακλαυσίθυρα, 150, 151.
πάροιθεν, 28, 42.
πέδιλα, 28, 40.
πέλαγος, 75.
πόθος, 159.
πομπαί, 166.
πόνος, 145.
πόντος, 76.
προσόδιον, 47, 52, 53.

σάκος, 28, 44.
σάμβαλα, 46, 51.
σημαίνειν, 100.
σιμοί, 171.
Σκιάποδες, 76.
σπλάγχνα, 82.
στάθμη, 104, 105.
Στεγανόποδες, 76.
στιβαρός, 84.
στυφελός, 32, 33.

ταρβεῖ, 28, 43.
τέττιγες, 126, 127, 131.
τρισέληνος, 258.
τρυφή, 118, 122, 123, 124, 129, 162.
τύχη, 205, 206.

ὕβρις, 117, 118.
ὑμέναιος, 53.
ὕμνος, 168.
ὕμνος κλητικός, 185.
ὑψίπυλος, 6, 7, 11.

φᾶρος, 29, 41.
φάσγανον, 28, 41.
φθόνος, 260.
φῶς, 28, 44.

χαλκοκνήμιδες, 23.
χθών, 28, 42, 43, 75.
χρυσόπτερος, 89, 90.

ψυχή, ψυχαί, 80.

INDEX AVCTORVM

Aelian, *N.A.*, 60, 61, 126, 137, 164, 177, 178; *V.H.*, 126, 137.
Aeschylus, *Ag.*, 35, 47, 57, 104, 161, 187, 192; *Cho.*, 230; *Eum.*, 104, 153, 157, 183, 194, 208, 230; *Pers.*, 40, 57, 80, 116, 166, 193; *P.V.*, 29, 73, 106, 114, 157, 166, 185, 191, 195, 219; *Supp.*, 35, 37, 153, 207; *fr.*, 40, 87, 194, 221.
Aesop, 63.
Aethiopis, 202.
Aetius, 107.
Agathias, 246.
Alcaeus, 29, 36, 37, 42–4, 51, 52, 113, 150, 200.
Alciphron, 257, 258.
Alcman, 73, 85, 161, 170, 194.
Alexander Aetolus, 97.
Alexis, 162.
Ammianus Marcellinus, 233, 234, 246, 265.
Anacreon, 29, 87, 116, 159.
'Andocides', 134, 136, 147.
Anthologia Palatina, 29, 160, 161, 167, 206, 210, 214, 219, 245–9, 250, 252–7, 259, 260, 262–6.
Antimachus, 40.
Antiochus, 56, 57.
Antiphanes, 116.
Apollodorus, *Bibl.*, 8, 97, 176, 189, 190, 203, 213, 217, 258; *Epit.*, 202.
Apollonius Dyscolus, 51.
Apollonius Rhodius, 184, 186, 202, 209, 230.
Aratus, 187.
Archilochus, 52, 59, 62–4, 67, 70, 71, 118, 171, 178, 182.
Aristeas, 72, 75, 80, 83–86.
Aristides, 73, 76, 90, 92, 95, 257, 258.
Aristophanes, *Ach.*, 257; *Av.*, 51, 63, 76, 90, 102, 151; *Eccl.*, 149, 154–60; *Equ.*, 60, 70, 131, 170, 179; *Lys.*, 38, 88, 89, 98, 132, 151, 153, 162; *Nub.*, 131, 151, 157, 158, 170, 257; *Pax*, 60, 132, 157, 166, 170, 257; *Plut.*, 143, 157, 242; *Ran.*, 47, 89, 90, 117, 148,
151, 176, 257; *Thesm.*, 41, 84, 151; *Vesp.*, 132; *fr.*, 132.
Aristotle, 51, 60, 61, 73, 149, 170, 174, 175, 178.
Asius, 111.
Athenaeus, 32, 34, 40, 48, 50, 67, 70, 87, 88, 102, 111, 112, 118, 122, 129, 130–2, 135, 138, 139, 147, 175, 178, 194, 200, 203, 205, 229.
Aulus Gellius, 219.
Ausonius, 258.

Bacchylides, 79, 90, 143, 146, 158, 161.
Bion, 158, 219.

Carmen Aureum, 263.
Carmen Naupactium, 84.
Carmina Latina Epigraphica, 214.
Cedrenus, 233–5, 244, 252, 259.
Chronicon Paschale, 233, 245–7.
Cicero, 107, 112, 139, 209, 228.
Clement of Alexandria, 48, 50, 119, 228, 243.
Codex Theodosianus, 235, 242, 251, 253, 254, 260.
Conon, 213, 217, 231.
Corinna, 34.
Critias, 191.
Cypria, 226.
Cyril of Alexandria, 246.

Damastes, 72.
Demetrius, 170.
Democritus, 35, 43, 55.
Demosthenes, 114, 134.
Didymus, 257.
Dio Cassius, 203, 259.
Dio Chrysostom, 63, 66, 89, 94, 95.
Diodorus Siculus, 49, 56, 136, 147, 190, 202, 209, 230, 258.
Diogenes Laertius, 121, 127, 165, 169, 205, 228.
Diogenianus, 117, 118.
Dionysius of Halicarnassus, 72, 190, 194.
Duris, 122, 123.

INDEX AVCTORVM

Empedocles, 37, 60, 78, 190.
Epicharmus, 37.
Erinna, 37.
Etymologicum Magnum, 47, 53, 186.
Eubulus, 152.
Eumelus, 46.
Eunapius, 242, 244, 248, 254, 255.
Euphorion, 97, 177, 231.
Euripides, *Alc.*, 29, 35, 140, 145, 222, 228; *Andr.*, 38, 144, 147, 173; *Bacch.*, 162, 170, 183, 190, 209, 219; *Cyc.*, 35, 71, 173, 183; *El.*, 36 107, 145, 157, 176; *Hec.*, 173, 207; *Hel.*, 79, 88, 93, 95, 106, 166, 171, 207, 209; *Heracl.*, 140, 144, 166, 173, 209; *Heraclid.*, 105, 157, 208; *Hipp.*, 80, 144, 171, 183; *Hypsipyle*, 193; *Ion*, 29, 35, 144, 145, 159, 173; *I.A.*, 107, 145, 159, 161, 173, 208; *Med.*, 173, 183; *Mel. Desm.*, 144, 145, 190; *Phoen.*, 106, 107, 141, 162, 209; *Supp.*, 29, 106, 191, 193, 207; *Tro.*, 173, 175; *fr.*, 38, 144, 162, 191.
Eusebius, 48, 234, 235.
Eusebius–Jerome, 41, 48.
Eustathius, 8, 41, 197, 246.
Eustratius, 59.

Fulgentius, 213, 216.

G.D.I., 187, 189, 198.
Galen, 257.
Gregory of Nazianzus, *Carm.*, 254; *Or.*, 236, 239, 248.

Harpocration, 137, 147.
Hecataeus, 72, 76.
Hellanicus, 72, 97, 165, 257.
Heraclides Ponticus, 58, 115, 126.
Heraclitus, 38, 100.
Hermesianax, 223, 225, 226, 230.
Herodas, 153.
Herodotus, 1, 15, 39, 41, 49, 51, 55, 70–5, 77, 78, 80, 85, 95, 96, 101, 102, 104, 108, 110, 114, 116, 119, 120, 127, 128, 141, 145, 164, 171, 179.
Hesiodus, 29, 34, 36, 55, 84, 88, 92, 96, 97, 118, 171, 176, 189, 191, 192, 195, 196.
Hesychius, 36, 43, 44, 126, 186, 193, 208, 242, 248, 257.
Hesychius of Miletus, 249.
Himerius, 90, 192, 235, 238, 258.

Hippias of Erythrae, 128.
Hippocrates, 170.
Hippon, 29.
Homer, *Iliad.*, A, 3, 8, 53, 83, 123; B, 2–4, 6–8, 23, 34, 109, 128, 144, 206; Γ 2, 3, 7, 22, 23, 34, 68, 208; Δ, 2, 6 7 22; E, 2, 3, 5, 130, 257; Z, 2, 3, 5, 6, 10, 64, 82, 96, 166; H, 4, 15, 23, 257; Θ, 2, 3, 7, 89, 115; I, 2–5, 7, 8, 84; K, 52, 126; Λ, 21, 23, 68, 82, 89, 257; M, 3, 7, 107, 120, 130; N, 2, 3, 5–8, 69, 130; Ξ 3, 8; O, 3–5, 8, 36, 68, 74, 130; Π, 2, 3, 5, 6, 10, 22, 85; P, 2, 4, 5, 52, 128, 257; Σ, 2, 3, 7, 20, 53, 69, 161, 257; T, 22, 144; Y, 2, 4, 257; Φ, 2–4, 6, 20, 22, 68, 160, 257; X, 3, 4, 257; Ψ 15, 21, 145, 173, 206; Ω, 2, 3, 22, 23, 53, 83; *Odyssey*, α, 3, 5, 88, 207; β, 2, 113; γ, 3, 5–7, 100; δ, 2, 3, 93; ϵ, 2, 3, 69, 79, 126, 166; ζ, 204; η, 3, 7, 166;; θ, 2, 113; ι, 2, 70, 83, 84, 198; κ, 6, 230; λ, 3, 5, 123, 193, 208; μ, 36, 208; ν, 5, 8; ξ, 5; o, 6; π, 100; ρ, 2; υ, 3; ϕ, 3, 77; χ, 2, 3, 52, 55, 166; ψ, 2, 7; ω, 2, 53, 171.
Homeric Hymns, 54, 55, 80, 89, 100, 123, 124, 140, 166, 209, 243.
Horace, 62, 150, 229.
Hybrias, 67.
Hyginus, 202, 226.
Hymn to Pan, 161.

Iamblichus, 115.
Ibycus, 160, 161, 227.
Inschriften von Priene, 258.
Inscriptiones Creticae, 189.
Inscriptiones Graecae, 17, 34, 35, 40, 41, 43, 44, 102, 107, 108, 126, 132, 140, 187, 203, 257.
Ion of Chios, 59, 65.
Isaeus, 35.
Isocrates, 89, 93, 134, 135, 140, 142, 145–7, 222.
Isyllus, 184.

John of Rhodes, 233.
John of Sardes, 53.
Julian, 233, 235–7, 240.

Lament for Bion, 223.
Libanius, 239, 247, 248, 251, 253, 254, 259, 264.

INDEX AVCTORVM

Linear B tablets, KN, 40, 41, 44; MY, 41; PY, 39–41.
Livy, 211.
'Longinus', 72, 74.
Lucan, 215, 258.
Lucian, 178, 179, 184, 221, 243, 257, 258.
Lucretius, 190.
Lycophron, 29, 92, 177, 206.
Lycurgus, 35.
Lysias, 114.

Macrobius, 219.
Malalas, 245.
Manilius, 204, 220.
Marcellinus Comes, 245.
Marianus, 203.
Maximus of Tyre, 74.
Martial, 202.
Melanippides, 186, 187, 209.
Menander, 60.
Menander Rhetor, 184, 185.
Mimnermus, 110.
Moschion, 191.

New Testament, 259, 260, 263.
Nicander, 29.
Nicolaus of Damascus, 49, 111, 128.
Nigidius Figulus, 214.
Nonnus, 203, 258.

Old Testament, 25, 193.
Oppian, 36, 60, 81, 177, 204.
Orphic Hymns, 206.
Ovid, 70, 176, 190, 202, 213, 215–17.
Oxyrhynchus Papyri, 88, 89, 139.

Pap. Mag. G., 243 n.
Parmenides, 78.
Parthenius, 219.
Paulinus, 258.
Pausanias, 35, 46–50, 53, 55, 56, 73, 77, 97, 129, 139, 143, 164–7, 178, 179, 206, 209, 213, 226, 228, 242, 243.
Pherecrates, 157.
Philetas, 231.
Philodemus, 97.
Philostorgius, 233, 236.
Philostratus, 76, 89, 171, 178.
Philoxenus, 170, 175.
Phlegon, 143.
Phocylides, pseudo-, 127.

Photius, 165, 184, 231.
Phrynichus, 47.
Phylarchus, 110, 111, 128, 178.
Pindar, *Ol.*, 35, 37, 52, 104, 105, 142, 143, 146, 177, 180, 185, 207, 208; *Pyth.*, 34, 35, 56, 57, 60, 73, 77, 80, 102, 104, 105, 116, 140, 142–6, 158, 161, 162, 174, 206–8, 227, 261; *Nem.*, 79, 88, 92, 142, 143, 145, 146, 161, 166, 174, 204, 206; *Isthm.*, 88, 90, 140, 144, 145, 209; *fr.*, 87, 140, 161, 174, 176, 200, 209, 219.
Plato, 35, 36, 63, 91, 92, 107, 117, 139, 142, 152, 165, 170, 188, 191, 207, 224.
Pliny the Elder, 25, 73, 74, 76, 139, 177.
Pliny the Younger, 177.
Plutarch, *Lives*, 134–40, 147, 157, 158, 203, 205, 259; *Moralia*, 47, 51, 53, 61, 77, 95, 133, 174, 177, 178, 221, 226.
Pollux, 111.
Polyaenus, 110.
Polybius, 115, 203, 205, 211.
Praxilla, 198.
Propertius, 21, 70.
Prudentius, 251.

Quintus Smyrnaeus, 202, 203, 208.

Rhesus, 130.
Rutilius Numalianus, 204.

S.E.G., 140.
S.I.G., 145, 188, 211.
Sappho., 36, 37, 42–4, 51, 52, 88, 89, 116, 128, 161, 183, 188, 200.
Schwyzer, *D.G.E.*, 34, 44, 107, 108, 187, 189.
Seneca, 213, 215, 217.
Servius, 202, 216.
Sextus Empiricus, 209.
Sibylline Prophecies, 204, 244.
Simias, 77.
Simonides, 38, 154, 206, 227, 243.
Socrates, 248, 249, 255, 260, 263.
Solon, 116–18.
Sophocles, *Ai.*, 35, 105, 144; *O,C,*, 28, 34, 73, 99, 208, 230; *O.T.*, 36, 38, 99; *Ph.*, 105; *Tr.*, 29, 37, 79, 102, 159, 166.
Sozomenus, 248, 250, 255.
Statius, 201, 217, 220.
Stesichorus, 40, 80, 88–91, 93, 116, 177.

INDEX AVCTORVM

Stobaeus, 64, 199.
Strabo, 7, 8, 49, 56, 73, 74, 76, 84, 110, 113, 114, 119, 165, 185, 190, 195.
Suda, 31, 32, 37, 52, 53, 69, 72, 74, 101, 120, 165, 166, 169, 173, 229.
Synesius, 246.

Tacitus, 211.
Tebtunis Papyri, 150.
Telestes, 170, 171.
Theocritus, 71, 104, 157, 161, 203, 206, 219, 230.
Theodectes, 208.
Theodoretus, 236, 237 256, 257.
Theognis, 29, 37, 55, 99, 101, 103-5, 107, 108, 113, 116-18, 152.
Theophanes, 246, 247, 252.
Theophrastus, 113, 257.
Theopompus, 112, 113, 117.
Thucydides, 4-5, 7, 49, 52, 101, 104, 107, 117, 124, 125, 134, 136, 137, 139, 146.
Timaeus, 49.
Timocles, 160.
Timotheus, 53, 82, 170, 172, 174.
Tragica Adespota, 36, 104, 170.
Tyrtaeus, 38, 56.
Tzetzes, 60, 61, 93, 223, 243, 258, 259.

Varro, 257.
Vatican Mythographer, 216.
Virgil, 70, 202, 204, 205, 207, 213, 214-16, 219, 221, 225, 227, 230, 231.

Xenophanes, 35, 55, 78, 85, 109, 114, 117, 120, 127.
Xenophon, 35, 43, 101, 104, 108, 152.

Zenobius, 59, 70, 102.
Zosimus, 234, 255, 264.

GENERAL INDEX

Abdul Hamid II, Sultan, 25.
Achaea, Mycenaean greaves found in, 18.
Achaeans, 14 ff.
Achilles, 22–3, 84; corslet of, 21; greaves, 20; shield, 53.
Acrocorinth, 4.
Adramyttian Gulf, 6.
Aelian, on statue of Arion, 164–5, 167 f.
Aeneas, description of arming, 130.
Aeolic, elements in Epic language, 52.
Aeolis, poetry bearing local stamp, 29; dialect words, 28, 36–7, 39; Mycenean survivals, 42–3.
Aesop, 63.
Agamemnon, 21–2, 84.
Agathias, 236.
Aglaophon, 139, 147.
Alaric, 242.
Alcaeus, 149.
Alcibiades, 134 ff.
Alcinous, 113.
Alcman, refers to web-footed race, 76.
Alexandria, and its troubles of 391 A D., 263–6.
Alexandrian erotic fragment, 150.
Alföldi, A., 73 n.
Allen, T. W., 27 n.
Alphabet, 51.
Aly, W., 182 n.
Alyattes, 110, 114, 119.
Amazons, 202–3.
Ammonius, 250.
Amoebaeic song, 149–50, 155.
Amphimachus, 128.
Anacreon, 167; love songs, 158, 160.
Anaxilas, 57.
Anderson, J. K., 119 n.
Andrewes, A., 49, 57, 58 n., 83, 127 n.
Antiochus of Syracuse, 56 f.
Antipater of Sidon, 205.
Apollo, 128.
Araithureë, 2.
Arcadia, dialect words, 28, 35–7, 40–1.
Arcadius, 246, 250, 252.
Arcado–Cypriot, 42.
Arcesilas of Cyrene, 101.

Archias of Syracuse, 48–9, 58.
Archilochus, and his spear, 67 ff.; in Zenobius, 59 ff., 62; compares himself to cicada, 63; date of, 80.
Archippus, 175–6.
Arctinus, 48, 50.
Arene, 2.
Ares, as father of Rome, 202–3.
Argos, and Alcibiades, 136; defeat at Mantinea, 137; dialect words, 28, 34, 36.
Ariarathes V, gift to goddess Rome, 211.
Arimaspea, 74 ff.; used by Hecataeus, Hellanicus, and Damastes, 72.
Arimaspians, 77, 84; war with Griffins, 73.
Arion, 51–2; alleged poems of, 173; and Corinth, 164–5, 177; and Dolphin, 164 ff.; connected with Lesbos and Corinth, 179–80; honoured by Periander, 51; hymn in Aelian, 168 ff.; known to Solon and Hellanicus, 179; monument on Cape Taenarum, 164–5.
Arisbe, 2.
Aristeas, of Proconnesus, 72 ff., 75; in *Arimaspea*, 73; claims supernatural powers, 74; poem personal, not heroic, 78.
Aristides, refers to Stesichorus, 90–1, 102.
Aristogeiton and Harmodius, 167.
Aristomenes, 54.
Aristophanes, 47; as song writer, 151–2; *Birds*, 175; on barley meal, 70; parodies love song, 161–3.
Aristophon, 139.
Artemis, 97.
Artemius, martyrdom of, 233 ff.
Asclepieum, 126.
Asius of Samos, 122 ff., 129; compared with Aristophanes, 130–2; date of, 132; *Genealogies*, 125; period he described, 132–3.
Askanie, 2.
Asteropaeus, 21.

GENERAL INDEX

Athens, 3, 6, 7; defeat at Mantinea, 137; dialect words, 28, 35–6; poetry bearing local stamp, 29.
Augeia, 2.
Augustus, alleged oracle to, 244.

Bacchiads, 48, 58.
Bahntje, V., 68.
Banti, L., 186 n.
Barley meal, 70.
Barrett, W. S., 171.
Beazley, Sir John, 178 n. 224 n. 227 n.
Bechtel, F., 27.
Bekker, Immanuel, 27.
Bellerophon, 52.
Bergk, T., 47, 59 ff., 89 n., 141.
Bethe, E., 51 n., 76 n., 123 n.
Bevan, E. R., 238 n.
Bieber, M., 175 n.
Birt, T., 201 n., 211.
Blegen, G. W., 1 n.
Boardman, J., 9 n., 24 n., 185 n.
Boeckh, A., 168 n.
Boeotia, dialect words, 28, 35; in chariot race 420 B.C., 136; poetry bearing local stamp, 29.
Bolton, J. D. P., 72 n. ff., 82 n.
Bosanquet, R. C., 182 n., 188 n., 191.
Boulter, C. D., 1 n.
Boxing, 159, 160.
Bracelets, 124, 128.
Bronze, date of first statues, 165.
Buck, C. D., 52 n., 197 n.
Bultmann, R., 260 n.
Bury, J. B., 205 n.
Buschor, E., 124 n., 128 n., 176 n.

Cadmus, of Miletus, 72.
Callinus, 118.
Calydon, 6.
Cameron, A. D. E., 263 n., 269 n.
Cameron, H. W., 18 n., 19 n.
Campbell, D. A., 67.
Carrière, J., 100, 103.
Caskey, J. L., 1 n.
Cassiotis, spring at Delphi, 242–3.
Catling, H. W., 18 n., 19 n.
Catulus, Quintus Lutatius, 203.
Cedrenus, Georgius, 233 ff.
Cerberus, 218, 222.
Chadwick, J., 2 n., 11 n., 19 n., 40 n., 73 n.
Chamaeleon, 87, 91–2; on Sappho, 200.

Chariot, as symbol of victory and glory, 206, 207.
Charon, 218, 222.
Charondas, 115.
Cheidos, 62.
Christianity, and Paganism, 264.
Chromius, 142.
Claudian, 241.
Cleon, 70.
Clitarchus, 70.
Clitor, dialect, 28–9, 31, 42.
Clonas, 53.
Codrus, 120.
Colophon, 114 ff.; date of destruction and fall, 119; drunkenness, 112; famous for cavalry, 110; government of thousand, 113, 114, 115; hairdressing, 128; luxuries, 111; probably destroyed by Persians, 119; tyranny, 110–11; Xenophanes on luxury, 109 ff.
Colophonians, 85; adornments of, 127; arrogance, 117, 118.
Constantine, 234 ff.
Constantius, 235 f.
Cook, A. B., 182 n., 186 n.
Cook, J. M., 119 n.
Copley, F. O., 150 n.
Corinth, 48; ally of Chalcis, 58; alone helped Sparta against Messenia, 58; and Arion, 164–5, 177; dialect of, 29, 41; Dolphin dances, 180; Mycenaean Greek survivals, 41; whether once Aeolian, 52.
Coronea, 142.
Cos, 8.
Crates, 175.
Cratinus, 130.
Cratisthenes of Cyrene, 206.
Crete, 3; dialect etc., 28–9, 34, 40, 43–5; Cretan hymn, 182 ff.
Croesus, 102, 112, 116, 119; and Delphic Oracle, 236.
Croton, 115.
Crusius, O., 164 n.
Cyclopes, 84.
Cyme, 115.
Cyprus, 186; dialect, 28, 35, 40–5; Mycenaean find of greaves, 18.
Cypselus, 48–9, 165.
Cyrene, 33.
Cyril of Alexandria, 239, 240.
Cyrnus, 99, 100, 105, 108, 118.
Cyrus, 119.

Dale, A. M., 92 n., 172 n., 222.
Dalmeyda, G., 134 n.
Damastes, used *Arimaspea*, 72.
Daphne, 234.
Darius vase, 128.
Davison, J. A., 67 n., 87 n.
Delos, 46 ff., 51, 52–4, 57, 80; evidence of greaves, 18.
Delphi, 57 f.
Delphic Oracle, 99 f., 116, 127, 233 ff., 241; restoration by Julian, 242–3; forgery for Christian ends, 244.
Demeter, Melinno's conception of, 209.
Demetrius I of Syria, gift to goddess Rome, 211.
Demosthenes (Athenian general), 70.
Demoteles, of Samos, 133.
Dempsey, T., 239 n.
Dendra, greaves found at, 18, 25.
Diagoras, Rhodian athlete, 208.
Dikte, 184 f.
Dindorf, F., 46.
Diogenianus, 31, 32.
Diomedes, 136, 147.
Dion, modern Lethada, 6.
Dionysia, festival of Greater, 137.
Dionysus, 51, 255.
Diores, 22.
Dirge, 53.
Dithyrambic style, 169–72, 174.
Divination, various methods, 105 f.
Dodds, E. R., 73 n. f., 209.
Dolphin(s) and Arion, 164; compared to puppies, 171–2; connected with Poseidon, 178–81; dances, 180; stories of rescues, 177–9.
Doria, M., 87 n.
Dorieus, 101.
Doris, 176.
Drachmann, A. B., 138 n.
Dunbabin, T. J., 46 n., 54 n., 56 n.
Duris of Samos, 122 ff.

Eagle, and fox (fable), 63.
Echinades, 3.
Edmonds, J. M., 67, 112.
Electra, 157.
Elegiac poems, scale and character, 120, 121.
Eleusinian mysteries, 107.
Elis, and duties of θεαρός, 108.
Emathia, 3.

Empedocles, 78.
Enalos of Lesbos, 178, 180.
Enispe (Arcadia), 7.
Enkomi (Cyprus), 18.
Epharmostus, 138.
Ephesus, Kouretes at, 195.
Epic language, its features, 52 f.
Epigrams, 166 f.
Epimenides, 85.
Epinicians, character of, 142–4; performance 138.
Epithets, confined to Troy, 3–5; suitable to Troy but applied elsewhere, 5–8; Homeric, refer to Mycenaean age, 9–10; conventional for places, 2–3.
Ergoteles of Himera, 138.
Erinna, 161.
Erythrae, 7; Sibyl and colonies, 49 f.; tyrants at, 128.
Eryx, 101.
Euboea, 6.
Eugenius, 264, 265.
Eumelus of Corinth, 46 ff., 49; Aeolic elements in language, 52; associated with Archias, 48–9; authenticity of poetry, 49, 50–1; date, 47–8; on Messenians, 58; prosodion and date, 57 f.
Eumolpidae, 107.
Euphorbus, 128.
Euripides, 134 ff.; characteristics, 144; conception of tyrant, 147–8; Epinieian at Athens, 139; its metre, date, 135–8, 141, 142; estrangement from Alcibiades, 148; influenced by Pindar, 142; life of, by Satyrus, 139; patriotism, 147, 148; plays against warlike policies, 135; plays performed in 415, 137; use of refrain, 153.
Eurydice and Orpheus, 80, 213 ff., 218; alternative versions, 219–32; associated with Alcestis and Protesilaus, 221.

Färber, H., 47 n.
Farnell, G. S., 169.
Farnell, L. R., 186 n.
Fish, depicted on stage, 175–6.
Flach, H., 46 n., 169 n.
Flamininus, Titus, and Paean, 203–4.
Flavianus, proconsul of Africa, 235.
Forrest, W. G., 58 n.

Förster, H., 136 n.
Fortune, and Palladas, 258, 259.
Fox, character etc., 60 ff.; and eagle (fable), 63.
Fraenkel, E., 104 n., 149 n., 231 n.
Frank, T., 231 n.
Franke, A., 253, 265 n.
Fränkel, H., 77, 112–13, 109 n.
Frazer, J. G., 147 n.
Friedländer, P., 166 n., 167 n.
Furtwängler–Reichold, 128 n.

Gaertringen, Hiller von, 234 n.
Galatea, 175.
Glaucus, and the Pythia, 104.
Goliath, greaves of, 25.
Golgoi, 186.
Gomme, A. W., 125 n., 130 n.
Gonoessa, 6.
Gortyn, 34, 37, 186.
Gow, A. S. F., 150 n.
Gratian, 245.
Gray, D., 10 n., 20.
Greaves, 14 ff.; believed by Pliny to be Carian invention, 25; bronze worn by Syrians, 24; bronze used by Mycenaeans, 19 f.; evidence for in Lefkandi, 17; fastening methods, 21; first appearance, 15; found in Central Italy, 24; made of leather? tin?, 22, 20; peculiar to Achaeans, 24; variety, 19; worn by Goliath, 25.
Greek dialects, 27 ff.; aim of compiler of Γλῶσσαι κατὰ πόλεις, 29; compared with Hesychius, 30; compiler's choice of archaic words, 45; date, 33 f.; derivation, 29, 31 ff.; historical background of words, 39 ff.; reliability, 33 ff., 38–9.
Gregory of Nazianzus, 239 ff.; author of 'oracle', 240–2; death of, 254.
Griffith, G. T., 211 n.
Grotius, 199.
Grüppe, O, 225 n., 227 n.
Guarducci, K., 182 n.
Guthrie, W. K. C., 182 n.
Gyges, 110–11, 119–20.

Hagemann, A., 20 n.
Hagesias, 142.
Hagesidamus, 138, 142.
Hagia Triada, 186.

Hair, dressing and adornment, 111, 125, 126.
Hampe, R., 18 n.
Hardt, van der, 168 n.
Harmodius and Aristogeiton, 167.
Harpagus, 119.
Harrison, E., 182.
Head, B. V., 186 n.
Headlam–Knox, 150.
Headlam, W., 259 n.
Hecataeus, used *Arimaspea*, 72.
Hedgehog, characteristics, 60 ff.; compared with lion, 59, 65–6; enemy of snake, 60, 64.
Helen, addressed in fragment of Stesichorus (?), 88; phantom at Troy, 91–3, 96–8; story of Egyptian visit, 93–6.
Helike, 3.
Hellanicus, 179; used *Arimaspea*, 72.
Hephaestus, 20.
Hera, of Samos, 123–4, 126–7, 129, 166.
Heracles, 8, 102; Palladas on, 256–9.
Herodas, 153.
Herodotus, on Aristeas, 72.
Hesiod, attacked by Stesichorus, 88, 92; subject of Palinode, 96–8.
Hesychius, 30 ff.
Hexameters, uses of, 123.
Hieron, 142–3.
Higham, T. F., 177 n.
Himerius, 90.
Hipparchus, 102.
Hippo Zarytus, bay, 177.
Hippocleas of Thessaly, 161.
Hipponax, on scent, 111.
Hissarlik, 1, 6, 8.
Hoffmann, O., 27, 34.
Homer, and Troy, 12, 13 ff.; attacked by Stesichorus, 88, 91–2; date 1, 9, 12, 14; epithets in general, 1 ff.; on greaves, 22, 23; style 10; use of Mycenaean epithets, 16 f.
Homolle, E., 234 n.
Honorius, 251.
Hoplite armour, 14, 15.
Horace, 150, 201.
Housman, A. E., 204 n.
Hudson-Williams, T., 68, 99.
Hungary, greaves found in, 24.
Huxley, G. L., 46 n., 54 n., 109 n., 119 n.

GENERAL INDEX

Hybrias, 67, 68.
Hyperboreans, 73.

Iasus, 177.
Ibycus, 51, love-songs, 156, 160–1.
Idaean cave, shield and picture of greaves, 24.
Ilberg, T., 179 n.
Images of gods and survival in Christian times, 249, 250–2.
Inscriptions, and dialects, 33.
Iolkos, 2.
Ion of Chios, on scent, 111.
Ionia, dialect, words, 28, 38, 41; local poetry, 29.
Iphigeneia, 97.
Iris, addressed by Stesichorus?, 89, 90.
Ismarian wine, 69, 70.
Ismene, 99.
Issedones, 72 f., 78 85.
Isyllus, Paean, 184.
Itanos (Crete), 187 ff., 195.
Ithaca, 2, 113.
Ithome, Mt., 34–5.
Ixion, 218.

Jacoby, F., 48 n., 80 n., 123 n.
Jaeger, W., 191 n.
Julian, emperor, 233 f., 237, 247–8, 264.
Julianus Scholasticus, 247.
Justinus, 32.

Kaibel, G., 125.
Kairos, worshipped as God, 258–9.
Keydell, R., 253 n., 256 n., 260 n., 264 n.
Khalandritsa, 18, 19.
Kinkel, G., 130 n.
Kleemann, M., 27 n.
Kleine, O. F., 91 n.
Klement, K., 179 n.
Knossos, 3, 11, 40–1, 186–7.
Koiranos of Paros, and dolphins, 178.
Kosay, Hamit, 24 n.
Kouretes, 189 ff.
Kranz, W., 116 n.
Kroll, J., 102 n.
Kroll, W., 169 n.
Kroyman, L., 56 n.
Kuban, silver mirror from, 83–4.
Kühner–Gerth, 82 n., 126 n.
Laconia, dialect words, 29, 38, 44, local poetry 29.

Lade, battle of, 120, 127.
Laestrygonian Lamos, 6.
Laius, 99.
Lampsides, O., 240 n.
Larisa, 2.
Lasserre, F., 62.
Latte, K., 27, 49 n., 182 n.
Lausus, 252.
Leaf, W., 10 n.
Lefkandi, greaves at, 17.
Lehrs, K., 169 n.
Lelantine war, 58.
Lemnos, 2.
Lenschau, T., 49 n.
Lesbos, 2, 52; dialect words, 36–7, 42–4.
Lesky, A., 76 n., 176 n.
Leumann, M., 27 n.
Lichas, son of Arcesilaus, 136.
Linforth, I., 229 n.
Liparion of Ceos, 143.
Lobel, E., 42.
Lobon of Argos, 169.
Locri, 115.
'Longinus', quotes *Arimaspea*, 74.
Lorimer, H. L., 15, 17 n., 18 n., 19 n., 22 n., 24 n., 73 n.
Love-duet, in Aristophanes, 149 ff.; 161–3.
Loy, R. van, 251 n., 253 n.
Luck, G., 245 n., 253 n., 263 n.
Luxury, disapproved of by Xenophanes, 117; leads to tyranny, 117.
Lycambes, 62, 63.
Lycia, 3.
Lycus, 147.
Lydia, influence on Samos, 129; luxury, 110, 116.
Lydians, effect on Colophon, 109.
Lyktos, 2.
Lyttos, 186–96 n.

Maeonia, 3.
Magnes, 111, 128.
Magnesia, its fall, 118, 119.
Mair, A. W., 177 n.
Mantinea, 2, 107, 137.
Marina, house of, 245 ff.; two of that name, 245–6.
Marisa, poem from, 150, 155.
Masson, O., 186 n.
Maximus of Tyre, on Aristeas, 74.
Medea, 158.
Megacles of Athens, 138.

GENERAL INDEX

Megara, 108.
Meister, R., 27.
Melanippides, 174.
Melicertes of Corinth, 178, 180.
Melinno, hymn to Rome, 199 ff.; date 210–12; method of construction, 201 ff.
Melos, and Athens, 416 B.C., 136, 137, 148.
Menelaus, 22.
Merhardt, G. von, 24 n.
Messenians, dialect, 51, 52–3; impious acts, 56; first war, 48, second war, 54, 56.
Metre, 155 *et passim*; Cretan hymn, 183–4; Sapphic stanzas, 201; Euripides' Epinician, 141–2; hymn of Arion, 172 f.; hexameters in Mycenean times, 10.
Meuli, H., 75 n.
Michelangeli, L. A., 132 n.
Milesians, 127.
Mimas, mt., 7.
Mimnermus, 120.
Minoan warriors, armour, 16.
Mithras, 255.
Momigliano, A., 206 n.
Monkey, and fox (fable), 63.
Moretti, L., 136 n.
Murray, G., 182 n., 194.
Musaeus, 102.
Muse, manner of address, 89, 90.
Mycenae, 4, 6, 7, 8 f.; fortifications at, 6.
Mycenaean, epithets for Troy, 11.
Mycenaean Greek, 27, 43; lack of word for greaves or shield, 21; not homogeneous language, 45.
Mycenaean Greek words, a-ne-mo, 11; ai-ka-sa-ma, 39; de-me-o-te, 11; di-pa, 40; e-te-do-mo, 40; e-to-wo-ko, 40; i-je-ro, 12; ki-ti-me-na, 2, 12; ko-wo, 41, 197; me-u-jo, 40; pa-ka-na, 41; po-ro, 11; pa-ta-ja, 44; pa-we-a, 41; pe-di-ra, 40; pe-di-ro, 40; pe-di-roi-, 40; ra-e-ja, 40; to-ko-do-mo; 11; wa-la-ka-ni-o, 186.
Myers, F. W. H., 224 n.

Neleus, 120.
Nemea, 147.
Nereids, 176.
Nerikos, 2.
Nicander, 30.

Nicosia, 18.
Nilsson, M. P., 182 n., 188 n., 194, 211 n.
Norden, E., 215 n., 227 n., 229 n.

Odysseus, 70, 80, 177.
Oldfather, W., 207 n.
Olympian Games, 127, 136–7, 134, 142–3.
Olympus, 204, 205.
Onchestos, 3.
Onomacritus, 102.
Oppian, on fishermen, 81.
Oracles, 101–2; and forgeries, 243–4.
Orestes, 157.
Oribasius, physician, 233–5, 243–4.
Orpheus, and Eurydice, 213 ff.; other versions, 219–32.
Overbeck, J., 179 n.
Ovid, on Orpheus, 213 ff.

Paean, 53.
Paeonia, 2.
Page, D. L., 17 n., 85 n., 87 n., 90, 150 n., 168 n.
Palaemon of Corinth, 178, 180.
Palamedes, 191.
Palladas, 245 ff.; concern at Theodosius' reforms, 255, 256; connection with Synesias, 265; dating of poems, 265; his age in 391 A.D., 265; conformity to Christianity, 262 ff.; mocks monks, 254; poems on Gessius, Maurus, Themistius, 265; on rumour, 264; Pythagorean influences?, 263; reliability of lemmata on his poems, 246–9, 263; whether Christian, 256–61; whether visited Constantinople, 248 f.
Palmer, L. R. 2 n., 19 n.
Pamphilus, lexicographer on dialects, 32.
Pan, 161.
Pandarus, 22.
Panyassis, 120, 125.
Paris, 22.
Parmenides, 70.
Parody, its value, 163.
Parry, Milman, 14, 16, 23.
Parthenon, 126.
Patroclus, 85.
Pausanias, date of Eumelus, 47–8.
Payne, H. G. G., 49.

GENERAL INDEX

Pazarli, find depicting greaves, 24.
Pedasos, 6.
Peek, W., 245 n., 265 n.
Pellana, duties of θεαρός, 107.
Penthesilea, 202–3.
Penthesilea-Painter, 128.
Periander, 51.
Pericles, 157.
Persians, language, 116; water drinkers, 112.
Pfeiffer, R., 33 n.
Pfister, C., 211 n.
Phalanthus, of Tarentum, 178.
Phalaris, 51.
Phantom, of Helen at Troy, 91–3, 95, 96.
Pheidolas of Corinth, at Olympia, 167.
Phemius (Homeric bard), 166.
Phere, 2.
Pherecrates, 157.
Philip of Macedon, 206.
Philostorgius, 236, 240, 242.
Philoxenus of Cythera, 174, 175.
Philoxenus of Leucas, 169.
Phintas, son of Sybotas, 47–8, 53, 54.
Phlius, 31.
Phocis, duties of θεαρός, 107.
Phrygian, music, 116.
Phrynichus, 151, 161, 176.
Phthia, 2.
Phyromachus, 140.
Pindar, 52, 58; influence on Euripides, 142.
Pisani, V., 94 n.
Pisthetaerus, 102.
Plutarch, reliability of, 140–1.
Poetry, how inscribed in 8th cent., 50–1; poetical words in common use, 27 ff.
Pollard, J., 49 n.
Polycrates of Samos, 133, 222.
Polygnotus, 139, 228.
Polyphemus, 175.
Poseidon, 144; and dolphins, 178–81.
Powell, J. U., 125 n., 150 n., 182 n., 204 n.
Praisos, 195.
Pratinos, 169.
Premerstein, A. von, 94 n.
Preuss, E., 94 n.
Prodicus of Phocaea, on Orpheus, 228.
Prosodion, normally sung to flute, 47, 53; by Eumelus, 48 ff.

Proteus, in story of Helen, 92–3.
Psammetichus I, oracle of 'brave man', 15.
Psychro, cave, 185.
Ptolemy, Philadelphus, 206.
Puppies, dolphins compared with, 171, 172.
Purple, clothes, 111.
Pylian cities, 84.
Pylos, 2, 3, 8, 11, 40, 70; Epano Englianos, 6; evidence of greaves, 17; fresco, 21 n., tablets, 19.
Pyromachus, 139.
Pythagoras, boxer from Samos, 127.
Pythermus, at Sparta, 111.

Ramesses III, 25.
Refrain, use of in Greek songs, 153, 154.
Reitzenstein, R., 167 n.
Rhegium, 51, 56, 57, 58, 115.
Rhipaean Mts., 73.
Rhodes, 36.
Rhys Roberts, W., 77, 78, 81.
Robert, C., 15.
Robinson, D. M., 224.
Rome, celebrated by Melinno, 199–212; daughter of Aesculapius, 203; daughter of Ares, 202; worshipped as goddess, 211 ff.
Rubensohn, N., 265 n.
Rumour, and Palladas, 264.

Salamis, 102.
Salii, 194.
Samians, dress, 124; history in Asius, 123, 124; luxury, 123–9.
Sandanis, 112.
Sappho, 111, 149, 160.
Satyrus, 139, 140.
Scherie, 2. 3.
Schliemann, H., 7, 8, 21 n.
Schmid, W., 263 n.
Schmid-Stählin, 46 n., 75 n., 92 n., 123 n., 175 n., 211.
Scholze, H., 247 n., 265 n.
Schröder, H. G., 234 n.
Schroeder, O., 173 n.
Schubart, W., 200 n.
Schulze, W., 27.
Schwenn, F., 195 n.
Scythians, 73, 85.
Seeck, O., 265 n.

280 GENERAL INDEX

Semonides of Amorgos, 111, 120.
Seneca, on Orpheus, 213, 217.
Septuagint, 37, 193, 197.
Serapeum, 250, 251.
Serapis, 255.
Shackleton-Bailey, D. R., 204.
Shield, Homeric treatment, 25.
Sicily, dialect words, 29, 37; Athenian expedition to, 134, 136, 137; treasury at Delphi, 227.
Sidonie, 8.
Silenus, 40.
Simonides, 52, 58.
Sisti, F., 87 n.
Sisyphus, 52, 218.
Smyrna, its fall, 119–20.
Smyth, H. W., 46 n., 140 n., 168 n., 169 n.
Snodgrass, A. M., 15 n.
Socrates, 157.
Solon, 70, 179; on tyranny, 117, 118.
Songs, accompanied by dances, 173, 174; role of refrain, 153, 154; solo, 174, 175.
Sounion, 3.
Sparta, 3, 108, 111.
Stadtmueller, H., 247 n., 257.
Statius, 201.
Statues, date of first bronze, 165.
Stella, L. A., 245 n., 260 n.
Sternbach, L., 260 n.
Stesichorus, 51–2, 87 ff.; second Palinode, 96–8; on phantom of Helen, 91–2; start of Palinodes, 88–90.
Stinton, T. C. W., 145 n.
Stobaeus, on Melinno, 199.
Streets, in Homeric age, 7–8.
Studniczka, F., 178.
Swoboda, H., 175 n.
Sybaris, 101.
Synesius, 69, 265.
Syracuse, 48.

Taenarum, cape, and Arion, 164 f.; cave, 218.
Tantalus, 217.
Taras, of Tarentum, 178.
Tarn, W. W., 211 n.
Tarne, 2.
Tebtunis, Papyrus, 150.
Tegea, decree of 218 B.C., 35; duties of θεαρός at, 108.
Teleclides, 130.

Teleclus, 56.
Telemachus, rescued by dolphins, 177.
Tenos, 107.
Terpander, 52–3.
Thales, 169.
Theagenes of Thasos, 145.
Thebe (Mysia), 3, 6.
Thebes, Boeotian, 6.
Thebes, Egyptian, 7.
Themis, in Cretan hymn, 194–5.
Themistius, 247, 254.
Theocritus, 157.
Theodoretus, 233 ff.
Theodosius, 241 ff., 246, 250–2; his edict, 242; policy towards Pagan gods, 250–1, 253, 264.
Theognis, 99 ff., 156; on tyranny, 117; whether θεωρός, 105, 107.
Theophilus of Alexandria, 248 ff., 255–6, 260, 262.
Therapna, 94.
Theseus, 97, 98.
Thessaly, dialect words, 28, 37, 38.
Thompson, E. A., 235–6 ff.
Thousand, oligarchies of a, 113–16.
Thrace, 2, 70.
Thrasybulus, 104.
Thucydides, son of Melesias, 157.
Timocles, 160.
Timotheus, *Persae*, 169–73, 176.
Tiryns, 4, 6, 21.
Tityus, 218.
Tityus cup, depicts bracelet, 178.
Toepfer, H., 49 n.
Torre-Galli, find of greaves, 24.
Treres, 118.
Tritons, 76, 176.
Trojan war, date, 1, 19.
Troy, 1 ff., 116; broad streets 7–8; deserted from *c.* 1100 to 750 B.C. 9; exceptional number of gates, 6–7; Homeric epithets for, 1 ff.; refounded by Greek colonists, 150–9; rising steeply, 6–7; site of, 1 ff.; subject for poetry, 10; winds, 7.
Troy VI, 3, 4, 7; destruction of by earthquake, 1; gates, 6.
Troy VI–VIIa, 10; contact with Mycenaean world, 9; dimensions, 4; evidence of horses at, 5, 25.
Troy VIIa, 3, 4; destruction of, by fire, 1, 5; Homeric city, 1; more populous than VI, 8.

GENERAL INDEX

Troy VIIb, 3; fewer horses at than Troy VI–VIIa, 5, 11.
Troy VIII, 3.
Troy IX, 6.
Tylisus, 34.
Tyranny, and luxury, 117, 118.

Ure, P. N., 49 n.

Valentinian I., 245, 264.
Veio, find of greaves, 24.
Ventris, M., 2 n., 11, 19 n.
Vermeule, E., 18 n., 20 n.
Vestinus, C. Iulius, 32.
Virgil, on Orpheus, 213 ff.
Visser, W. J. D., 95.
Vürtheim, J. J. G., 89, 94 n.

Wackernagel, J., 125.
Wade-Gery, H. T., 73 n.
Walbank, F. W., 205 n.
Waltz, P., 253 n.
Way, A. S., 82.
Weber, L., 167.
Webster, T. B. L., 10 n., 17 n., 57 n.
Weizsäcker, P., 178 n.
Welcker, F. G., 169 n., 210 n., 211.
Wellmann, M., 46 n.
West, M. L., 182 n., 196 n.
White, J. W., 184 n.

Wilamowitz–Moellendorff, U. von, 46 n., 51 n., 92, 182 ff., 113, 115, 131, 154, 172 n., 193, 192, 208 n., 228.
Wilkinson, L. P., 201–2 n.
Willetts, W. E., 182 n., 185 n., 188 n., 194.
Winniczuk, L., 210 n.
Wolff, G., 239 n.
Women, position of in Greece, 149.
Wright, W. S., 234 n.

Xenophanes, 78, 107, 125; connected with Elea 119; disapproved of luxuries, 117, 118; on impact of Barbarians on Greeks, 109.

Young, D., 49.
Yugoslavia, greaves found in, 24.

Zacynthus, 177.
Zenobius, 59.
Zenodotus, on dialects, 32.
Zeus, 128, 185 ff.; as 'leaping' god, 193–4; cult of youthful Zeus, 186–8; Diktaios, 188, 196; Ithomatas, 54, 55.
Ziegler, K., 226 n.
Zuntz, G., 147 n.

PRINTED IN GREAT BRITAIN
AT THE UNIVERSITY PRESS, OXFORD
BY VIVIAN RIDLER
PRINTER TO THE UNIVERSITY